LANGUAGE DEVELOPMENT
FROM BIRTH
TO THREE

Moshe Anisfeld
Yeshiva University

Psychology Press
Taylor & Francis Group

New York   London

Permission has been granted to quote from the following sources:

THE CONSTRUCTION OF REALITY IN THE CHILD, by Jean Piaget. Translated by Margaret Cook. ©1954 by Basic Books Inc., Publishers. By permission of the publishers. And by permission of Routledge & Kegan Paul Ltd.

NEW DIRECTIONS IN THE STUDY OF LANGUAGE, edited by E. H. Lenneberg, published by THE MIT PRESS, 1964, by permission of Publisher.

PLAY, DREAMS AND IMITATION IN CHILDHOOD by Jean Piaget, Translated by C. Gattegno and F. M. Hairston, by permission of W. W. Norton & Company, Inc. All Rights Reserved 1951, Norton Library Edition, 1962. And by permission of Routledge & Kegan Paul Ltd.

An article by D. Horgan entitled, "Learning to tell jokes: A case study of metalinguistic abilities," which appeared in the *Journal of Child Language,* 1981, *8,* 217–224, published by Cambridge University Press, by permission of Publisher.

First Published by
Lawrence Erlbaum Associates, Inc., Publishers
365 Broadway
Hillsdale, New Jersey 07642

Transferred to Digital Printing 2009 by Psychology Press
270 Madison Ave, New York NY 10016
27 Church Road, Hove, East Sussex, BN3 2FA

ISBN 0-89859-284-4
ISBN 0-89859-625-4 (pbk.)

Library of Congress Catalog Number: 83-82493

Publisher's Note
The publisher has gone to great lengths to ensure the quality of this reprint but points out that some imperfections in the original may be apparent.

To
My Mother
My Wife
My Children

Contents

Preface

This book presents a synthesis of two areas of research: infant cognition and early language development. It treats the development of language, which begins in the second year, as continuous with the development of the symbolic capacity, which takes place in the first year. The juxtaposition of the linguistic period with the prelinguistic period results in a sharper portrayal of each of these periods.

The aim of the book is to provide a sophisticated understanding of the development of symbols and language without requiring a background in the scientific study of children or language. In pursuance of this goal, I develop the ideas gradually and make explicit the fundamental insights of earlier scholars that are taken for granted in current work. A glossary is appended to help clarify concepts used in the text.

The book is intended for a wide audience, including students in courses on language development and child psychology, as well as professionals in these fields, and in the fields of education, linguistics, and pediatrics. Educated parents will also find the book useful in providing the foundations for effective practices that enhance their children's linguistic and cognitive development.

Work on the book started in earnest during my sabbatical leave in the Department of Psychology at the Hebrew University of Jerusalem during 1976-1977. I am grateful to I. M. Schlesinger for his hospitality and for reacting constructively to a couple of preliminary chapters. I also wish to express my gratitude to other friends and colleagues who read chapters along the way and gave me the benefit of their criticisms. They include: Hans Furth, Michael Gertner, Shoshana Goldman, Allan Goldstein, Charles Greenbaum, David Lewkowicz, Rita Neugut, Sue Rose, Phyllis

Ross, Benny Shanon, and Joyce Weil. Two anonymous reviewers also provided enlightening comments. I am particularly grateful to Richard Steiner for his close reading of the chapters concerned with speech and its acquisition. I am thankful to Elizabeth Anslow for making the initial version of the sketch that appears on the cover. Special thanks are due to Robert Lummis, Director of the Scientific Computing Center of the Albert Einstein College of Medicine of Yeshiva University, to Associate Director Arthur Rosenthal, and to their staff for opening for me the rich resources of the UNIX system for text processing. I also thank Dr. I. Bretherton and Dr. P. D. Eimas for checking my reading of figures in graphs of their articles. Finally, I owe the greatest debt of gratitude to my family. My wife, Elizabeth, read and commented on practically every one of the numerous versions I brought home from the Computing Center. My son, Shimon, gave me the benefit of his meticulous reading of various chapters in preparation and of the galleys and page proofs. My daughters, Miriam and Rachel, helped with proofreading and with the checking of references and quotes. Beyond this direct assistance, my wife and children gave me much more. They helped me—by being who they are—to develop intuitions about children that guided me throughout this project. This book is dedicated to them and to my mother, who through the calamitous tragedies of war retained the education of her children as the highest priority.

Moshe Anisfeld

LANGUAGE DEVELOPMENT FROM BIRTH TO THREE

1
Introduction

In the course of the first 3 years of life the child becomes transformed from a squirming, crying, and impulsive creature into a thinking and talking human being. This book tells the story of this fundamental transformation, tracing the small steps and the large leaps that children take in achieving it.

The story of development that unfolds in the following chapters has the quality of a good drama. In the flow of developmental events, as in the sequencing of scenes on the stage, there is anticipation and continuity. Every major change in functioning has been prepared for by antecedent events. The antecedents are often not appreciated at the time of their occurrence; their full significance emerges only when they are viewed from a broad developmental perspective. We see, for instance, that such behaviors as sucking and grasping, which appear intellectually inconsequential, serve an important function in the development of thinking and in the preparation for language. We also see that the distorted speech of the toddler reflects internal patterns and constitutes a step toward the acquisition of the standard speech of the community.

The material I draw on includes **observational** and **experimental studies**, as well as formal **linguistic studies**. In observational research the investigator observes the natural behavior of children—be it speech, play, or interaction with the mother—records the observations, and analyzes them in search for patterns and trends. The methods of recording and analysis can vary. Some investigators write down what they see or hear; others use recording devices, such as video equipment. The analysis may involve impressionistic summaries, quantitative statistical calculations, or a combination of both. A noteworthy type of observational study is the **diary study**, in which the investigator observes a child, often his or her own, on a regular and continuous basis over a period of time, which may range from a few months to a few years.

Experimental studies, in which specific behaviors are examined under prede-signed conditions, are harder to conduct with infants and toddlers than with older subjects. But some ingenious methods have been developed in recent years, and they have produced results that contribute to our understanding of human development.

Also used in this book are the studies of linguists concerning the structure of language. In studying the structure of language, linguists do not typically test subjects or make observations on them. Rather, they try to develop an account of the structure of specific languages and of language in general by analyzing com-monly observed phenomena. We use the work of linguists concerning the struc-ture of language, because in order to understand how children acquire language, we need to know something about what it is that they are acquiring.

The most important source material for the present book is the work of the Swiss psychologist Jean Piaget. Piaget, who died in 1980 at the age of 84, is generally acknowledged as a great developmental psychologist. I draw particu-larly on Piaget's theory of infant development, which is based on a study of his three children. In his work Piaget combines keen observation of naturally occurring behaviors with creative experimental interventions.

This book tries to synthesize the different strands of research, coming from different disciplines, using different methodologies, and deriving from different theoretical orientations, into a cohesive picture of development. My approach is based on Piaget's conception of development and is anchored in current thinking concerning the nature of human information processing. In some respects it is similar to the approach of Werner and Kaplan (1963). I make three basic assump-tions: that similar behaviors can derive from processes at different levels of mentation, that there are both gradual and abrupt changes in development, and that children do not absorb passively the language of their community but con-struct it actively for themselves.

The substance of the book is presented in three parts. Part I, which contains Chapters 2-4, deals with the formation and socialization of the symbolic capac-ity. Chapter 2 lays the groundwork for the study of symbolic development. It clarifies the concept of symbol and relates it to other concepts. Chapter 2 also provides a preview of the nature of presymbolic mentation in infancy. Chapter 3 traces the steps infants go through in advancing from presymbolic thinking to symbolic thinking. In the presymbolic stage infants cannot represent objects and people internally and therefore do not realize that they have substance and per-manence. For instance, young infants have no notion that their mothers continue to exist when they are not in sensory contact with them. The symbolic capacity, which is developed gradually in the course of the first 18 months, makes possible the construction of reality and the acquisition of language to represent it. Chapter

4 describes how words are learned and how their meanings change to approximate gradually the meanings of adults.

The use of sentences represents a higher level of symbolic capacity than the use of single words, and sentences appear in children's speech after single-word utterances. Part II, which contains Chapters 5-7, deals with the nature of early syntax and its development. Chapter 5 analyzes the nature of sentences in mature form and thus provides the necessary background for the study of syntactic acquisition. Chapter 6 describes the characteristics of children's early sentences, and Chapter 7 examines the developments that foreshadow the emergence of syntax and the factors that facilitate its growth. It describes how toddlers organize for themselves the task of learning to form sentences. Some children, for instance, divide the task of sentence construction into manageable parts and concentrate their efforts on learning each part separately.

Part III, consisting of Chapters 8-10, is concerned with the development of speech and morphology. Chapter 8 gives an introduction to the nature of human speech, providing background information needed for the following two chapters. Chapter 9 discusses children's acquisition of morphology. Morphology deals with the structure of words and involves such things as the use of inflections (e.g., the plural *s*). Chapter 10 discusses how children acquire the sound system of their language, and the ability to perceive sounds and to articulate them. The chapters of Part III, like the preceding ones, highlight the child's active part in learning language. We see, for instance, that children's pronunciation errors are creative attempts to construct a sound system on the basis of what they hear. Similarly, such childish renditions as *doed* (for *did*) and *mans* (for *men*) are mistakes only from the adult's point of view. From the child's perspective, they reflect discovery of inflectional generalizations.

The ordering of parts in the book is designed to reflect the chronological order of development. In this connection, a comment is in order on why I placed the chapters on speech and morphology after the chapters on syntax. Morphology emerges after the onset of syntax and therefore belongs after syntax in the exposition. Speech development begins before syntax, but I put it together with morphology because of the affinity of the concepts used in the two areas. Also, from a pedagogical point of view, it seems advisable to move gradually to increasingly more technical aspects of language; hence the progression from words, to sentences, to speech and morphology. In addition, it is appropriate to conclude the course of development traced in this book with the chapter on the acquisition of speech, because this chapter spans the entire age range (0-3 years) covered in the book.

THE EMERGENCE AND
SOCIALIZATION OF THE
SYMBOLIC FUNCTION

2 Representation, Language, and Infant Mentation

*Sensory-motor intelligence aims at success and not at truth. It is
an intelligence which is only "lived" not thought.*

Jean Piaget

As adults we hold in our memories a vast amount of knowledge. The acquisition
and storage of knowledge depends on the capacity for internal representation and
on the availability of a system of mental codes. This book analyzes how the foundations of the representational capacity and of language as a map of reality are
laid down in the first 3 years of life. As a preparation for this analysis the present
chapter sketches the nature of internal representation in mature form and, in comparison, provides an introduction to infant mentation.

INTERNAL REPRESENTATION

The concept of **representation** (more precisely referred to by the terms *mental
representation, internal representation*) is central to the study of cognition.
Therefore, I attempt to explicate this concept at the outset.

When I stop my car on reaching a barricade, I am responding directly to the
physical obstruction. But when I stop the car at a red light, it is not because the
red light by virtue of its own physical properties prevents me from driving
through, but rather because it stands for or represents a traffic regulation. Children start going back to their classes when they hear the school bell, not because
of the acoustic properties of the sound of the bell, but because of what the bell
has come to mean for them. There are numerous other instances in our daily lives

where we respond to things and events by virtue of their representational, rather than their intrinsic, qualities. But language constitutes our main and most highly developed representational system. To appreciate the nature of representation afforded by language, distinctions have to be made between different levels of representation. I turn to this topic in the following section.

Signs and Symbols

Representation involves two entities: a representing entity, a **signifier**, and a represented entity, a **signified**. The level of representation depends on the characteristics of the signified entity. One type of signifier, the **sign**, relates directly to an immediate, specific object or event. Another type of signifier, the **symbol**, relates to a concept, not directly to an object or event. The philosopher Susanne Langer (1951, chaps. 2-3) characterized the difference between signs and symbols by saying that signs direct our attention and action to things, whereas symbols are vehicles of conception. They bring ideas to our minds instead of preparing our limbs and senses for reaction.

Symbols require higher intelligence, whereas signs are used throughout the animal kingdom. For example, animals use signs to inform each other of imminent danger. In fact, there is a training procedure known as classical conditioning that can be used to develop sign representations in animals (and humans, as well). This procedure was developed by the Russian physiologist I. P. Pavlov (1927) in experiments he conducted with dogs. In a standard experiment he would sound a metronome and then immediately give the dog some food. After a number of such occurrences, the dog would exhibit anticipatory food reactions (e.g., salivation) to the sound even before receiving the food. The dog thus reacted to the sound not for any inherent properties of its own, but in terms of what it stood for. Generally, stimuli that do not elicit strong reactions in their own right can become conditioned representations in this way.

For the dog that has been conditioned the sound of the metronome anticipates food, and its sole function is to prepare for the immediate intake of food. Similarly, the school bell creates for the child an expectation that classes are about to start (or to end). Familiar footsteps indicate the approach of a particular individual. These are all signs, functioning to prepare and orient directly toward action.

Symbols, on the other hand, have a conceptual function. Words are symbols. The word *food,* for instance, does not necessarily make one salivate or hungry; rather, it activates the concept of food in one's mind. The sound of a fire alarm arouses fear and makes people run outside. It is a sign. In contrast, the phrase *fire alarm* need not give rise to a fear experience; it may merely evoke the conception of fear.

Although words are primarily designed to be used as symbols, they can be used, and occasionally are used, as signs. That is, words can be used not in their conceptual function, but as stimuli that automatically elicit certain responses and as responses that are automatically elicited by certain stimuli. This is evident particularly in the case of social routines, such as "hello" as an automatic response when picking up a telephone and "thank you" as a stimulus that automatically elicits "you're welcome." Also, the exclamation "fire!" may have the same effect as the sound of a fire alarm.

We see in Chapter 4 that children use words initially as signs and only gradually shift to using them as symbols. This shift was described dramatically by the deaf and blind Helen Keller (1902/1954):

> We walked down the path to the well-house, attracted by the fragrance of the honeysuckle with which it was covered. Some one was drawing water and my teacher placed my hand under the spout. As the cool stream gushed over one hand she spelled into the other the word *water,* first slowly, then rapidly. I stood still, my whole attention fixed upon the motion of her fingers. Suddenly I felt a misty consciousness as of something forgotten—a thrill of returning thought; and somehow the mystery of language was revealed to me. I knew then that "w-a-t-e-r" meant the wonderful cool something that was flowing over my hand. That living word awakened my soul, gave it light, hope, joy, set it free! There were barriers still, it is true, but barriers that could in time be swept away.
>
> I left the well-house eager to learn. Everything had a name, and each name gave birth to a new thought. As we returned to the house every object which I touched seemed to quiver with life. That was because I saw everything with the strange, new sight that had come to me. (p. 28)

It seems that before her sudden recognition of the symbolic potential of words, the word *water* had been for Helen Keller merely an event connected with actual pouring or drinking of water, not very different from other physical accompaniments, such as the sensation of water on the hand. The grasp of the symbolic function of words gave Helen Keller exhilarating joy as it freed words from their attachment to things and actions, and allowed them to serve as instruments of thought and imagination. It is the symbolic function that enables words to transcend reality and to be used to tell lies, to talk about imaginary situations, and to discuss creative ideas.

Words as symbols thus differ from signs by what they signify. Symbols signify concepts, whereas signs signify concrete things and actions. Because symbols signify concepts, their tie to their signifieds is more lasting than the tie of signs to their signifieds. For the sound of a metronome to retain its status as a sign of food, food has to follow it consistently. If on several occasions food is not provided, the sign properties of the sound will become extinguished; the dog will not salivate on hearing the sound. But the tie between a word-symbol and the concept it signifies is not so easily broken. Even if an individual's request for whiskey is consistently denied, he will not lose the meaning of the word, although he may stop using it.

There is a deeper sense in which words have a vitality of their own. Language is a system, and each component in it is sustained by its place in the system. Once a word establishes itself as part of the speaker's lexicon, it does not depend for its existence on constant pairing with its referent. (The signified of a word is called its **referent**.) Moreover, the semantic boundaries of words are not defined solely through referent association. The words an individual knows relate to one another in a system of relations where the meaning of each word constrains and shapes the meanings of its neighbors. For instance, some children use the word *doggie* initially as a name for four-legged animals in general. Later, when they learn other animal names, *doggie* seems to become spontaneously more restricted. The point is that vocabulary items are learned and maintained not as isolated entities but as members of a system. The fuller ramifications of language as a system will become evident in the course of this book.

Finally, two comments are in order. First, for expositional purposes I have used the sign-symbol distinction as a dichotomy. But actually there is a continuum, signifier-signified relations being more or less symbolic. Second, in current psychological usage the term *representation* normally refers to symbolic representation, unless specifically qualified as in *sign representation*. I follow this usage here, except when context obviates the need for qualification.

Concepts and Instances

I have said that words as symbols serve as signifiers for concepts, not for things. But what is a verbal concept? The term **concept** has a broader meaning in psychological discourse than in everyday language. In the psychological sense, not only truth, happiness, and education are concepts but also table, ball, and sleeping. In psychology the term **category** is often used as a synonym for *concept*.

The essential characteristic of all concepts is that they are generalized entities. Thus, the word *table* as a mental entity does not refer to any particular table or even to a finite set of actual tables. Rather, it refers to the concept of table. A concept is an open and productive entity, providing criteria for the admission of new members. Thus, when presented with new pieces of furniture, which they have not seen before, individuals are able to tell which are tables and which are not.

Basic Concepts   Objects can normally be categorized on different levels of abstraction (e.g., fruit, apple, McIntosh apple; vehicle, car, sports car; bird, eagle, bald eagle). However, the intermediate level, represented in the examples by *apple, car,* and *eagle,* is the level that is more useful in everyday life than either the superordinate level or the subordinate level. Rosch, Mervis, Gray, Johnson, and Boyes-Braem (1976) referred to this level as the "basic" level. They demonstrated that words on this level had a privileged status in several experimental tasks.

One of these tasks required college students to verify pictures against names of objects. Subjects were first presented with a name; then they were shown a picture and asked to press one key if the picture was an example of the name and another key if it was not. The keys were connected to timing devices, which allowed the investigators to measure the subjects' reaction times. Rosch et al. found that the verification of the basic-level names was faster than that of names on the other two levels. The reaction time for the basic-level names was 556 milliseconds (msec), for the superordinate names 610 msec, and for the subordinate names 650 msec. The shorter reaction time for the basic-level names suggests that the subjects experienced greater ease in categorizing the pictures in relation to the names on this level than in relation to the names on the other two levels.

Also, children's early vocabularies are characteristically drawn from the basic level. The superordinate terms are too abstract, and the subordinate terms are too specific. The basic terms are just right to distinguish objects from one another in a functionally useful way.

The Fuzziness of Concepts   Philosophers and psychologists have for a long time been interested in discovering what knowledge of concepts (on any level) consists of and how this knowledge is represented in the mind. Although some progress has been made on these issues, much remains to be discovered. In what follows, I present an approach to concepts that will be useful for understanding the developmental issues pursued in this book.

Natural human concepts are not defined in rigorous ways; we do not have explicit lists of defining attributes even for the most common concepts. Our knowledge of concept attributes and of their internal organization is intuitive and vague. Natural human concepts lack sharp boundaries; they shade into one another; they are fuzzy. Consider *table* again. What is it that we know about the concept of table? It is defined in the dictionary as "a piece of furniture consisting of a smooth flat slab fixed on legs." This definition suggests what *table* means, but does not fully circumscribe it. It is not sufficient to distinguish tables from a variety of other objects such as those called *stool, bench, counter, desk, platform,* and *stand.* It may be assumed that our internal implicit definitions are even fuzzier than the explicit dictionary definitions.

Various writers have argued that functional uses must be included in the definition of concepts, especially those involving human artifacts. As Sapir (1933/1951) clearly stated: "No entity in human experience can be adequately defined as the mechanical sum or product of its physical properties" (p. 46).

Miller and Johnson-Laird (1976) offered a functional definition of *table* and commented on it:

"A table is used for working or eating or playing games; the top is used to support various smaller objects required in the course of those activities." From this functional definition it is possible to infer what tables should look like. A table should have a WORKTOP, a surface that is horizontal so that objects will not roll or slide off and flat so that objects can stand on it. Moreover, the surface would be useless if it were not firm and at a convenient height from the floor (not horizontal upside down), so rigid legs are required to support it. (p. 229)

The inclusion of functional attributes improves the definition of concepts, but it does not alter their fuzzy character. The demarcation line between *table* and *counter* or *table* and *desk* still remains vague.

The fuzziness of concepts can be understood by thinking of defining attributes in probabilistic terms. That is, the attributes do not apply in an all-or-none fashion, but in a probabilistic more-or-less fashion. For *table* the attributes of high probability would include "being used for working or eating or playing games," "having a rigid surface," and "being elevated off the ground." It is hard to imagine a table without these attributes. The attribute "held up from the ground by legs," although usually characteristic of tables, has lower probability, because there are tables that use means of support other than legs. The attribute "being made out of wood" would seem to have even lower probability. Similarly, in the definition of the natural concept *robin,* the attributes "is a biped," "has wings," and "has distinctive colors" have higher probability than the attributes "perches in trees" and "is not domesticated" (see Smith, Shoben, and Rips, 1974).

It is time now to make explicit a distinction that has been implicit throughout the discussion, namely, the distinction between concepts and instances (see Anisfeld, 1968). The things we see and use are exemplars or instances of concepts. The concepts themselves are not observable; they are abstractions that exist only in our minds. A concept is an abstraction in the sense that it is more general than any given instance; it can cover an infinite number of different instances, as long as they possess the defining attributes. Every actual table must have a certain physical height, but the concept *table* has associated with it only a range of heights; every table must have a certain color, but the concept does not have a color attribute. Concepts do not fully specify their instances, because in addition to possessing the attributes characterizing the concept, instances also have properties that are incidental to the concept.

Individual items differ in how typical they are as instances of a particular concept. Some tables are more typical instances of the concept *table* than others. The issue of typicality or prototypicality has recently received attention from Rosch and her co-workers on the level of the relation of lower order concepts to superordinate concepts. In one study (Rosch, 1973) where subjects were asked how good different subcategories were as examples of certain supercategories, the following mean rank order of prototypicality emerged. For the supercategory *fruit* the order was: apple, plum, pineapple, strawberry, fig, and olive. For *disease* the order was: cancer, measles, cold, malaria, muscular dystrophy, and rheumatism. For *bird* the order was: robin, eagle, wren, chicken, ostrich, and bat.

Another study (Rosch & Mervis, 1975) found that the prototypical instances had more attributes in common with other instances of the supercategory than the peripheral instances. Thus, most birds fly, and so do robins. Robins are therefore judged as highly prototypical. In contrast, chickens do not fly, and they receive lower prototypicality ratings. Rosch and Mervis also found that the more prototypical instances tended to be more exclusively associated with a single category. Thus, chicken is classifiable not only as bird but also as poultry and meat, whereas robin is only a bird. Another factor that seems to contribute to making an instance relatively more prototypical is its commonality. Thus, it would seem that malaria had a lower rank than cancer as a disease, partly because the research was conducted in the United States where the latter is much more common than the former.

The Functions of Categorization

There is great utility in conceptual grouping. Without it, we would have to respond to each discriminable event as unique, and as Bruner, Goodnow, and Austin (1956) pointed out ''we would soon be overwhelmed by the complexity of our environment'' (p. 1). Conceptual grouping or categorization reduces the environment to manageable proportions.

Categorization is involved in all aspects of our lives. When one encounters an object and sees it not merely as a round, blue, elongated, pointed thing, about 20 cm long and 1 cm in diameter, but as an instance of the category *pencil,* one can bring to bear a wealth of information on this simple sensory experience. One knows its texture before touching it, its uses without exploring it, its manner of repair before it breaks, and its monetary value without trading it. Categorization thus facilitates prediction. It also aids memory. If one wants to remember the presence of the aforementioned object in a particular location, the conceptual category reduces the memory load. Instead of remembering the full sensory description, one can simply enter it into the memory store by the conceptual code of *pencil.* Note that we do not know how *pencil,* or any other concept, is represented internally. It could be represented as an image, as a description of attributes, or in some other way (Farah & Kosslyn, 1982). But we assume that it is represented in some abbreviated, summary fashion.

Categorization is also at the heart of the perceptual process. The very act of perceptual recognition entails placing an object in a preexisting category. When I meet someone on the street and identify him as John Smith, what I am doing is placing the individual in a category on the basis of partial information. The category is much richer than the immediate percept in front of me. Obviously, the category contains information concerning the social place of the individual, which the percept lacks altogether. But even with respect to physical characteristics, the percept contains only a small portion of the total categorical information. The individual I meet may have his head covered, but I know that he has black hair. He may not be talking now, but I know what his voice sounds like, and so on. Because perception is an inferential process, mistakes are possible. Thus, I meet someone who I think is John Smith, only to realize later that he was really Bill Brown.

Individuals are normally not aware of the extent of involvement of categorical knowledge in their perception. For instance, on clearly hearing the lyrics of a familiar song, one does not have the subjective experience of enriching the impoverished acoustic signal by prior knowledge. But this is in fact what happens, as becomes evident when one experiences difficulty making out the words of a new song.

Categorization is also involved in problem solving. Common observation and psychological experiments suggest that an individual's ability to solve a problem is often dependent on his or her ability to reclassify objects in terms of new categories. Thus, for instance, Glucksberg and Danks (1968) gave subjects the task of completing an electrical circuit. The problem was that they were not given enough wire, and even though they could use the metal blade of a screwdriver, people do not normally think of screwdrivers as functioning to complete electrical circuits. There were two groups of subjects in this experiment. For one group, the only label mentioned was *screwdriver*. For another group, reference was also made to *handle* and *blade*. Glucksberg and Danks found that the latter group did better than the former. The categorization suggested by *blade* was more conducive to orienting subjects in the right direction for the solution than just *screwdriver*. Categorization thus has a directive function in problem solving. Habitual forms of categorization may be a hindrance to problem solving, which one can overcome only by having the flexibility to shift categories.

INFANT MENTATION

The main point that has emerged from the discussion so far is that we organize our experiences of objects (as well as actions and qualities) into categories. Categorization, which is so natural to us and taken so much for granted, is alien to the infant. True, categorization builds on sensitivity to similarities and differences, and even infants do have such sensitivity. Infants, however, have little interest in categorization per se. The following subsections provide a general characterization of the noncategorical-nonsymbolic mentation of infants and a brief discussion of their transition to the symbolic-linguistic mode of operation.

Sensorimotor Intelligence

As adults we can think of objects and classes of objects even in their absence. I can easily conjure up an image of the chair I sit on at my desk, even when I am not there. I can discuss the properties of the class of objects called *chair,* even if no single instance is in front of me. I can do this because the concept *chair* is somehow represented in my mind. There is other knowledge, however, that is not as readily accessible outside of its behavioral context. For example, I know how to touch-type; that is, when I sit at the typewriter, I can type without looking at the keys. My fingers depress the correct keys blindly. But when not at the typewriter, I cannot tell which keys "belong" to which fingers. Even when my fingers rest on the typewriter keyboard, it is only with great effort and uncertainty that I am able to come up with this information. Yet, in the course of typing my fingers select the right keys rapidly and without any hesitation. It is as if my fingers know how to type. Evidently, there is a kind of knowledge that exists as part and parcel of the context of its usage and is not otherwise available. Many of the skills that involve motor components fall into this category. We often know which direction to turn a key to open a door when the key is in the keyhole, but not when we have to tell someone else how to do it. We know how to get to a friend's house, even though we may not be able to describe the route.

One gets a glimpse of the nature of infant mentation when one considers that it is closer to the procedural knowledge of how to type than to knowledge of words and concepts. Piaget has characterized infant mentation as **sensorimotor**. That is, the knowledge that young infants have of objects is in terms of the sensorimotor impressions the objects leave on them and the sensory and motor adjustments the objects require. For young infants objects do not have an existence independent of their reactions to them. Adults do not have any knowledge in this pure sensorimotor form. All adult knowledge, even that with a heavy sensorimotor component, is colored with abstract notions of reality. Thus, the typist who cannot identify the letters on the keys when away from the typewriter knows that there are keys that exist independently of the typing activity. Not so in the case of young infants; for them the very reality of objects is defined in terms of their sensations and actions toward them.

Sensorimotor intelligence is primarily focused on action, not on classification and organization. Classification exists only as an incidental byproduct of sensorimotor activity. Each particular pattern of sensorimotor activity toward particular objects is organized as a repeatable **scheme**. The different objects that served as stimuli for the exercise of a particular scheme are tied together by this experience. Thus, there are sucking objects, grasping objects, and so forth. Things are not classified objectively, but by reference to the infant's reactions to them.

Transition to Symbolic-Linguistic Functioning

Sensorimotor development leads gradually to the transition to symbolic-linguistic functioning, typically, in the middle of the second year. This transition is not an easy one. For the child steeped in sensorimotor thought, linguistic representation constitutes a totally new approach to the world. Sensorimotor representation is based on the child's own actions and sensations, and it groups ob-

jects in terms of the schemes that they engage in the child. In contrast, linguistic representation is based on arbitrary, social conventions, and it classifies objects in terms of their objective attributes. The child, thus, has to gain an understanding of the different nature of linguistic representation. Symbolic-linguistic representation indeed brings about a complete reorganization of the child's view of the world. Piaget (1952/1963, pp. 240-241) suggested that in the initial period of adjustment to this new mode of operation, children may actually regress to lower levels of functioning than they achieved at the end of the sensorimotor period. It takes time to translate the understandings acquired on the sensorimotor level into the symbolic-linguistic level.

THE PROCESSES OF GROWTH

What are the processes by which children grow out of sensorimotor mentation and develop increasingly higher levels of representation? Piaget proposed that three processes, **assimilation**, **accommodation**, and **organization**, are responsible for all growth and development, indeed, for all biological adaptation (see, e.g., Piaget, 1954/1981). It is important for us to become acquainted with these processes in preparation for the following chapters.

Assimilation and Accommodation

Assimilation is the process by which external stimuli are taken in and interpreted by the organism. There is assimilation on different levels, depending on the operations involved. Infants tracking a visual object with their eyes are assimilating it visually. The internal structures responsible for the head and eye movements are said to constitute the assimilating schemes. An adult engaging in similar visual behavior goes beyond the visual assimilation to richer, more conceptual assimilation. For the adult the moving object is a Chevy, and it is embedded in the framework of knowledge about transportation, makes of cars, traffic rules, and so on. Perceptual categorization, which was discussed in the first part of the chapter, is thus a special case of assimilation.

Assimilation is the process that turns sensory data into psychological experience and knowledge. Accommodation is the process whereby internal structures are adjusted to facilitate adaptive assimilation of incoming stimuli. Assimilation in and of itself does not necessarily bring about an appropriate or veridical interpretation of environmental stimuli. In fact, if not for accommodation, the assimilation of new stimuli would always be at least mildly distortive of the true character of those stimuli, because the assimilating structures were developed on the basis of previous experiences and are therefore biased toward them.

Learning and adaptive behavior in general are characterized by a close interplay between assimilation and accommodation. In every adaptive action there are both assimilation and accommodation. But the balance between the two processes varies depending on the nature of the stimulus involved and on what the individual does with it. In a habitual response to a well-known stimulus, assimilation predominates. In this case the particular stimulus is taken in smoothly by a previously developed scheme; it requires little accommodation. (Even here general accommodation is involved in attending to that particular stimulus in that particular context, and in selecting it for response, but there is little specific accommodation in the actual processing of the stimulus.) At the other extreme, totally new stimuli beyond the grasp of the individual (i.e., stimuli that cannot be assimilated by existing structures even in a distortive way) also lead to little specific accommodation.

Only stimuli that are moderately novel call forth both assimilation and accommodation. Their resemblance to old stimuli makes them assimilable by old schemes; however, because they do not fit well into the schemes not tailored for them, they set the process of accommodation into operation. This dynamic interplay between assimilation and accommodation explains why developmental changes, and learning in general, are gradual. In order for accommodation to produce changes, there must be assimilation, but in order for assimilation to operate on the new, change-inducing information, this information must have an anchor point in old information (i.e., it cannot be totally new).

As an analogy to the interplay between assimilation and accommodation, consider a container with a flexible opening into which oval objects had been inserted. As a consequence of this particular use, the opening developed an oval shape. Now, one wishes to insert a round object, a ball, into the container. The attempt will succeed—that is, the opening will adjust itself to the new shape (accommodation)—only to the extent that the new object can be pressed into the opening (assimilation) to exert pressure on it. Without this initial contact, no adjustment is possible. There is no accommodation without assimilation.

Assimilation and accommodation are basic biological processes governing the adaptation of all organisms to their environment. Consider the process of eating. It starts when the organism perceives something (via vision, smell, or touch) and interprets it as food. That is, an external object is assimilated to an internal eating scheme. One of the first steps in the execution of the eating scheme involves grasping the food, and if it is different from previously grasped objects, accommodation sets in. The interplay between assimilation and accommodation continues as the food is taken into the mouth, is chewed, and passes through the digestive tract to the stomach. In such bodily adaptations as eating and grasping, physical organs are involved in the processes of assimilation and accommodation. For other, more psychological adaptations there are no organs. But there must be mental structures, which are no less real for not being embodied in observable organs.

Let us turn now to psychological examples of the operation of assimilation and accommodation. When a person sits down at her desk to write with a pen she has used many times, the writing behavior itself does not involve any kind of accommodation. But if she were to use a pen with a much broader circumference than usual, adjustment (i.e., accommodation) would be required. This accommodation is possible only because she has an initial approach, via the patterns developed for holding ordinary pens, to the new pen. If she were not able to take hold of the new pen, no learning would be possible. That is, without initial assimilation, no accommodation is possible.

Or consider Johnny learning to hold a pencil and write with it. Initially, he applies to the pencil the pattern of finger flexion that he has developed for grasping and holding other objects; he assimilates the new stimulus to familiar schemes. But gradually he learns the holding pattern appropriate for writing. For this to happen, the holding scheme has to become refined and differentiated by the process of accommodation.

In the pursuit of intelligent interaction with the environment, assimilation is the process that uses available structures to take information in, and accommodation is the process that brings about modifications in those structures when necessary. The balance between the two forces varies depending on the activity involved. In routinized behaviors, assimilation predominates; in novel behaviors and in learning, assimilation and accommodation are in a more balanced state. They are, to use Piaget's term, in equilibrium.

Organization

In the preceding discussion internal cognitive growth was seen in the context of interaction with the environment. The emphasis on environmental effects is justified when one deals with infants, as I do in much of this part. But internal activity not in immediate response to stimulation must not be ignored. The internal structures that develop do not exist in isolation from one another. They are dynamic entities that interact with each other and organize themselves into a coordinated system of relations.

Organizational processes, although present even in infancy, become the dominant forces of cognitive development with the onset of the symbolic-linguistic function in toddlerhood. Chapters 4 through 10 show how children impose an organization on every aspect of language that they acquire. Language is a system, and it is acquired as a system.

3 Development of the Symbolic Function

> *I think the most creative period of human life is between birth and eighteen months.*
>
> Jean Piaget

Most children begin to use language productively in the second half of their second year. Why do they begin then? Why not earlier? This question can be approached from a variety of perspectives. Taking a neuropsychological perspective some have sought to relate the onset of language to the maturation of the central nervous system (see, e.g., Lenneberg, 1967). One can also take a phonetic perspective, as I do in Chapter 10, and examine the development of vocal control mechanisms that lead up to recognizable speech. But the present chapter takes a cognitive perspective and considers the conceptual prerequisites for language. It outlines the stages children pass through in their attainment of the symbolic function.

As we have seen in the previous chapter, language does more than provide labels; it actively participates in the shaping and organization of our representation of reality. Children cannot use language in its symbolic-representational function until they have developed the capacity for internal representation of objects and people. The foundations of the representational capacity, which are laid down in the first 18 months, are charted in this chapter.

The discussion is based primarily on the work of Jean Piaget. Through original research and theorizing spanning more than 5 decades, Piaget was able to illuminate the nature of human knowledge and its development in children. To understand infantile cognitive operations properly, one has to guard against imposing adult modes of thinking on the child. One could not have a better guide than Piaget in this effort of psychological distancing. I draw particularly on

Piaget's trilogy on infancy: *Play, Dreams and Imitation in Childhood* (1951/1962), *The Origins of Intelligence in Children* (1952/1963), and *The Construction of Reality in the Child* (1954).

Piaget has divided intellectual development into four broad stages: the sensorimotor stage, from birth to the end of the second year; the preoperational stage, from 2 to 6; the concrete-operational stage, from 7 to the beginning of adolescence; and the formal-operational stage, from adolescence onward.

Children in the sensorimotor stage do not think symbolically. Preoperational children do think symbolically, but their thinking is not yet analytic. For instance, if shown a row of buttons and asked to make another row that has the same number of buttons, preschool children make a row whose end points coincide with those of the model row, but they are not concerned with insuring a one-to-one correspondence between the two rows. Preoperational children are satisfied with global, perceptual correspondence. By contrast, concrete-operational children perform correctly on this kind of task because they possess the conceptual tools to analyze wholes into component parts. However, though concrete-operational children can solve concrete problems, their ability to manipulate abstract ideas is rather limited. It is not until adolescence that children acquire formal operations and the capacity for hypothetical thought.

Although the sensorimotor stage is the shortest of all stages, its contribution to human development is fundamental. It is in the course of this stage that the child truly becomes a thinking creature. In fact, the advances occurring in the sensorimotor period are so great that Piaget was able to distinguish six substages within this period. Each subsequent substage brings the child closer to symbolic functioning, which is the main achievement of this entire period. To provide a sharper view of the steps in symbolic development, I group together Piaget's substages 1 and 2, and 4 and 5. For the sake of simplicity the substages are usually referred to as stages, and I follow this practice in my exposition. Table 3.1 provides a summary of the main characteristics of the stages outlined.

The chronological ages associated with the sensorimotor stages vary somewhat for different children. The ages that I give are intended to *suggest* the age ranges corresponding to the different stages; they should not be interpreted too strictly. Piaget's practice is to indicate age by three numbers, which stand for years, months, and days. For example, 1;3(15) means 1 year, 3 months, and 15 days. This book follows Piaget's notation.

STAGES 1–2 (FIRST HALF OF FIRST YEAR):
NO REPRESENTATION;
ONLY SENSORIMOTOR MEMORY

This section begins the story of the development of the capacity for symbols and language. It contains four subsections. The first provides a characterization of the child's level of functioning at the initial sensorimotor stages; the second fo-

TABLE 3.1
Outline of the Sensorimotor Stages

Stage	General Characterization	Reaction to Objects	Imitation	Make-Believe Play
1-2	Sensation and action dominate. Intermodal coordination established by the end of Stage 2.	Infants track moving objects and grasp objects in sight. Infants look for objects that they lost sight of only in the places where the objects had been seen.	Only sporadic imitation of familiar human models occurs.	None.
3	Beginnings of sensorimotor representation.	Object is modality specific: visual object, auditory object, etc. No manual search for objects apprehended visually. No identification of people and objects; only a reaction of familiarity on the basis of reevocation of previously exercised schemes.	Infants exhibit systematic imitation of human models. Imitation of nonhuman models begins to occur and evidences some representational distancing.	Not distinct.
4-5	Infants exhibit a clear interest in the representation of reality. They explore the environment, and begin to develop a view of reality that is not self-referenced.	Infants view objects as intersects of different sensory schemes: visual-auditory object, visual-prehensile object, visual-auditory-prehensile object, etc. Infants search manually for covered objects and attribute causality to objects. Infants recognize persons as social, as well as physical, beings, and become conscious of their own selves. Genuine communication begins to take place.	Infants imitate new and invisible gestures.	Infants show beginnings of make-believe play.
6	Representation clearly distinct from sensation and action.	Infants search manually even for objects hidden in complex ways.	Infants are capable of deferred and complex imitation.	Full-fledged make-believe play occurs.

cuses on infantile memory; the third looks for the seeds of future developments; and the fourth provides an overview.

General Characterization

The child starts the process of cognitive development equipped with sensory capacities, inborn reflexes, and the operating principles of assimilation and accommodation. To see how reflexes can serve as points of departure for cognitive growth and the development of internal representation, consider the sucking reflex, which appears immediately after birth. Piaget (1952/1963, p. 25) reports that two of his children sucked their fingers within an hour after birth. In the course of the first few weeks of life, different schemes develop from this single reflex through the process of accommodation. Different objects arouse significantly different kinesthetic sensations in the lips and require different sucking motions. On the basis of repeated sucking experiences with different objects, new sensorimotor sucking patterns develop. The biggest differentiation is probably between nutritional sucking and nonnutritional sucking. Nutritional sucking requires complex organization as it involves fine regulation of suction force and coordination of swallowing with breathing. The infant develops a nursing scheme, which in addition to the sucking reflex includes anticipatory orientation, body posture, head position, eye movements directed to the proximal part of the mother's body, kinesthetic responses to the breast, and so forth.

The schemes that infants develop provide them with the tools that enable them to discriminate among different objects and to recognize familiar ones. Piaget (1954) reports that: "The nursling, from the second week of life, is capable of finding the nipple and differentiating it from the surrounding teguments . . . So also, after the fifth to the sixth week of life, the child's smile reveals that he recognizes familiar voices or faces whereas strange sounds or images astonish him" (p. 5).

When infants react differently to different objects, it may seem to the observer that they are identifying the objects and distinguishing among them. But actually, Piaget claims, infants have no experience of independent objects, only of their own sensations and reactions to objects. He maintains that infants do not have **object permanence** or an **object concept**. That is, they do not have the idea that the world is populated with objects that have substance and permanence. For infants, objects exist only when they act on them and only in terms of the specific action schemes they apply to the objects. Infants experience only sensorimotor actions, not things. They differentiate among objects only if and to the extent that the objects elicit in them different sensorimotor schemes. Thus, infants do not distinguish between the nipple and the surrounding area as such; they distinguish only between the kinesthetic and visual sensations and motor reactions that the two activate in them.

Piaget would also interpret infants' recognition of their mothers (shown by smiling, cooing, etc.) in sensorimotor terms. Through repeated encounters, infants interconnect the different sensations and reactions elicited by the mother. Because of the interconnectedness, elicitation of one of the components leads to anticipation of the others in the sequence. Thus, the sight of his mother is likely to activate in Johnny the particular tactile-kinesthetic sensations involved in being held by her, which in turn are likely to trigger the complex of sucking sensations and gestures, which in turn are associated with the satisfaction provided by the inflow of milk. When hungry, Johnny may therefore calm down on seeing his mother, because he anticipates the other events in the habitual sequence. An adult observing this type of behavior is tempted to interpret it in adultomorphic terms and to attribute to Johnny **perceptual identification** of his mother. But Piaget insists that this approach is superficial and must be resisted. Infants have no cognizance of people or any other objects; only their own sensations and motor reactions are functional for them. Infants do not have an object concept because they have no representational capacity, and hence no way to represent objects internally. Our knowledge of the existence of a world populated with objects is so compelling that it is hard to imagine anyone not sharing this knowledge. But we know reality only because we are able to represent it internally. Without representation there can be no knowledge of reality.

Piaget's argument is that although in the first three stages infants behave as if they had memory of objects and people, they actually remember only their own actions and sensations in response to these stimuli. Piaget's strongest evidence is for infants of Stage 3, who can be more readily tested. That evidence is presented later when Stage 3 is discussed. In the meantime an experiment conducted by Bower (1974, pp. 191-193) with infants in the age range of 12–16 weeks can be cited in support of Piaget's argument.

Bower began the experiment by presenting the infants with a toy train in one location (A) and moving it to another location (B). The train stayed at B for 10 seconds and then moved back to A. After a number of $A \rightarrow B \rightarrow A$ sequences the infants tracked the train visually as it moved from one location to the other. At this point Bower moved the train not to B but to a new location (C). The infants' reaction to this change was revealing. Instead of following the train to C, they looked for the train in the customary B location and showed signs of disappointment when they did not find it there. If the infants had a conception of the train as an independent object in space, their failure to adjust to its altered position would indeed be puzzling. But this behavior makes sense on the assumption that what was real for the infants was not the train itself but the visual sensations it evoked in them and the pattern of head and eye movements involved in tracking it. The train merely served as an opportunity for the pleasurable exercise of these activities. The absence of the train from its usual destination constituted an interference with the operation of an enjoyable active scheme, and therefore aggravated the infants. They remembered the visual image of the train and the associated pattern of head and eye movements; when these movements failed to produce the desired sensation, the memory of what should be conflicted with what was.

More on Sensorimotor Memory

The preceding discussion attempted to answer an apparent paradox, namely, how it is possible for infants to recognize objects when they do not even have an idea that objects exist. The answer given was essentially that infants remember not objects as such but the sensations and responses objects evoke in them.

Research on infant recognition memory is consistent with this interpretation. This research can be exemplified by the work of Fagan (e.g., 1970, 1973). His method, like much of the research on infancy, is based on the tendency of infants to prefer novel stimuli over familiar ones. A Piagetian explanation of this tendency would be in terms of assimilation-accommodation. Because infants like to exercise their accommodative capacity, they are more attracted to novel stimuli, which require substantial accommodation, than to familiar stimuli, which require little accommodation. Whatever the explanation for the preference for novel stimuli, this preference can be used to test infant memory. To test whether infants retain a stimulus they have been exposed to, that stimulus is paired with a novel stimulus. If the infants attend more to the novel stimulus, one can conclude that they have retained the stimulus they were familiarized with.

Using the **paired-comparison technique** Fagan tested infants in the age range of 3–6 months. In one experiment (Fagan, 1970) the infants were first shown a visual pattern for 2 minutes. The familiarized pattern was shown again along with a new pattern 2 hours after this familiarization phase. The experimenter measured the length of time the infants fixated their gaze on each of the two patterns. The results show that the fixation durations were longer for the novel stimuli than for the familiarized stimuli, indicating retention over a 2-hour period. Another experiment (Fagan, 1973) demonstrated retention of patterns for periods of up to 48 hours and of photographs of human faces for up to 2 weeks. Such long-range memory is indeed very impressive but, as I have suggested, can be interpreted as a sensorimotor phenomenon. Fagan (1977) himself also thinks of infantile memory in sensorimotor terms: He uses such concepts as orienting and fixating responses to interpret his results.

Adult analogues of sensorimotor memory can be seen in the recognition of individuals as familiar without being able to identify them. You have probably had the experience of meeting someone and feeling that you have seen the individual before, but not being able to recall who he or she is. Even this type of recognition is, however, only a remote approximation to the infant's recognition. As an adult you knew that there was an individual in front of you; you even knew that the individual was a child, a male, and so on. Infants, on the other hand, have no such knowledge; they merely have an experience of **familiarity** as a result of the reevocation of previously experienced sensorimotor schemes.

Another way to characterize the memory of infants is to say that they have recognition-memory capacity, but no recall capacity. They recognize something as familiar when it evokes in them schemes that require little accommodation. But they have no recall capacity because recall requires mental representation, which they do not possess. Infants can sense objects and react to them appropriately when they are in contact with the objects, but they cannot evoke objects in their absence.

Piaget's (1951/1962, chap. 7) discussion suggests that one reason why infantile experiences, especially in the emotional domain, have such profound effects and are so hard to modify is that they are retained as sensorimotor impressions, which unlike categorically coded memories are not directly subject to conscious inspection and analysis.

Piaget's claims about infant memory have far-reaching implications. They imply, for instance, that when infants are not in sensory contact with their mothers, the mothers as such do not exist for them. Understandably, there has been resistance to Piaget's revolutionary ideas about infant mentation. Skeptics are concerned about the lack of critical evidence in support of the theory. Although this is true, it is also the case that Piaget's is the only theory that incorporates a large array of disparate observations into a coherent framework.

To appreciate the difficulty in testing directly the notion that infants have only sensorimotor memories, consider an experiment (Ungerer, Brody, & Zelazo, 1978) that claims to have found evidence for nonsensorimotor memory in neonates. In this experiment 2- to 4-week-old infants heard from their mothers, for 13 days, 60 times each day, either the word *beguile* or *tinder*. The infants' recognition of the words was tested at four different intervals following exposure. In the tests the infants heard from a tape recorder the trained word and one other word. In each test the infants heard six recordings of each word, half made by the mother and half by an unfamiliar female speaker. Ungerer et al. (1978) credited an infant with recognition of a word if he or she exhibited any of the following behaviors when the word was heard: ''large nondirectional eye movements, sustained lid widening or raising of brows, or head-turning toward or away from the sound source'' (p. 180). Using these indicators Ungerer et al. found higher recognition reactions for the familiarized word than for the unfamiliarized word on one of the four tests. (The authors claim to have found significant differences on all four tests. However, only one of the tests yielded significance beyond the .05 level on a two-tailed test, which is normally considered to be the minimally acceptable level of significance.) These marginal results are rendered even more shaky by the deficiency of the tests in reliability.

But even if the results were strong and reliable, they would not contradict Piaget's conception of memory in infancy. There is nothing in the results to indicate that the infants recognized the sounds themselves as familiar rather than their own auditory sensations and associated bodily orientations. What I am saying is that the infants had an experience of familiarity when they heard the previously exposed word because it activated in them a familiar sensorimotor scheme consisting of a particular auditory sensation and associated motor responses. In fact, it may very well be that the signs that Ungerer et al. took as indicating recognition were the very ones that had occurred during the original exposure of the word.

The Ungerer et al. experiment highlights the problem in designing critical experiments to decide whether infant memory is sensorimotor or representational, namely, that the two postulated types of memory often result in similar manifest behaviors. In particular, both can account for experiences of familiarity. It must be further pointed out that Ungerer et al. make the mistake of thinking of sensorimotor memory as peripheral. That is, they assume that sensorimotor memories are located in the infant's eyes, ears, skin, and musculature. The term *sensorimotor*, however, refers to the content of memory, not to its neuroanatomical locus. Piaget did not concern himself with the question of locus. But it is clear that sensorimotor memories cannot be peripheral. The peripheral memories, called "icons" in the visual modality and "echos" in the auditory modality, that have been identified have durations in the order of seconds (see Neisser, 1967; Sakitt, 1976). Obviously, any memory lasting minutes, not to speak of hours and weeks, must be located in the central nervous system.

From Intermodal Coorientation to Multimodal Representation

In the first two stages infants are wound up in their own sensations and actions, evidencing little awareness of the existence of an external reality or of themselves as separate beings. Yet an internal representation eventually evolves, and the basis for it is present in the earliest stages.

Mature representation of objects contains information about their various properties, including their characteristics in different sensory modalities. **Multimodal representation** makes possible anticipation and planning. Even though one may at a given moment experience an object only through a single modality, one can and does anticipate its characteristics in other modalities. Thus, on seeing a new piece of chalk, one knows (implicitly) how much force one needs to exert to lift it before attempting, and one knows how widely one needs to open one's hand to grasp it before touching it. Young infants are far from having such multimodal representation of objects. But they have the rudiments that make the development of such a representation possible.

Even newborn infants move their heads and eyes, under certain conditions, in the direction of a sound (e.g., Mendelson & Haith, 1976; Muir & Field, 1979). However, this behavior seems to be little more than an orientation toward additional stimulation. Turkewitz and his co-workers have pursued the hypothesis that young infants are not as responsive to the qualitative characteristics of stimulation in different modalities as to their quantitative characteristics (e.g., their intensity). In fact, it has been demonstrated that young infants sometimes react to stimulation in different modalities as interchangeable. Thus, for instance, Lewkowicz and Turkewitz (1981) presented 1- and 2-day-old infants simultaneously with two light patches of different intensities and noted their looking preferences. Experimental infants received auditory stimulation just prior to exposure to the light patches; control infants did not. The results show that the experimental infants looked more at lower-intensity patches than the control infants. Apparently, the infants who had auditory stimulation needed less additional visual stimulation to produce the optimal total amount of stimulation. Thus, the neonates in this experiment did not seem to respond to the unique qualities of the visual and auditory stimuli, but rather to their common characteristics as sources of arousal.

Although the early **intermodal coorientation** does not even presuppose cognizance of separate sense modalities, it can nevertheless be viewed as the starting point in the development of **intermodal coordination** because as Mendelson and Haith (1976) note it predisposes the infant "to learn about spatially related events" (p. 55). Intermodal coordination becomes manifest around 3 months. Piaget (1952/1963, pp. 81–87) observed that at about 3 months infants turn their heads when they hear voices for the purpose of seeing the speaker. Coordination between eye and hand appears later than between eye and ear, but by the middle of the first year, infants are typically able and eager to grasp things they see and to look at things they hold (Piaget, 1952/1963, pp. 88–121).

The intermodal coordinations are a basis for expectations and therefore advance the construction of the object concept. As Piaget (1954) explained: "It is clear that such coordination endows sensory pictures with a greater degree of solidity than when they are perceived through a single kind of schemata: the fact of expecting to see something instills in the subject who listens to a sound a tendency to consider the visual image as existing before the perception" (p. 8).

Gradually, infants come to realize that particular sight experiences go together with particular sound experiences, with particular tactile experiences, and so forth, and they draw the conclusion that such constellations of experiences are due to the characteristics of independent objects. They learn that their actions do not create reality, but merely use it. Sinclair (1975) put this point somewhat differently: "It is only gradually, by performing the same action on a number of different objects (e.g., shaking rattles, spoons, dolls, etc.) and different actions on the same object (e.g., shaking, licking, throwing a rattle) that action and object become differentiated'' (p. 236).

Overview

At birth infants have at their disposal crude sensory and motor abilities. On the basis of these they develop, through the mechanisms of assimilation and accommodation, more refined sensorimotor action patterns or schemes, which enable them to interact adaptively with the environment. In the first 6 months infants learn to focus on objects and to follow their movements. They can coordinate different sensory and motor activities, such as grasping a pacifier they see and putting it in their mouths for sucking. The sensorimotor schemes become increasingly better established and more refined as infants increase their interaction with the environment and widen the range of their contacts.

In the first stages infants develop skills for interacting with people and objects, and they form social-emotional attachments, but there is no awareness of the existence of people and objects. They have no internal representation of reality; they have only sensorimotor memory, which is an automatic byproduct of sensorimotor engagement. Infants' sensorimotor memories of people and objects serve as the basis for the experience of familiarity when they reencounter previously experienced stimuli. Infants also have no awareness of themselves as separate, independent beings, even as they are wrapped up in their own sensations and motor reactions. As Piaget (1954/1981) has said: ''The infant's primary narcissism is a narcissism without a Narcissus'' (p. 38).

The intermodal coordinations, which are well established by the end of the first two stages, help in the separation of object from action and in the development of object representation.

STAGE 3 (THIRD QUARTER OF FIRST YEAR): BEGINNING OF SENSORIMOTOR REPRESENTATION

In the first two stages infants act out sensorimotor schemes but display little interest in the schemes themselves or in the objects to which they are applied. Such interests become clearly evident in the third stage. By the third stage infants have developed considerable manual skills, and they enjoy exercising and improving them. They grasp and handle objects and inspect them, eager to learn about their characteristics. Piaget (1954, p. 258) considers the interest in improving the grasping ability and other manual skills to be the criterion for the advent of the third stage. He (Piaget, 1954, pp. 231–232) describes the fascination his children exhibited in their hand movements. For instance, in her eighth month his daughter Jacqueline devoted a great deal of attention to the opening and closing of her hands. Piaget sees this behavior as a sign that Jacqueline was beginning to become aware of her hands and of the power she exercised over them.

The level of functioning characteristic of this stage can be exemplified through an examination of three types of behavior: reaction to vanished objects, causal behaviors, and imitation.

Reaction to Vanished Objects

In the preceding stage infants would usually not look for objects that went out of their sight or fell out of their hands. It is as if the objects ceased to exist. When Stage 2 infants wanted to reexperience a pleasant stimulus that disappeared from their field of vision, the most they would do would be to repeat the behavior that proved successful before (i.e., they would turn to the location where the stimulus was previously seen). Stage 2 infants would not, however, mobilize new behavior to locate the desired stimulus (i.e., they would not look in locations where the stimulus had not been seen).

Piaget (1954, pp. 10–11) reports, for instance, that his daughter Lucienne repeatedly exhibited the following behavior when she was 3–5 months old. She would catch a glimpse of her father in a particular location and smile vaguely in recognition. She would then look away, but keep returning to the original location. When her father was not in the expected location, she would show signs of disappointment, such as crying, but would not look for him elsewhere. Apparently, what Lucienne remembered was that a particular head-turning produced a pleasant sight. She did not localize the source of the pleasure in an external object, believing instead in the efficacy of her own gestures. According to Piaget (1954) young infants seem to believe that: "a certain complex of efforts, tension, expectation, desire, etc., is charged with efficacy" (p. 229), without really knowing how or even being conscious of themselves as the sources of the effort.

In the third stage there is a beginning of separation of object from action. Infants now look for a lost object in new locations, no longer restricted to the particular location in which the object was initially seen. For instance, Piaget (1954, p. 15) reports that his son Laurent, 0;6(7), looked in different directions for a matchbox that he dropped.

However, although the search for lost objects is no longer limited to a particular location, it is limited to a particular sense modality. Thus, infants do not attempt to search with their hands for an object that has disappeared from their sight. At this stage an object perceived visually is apprehended only as a sight experience and is retained as such after it disappears. The disappearance is experienced by the infant as interference with the operation of a visual scheme that had just been active. The infant therefore engages in visual search to recover, as it were, a visual "aliment." That is, the object functions as a kind of nourishment or fuel that the scheme seeks. But not having a concept of an object as independent of the particular mode of its perception, the infant does not engage a tactile-motor scheme to aid in the search.

This description of Stage 3 mentality rests largely on Piaget's discovery that at this stage infants do not search underneath covers to recover desired objects that they have watched disappear. One example (Piaget, 1954) should suffice on this point:

> At 0;7(28) Jacqueline tries to grasp a celluloid duck on top of her quilt. She almost catches it, shakes herself, and the duck slides down beside her. It falls very close to her hand but behind a fold in the sheet. Jacqueline's eyes have followed the movement, she has even followed it with her outstretched hand. But as soon as the duck has disappeared—nothing more! It does not occur to her to search behind the fold of the sheet, which would be very easy to do . . . But, curiously, she again begins to stir about as she did when trying to get the duck and again glances at the top of the quilt. I then take the duck from its hiding-place and place it near her hand three times. All three times she tries to grasp it, but when she is about to touch it I replace it very obviously under the sheet. Jacqueline immediately withdraws her hand and gives up. (pp. 36-37)

Children fail to remove covers to get at desired playthings because, as Piaget (1954) is fond of saying, at this stage the object is still at the disposal of the action, and the action of cover removal was not part of the initial apprehension of the object. According to Piaget (1954): "The child's universe is still only a totality of pictures emerging from nothingness at the moment of the action, to return to nothingness at the moment when the action is finished" (p. 43).

Although Stage 3 infants do not search manually for an object that has been covered while they were viewing it, they do search manually for it if they had manual contact with it. Piaget (1954, pp. 21) reports, for instance, that when a watch Jacqueline, 0;8(20), was holding was pulled out from her hands, she stretched out her arms to search for it, without looking for it visually.

If an object you were viewing was suddenly hidden, you would engage nonvisual activities to recover it because the visual information gives you the basis for the inference that the object exists somewhere and is accessible to other senses besides sight, even though you had only sight contact with it. But infants do not have a concept of an object as independent of the modality currently in contact with it. Because of this, they cannot go beyond the data of their senses. Therefore, when the object is actually in sight, they reach out for it because they have learned that visual stimuli can be grasped. But when the object is covered, there is only a memory of a visual stimulus, which would give rise to manual search only when used as a basis for an inference that an independent substantive object exists. Because at the third stage infants are not yet able to make such an inference, their mode of search is tied to their initial mode of apprehension. A vanished object is searched for visually if it was seen before its disappearance and manually if it was touched; but manual search following visual contact or visual search following manual contact is unlikely.

I have said that the infant retains the object in terms of the specific modality through which it was experienced. What happens when an object is experienced both visually and manually? It seems that in this case the object would be registered as a visual object, because vision predominates. An experiment by Gratch (1972) demonstrates the complexities involved in intermodal relations. In this study babies aged 6-7 months participated in one of four experimental conditions. In all conditions the infants were initially shown a rubber hammer. The four conditions differed in what happened afterwards. In the first condition time was allowed for the infant to grasp the hammer. After the infant got hold of the hammer with his or her hand, the hand was covered with a transparent cloth. The second condition was similar to the first, except that the hand was covered with an opaque cloth. In the third condition the toy was covered with an opaque cloth as in the second condition, but the covering occurred as the infant was reaching for the toy, before he or she could get hold of it. In the fourth condition the toy was covered with an opaque cloth even before the infant started reaching for it.

Gratch's results show that in the last two conditions no infant attempted to recover the toy. These conditions thus replicate the typical Stage 3 findings. In the first condition virtually all infants removed the hand from under the cover with the toy in it. Apparently, the sight of the hand served as a cue that triggered the tactile experience of the toy in it. In the second condition about half of the infants removed the hand with the toy in it, and the other half either left both the hand and the toy under the cover or else just removed the hand, leaving the toy behind. One possible explanation for the failure of half of the infants to retrieve the toy is that they registered it as primarily a visual event; therefore, they did not engage manual means to make it reappear.

The design of Gratch's experiment and his findings are summarized in the following tabulation:

Condition	Type of Cover	When Covered?	How Many Retrieved Toy?
1	transparent	after got hold of toy	all
2	opaque	after got hold of toy	half
3	opaque	when reaching for toy	none
4	opaque	before reaching for toy	none

More on Vanished Objects

The most dramatic finding concerning Stage 3 is that infants do not remove a cover to get at a desired object that has been hidden while they were watching. This finding was interpreted by Piaget as reflecting the failure of infants to view objects as having substantive permanence, as being independent of their own actions. Bower (1974, chap. 7) has produced evidence showing that infants who do not pass the standard cover-removal test can do other things, which to him suggest that they do have an object concept. A critical examination of this research should deepen our understanding of the Stage 3 level of development.

In one experiment reviewed by Bower (1974, pp. 188–189), an object that infants had viewed was covered. When the cover was removed the object either reappeared or did not reappear. Heartrate changes suggested that the infants were more surprised by the nonreappearance than by the reappearance. If the object ceased to exist for the infants when it went out of sight, why were they surprised—asks Bower—by its nonreappearance? The answer is that the object does not cease to exist when it is out of sight. Out of sight is not entirely out of mind. True, the object is not registered and retained as an independent object, but it is registered and retained as a sight stimulus (i.e., as an occasion for the engagement of a particular viewing scheme). When the object was not there after removal of the cover, the infants were surprised because the recently active viewing scheme missed its aliment (i.e., the occasion for its operation). Infants do not, however, act to remove a cover to obtain a toy, because what they retain as being under the cover is a sight aliment, not an autonomous object that can be not only seen, but also touched, grasped, put in one's mouth, and so forth.

In another experiment Bower (1974, pp. 204–205) found that infants who would not remove a cup to find a desired object when the cup was opaque would do so when the cup was transparent. Why? One might as well ask why infants reach out for an object they see—and this they do even before the third stage, as I indicated earlier. The answer is that the child has learned that when a visual scheme is active in the presence of a visual stimulus, it is an opportunity for other schemes, including prehension schemes, also to become active. Infants reach for an object under a transparent cover as they would for any other visible object. Once the hand is aroused into action there is no reason why it would not act to remove an obstacle on the way to the desired object.

Finally, Bower (1974, pp. 207–208) reports that when a screen is placed between infants and a desired object, they remove it and reach for the object, even though they do not remove a cover placed on the object. This finding is also fully consistent with Piaget's view. In fact, the phenomenon was first noted by Piaget (1954, p. 33). He reports that Laurent, 0;7(28), would lower a cushion which blocked his view of his father if it was positioned next to him (10 cm from Laurent's face) but not if it was positioned next to his father (20-30 cm away from Laurent). Why this difference? It appears that when the cushion was next to him, Laurent saw it as interfering with his vision, and he acted to remove an obstacle to the exercise of his visual perception. But when the cushion was at a distance from him it did not block his vision; it occluded the object and not having an object concept, he had no reason to act to remove it.

In the preceding paragraphs I attempted to reinterpret Bower's findings in terms of Piaget's theory. Bower (1974, chap. 7) himself proposed what he claims to be an alternative interpretation in terms of spatial relations. But the development of the concept of space is intimately tied to the development of the object concept, as Piaget has duly emphasized in his chapter on space (Piaget, 1954, chap. 2) which follows directly the chapter on objects. Piaget sees the two lines of development as interdependent because they derive from common processes. The elaboration of this point would take us too far afield; the interested reader is urged to compare Piaget's discussion of space (Piaget, 1954, chap. 2, note especially p. 130) with Bower's (1974, chap. 7).

Causal Behaviors

We saw in the previous two subsections that in the third stage infants begin to have a representation of objects. This representation is, however, still basically in terms of their own action schemes. The force of their own action is still so dominant in forming the world of infants that they can sometimes be observed to expect things to appear and events to happen magically through mere execution of an action, as in the following examples from Piaget's (1954) children:

> Laurent, at 0;7(5) loses a cigarette box which he has just grasped and swung to and fro. Unintentionally he drops it outside the visual field. He then immediately brings his hand before his eyes and looks at it for a long time with an expression of surprise, disappointment, something like an impression of its disappearance. But far from considering the loss as irremediable, he begins again to swing his hand, although it is empty; after this he looks at it once more! For anyone who has seen this act and the child's expression it is impossible not to interpret such behavior as an attempt to make the object come back. Such an observation . . . places in full light the true nature of the object peculiar to this stage: a mere extension of the action. (p. 22)

The typical case described by Piaget (1954, chap. 3) in his chapter on causality involves the generalization of gestures that proved successful in a certain situation to other, inappropriate situations. For instance, Laurent, 0;7(7), watches delightedly his father drumming with his fingers on a tin box. When the drumming stops, Laurent looks at the box and "claps his hands, waves goodbye with both hands, shakes his head, arches upward, etc. In short, he uses the whole collection of his usual magico-phenomenalistic procedures" (p. 244). In another example, Jacqueline, 0;8(9), is lying and looking with lively interest at a saucer swung in front of her. When the swinging stops, she arches herself upward, repeating the gesture many times. When swinging ensues, she manifests "great satisfaction; otherwise, an expression of disappointment and expectation" (p. 238). The gesture of arching up, which Jacqueline used to express pleasure and to make her bassinet shake, thus became endowed with powers to produce any and all effects. It had **magical efficacy**.

Imitation

Infants' use of sensorimotor schemes for representational purposes is clearest in their imitative behaviors. While in the previous stage imitations were sporadic, now they are systematic and appear to be deliberate. The imitative act is preceded by careful observation of models and concentration on their gestures. Infants are now likely to imitate not only their parents but other people as well. Thus, Uzgiris (1972) found that not until the age of 7 months could she elicit gestural imitation from all 32 infants whom she studied longitudinally from the age of 1 month. The purposeful, systematic imitation that occurs in Stage 3 is obviously representational because it attempts to represent the model's behavior. The representational level of Stage 3 imitation is, however, limited because it is characteristically derived from action. Thus, the imitations of the third stage are generally confined to actions the infant had previously performed spontaneously; new behaviors are usually not imitated. Piaget's children imitated mainly sounds and manual activities at this stage. For instance, they imitated the hitting and scratching of objects and such sound sequences as *bva, pfs,* and *mam.*

Even with practiced behaviors, infants in the third stage are restricted to the imitation of complete patterns of behavior; they are not able to imitate parts of a pattern. The part is embedded in the whole and cannot be isolated from it. For instance, Jacqueline, 0;7(22), did not seem able to imitate hand opening and closing, even though this action constituted part of grasping, which she easily performed and imitated (Piaget, 1951/1962, pp. 22-23). Being able to perform movements physically is thus not a sufficient condition for being able to imitate them. Imitation requires an internal scheme of the movements to guide their execution. Jacqueline could not imitate hand opening and closing because she did not have available this pattern as an independent psychological entity, as a separate scheme. On the psychological level hand opening and closing was a new behavior, and she could not imitate it. Traces of functional inseparability of parts from wholes can be found in the difficulty children have in reciting the alphabet from a point other than the beginning and in the difficulty piano players have in performing parts of a musical composition.

The inability of the infant at the present stage to imitate new behaviors and parts of old behaviors reflects the dependence of scheme formation on action. Stage 3 imitation cannot initiate the construction of new schemes; these have to evolve in the context of the infant's spontaneous interaction with the environment. Infants cannot imitate new and partial behaviors because they do not have schemes to guide such performances, and they cannot construct such schemes at will because they are capable only of action-derived representation.

With all its limitations, Stage 3 imitation is a form of representation. Its representational character is clearly evident in the imitation of nonhuman models, which makes its first appearance in the third stage. For instance, Piaget (1952/1963, p. 186) reports that when Lucienne, 0;6(12), saw her toy parrots suspended from a new place (the chandelier), she briefly shook her legs without making any attempt to reach them. He notes that Lucienne had the habit of shaking her toys and interprets her leg shaking as a form of **motor recognition**. That is, Lucienne "labeled" motorically what she saw; her leg shaking represented the parrots. This representational behavior was not symbolic yet, because the representing activity was in the form of the action normally associated with the thing being represented. Still, there was the beginning of distancing between the signifier and the signified, because of the difference in the object being shaken (herself instead of the parrots) and manner of shaking (in a different way and for a shorter duration than when actually handling the parrots).

Summary

In Stage 3 infants develop imitative skills. Their imitation is systematic and it shows signs of being designed to gain a better understanding of the environment. There is also the beginning of imitation of nonhuman models. Infants thus begin to use sensorimotor schemes not only to act on things but also to represent them motorically. However, their representations are not yet symbolic; they derive from the actions toward the things represented. Stage 3 infants do not yet have the capacity to construct sensorimotor schemes directly for representational purposes, even with the aid of a model and even when the action is in their repertoire. They can, however, alter (e.g., abbreviate) action patterns when they use them for representational purposes. This marks the beginning of the ability to separate representation from action.

Because representation of objects is still tied to the particular sensorimotor schemes they evoke on particular occasions, infants do not yet acknowledge the independent existence of objects, and consequently do not search manually for seen objects. Infants' self-referenced orientation to the world is also evident in the domain of causal behaviors. When infants want something to happen, they produce behaviors that proved successful before, even if the behaviors are entirely inappropriate to the situation at hand.

STAGES 4-5 (FOURTH QUARTER OF FIRST YEAR AND FIRST QUARTER OF SECOND YEAR): BEGINNINGS OF DETACHED SENSORIMOTOR REPRESENTATION

In Stages 4-5 children begin to develop representational notions of objects that are separate from the actual specific sensorimotor actions toward them. They begin to realize that objects have certain substance and permanence and that they continue to exist not merely as extensions of the actions in which they were just involved, but as independent entities. I examine this level of development in six domains: reaction to vanished objects, causality, imitation, exploration, cross-modal transfer, and social representation.

Reaction to Vanished Objects

In the fourth and fifth stages children show an increasing appreciation for the autonomy of objects. This change is reflected in their behavior in the search-for-vanished-objects task, discussed in this subsection, and in their causal behaviors, discussed in the next subsection.

The behavior of Stage 4-5 infants in the search task contrasts with the behavior of Stage 3 infants. In these stages, when a desirable object an infant was viewing is hidden underneath a cover, the infant removes the cover. Apparently, an object seen is now appreciated as more than an opportunity for the exercise of a particular visual scheme. Even though it was assimilated via a visual scheme, the object now has enough of an independent identity to command a new scheme (i.e., the visual-motor scheme involved in the manual search). The search for hidden objects reveals that an object seen is not retained exclusively as a visual object. The child can now conceive of the object as a point of convergence for visual and tactual (as well as other) schemes. The capacity for intermodal coordination of schemes that developed in the previous stages is now utilized for the construction of a **multimodal object**.

However, the multimodal object is still heavily subject to the influence of immediate sensorimotor experiences, as is evident from the so-called **Stage 4 error** that Stage 4 children commit. The typical situation in which the error occurs is as follows (Piaget, 1954):

> Suppose an object is hidden at point A: the child searches for it and finds it. Next the object is placed in B and is covered before the child's eyes; although the child has continued to watch the object and has seen it disappear in B, he nevertheless immediately tries to find it in A! (p. 50)

The Stage 4 error occurs because the child identifies the object with the particular constellation of sensorimotor activity involved in its initial encounter.

The Stage 4 error has aroused the interest of several investigators, who have studied it with standardized procedures and large numbers of subjects (for references, see Harris, 1975). These experiments have yielded results that are in general agreement with Piaget's conclusions. I now consider two of these studies.

One study (Gratch, Appel, Evans, LeCompte, & Wright, 1974) tested 48 infants in the age range of 0;7(13)-0;10(16). Each of the subjects went through the following sequence. First, a toy was placed in one of two wells (A) in a tray, and the well was covered. This procedure was repeated until the infant uncovered the toy five consecutive times. Following this part of the procedure the toy was placed in the other well (B) and covered, while the tray was out of the subjects' reach. It was moved to within reach after designated intervals, which differed for different groups of subjects. These intervals were 0, 1, 3, and 7 seconds. The results show that at all intervals except 0 the infants exhibited a tendency to make the error of looking for the toy in the initial well (A). In the 0 condition the infants did not make the error; they reached directly to well B for the toy.

It appears that in the intervals of 1 to 7 seconds the sight of the object in B triggered the memory of the object in A with the attendant recovery procedure. Because the mode and place of recovery constituted for the infants part of the representation of the object in memory, they attempted to reapply the original means of recovery of the object. But at 0 delay there was no time for the activation of the original memory, and the infants responded to the toy in B as a new stimulus. Therefore, they went directly to B.

The experimental manipulation in the Gratch et al. study was in the second phase of the experiment. A study by Frye (1980) with 9-month-old infants introduced a manipulation in the interval between the first and second phase. The length of the interval was held constant, being 90 seconds in one experiment and 180 seconds in another experiment, but the infants were subjected to different experiences during the interval. In the control condition, resembling the standard Piagetian procedure, the infants had no access to the toy during the interval, while in the experimental conditions they manipulated the object in a new way during the interval. Frye found that the incidence of the Stage 4 error was substantially lower in the experimental conditions than in the control condition. For instance, in one experimental condition the object was placed on a support after completion of the first phase, and the infants obtained it by pulling the support. In this condition, 8 out of 10 infants searched in B when the object was placed there after the interval; only 2 went back to A. By contrast, in the control condition only 3 out of 10 infants searched directly in B; 7 searched first in A. Apparently, the different manipulations of the object during the interval in the experimental conditions helped dissociate it in the child's mind from its initial mode of recovery.

In Stage 5 infants search in B in situations that made them search in A in Stage 4. But even in Stage 5 infants search in B only when they see the transfer of the object from A to B, not when the displacement is invisible. An invisible displacement situation might be arranged by placing a toy in an open box, putting the box under a cover, emptying the box under the cover, and withdrawing the box. In this situation the child will typically not search for the toy under the cover even after he or she realizes that it is not in the box. As Piaget (1954) explains, at this stage:

> the object is certainly dissociated from its phenomenalistic and practical context and consequently endowed with substantial and geometric permanence. But from the moment that the displacements are too complicated . . . the object again be-

comes dependent on the context of the whole and on the practical schema leading to its possession. (p. 78)

This problem arises from insufficient autonomy of the internal object-representation. When the object's autonomy becomes consolidated in the next stage, the child will be able to find an object even when it is invisibly displaced.

Causal Behaviors

In the fourth and fifth stages infants gain an appreciation not only for the independent existence of objects and people but also for their independent causal powers. In contrast to Stage 3 children, who have no conception of causal forces outside themselves, Stage 4 children grant others elementary autonomy. Comparative examples (Piaget, 1954) should clarify this difference. At 0;7(8) Laurent enjoys watching his father scratching a cushion. The father stops and places his hand between the cushion and Laurent's hands "in such a way that if he pushed it slightly it would press against the cushion" (p. 245). But Laurent does not do that. Instead, he tries a variety of other means to reactivate the previous phenomenon. He strikes the cushion, arches his back, and swings his hand. Finally, he grasps his father's hand. "But it is only in order to strike it, shake it, etc., and he does not once try to move it forward or put it in contact with the cushion" (p. 245). In contrast, at the age of 0;9(6) Laurent directs his father's hand to the bars of his bed "to urge me to scratch them as I was doing just before" (p. 261).

In the earlier episode Laurent recognized vaguely that the father's hand had something to do with the scratching effect, but he did not appreciate its causal role. By contrast, in the later episode Laurent did recognize that the father's hand was responsible for the scratching.

The causal autonomy that children attribute to others is not complete in the fourth stage. Although they appreciate that others can make things happen, they still consider their own movements as necessary to initiate the effects produced by others. There is a change in this respect in the fifth stage. Children now recognize that it is sufficient for them to communicate their desires to bring about an effect; they no longer need to start the action. This is when instrumental interpersonal communication begins. Thus, when Jacqueline, 1;0(3), wants her father to continue blowing into her hair, she simply places herself in position in front of him (Piaget, 1954, p. 275). Common methods of communication at this stage include pointing, calling, and handing things over to adults to be opened, fixed, and so on. Such communication reflects, of course, a measure of symbolic development, as children refer to the things they want by means other than the sensorimotor actions associated with them. We come back to communication later, but now we have to return to noncommunicative causality.

By the fifth stage children's grasp of external, objective causality is such that they attribute it not only to people, who are major causal agents, but to inanimate objects as well (sometimes inappropriately). For instance, they put balls on inclines, or even level surfaces, and expect them to roll on their own (Piaget, 1954, pp. 274-275). At this stage children actively seek to understand the causes of movements they observe. For instance, Jacqueline, 1;3(9), is presented with a clown whose arms move and activate cymbals when his chest is pressed. She grasps the clown and searches all over his body for the cause of the cymbal movement.

The recognition of the permanence of objects and of their independent causality in the fourth and fifth stages constitutes a significant advance over the third stage. It marks the beginning of the emancipation of representation from action, because objects become autonomous only to the extent that children represent them independently of their own actions. The advance in representational capacity is also evident in children's imitations, to which I turn next.

Imitation of Invisible Gestures

In the fourth and fifth stages infants can imitate behaviors they have not themselves performed. Because the ability to imitate a particular behavior depends on the availability of a scheme that can assimilate that behavior and control its execution by the imitator, infants' imitation of new behaviors indicates that they can construct schemes in the imitative situation. Schemes need no longer evolve in the context of spontaneous action. The ability to construct schemes purposefully makes genuine representation possible, and representation now begins to evolve on a secure path. Children become able to imitate behaviors such as facial gestures, which they cannot see themselves perform. The cognitive advance marked by the imitation of **invisible gestures** can be more easily understood by first analyzing the processing involved in the imitation of visible gestures, which became solidifed in Stage 3.

In visible imitations infants see the model perform a certain action and assimilate it to the visual scheme activated by their own performance of that action. To be sure, the two visual experiences are not identical, but presumably there is enough of a commonality in essentials to evoke the same visual scheme. The visual scheme has associated with it a motor scheme, because when infants see themselves doing something they also have at the same time kinesthetic sensations attendant on their motor performance. The visual component and the motor component are integrated into a complex sensorimotor scheme, in which there is mutual guidance and cuing of one component by the other. The imitation of visible gestures is thus possible because when the visual component becomes activated by the model's behavior, it arouses the full visuomotor scheme, which can then guide the infant's imitation.

According to the foregoing analysis imitation of visible gestures depends on the similarity between the visual experience of seeing the model perform a certain action and the visual experience of seeing oneself perform that action. Analogously, the similarity between the auditory experiences associated with hearing oneself and hearing the model can serve as a basis for vocal imitation. But how is imitation of invisible gestures, which begins to occur at Stages 4-5, possible? To find an answer, I examine some of the actual imitations that Piaget has reported for Jacqueline.

Jacqueline's learning to imitate movements involving the mouth is both typical and instructive (Piaget, 1951/1962, chap. 2). In the ninth month she began to show great attentiveness to her father's mouth. In this period she imitated a variety of speech sounds, and the interest in the mouth may have been an attempt to understand the process of speech production. On one occasion Jacqueline moved her lips and produced a slight noise with her saliva through the friction of her lips against her teeth. Her father immediately reproduced both the lip movement and the sound. However, a few days later, he produced only the lip movement, leaving out the sound. Watching him carefully, Jacqueline imitated the lip movement several times. Jacqueline thus imitated the invisible gesture of lip movement. But how was this possible? How did she associate her lip movement with the model's lip movement? When she saw the model she had a visual image of his lip movement, and when she performed the action herself she had a kinesthetic image. The kinesthetic image is connected, through past experience, with the motor program that controls the lip movement. But how does the visual image become connected to the motor program? The answer that Piaget (1951/1962, p. 42) gives is that the sound served as a cue that connected the visual scheme with the kinesthetic-motor scheme. (Piaget refers to this kind of **indicator cue** as an "index.") Jacqueline was able to match up the visual scheme with the motor program because both were accompanied by the same sound.

The critical difference between this kind of **inferential learning** and **habitual-associative learning**, of which the conditioning paradigm is typical, must be highlighted. What the subject learns in associative learning is to emit a certain response in the presence of certain stimuli. Therefore, when the stimulus situation changes through the removal of a critical element, the response is no longer elicited. By contrast, in inferential learning, learners do not respond directly and automatically to stimuli; rather, they respond to the information that the stimuli provide. Thus, what Jacqueline has learned in the preceding episode is the equivalence between her father's lip movement and her lip movement. The sound served to suggest this equivalence; once it fulfilled this function, the sound was no longer needed to elicit the lip movement behavior. What Jacqueline has done is to *classify* as belonging together behaviors that on a sensorimotor basis are very different. This type of classification is, as we saw in the previous chapter, at the root of human concept formation. Jacqueline is also likely to have learned something more general than the equivalence of the two lip movements, namely, that her mouth and her father's mouth are homologous (see Guillaume, 1926/1971, p. 82). This knowledge can serve as a basis for the imitation of a variety of gestures involving the mouth.

The characteristics of inferential learning and the role of indicator cues can be seen quite dramatically in Jacqueline's learning to imitate tongue protrusion. A month after the lip-movement imitation just described, Piaget tried to get Jacqueline to imitate tongue protrusion. For three weeks she imitated the model's tongue protrusion by biting her lips. The turning point came when an indicator cue became available, seemingly by chance. One day, Jacqueline spontaneously stuck out her tongue while saying *ba . . . ba*. Her father seized the opportunity and immediately reproduced both the tongue protrusion and the sound. Jacqueline then imitated the same behavior. After a few more mutual imitations, her model turned to tongue protrusion without sound. Jacqueline succeeded in doing the same, but on several occasions preceded tongue protrusion with the old behavior, lip biting. Then a week later lip biting dropped out completely and tongue protrusion alone remained.

Jacqueline did not need to learn to stick out her tongue; she had done this many times, and she had a well-established motor scheme to control the gesture. She probably also had an appropriate visual scheme to interpret the model's gesture. But the visual tongue-protrusion scheme was connected to a motor lip-biting scheme, not to a motor tongue-protrusion scheme. The correct connection was finally made when a common sound accompanied both Jacqueline's and the model's tongue protrusions. Again, once the indicator served its role of pointing to the equivalence of the model's gesture and the child's gesture, it became superfluous. There was an added complication here in that Jacqueline had to eliminate lip biting from the imitation of tongue protrusion. She accomplished this without much difficulty. What Jacqueline learned in this episode was that her tongue and her father's tongue are homologous and that their tongue protrusions are similar behaviors in relation to their own bodies.

Children can be seen to grope actively to achieve accurate imitations. This is well illustrated in Jacqueline's attempts to imitate eye rubbing (Piaget, 1951/1962, pp. 36-37). At 0;11(2), Jacqueline rubbed her eyes with the back of her hand, and her father reproduced this behavior. She then tried to imitate him but did not succeed, even though she had produced this behavior spontaneously many times before. The spontaneous behavior, however, did not require knowledge of the correspondence between the model's eyes and her own, which the imitation did. Arriving at the correspondence was not simple, because she had only a visual experience of the model's eyes and only a tactile-kinesthetic experience of her own eyes. Nevertheless, in the course of 19 days this imitation was fully mastered. Piaget (1951/1962) reported:

At 0;11(16) . . . I rubbed my eyes in front of her just after she had rubbed her right eye. She laughed, as if she had understood, then, watching with great interest what

I was doing, she passed the back of her hand to and fro in front of her mouth. There was thus confusion between the eye and the mouth, as there had been two days earlier, when J. opened and closed her mouth instead of her eyes. But this time J. seemed to be dissatisfied with her assimilation, for she next slowly moved the back of her hand against her cheek, still rubbing and watching me all the time, as if looking for the equivalent of my eyes on her own person. She found her ear, rubbed it, then came back to her cheeks and gave up the attempt. Five minutes later she again spontaneously rubbed her right eye, but for a longer time than before. I immediately rubbed my eyes and she again watched me with keen interest. She then again began to rub her mouth, then her cheek, as if she were investigating, keeping her eyes on me all the time. (p. 36)

Five days after this episode Jacqueline finally succeeded in imitating eye rubbing accurately. The imitative behavior was distinct from instrumental eye rubbing (in response to an itch); in imitation, the hand passed only lightly over the corner of the eyebrow.

Three points deserve mention concerning this eye-rubbing imitation. First, it should be noted that Jacqueline had the interest to persist in trial-and-error experimentation until she hit on the target behavior. Second, the learning process would not have taken place if the model's behavior were so novel that Jacqueline could not have assimilated it to an approximate scheme, i.e., if she had not interpreted it as involving hand motion on the face. The approximate assimilation made possible the process of accommodation which ultimately resulted in the desired behavior. Third, it seems that Jacqueline knew when she was off target. How did she? It appears that the episodes in which the father reproduced immediately the eye rubbings initiated by Jacqueline played a facilitating role here, because they enabled her to connect the visual image of the father's performance to her tactile-kinesthetic experience. When she rubbed her mouth or cheek in an attempt to imitate the model, she knew that she had not done the right thing because the sensation was different from her initial eye-rubbing sensation, which became connected to the model's behavior. This explanation rests on the assumption that Jacqueline knew that her father was imitating her. In view of their numerous mutual-imitation games, this assumption does not appear unlikely. In addition, it is possible that her father's facial expression told Jacqueline whether her imitation was accurate or not.

Whatever the precise learning process, the achievement of faithful invisible imitation is a manifestation of the capacity to conceive of objects and events as transcending the particular schemes through which they are assimilated. In the case of the eye-rubbing imitation, for instance, Jacqueline must have realized on some level that what she did on her face was the "same" as what her father did on his face, even though the two engaged in her different schemes.

According to the present analysis the imitation of invisible gestures is an advanced sensorimotor ability that marks the transition toward genuine representation. In imitating an invisible gesture children represent a visual scheme (i.e., what they see the model do) by means of a motor scheme (i.e., the scheme guiding their own performance of the gesture). The signifier—the child's action—is thus expressed in terms that are different from the signified—the child's perception of the model's action. Although this representation is not yet fully symbolic, because the signifier is constructed on the basis of the signified, there is a significant advance here. In the previous stages infants' "knowledge" of the world consisted merely of the sensorimotor events that were involved in their encounters with it. Now, they actively construct representations by a process of inferential learning. They begin to utilize environmental events as sources from which information can be derived, and not merely as stimuli to be reacted to. We are witnessing here the launching of the human being as an **information processor!**

In view of my analysis of the process, it should not be possible for invisible imitation to occur much earlier than Piaget reported for his children (i.e., at about 8-9 months). A report (Meltzoff & Moore, 1977) claiming to have demonstrated that neonates can imitate such gestures as tongue protrusion and mouth opening did not withstand close scrutiny (Anisfeld, 1979; Jacobson & Kagan, 1979; Masters, 1979). The critics pointed to methodological and statistical weaknesses in the original report. On the other hand, a longitudinal study of the imitation of 12 infants between the ages of 1 month and 24 months provided support for the sequence of development postulated by Piaget (Uzgiris, 1972). Moreover, a careful study by Hayes and Watson (1981) failed to replicate the Meltzoff and Moore findings.

The Functions of Imitation

In the discussion so far I examined what Stage 4-5 infants can imitate and how they do it. I now consider why infants imitate. In Stages 1-3 infants imitate only behaviors that they have manifested spontaneously before. Their motivation seems to be to act out pleasurable schemes. The model's behavior activates an existing scheme, and the scheme is produced for the sheer pleasure of executing it. Babies love to repeat familiar actions.

The function of imitation seems to change in Stage 4 when infants begin to imitate new behaviors, and their imitations are accompanied by clear intentionality and mobilization of effort. Piaget and others (see Yando, Seitz, & Zigler, 1978) have suggested that children at the fourth stage and beyond imitate in order to learn and to gain competence. The main evidence for this motivation is the selectivity in children's imitations. Children primarily imitate behaviors that they are in the process of acquiring (see Harnick, 1978; Largo & Howard, 1979). That is, they are not likely to imitate behaviors well within their repertoire; these are too routine to arouse much interest. In Piagetian terms, routine, well-practiced behaviors do not arouse much interest because they call forth little accommodation. Nor are infants likely to imitate behaviors too novel to be assimilable by existing schemes. Rather, infants tend to imitate behaviors that are moderately novel (i.e., behaviors that can be assimilated, but require accommodation). This selectivity suggests that early imitation serves a learning function, that is, infants imitate to advance their comprehension and mastery of behaviors that interest them. Kagan, Kearsley, and Zelazo (1978, pp. 124-125) suggested that children imitate to test their ability to carry out actions that they have not performed routinely before.

The foregoing disucussion focused on the cognitive dimension of imitation in infancy. There is also a social-interactional dimension to infant imitation (see Uzgiris, 1981; Yando et al., 1978). Thus, infants, like older children and adults, show selectivity not only in what they imitate but also in whom they imitate. Valentine (1930) long ago emphasized the importance of the "imitatee," noting that although his daughter imitated a variety of models, it was her mother who "set her off" as none other could. He suggested that the child enjoyed interacting with her mother, finding the mother's actions "supremely interesting."

In a quantitative study of imitation conducted in the spirit of the interpersonal approach to the analysis of imitation, Pawlby (1977) observed the interactions of eight mother-infant dyads in weekly play sessions. The observations started when the infants were 26 weeks old and continued till the 43rd week. The results are based on an analysis of the videotape recordings of 10-minute portions of each session. Pawlby found that an average of 16% of the time in each session was spent in either mother imitating infant or in infant imitating mother. Pawlby also found that mothers imitated their infants four times as often as the infants imitated their mothers.

These findings suggest the possibility that the tendency of infants to imitate is induced, or at least reinforced, by the tendency of their mothers to imitate them. Studies with older subjects (see Yando et al., 1978, p. 18) have shown that individuals find it gratifying to be imitated and that they become favorably disposed toward those that imitate them. Assuming that these findings can be generalized to mothers and infants, their reciprocal imitations would seem to have the potential of strengthening the bond between them and inducing further imitations.

Most of the imitations recorded by Pawlby (94%) fell into two broad categories: vocalizations, including both speech and nonspeech sounds (e.g., laughter and whimper), and manual activities, including hand gestures (e.g., hand clapping) and object manipulation (e.g., grasping and pushing toys). The following tabulation summarizes the relative incidence of the two categories in infant imitations and mother imitations:

	Infants' Imitations of Mothers	Mothers' Imitations of Infants
Vocalizations	23%	72%
Manual activities	77%	28%

It is clear that the mothers imitated their infants' vocalizations more than their manual activities, whereas the infants imitated the mothers' manual activities more than their vocalizations. The mothers were apparently motivated by their concern for their children's language development. However, the children, who were between 4 and 10 months, had not yet developed a strong interest in speech, but were absorbed in practicing manual gestures.

The eagerness of children in Stages 4-5 to learn about the world is particularly evident in their exploratory behavior, to which I now turn.

Exploration

Infants show an interest in the environment and explore it before they reach Stages 4-5. But in the first three stages their exploration of different objects is undifferentiated. They follow objects visually, focus on them, mouth them, and handle them manually (see, e.g., Belsky & Most, 1981), but they do not evidence direct interest in the specific characteristics of different objects. The predominant interests seem to be in exercising schemes and in obtaining stimulation rather than in gaining knowledge and understanding. With the onset of Stages 4 and 5, exploration becomes more directed and object specific.

Observers (e.g., White, Kaban, & Attanucci, 1979) have noted an increase around the age of 1 year in sustained staring at people and objects with an apparent desire to understand them and their functions better. In a study of 32 children, 8 each at the ages of 9, 12, 15, and 18 months, Belsky, Goode, and Most (1980) found longer exploratory episodes in the 12-month-olds than in the 9-month-olds, with little increase thereafter.

Piaget (1952/1963, chap. 5) describes in detail exploratory activities designed to gain an understanding of the environment. For instance, he reports that Laurent, 0;10(11), lay on his back and dropped things from his hand, deliberately varying the position of his hand to observe the consequences. When an object fell to a new place, he would let it fall again to the same place several times before moving on. Another example of intense object exploration can be drawn from Piaget's observations of Jacqueline. While examining a new box at 1;2(8), she accidentally pressed on the edge, making the box tilt. This result fascinated her, and she set out to manipulate the box in an apparent attempt to try to understand the cause of the tilt.

Parents are familiar with more obvious exploratory activities, which are attendant on the achievement of locomotive skills, first through crawling (around 7 months) and then through walking (around 1 year). As soon as they are able to move around, babies begin to "get into everything." Even the cuts and bruises that they suffer along the way do not seem to deter them from taking advantage of the vast opportunities for exploration that locomotion opens up. Appleton, Clifton, and Goldberg (1975) write that the infant who achieves mobility:

> is no longer at the mercy of the immediate locale and what others have placed within reach . . . New aspects of the environment become accessible . . . People

and objects can be approached as a result of his or her own movements. Withdrawal from situations which are unpleasant or uninteresting is another new possibility. If a ball rolls away, the infant can follow it; if the toy within reach becomes boring, he or she can look for another one. (p. 143)

Normally reserved scholars describe in superlatives the child's bursting curiosity in the second year. Mahler, Pine, and Bergman (1975) quoted approvingly the statement that in this period the child has "a love affair with the world" (p. 70). Allport (1961) characterized the child in the second year as having "a fierce passion to manipulate objects" (p. 118).

Children's attempts to understand their environment and to control it are carried out in Stages 4-5 through active manipulation. In Stage 6 children become able to manipulate things internally. For instance, a Stage 5 child has to engage in extensive trial and error to get a stick through the bars of a playpen, but a Stage 6 child can solve the problem essentially through mental contemplation (Piaget, 1952/1963, pp. 305 & 336).

Children explore in order to gain a better grasp of the notions they have discovered. Thus, the attainment of the object concept motivates activities designed to understand the characteristics of objects better. Piaget (1954, pp. 152-203) reports many examples showing his children covering and uncovering parts of their bodies, turning objects around and inspecting them, putting things in containers and taking them out, and turning their heads slowly and deliberately to view objects from different angles. According to Piaget (1954) the child's intense interest in object exploration makes it "difficult to interpret his experiments . . . as other than experiments in solid geometry" (p. 157). Piaget and other writers (e.g., Stern, 1924/1975, pp. 97-98) project an image of the child reminiscent of a scientist who has come up with an exciting hypothesis and is eager to investigate it.

As has been pointed out by White et al. (1979), child curiosity develops and flourishes when parents provide opportunities for exploration and are available as "consultants" to explain, guide, and offer assistance when the child is "stuck." Escalona (1968, p. 47) made a similar point when she talked about the mother "illuminating" the environment for her child. Given the important role that curiosity plays in development, it is not surprising that children who were privileged to have such appropriate attention from their parents were found by White et al. to be intellectually more advanced (at the age of 3 years when their mental development was assessed) than children who were not so privileged.

Searching for specific maternal behaviors that promote exploratory behavior, Belsky et al. (1980) found a correlation of .61 ($p < .001$) between the mothers' tendency to engage in attention-focusing behaviors and the children's tendency to explore. The attention-focusing behaviors they observed involved pointing at objects, tapping them, demonstrating a particular activity to the child (e.g., dialing a toy telephone), and physically guiding the child's hands through a particular activity (e.g., putting the child's hand on a milk bottle to pull off the cap).

Such behaviors increase children's range of interests and facilitate their explorations. Children's increased explorations further encourage their mothers to redouble their efforts.

Feuerstein (1979) has encapsulated the role of parents and other caregivers in the child's cognitive development in his concept of "mediated learning experiences." For individuals to be able to use physical and social experiences beneficially, they need to have had the initial guidance of a concerned adult to provide them with direction and effective learning sets. According to Feuerstein (1979) the adult caregiver fulfills this critical function when he "interposes himself between the child and external sources of stimulation" (p. 71), focuses the child's attention on selected experiences, and interprets them for the child. Feuerstein (1979) considers "absence, paucity, or ineffectiveness" (p. 70) of mediated learning experiences to be at the core of cultural deprivation, and he has developed assessment and remediation techniques based on this concept.

Cross-Modal Transfer

The four categories of behavior (reactions to vanished objects, causality, imitation, and exploration), through which I have so far described the symbolic level of Stages 4 and 5, were based largely on Piaget's own writings. In this and the next subsection I discuss phenomena that have been investigated outside the Piagetian framework. I attempt to reinterpret them in terms of the Piagetian approach to symbolic development.

An adult may acquire a particular piece of information through a single modality, but that information does not remain modality specific. A dramatic example of the supramodal nature of our knowledge can be seen in our ability to identify letters of the alphabet when they are traced on our backs, even though they have not been learned as tactile entities. Evidently, we have what has been called a cross-modal transfer ability.

At what point in chronological development can one expect cross-modal transfer to appear? No transfer can be expected when the infant sees objects solely in terms of the particular sensorimotor schemes that they engage. For transfer to occur, objects must not be represented exclusively in terms of the sensorimotor schemes that made contact with them; they must be represented more generally. In other words, cross-modal transfer should be demonstrable in Stage 4 infants, but not earlier. Support for this prediction comes from experiments by Gottfried, Rose, and Bridger (1977) and Rose, Gottfried, and Bridger (1981).

Gottfried et al. (1977) tested 26 infants in the age range of 0;11(25) to 1;1(28). Although the infants were not given the standard Piagetian tasks to determine their sensorimotor stages, we can assume from their ages that they were in Stages 4 or 5. Using the paired-comparison technique, Gottfried et al. first gave the infants a geometric shape either to feel in their mouths or to palpate with their hands for 30 seconds. The infants were prevented from seeing the object in this familiarization phase. Then in the test phase the familiarized stimulus was exposed visually along with a novel stimulus, and the direction of the infant's visual fixations and reaching attempts was noted. If the tactile experience had no visual relevance, the fixations and reaching gestures should be equally directed to the two stimuli. However, the results show a preference for the novel stimuli. In the manual condition the infants fixated 56% of the time on the novel stimulus and reached for it in 68% of the cases; in the oral condition the corresponding figures were 63% and 77%. These results indicate that the shapes with which the infants were familiarized tactually remained familiar when shown visually. For these infants, then, the objects touched or mouthed were not merely tactile objects but visual objects as well.

By contrast, Rose et al. (1981) obtained no evidence of cross-modal transfer when they used the same procedure with 6-month-old infants. Their attempts to modify the procedure so as to make it more likely to yield positive results succeeded only in producing statistically marginal evidence for cross-modal transfer in 6-month-olds. The difference between the two age groups makes sense from the Piagetian point of view that we are pursuing here. For the 6-month-olds, who were probably not yet at Stage 4, the internal memory of the shapes was modality specific. Because they experienced the shapes primarily as tactile stimuli, they retained them as such. The situation was different for the older infants. Even though they had experienced the shapes only tactually, their internal representation of the shapes was not that specific. At Stages 4 and 5 the internal representation of objects is not strictly tied to the specific modality of contact. Representation now begins to be symbolic.

Social Representation

Stages 4 and 5 constitute a turning point not only in children's conception of the physical world but also in their conception of the social world. I discuss different aspects of this topic in this subsection.

Person Permanence In the discussion so far no distinction has been made between people and inanimate objects. We proceeded on the assumption that persons, like other objects, become objectified in the fourth and fifth stages. Is this assumption justified? After all, people are the most important and interesting objects in the child's environment. Children might therefore begin to attribute permanence and causality to people before they attribute these qualities to other objects. Piaget (1954, chap. 3) considered this question, and his answer is essentially that the person concept is not significantly ahead of the inanimate-object concept, although experience with persons provides an important impetus for the development of the object concept in general. Piaget maintains that infants do not make the transition toward considering people as having independent reality until Stage 4.

Piaget discusses the phenomenon of "causal imitation," which might at first appear to suggest that people are endowed with reality earlier than other objects. He notes that his children would imitate their parents for the purpose of making them continue an activity they had stopped. This type of imitation, which was restricted to people, occurred even before Stage 4. For instance, Jacqueline, 0;7(27), started striking a quilt as soon as her mother stopped, and she did not quit until the mother resumed the activity. It is worth quoting an observation to demonstrate how Piaget (1954) determined that a particular imitation had a causal purpose:

> At 0;8(10) Jacqueline coughs, I cough in response, and she laughs at my imitation. To make me continue she then coughs again, at first normally, then harder and harder and faster and faster. The manner in which she looks at me with an expression of desire and expectation, and the way she regulates her coughing in proportion to my silence, leaves little doubt as to the purpose of this behavior. (p. 250)

Piaget insists that one must resist the temptation to interpret such behaviors as indicating that the infant sees people as independent causal agents. Causal imitation is really not fundamentally different from causality by magical efficacy; the autonomy of persons does not emerge before the autonomy of other objects. According to Piaget (1954): "The only difference is that in the case of the object the child uses any means that chance reveals to him, whereas in the case of persons causality takes a precise form prescribed by the convergence of another person's body and his own—the form of imitation" (p. 253). What Piaget seems to be saying is that his children used imitation of people as a form of causality quite early because it proved effective, not because they recognized people as causal agents. They merely learned as a matter of empirical observation that imitation of people is effective in bringing about desirable results. The effectiveness of imitating adults as a form of causality arises from the correspondence between the child's body and the bodies of adults.

There have also been experimental investigations of the question of person permanence. A study by Bell (1970) with infants aged 8 to 9 months has been widely cited as providing evidence that children recognize the permanence of their mothers and of people in general before they recognize the permanence of other objects. Bell's results, however, lend themselves to an alternative interpretation.

In her experiment Bell administered to her subjects Piagetian hidden-object tests as well as parallel tests using the mother as the hidden object. She found that most of the infants tested (23 out of a total of 32) performed at Stage 5 level on the hidden-object tests and at Stage 6 level on the hidden-mother tests. (On a few occasions the experimenter served as the hidden person instead of the mother, but the results for these few cases are not reported separately.)

Bell interpreted her results to mean that the infants had a more advanced representation of their mothers than of other objects, but this interpretation is not necessarily correct. A crucial distinction must be drawn between spontaneous search for hidden objects and learned search. It would certainly not be very difficult to train even young infants to remove a cover when they see something that they desire being hidden underneath it. Cover removal following training would not constitute evidence for the possession of an object concept; it would merely indicate that the infants had learned to respond in particular ways to particular stimuli. Only when infants engage in search without having specifically learned to do so can inferences be made about their object concept. In the case of the mother it is quite likely that the infants' search behavior in the testing situation was a transfer from peekaboo-type games as well as from experiences of coming upon their mothers in hidden places while crawling.

Aside from interpretive questions, there is also a methodological problem with the Bell experiment in that the manner of hiding the mothers and the objects was different. The objects (small toys) were hidden under 6 x 8-inch felt pads, whereas the mothers hid behind such things as doors, couches, or a 1.5 × 6-foot screen. Jackson, Campos, and Fischer (1978) conducted a systematic study with infants in the age range of 6-8 months in which they equated the hiding places of persons and objects (both were large boxes of the sort used in a puppet theater). Under these circumstances infants were no more likely to search for persons than for objects. Jackson et al. also found a weighty practice effect. Infants who had taken the search tests at 6 months did much better when they were retested at 8 months than 8-month-old infants who had not been tested before. Apparently, the infants who had taken the test at 6 months remembered the search experience and benefited from it at 8 months. This supports our learning hypothesis.

The available experimental findings are thus not inconsistent with Piaget's position that persons do not have an inherently significant advantage over objects in establishing their independence. However, children's interaction with persons does serve a critical role in helping them arrive at the object concept. People are the most important, independently active objects in the children's environments, and it is through people that children gain the general idea of an independent reality (see Piaget, 1954, p. 254). People lead in the child's construction of reality, but they do not gain reality status substantially earlier than other objects.

It must also be recognized that in the last quarter of the first year, the child's distinction between social and physical reality is not as clear as it will become later. In fact, because of the primacy of people in children's lives, their initial view of inanimate objects tends to have a personal flavor. The process of depersonalization of the physical world is slow. Children continue into the early school years to attribute humanlike characteristics to remote objects (e.g., the sun), which they cannot understand (Piaget, 1929/1979). According to the philosopher John Macmurray (1961) the child constructs a separate physical world by noticing that it differs from the world of persons:

> The non-personal is discriminated within the unity of the personal as a negative. It
> is that in the Other which does not respond to my call. If I am to enter into active

relation with it then I must go to it; it will not come to me. The relation I have with it lacks the mutuality of a personal relation. It is, then, that which can be moved, but which cannot move itself. (p. 81)

One of the behaviors that is restricted to people from the start is communication. I turn to this topic next.

Communication   We saw that in Stage 4 children use people as if they were tools needing to be physically activated to produce results. By Stage 5 children have achieved a good grasp of the unique status of people as social beings through whom one can procure goods and services by means of communication, thus obviating the need for direct action. They appreciate now that if one wants to use an object as an instrument, it has to be acted on directly, whereas people can be made into instruments through communication. For instance, if one wants to get a distant object with a stick, one has to get hold of the stick physically and perform the pulling action with it. But in the case of an obliging adult, it is suffi-cient to ''ask'' by pointing, looking in the appropriate direction, calling, and so forth.

The Piagetian position that the emergence of genuine communication is de-pendent on the establishment of the object concept can find support in the results of a longitudinal study by Sugarman-Bell (1978) of four children between 9 and 14 months. Sugarman-Bell (1978) classified the children's behavior into three categories:

1. Person-oriented acts (e.g., child looking at or smiling to adult).
2. Object-oriented acts (e.g., child attempting to get something from an adult's lap, without paying any attention to the adult).
3. Coordinated person-object orientation (e.g., child ''touches adult's arm—adult acknowledges child—child reaches toward object in adult's lap'') (p. 54).

In the first two behaviors the orientation is either to people or to objects, but in the third the orientation is to people in relation to objects; it involves communica-tion, not merely interaction. Sugarman-Bell found that prior to Stage 5, the chil-dren exhibited primarily the first two types of behaviors; only at Stage 5 did the third type of behaviors become noticeably present. This is in accord with Piaget's conclusion that distinct instrumental social communication does not emerge until the fifth stage.

Some investigators have concentrated on close examination of specific com-municative gestures. Murphy and Messer (1977), for instance, analyzed the pointing behavior of 24 lower-middle-class mother-infant pairs. Half of the in-fants were 9 months old and half were 14 months old. The mother and infant were seated alongside each other facing three hanging toys. Murphy and Messer found that the mothers of both age groups exhibited a fair amount of pointing, but only the older infants looked consistently in the direction pointed to by the mother. Similarly, the older infants exhibited some pointing behavior themselves, but the younger infants exhibited virtually none. Pointing represents the object by a method other than action toward it, and therefore could only have been appreciated by the older infants who, judging from their ages, are likely to have been in the fifth stage of sensorimotor development.

I have interpreted the emergence of social communication in terms of the dawning appreciation of the independent existence of persons as physical and social beings. Another approach seeks the roots of communication in mother-infant interaction (see Lock, 1978; Markova, 1978; Schaffer, 1977). R. A. Clark (1978), for instance, suggested that mother-infant give-and-take interchanges serve as a basis from which gestural communication and, later, linguistic communication develop.

Murphy and Messer (1977) revived the suggestion of Latif (1934) that reaching develops into pointing through maternal mediation. When an infant reaches toward an unattainable object, the mother interprets this behavior as an indication that the infant wants the object, which she then provides. In this way the reaching gesture gains signal value and gradually becomes abbreviated into a pointing gesture, which is later substituted by a word. The sequence of gradual refinement and symbolization of forms of indication can be sketched as follows: whole body reaching orientation → reaching hand gesture → pointing → reaching or pointing and naming → naming. Although this sequence seems chronologically valid, it remains to be determined whether there is a causal connection between successive links in the sequence. With respect to this issue, it must be noted that reaching develops in the first trimester of the first year, and pointing does not emerge until many months later. It would therefore seem to follow that even if pointing does grow out of reaching, this transformation does not take place until infants are ready for it in terms of their capacity to deal with symbolic representations.

In contrast to the investigators who seek the origins of social communication in social interaction, my position is that the emergence of social communication cannot be understood outside the context of the child's overall cognitive development. Genuine communication occurs in the fifth stage when children are able to separate objects from actions and means from ends. It is then that they can adjust their communicative means to achieve their goals.

What I am saying is that prior to the attainment of the symbolic capacity, no genuine communication is possible. There is no denying, however, that when the child becomes capable of symbolic communication, the earlier social interactions profoundly influence its manner and content. Children who had unpleasant early experiences in interaction with their mothers are not likely to want to or to be able to communicate with them effectively when they become cognitively ready to do so.

The Self   During the fourth-fifth stages, when children become conscious of the autonomy of objects and people, they also become conscious of themselves as separate, independent beings. Before the dawning of the representational capacity, when infants cannot represent reality internally, they cannot represent themselves either. The self evolves gradually. Young infants cannot clearly demarcate the internal from the external. When the hands of 4-month-old infants are held tightly, they struggle, indicating consciousness of the sensation, but look all around for the source of the sensation, indicating failure to distinguish between the self and the nonself (Piaget, 1951/1962, pp. 201-202).

Children's evolving sense of self can be seen from their behavior when put in front of a mirror (see Asch, 1952, p. 284; Guillaume, 1926/1971, pp. 150-154; Lewis & Brooks-Gunn, 1979; Piaget, 1951/1962, p. 56; Preyer, 1889/1973, pp. 189-207). In the first year infants tend to react to their own images as they would to any other sight; they look at them and touch them. It is not until the second year that children show an appreciation for the representational relation between the image and their own selves. In the second year children enjoy making various gestures and grimaces at the mirror with the obvious expectation of seeing them reflected in the mirror.

Children's awareness of their bodily selves is part of a more general concept of self that includes continuity of memories and a sense of social-personal identity. The studies in this area come primarily from psychoanalytically oriented investigators. The most important is that of Mahler et al. (1975), which is based on careful observation of infants and their mothers in an experimental nursery. The main sample in this study included 21 infant-mother pairs, who were observed continually from 2½ months to 31 months, yielding hundreds of hours of observation, much of it recorded on film and thoroughly analyzed. No quantitative-statistical data are reported from this study. Instead, the authors present the theoretical conclusions they have reached from their work. Even though the absence of quantitative results precludes an independent evaluation of the validity of the theory developed by Mahler et al., their ideas do inspire confidence because of the massive amount of work involved and the obvious insights that emerged.

I attempt in the following paragraphs to incorporate the insights of the psychoanalytic investigators into the Piagetian framework presented in this chapter. Like Piaget, these writers hold that infants are initially undifferentiated from their environment, although in the psychoanalytic approach this undifferentiation is seen primarily in terms of the relation of infants to their mothers.

The growth of the self goes hand in hand with the child's increasing appreciation and exploration of the environment. In interacting with their environment,
children learn not only about objects and people but also about their own powers
and limitations. It can be assumed that the achievement of locomotive skills (first
crawling and later walking), which makes it possible for children to get to desirable objects and places on their own, gives them a strong sense of power and mastery. However, children are not exclusively dependent on locomotion for a sense
of mastery. They can derive it from their expanding skills in the manual, visual,
and other domains. But however they experience it, mastery would seem central
to the self-concept (see Macmurray, 1961). In a sense, "I do, therefore I am."

Guillaume (1926/1971, pp. 137-138) emphasized the role of imitation in the
achievement of self-awareness. As we have seen in the discussion of imitation, it
is in the course of imitating others that children learn about their invisible body
parts and their resemblance to the body parts of their models.

Mahler et al. (1975) placed heavy emphasis on the role of the mother in
facilitating the formation of self-identity. Mothers serve a facilitating role when
they encourage their children to move around on their own, but are available
when they stumble and need help. Because of children's initial insecurity in
venturing out to explore the unknown, they need to feel confident that the mother
is there to provide physical and emotional support. Mahler et al. describe graphically how children crawling or walking away from their mothers keep glancing
back for reassurance, occasionally returning for "emotional refueling." Sorce
and Emde (1981) have shown that the physical presence of the mother is not
enough to facilitate exploratory behavior. The mother has to be emotionally
available; she has to be sensitive to the infant's signals and must respond to them
promptly and appropriately.

Mothers also engage in behaviors that are more directly intended to enhance
the child's sense of self. The pride and joy that mothers (at least in Western
middle-class societies) typically express in reaction to displays of their children's
achievements cannot but infect the children. The mother who interrupted the
puzzle-board play of her 11-month-old daughter to tell her how well she was
doing was assigning ego significance to the child's activity and was thus helping
the child construct her self (Shotter, 1978, p. 68). Going beyond the early phase
of ego formation, sociologists (e.g., Mead, 1934) have emphasized that an individual's sense of self-identity and worth largely reflect society's evaluation
(through the agency of parents and peers) of him or her.

Children's awareness of their skills and power, reinforced by parental praise,
leads not only to the development of a sense of self but also characteristically to
an overinflated, exaggerated self. Normal toddlers walk proudly with their heads
up as masters of the universe. In Lichtenberg's (1975) words: "sensorimotor activities that take place before the gaze of the appreciative parent contribute important imagery to the sense of self grandiosity and omnipotence" (p. 469). In
time, the waning of the novelty of the child's accomplishments and the encounter

of new challenges and inevitable frustrations, reinforced by the process of socialization, lead to the deflation of the self to realistic levels.

One other point has to be taken up before leaving the topic of the self. In classical psychoanalytic theory tolerable delays in the gratification of the hunger need constitute a critical precursor to the differentiation of the self. In her summary of this position, Escalona (1968) says: "Psychoanalytic theory proposes that the very young infant is impelled to a first awareness of the discrepancy between the self and a surrounding field when unpleasure due to hunger does not subside at once, so that the infant is forced to register the fact that food and satisfaction reach him from the 'outside'" (p. 39).

There is a parallel in Piagetian theory to the notion of hunger frustration. It is the tension between assimilation and accommodation. An object not adequately assimilated produces pressure for accommodation. Accommodation is thus the process through which the external environment impresses itself on the infant. If the infant were truly the maker of all things, there would be no need for accommodation. From this broader perspective, hunger frustration does not seem necessary for the attainment of the differentiation between the self and the nonself. In most environments there are enough changing and novel stimuli (from the point of view of the infant) to engage the accommodative process constantly. There is thus a basis, without hunger frustration, for the acknowledgment of an independent external reality and the separation of the self. Asch (1952) has made a similar point:

> Of prime significance in this development [of the self] is activity with objects and the resistance they offer. In the course of action, the individual forms a conception of the properties of things, of their stubborn character, and of their separateness from him. Did objects lack this independence, if they obeyed our bidding without fail, there would be no evidence to support a differentiated self; effortless, automatic activities of breathing or scratching do not easily gain a self-referred character. While meeting the opposition of things to efforts, which he does not initially grasp as his, and while encountering obstacles and disappointments, the individual comes to differentiate himself from things. (pp. 284-285)

Summary

In Stages 4-5 children move to an objective view of the world. They begin to realize now that there is a reality that is not totally dependent on their actions, and they show a great deal of interest in exploring that reality and in learning about it. Their representation of reality is still sensorimotor in character, but it is clearly separated from nonrepresentational sensorimotor activity. Children are now able to work directly on the construction of representational schemes (e.g., in the context of imitation). Representation need no longer be a byproduct of other behaviors. The emerging representational capacity makes possible the rudimentary formation of the self and of the social and nonsocial object.

STAGE 6 (LAST THREE QUARTERS OF SECOND YEAR): INTERNAL REPRESENTATION ESTABLISHED

The final stage of the sensorimotor period marks a clear advance over the previous stages. Sensorimotor schemes have now evolved to the point where they can be distinctly dissociated from the things and actions that they represent. They can be evoked internally even in the absence of their "referents." Children now search for objects even if invisibly displaced. They can do this because objects are retained as autonomous entities abstracted away from the specific circumstances of their encounter. In the sixth stage children are capable of internal representation in the full sense of the term (Piaget, 1954, p. 85). The child's achievements in Stage 6 can be seen in imitation and gestural representation and in play.

Imitation and Gestural Representation

The emergence of internal representation at Stage 6 is reflected in the appearance of deferred imitation. Children are no longer restricted to immediate reproduction of the model's behavior; they can now imitate after some delay. For instance, at 1;4(3), Jacqueline observed a little boy throw a temper tantrum. According to Piaget (1951/1962) she watched him in amazement, "never having witnessed such a scene before" (p. 63). Twelve hours later she imitated the full details of the scene she had witnessed. She must have encoded and retained the temper tantrum internally without recourse to external action.

The child's facility in mental representation can also be seen in representational acting out of complex behaviors. Piaget (1951/1962) gives the following example:

> At 1;3(8) J. was playing with a [toy] clown with long feet and happened to catch the feet in the low neck of her dress. She had difficulty in getting them out, but as soon as she had done so, she tried to put them back in the same position. There can be no doubt that this was an effort to understand what had happened: otherwise the child's behaviour would be pointless. As she did not succeed, she put out her hand in front of her, bent her forefinger at a right angle to reproduce the shape of the clown's feet, described exactly the same trajectory as the clown and thus succeeded in putting her finger into the neck of her dress. She looked at the motionless finger for a moment, then pulled at her dress, without of course being able to see what she was doing. Then, satisfied, she removed her finger and went on to something else.
>
> In imitating in this way with her finger and her hand the shape and movement of the clown, J. was doubtless merely trying to construct a kind of active representation of the thing that had just happened and that she did not understand. (p. 65)

Piaget (1952/1963) discusses in detail another example of representational acting out in which the representational purpose of the child's behavior seems more evident. At 1;4(0) Lucienne tried to get a chain out of a matchbox which was not open wide enough to get the chain out. She tried to retrieve the chain with her finger—a procedure which had succeeded before when the opening was wider—but failed. She then abandoned her attempt to get the chain out, watched the slit attentively, and opened and closed her mouth several times, successively increasing the width of the mouth opening. "Soon after this phase of plastic reflection, Lucienne unhesitatingly puts her finger in the slit and, instead of trying as before to reach the chain, she pulls so as to enlarge the opening. She succeeds and grasps the chain" (p. 338). Piaget considers the opening and closing of the mouth as thinking out the situation, quite akin to what an adult would do with words or mental imagery. To solve the problem Lucienne did not restrict herself to the trying out of different actions; she also contemplated the situation. She conceived of the possibility of widening the opening before she actually tried it. This external, gestural reflection is still practical sensorimotor thought because it takes place in the context of a specific difficulty and is directed toward its immediate solution. Nevertheless, this type of behavior has the earmarks of thinking because, once started by an external stimulus, it is internally maintained and guided.

Gestural representation declines as children become capable of verbal representation. Bretherton, Bates, McNew, Shore, Williamson, and Beeghly-Smith (1981) compared the use of words and gestures by children at the ages of 13 and 20 months. Bretherton et al. exposed their subjects to two toy objects at a time (e.g., a toy telephone and a cup) and instructed them to get one of them (e.g., "Get the telephone"). The children were shown a total of eight objects (bottle, car, cup, doll, shoe, spoon, teddy bear, and telephone).

To measure the children's comprehension Bretherton et al. counted the number of objects they retrieved. As would be expected the 20-month-olds retrieved more objects than the 13-month-olds, the mean comprehension scores being 4.7 and 3.2, respectively. Of greater interest to us here are the differences between the two age groups with respect to two other behaviors that were quantified in this study, gestural encoding and verbal encoding:

1. Gestural encoding. Children were considered to be encoding an object gesturally if they greeted the object they retrieved with an appropriate gesture (e.g., held telephone to ear, rolled car back and forth, hugged, patted, and kissed doll and teddy, and put shoe to feet).
2. Verbal encoding. Children were considered to be encoding the object verbally if they vocalized some relevant word in response to the object (e.g., said *cup, juice,* or *yum* while getting or holding cup).

The mean scores obtained by the two age groups in these two categories are:

	13 mo.	20 mo.
Number of appropriate gestures	5.6	3.9
Number of appropriate vocalizations	2.7	4.6

This tabulation shows that gestural responses were relatively more common at the younger age, and verbal responses relatively more common at the older age. Both the gestural and verbal responses are overt forms of object encoding. Thus, the results show that as language develops, it takes the place of motor gestures as a medium of encoding.

Play

Play is an activity done for the pleasure of doing it, not (consciously) as a means to an end. In Piagetian terms play is characterized by the predominance of assimilation over accommodation. That is, in play the child exercises previously acquired schemes without much need or desire to accommodate them to the demands of external reality.

There are different levels of play depending on the child's level of mental development. In the first three sensorimotor stages, play activities are extensions of adaptive activities. After infants have learned to do something, they may continue doing it for the pleasure of the action. Piaget (1951/1962) describes, for instance, Lucienne's swinging of hanging toys:

> At first, between 0;3(6) and 0;3(16), she studied the phenomenon [of swinging objects] without smiling, or smiling only a little, but with an appearance of intense interest, as though she was studying it. Subsequently, however, from about 0;4, she never indulged in this activity, which lasted up to about 0;8 and even beyond, without a show of great joy and power. In other words assimilation was no longer accompanied by accommodation and therefore was no longer an effort at comprehension: there was merely assimilation to the activity itself, *i.e.*, use of the phenomenon for the pleasure of the activity, and that is play. (p. 92)

In the fourth-fifth stages children exhibit higher level play than they did in the previous stages. The representational capacity that begins to take root in these stages makes possible glimmerings of **make-believe play**, as in the following example (Piaget, 1951/1962) from Jacqueline at 0;9(3). Sitting in her cot and doing various things, Jacqueline happened to seize her pillow.

> As she was holding the pillow, she noticed the fringe, which she began to suck. This action, which reminded her of what she did every day before going to sleep,

caused her to lie down on her side, in the position for sleep, holding a corner of the fringe and sucking her thumb. This, however, did not last for half a minute and J. resumed her earlier activity. (p. 93)

In lying down, Jacqueline did not intend to go to sleep, merely to represent going to sleep. This, however, was only a primitive form of representation as can be seen clearly by comparing this episode with a later episode (Piaget, 1951/1962), which Jacqueline exhibited at 1;3(12), when she was in the sixth stage:

> She saw a cloth whose fringed edges vaguely recalled those of her pillow; she seized it, held a fold of it in her right hand, sucked the thumb of the same hand and lay down on her side, laughing hard. She kept her eyes open, but blinked from time to time as if she were alluding to closed eyes. Finally, laughing more and more, she cried "Néné" (Nono). The same cloth started the same game on the following days. At 1;3(13) she treated the collar of her mother's coat in the same way. At 1;3(30) it was the tail of her rubber donkey which represented the pillow! And from 1;5 onwards she made her animals, a bear and a plush dog also do "nono." (p. 96)

The differences between the two episodes are quite apparent. In the later episode Jacqueline was conscious of the make-believe nature of her play (as indicated by her laughing), and she deliberately controlled its different elements, varying at will the **pretend substitutions**. The earlier episode, on the other hand, happened by chance, and it seemed to be an automatic, momentary reactivation of part of the going-to-sleep routine, rather than a planned reenacting. The earlier episode represented actual going to sleep by acting out part of it, whereas the later episode represented going to sleep through systematic pretend substitutions: The cloth stood for the pillow, and the blinking for the eye closing of real sleep. Later on, Jacqueline used her toy animals to represent her own going to sleep. By this she revealed that her self was sufficiently objectified to be capable of symbolic representation.

Piaget (1951/1962) also reports a Stage 6 going-to-sleep episode for Lucienne, 1;0, in which a mere hand gesture substituted for the pillow:

> She was sitting in her cot when she unintentionally fell backwards. Then seeing a pillow, she got into the position for sleeping on her side, seizing the pillow with one hand and pressing it against her face . . . she smiled broadly . . . She remained in this position for a moment, then sat up delightedly. During the day she went through the process again a number of times, although she was no longer in her cot; first she smiled (this indication of the representational symbol is to be noted), then threw herself back, turned on her side, put her hands over her face as if she held a pillow (though there wasn't one) and remained motionless, with her eyes open, smiling quietly. The symbol was therefore established. (pp. 96-97)

In these examples we see increasing separation of the pretend substitutions from the real-life situations that they represent. A pillow need not be represented by a pillow or anything resembling it or associated with it, and pretend actors need not be the children themselves (e.g., Jacqueline made a toy bear put itself to sleep).

In the pretend going-to-sleep episodes just cited, symbolic status was assigned to objects by means of pretend action. Thus, Jacqueline made a rubber donkey represent a pillow by pretending to lie on it. As children develop language it can take the place of action in giving symbolic status to pretend substitutions. Thus, Piaget (1951/1962) writes that Jacqueline, 1;9: "saw a shell and said '*cup*.' After saying it she picked it up and pretended to drink . . . The next day, seeing the same shell, she said '*glass*,' then '*cup*,' then '*hat*' and finally '*boat in the water*'" (p. 124). Each of these make-believe acts, on its own and even more so in their combined variability, was possible because Jacqueline indicated verbally the role of the shell.

Experimental-quantitative research has accumulated in recent years in support of Piaget's analysis of pretend play (e.g., Belsky & Most, 1981; Jackowitz & Watson, 1980; Largo & Howard, 1979; Nicolich, 1977; Watson & Fischer, 1977; see also review by Fein, 1981). The experimental research concentrated primarily on the child's choice of pretend substitutions. The general tenor of the methodology and findings can be exemplified by the study of Watson and Fischer, who analyzed the play behavior of 12 children in each of three age groups: 14 months, 19 months, and 24 months. The children came with their mothers to an experimental playroom in which their play was videotaped. They were induced to engage in pretend play by the experimenter's modeling of such play. The children's play behavior was classified into four categories in terms of increasing distance of the substituting agent from the real agent. The least distance occurs when children act out themselves in pretense a certain behavior that they went through in real life, as when Suzie puts her head on a pillow to pretend to go to sleep. More distant is a pretense in which children apply to *others* behaviors that they themselves experienced in real life, as when a child puts a doll on a pillow pretending to put it to sleep. The substitution moves further away from reality when the substituting other is unrealistic, as when a child pretends to put a block to sleep. The most distant substitution in Watson and Fischer's scheme occurs when the substituting other is made to act as an agent, as when a child pretends to make a doll put itself to sleep.

The results, presented in Table 3.2, indicate that as children get older they exhibit increasingly more distant types of substitution. Thus, 75% of the 24-month-olds engaged in make-believe play in which another was an active agent, but none of the 14-month-olds engaged in this type of play. Similar results were obtained by Belsky and Most (1981) using nonmodeled, free play.

TABLE 3.2
Percentages of Children Exhibiting Different Types
of Play at Different Ages

Type of Agent	14 months	19 months	24 months
Self	58	50	50
Realistic other—passive	42	58	58
Unrealistic other—passive	25	58	75
Realistic other—active	00	42	75

Note: The data are from Watson and Fischer (1977). A child was credited with a particular category of play if he or she exhibited at least one
instance in that category.

Overview and Prospects

In the sixth stage children exhibit deferred imitation, imitation of complex new activities, and pretend play; in addition, their faith in object permanence cannot be easily shaken. What these phenomena have in common is that they require internal representation. One cannot hold something in mind to be acted on later as in delayed imitation without representing it internally during the interval. Imitation of complex new activities calls for the internal construction of new schemes and the reorganization of old ones—a process that requires a fairly high level of representational capacity. Make-believe play assumes a two-term relation: a "real thing" (the signified) and its make-believe substitute (the signifier). The real thing must be held internally in order for it to be imitated in play. Internal representation gives children the confidence to maintain belief in the existence of an object that has been seen, even when it is difficult to find.

The internal representation being postulated for the sixth stage of the sensorimotor period is not in terms of images or concepts, but rather in terms of sensorimotor schemes. That is, children can now think freely about the world in terms of the blueprints of potential action on it. To some extent they can also manipulate their representations internally.

As children advance in their representational capacity, the sensorimotor mode, tied as it is to the world of sensation and action, becomes too limiting as a medium of representation. Children are now ready for a more autonomous medium of representation. Fortunately, language is available for them as a biological predisposition and as a social given. It provides ready-made symbols (i.e., words) that children can use to represent ideas they have acquired on the sensorimotor level. Language also guides children in the formation of new categories and, as we have seen, helps them expand their pretend play. There is no question that through language children enter into a new stage of symbolic development with vast potential. In Piaget's (1951/1962) words: "It is thus legitimate to consider the intervention of the social sign [the word] as a decisive turning-point in the direction of representation" (p. 99). (Note that Piaget uses *sign* in our sense of *symbol*.) In the following chapters we see how children acquire increasingly more symbolic aspects of language.

AGES AND STAGES

The description of the substages of sensorimotor development in this chapter may have given the reader the impression that the different categories of behavior described under each stage appear uniformly at the same time in the sequence of development. This impression must now be corrected. In human behavior things are never that clean and orderly. There is unevenness and heterogeneity in development as there is in other psychological spheres. Performance in any one behavioral domain is determined not only by general factors, such as level of symbolic development, but also by specific factors relevant to that domain, including specific abilities, interests, and experiences. Piaget (1952/1963, p. 164) notes, for instance, that Jacqueline did not begin to pull on strings to activate distant objects until her eighth month, whereas her brother Laurent engaged in such behaviors in his fifth month. Piaget relates this difference to Jacqueline's 3-month lag in grasping seen objects. In some other domains Jacqueline was ahead of Laurent. For instance, she was able to imitate tongue protrusion at 0;9(12), but Laurent did not acquire this skill until a month later (Piaget, 1951/1962, pp. 32 & 40).

Not only is there heterogeneity in performance across different behavioral domains, such as imitation and grasping, but even within a single domain there is variability across different tasks. Piaget (1954, pp. 298-308) discusses this issue with reference to the development of causality. He observed that even in the sixth stage his children occasionally exhibited forms of causality characteristic of earlier stages. For instance, at 1;6(8), Jacqueline watches how a toy lamb placed on top of a rolled-up quilt is made to slide down by striking the quilt. After she is allowed to imitate this behavior, the lamb is placed on a table clearly separated from the quilt. However, Jacqueline continues to strike the quilt to make the lamb move. Piaget attributes this Stage 3 behavior to the novelty of the situation and Jacqueline's lack of understanding of how the striking made the toy descend.

Similarly, Piaget explained that Lucienne, 1;4(20), blinked her eyes to make lights go on and off because she did not understand the mechanics of illumination. Piaget concludes that each new stage is marked by the emergence of new capacities, but the child may not be able to exercise these new capacities under all circumstances. It takes time for an emergent ability to consolidate and to generalize to a wide range of tasks. Piaget refers to the gap in performance on different tasks as a **decalage**, a temporal displacement.

The point I made about the dependence of performance on local task characteristics is demonstrated quite clearly in a study by Rader, Spiro, and Firestone (1979). Rader et al. gave 10 infants in the age range of 5 to 6 months two cover-removal tasks: one with a washcloth as a cover and another with a sheet of manila paper as a cover. They found that three infants did not remove either cover, one removed both, and six did not remove the washcloth but did remove the paper. Rader et al. suggest that the paper was motorically easier to remove than the washcloth. Whatever the explanation, this experiment demonstrates the dependence of performance on the specifics of the task. Task characteristics are especially important in the initial period of acquisition of a particular capacity. As the capacity becomes better established, task peculiarities become less relevant.

Two interrelated problems were raised in the foregoing paragraphs with respect to the stage concept. One concerns variability among children and the other variability among tasks. I emphasized that individual differences militate against perfect synchrony among different behavioral domains. Thus, one child may be more interested and skilled in vocal imitation and another child more in manual activity. Therefore, when we say that a child has reached a certain stage of symbolic development, we are merely saying that he or she has acquired the potential for success in tasks requiring that level of symbolism. We cannot say whether or not the child will be able to manifest this potential in a particular domain. That would depend on additional factors, including specific capacities, interests, and experiences. We have also seen that of two tasks requiring the same symbolic capacity, one may be inherently easier than the other. Recognizing these constraints, one can see considerable orderliness and consistency in human development. (For a discussion of the stage concept as it applies to the entire developmental spectrum, not just infancy, see Flavell, 1982, and references therein.)

I now examine some research that relates to the issues I have been discussing in this section. On the basis of Piaget's work, Uzgiris and Hunt (1975) designed an instrument to assess mental development in infancy. They devised scales to assess functioning in six domains, including imitation, object permanence, and causality. Piaget divided the period of infancy into six stages. Uzgiris and Hunt refined Piaget's stages and identified intermediate steps in the continuum of development. They administered their tests to 84 infants ranging in age from 1 to 24 months and found that the tests correlated highly (above .80) among themselves as well as with age. These correlations mean that with increasing age infants perform better on all tests. The correlations do not, however, indicate that a *particular* step on one scale co-occurs with a particular step on another scale. Such precise synchrony is not to be expected in view of the individual and task variability previously discussed.

A comment is in order here on the widespread practice, also engaged in by Uzgiris and Hunt, of partialing out age statistically from the correlations between different cognitive tasks. Uzgiris and Hunt calculated such partial correlations and were disappointed when the initially high correlations among the six tests disappeared. This approach seems unwarranted. A partial correlation is normally used to eliminate potentially spurious effects. Assume a test of reading and a test of arithmetic were given to children between kindergarten and fifth grade, and the correlation between the scores on the two tests was found to be very high. Before rushing to the conclusion that reading and arithmetic draw on common abilities, one would have to check whether performance on each of the tests correlated with age. If this turned out to be the case and if partialing out the age factor eliminated the correlation between the two tests, then the conclusion about common abilities would not be warranted. One could reasonably argue in this case that the variation in age created an *artificial* correlation between the two tests, because the older the child, the greater was his or her exposure to both reading and arithmetic. In the case of infants, however, no one would claim that age is an artificial factor. Infants are not specifically taught causality or object permanence. We assume that the reason these two tests (as well as other tests) correlate is that as infants get older their level of mentation advances, making possible higher levels of performance on both tasks. In this case age is an essential factor, and it should not be partialed out. Thus, my conclusion is that the high correlations and the considerable homogeneity in performance across the different sensorimotor domains suggest that what develops is a general capacity, namely, the representational capacity.

A GENERAL SUMMARY OF SENSORIMOTOR DEVELOPMENT

The course of development that culminates in the genuine representation of the sixth stage may now be briefly summarized. Infants begin life with inborn reflexes and the processes of assimilation and accommodation. Through interaction with the environment, the initial reflex schemes become differentiated and modified. The infant's schemes function in the first two sensorimotor stages (from birth to 6 months) primarily in the service of reactivity to environmental and internal stimuli. At this point infants have no representation of objects. What they remember is essentially a potential for particular actions in response to particular stimuli.

Gradually, infants develop an increasing interest in the schemes themselves, not just in using them instrumentally. In the third stage (from 7 to 9 months) they imitate behaviors that are guided by familiar schemes, and they engage familiar schemes in play. Sensorimotor schemes thus begin to function as vehicles of representation, not merely as instruments of action. However, at this stage "representation" is totally dependent on instrumental action and reproduces it faithfully.

The transition toward separation of representation from action takes place in Stages 4-5 (10 to 15 months). In these stages children begin to represent reality and therefore begin to be able to appreciate the independent existence of objects and people. Children now learn inferentially; they imitate new behaviors; and they eagerly explore the environment. In these stages the internal representations are still derived from instrumental actions, although in altered and abbreviated form.

Children reach the sixth and final stage of the sensorimotor period (sometime in the second quarter of the second year) when they are able to construct representational schemes that do not directly derive from action, but rather serve as blueprints for it. In the sixth stage children manifest deferred imitation and genuine make-believe play. The next step, beyond the sensorimotor level, involves linguistic representation, to which I now turn.

4 The Socialization of Verbal Symbols

The infant produces speech sounds and responds to speech throughout the first year of life. But the use of speech to make reference occurs only around the first birthday (see McCarthy, 1954, pp. 523-526). This marks the beginning of a new period in the development of language, which I designate as the **referential period**. In the beginning of the referential period children produce only single-word utterances. Around the second birthday they start producing sentences, marking a qualitative advance in the development of language. Isolated words have **lexical meanings**, as in a dictionary; when they interact with other words in sentences they take on in addition **grammatical** or **syntactic meanings** (e.g., that of "subject" and "object"). This chapter analyzes the development of the lexical meanings of words up to about the age of 3. Subsequent chapters deal with sentences and the syntactic meanings that they express.

This chapter consists of four parts. The first part divides early word meanings into three levels. The second analyzes the functions of early words. The third considers the factors involved in word learning, and the fourth examines lexical development in relation to other aspects of the child's development.

LEVELS OF MEANING

In the three sections that follow an attempt is made to chart developments in the child's conception of the nature of word meaning. No comprehensive theory exists on this subject, but there is enough evidence in the literature to suggest an analysis of early word meaning into three levels. (Bates, Camaioni, & Volterra, 1975, seem to be oriented toward a similar analysis.) The first level characterizes children's use of words at the end of the first year and at the beginning of the second year, and it bears strong imprints of sensorimotor intelligence in Stages 4 and 5. The second level reflects the separation of representation from action, which crystalizes in sensorimotor Stage 6, around the middle of the second year. At the second level, words function as subjective, personal symbols. At the third level, which normally begins in the second half of the second year, the child reveals an appreciation for the social-conventional nature of the meanings of words.

The three levels are chronologically sequential only in a broad sense. Although there seems to be a dominant level of operation in a given time period, a child may operate in some cases on a level that is higher or lower than the dominant level. We have seen in the outline of the stages of sensorimotor intelligence in the previous chapter that sporadic snatches of advanced behavior patterns emerge before their systematic appearance. I also noted the complementary phenomenon: that lower forms of behavior persist in later stages when children characteristically engage in more sophisticated behaviors. In view of the complexity of language and the vagaries of children's exposure to it, the overlap between forms of behavior may be expected to be even more pronounced in the case of early language than it is in the case of sensorimotor functioning. It must also be noted that because of the novelty of the linguistic mode of representation, children's initial linguistic functioning may be at a lower symbolic level than they demonstrate in more familiar domains, such as pretend play. The three sections that follow describe how the child gradually "shakes off" the sensorimotor mode of representation and takes on the linguistic mode.

First Level: Presymbolic Uses of Words

The words that appear early, around the first birthday, are often not used as symbols. The hallmark of a word used as a symbol is that it labels an open class of referents and is not merely a verbal response to a particular stimulus or a stimulus for a particular nonverbal response. The early words have a sign character. They seem to be part and parcel of certain behavioral routines and are not separable from them. They lack the freedom to disengage themselves from the contexts in which they are embedded. They are **context bound**.

The first two subsections elaborate on and exemplify the nature of the first level of word meaning. The first subsection is concerned with word "comprehension" and the second with word production. A third subsection then considers the relation between comprehension and production, and a fourth projects future developments.

Manifestation of Level 1 in Comprehension Many of the show off acts that parents train their very young children to perform in response to verbal commands involve nonsymbolic uses of language. Some examples can be given from a study by Huttenlocher (1974). One child, Wendy, 0;10(13), responded to her mother's "say goodbye" by raising her right hand and opening and closing it several times. To "make bangbang" she responded by banging a spoon on a bowl in front of her. The mother's words served for Wendy as cues to elicit the particular action patterns. Other cues, such as turning on a particular light, could have served just as well. There is no linguistic comprehension here, but merely an association between a vocal stimulus and a nonverbal response. The association is direct, automatic, and relatively rigid. That is, behaviors such as hand waving and banging are typically elicitable only under circumstances that resemble the situation in which the responses were trained. Characteristically, children do not themselves produce the utterances to which they have learned to respond in this manner. The parent's utterances were not learned as items of knowledge but as stimuli to be responded to. The child's behavior was acquired as part of a ritual interaction in which the vocal element was part of the stimulus situation, and it cannot be isolated from that situation.

Reich (1976) has analyzed in similar terms his son's early behavioral responses to verbal stimuli. At 8 months Adam would respond to "Where's the shoes?" by crawling over to his mother's closet where her shoes were kept. The response pattern was so narrowly defined that he would bypass his mother's shoes if encountered on the way to the closet. It took him approximately two weeks to learn to respond to the question in relation to shoes in the father's closet, two more weeks to shoes on the bedroom floor, and again two weeks to shoes on the parents' feet. Reich (1976) summarizes by saying: "It appears that the very first word meanings are formed by associating a sequence of sounds with essentially everything that is perceptually and functionally salient about the objects or actions in the environment that co-occur with that word" (p. 120).

In fact, young children may not consider either the word or its nominal referent as essential elements in the connection they have formed. Luria (1982, pp. 47-48) gives some examples from the work of others on this point. Thus, a 1-year-old Russian child was trained to turn his face to a portrait of Lenin when asked "Where is Lenin?" To the observer it seemed that the child learned to connect the word *Lenin* with the portrait. But the child continued to turn his face to the same place even after the portrait was removed, showing that for him the question became associated with the total act of head turning. The portrait proved to be incidental in this association. Similarly, on the verbal side the child may not be responding to the critical word but rather to the global pattern of the utterance. Luria gives an example of a 1-year-old French child who was trained to respond to "Ou est la fenetre?" (Where is the window?) by turning to the window. However, he continued to turn to the window even when the question was asked in German, to which he had had no exposure. Apparently, the child responded not to the individual words but to the questioning intonation produced in the appropriate context.

Snyder, Bates, and Bretherton (1981) contributed quantitative evidence on the incidence of context-bound word uses. Through intensive interviews with the mothers of 32 children, whose mean age was 1;1, Snyder et al. obtained information as to the words the children comprehended and produced and the contexts in which they exhibited these competencies. On the basis of this information Snyder et al. classified the uses of each word as contextually restricted or contextually flexible. Of the instances of word comprehension that could be clearly classified into these two categories, 66% were restricted. As an example of a context-restricted response, Snyder et al. cite a child who obeyed the request "Spit it out" only when the mother's hand was under his mouth. Snyder et al. also found cases in which children obeyed utterances only when spoken by the mother in a particular tone of voice.

Manifestation of Level 1 in Production   In their standard symbolic uses words have an autonomous status; they stand apart from the objects and actions that they represent. One of the manifestations of the autonomy of symbolic words is that they can be freely generated in a wide range of circumstances. (For instance, *chair* can be evoked by the question "What is the name of the thing you are sitting on?" even though it may never have been specifically associated with that question.) In contrast, children's early words are nonsymbolic because they function primarily as responses to specific stimulus contexts. When young children encounter the situation in which they had learned a particular word, they emit the word more or less automatically. But the word does not seem to be available in new situations. This type of behavior gives early speech the appearance of ritual, compulsive acts. In the study by Snyder et al. (1981), 48% of the children's utterances were context restricted.

Examples of nonsymbolic, context-bound uses of words can be found in Bloom's (1973) report of the early language of her daughter Allison. Bloom (1973) reports that at 9 months Allison used the word *car*: "to refer only to a car moving by on the street below, as she watched from the living room window" (p. 72). Similarly, at the age of 1 year Allison used *flower* and *dog* in specific situations. She used *flower* for one week when in Florida and *dog* during one summer in the country. Allison discontinued using these words when she returned to her home environment. These words were responses to the sight of flowers and dogs in the particular situations, and they were not available in the drastically different situation of the home environment.

Greenfield and Smith (1976, pp. 81-83) have referred to these context-bound types of utterances as "performatives." A typical example is the use of *bye-bye* by Nicky, one of their two subjects. Nicky said *bye-bye* at 1;1(19) as he waved his hand when his father left for work. It was some time before he would utter *bye-bye* without waving. Evidently, for Nicky, *bye-bye* did not represent taking leave, but rather was part of the complex of behaviors associated with the father-leaving situation.

In an observational study of a boy, David, between the ages of 12 and 16 months, Carter (1979) found that certain verbal sounds (usually not actual words) tended to co-occur with certain gestures. Three sounds, *m*, *l*, and *d*, were particularly prominent. David would often utter the *m* sound when he was reaching toward an object. The function of the sound was apparently to obtain adult assistance in getting the object. He would utter the *l* or *d* sound when he was pointing to an object or holding it. The function of these sounds was apparently to draw adult attention to the object. The attentional and the aid-seeking sounds occurred only in the context of the particular orientations toward the objects. Thus, the sounds functioned nonsymbolically.

At the first level, which I have been discussing, children use words as signs rather than as symbols. I indicated in Chapter 2 that in adult language as well, words are sometimes used in sign functions. The difference is that adults have the capacity to use words symbolically—and normally use them in this way—whereas children at the first level are to a large extent confined to the sign function. Another related point needs to be made concerning the comparison of first-level word meaning with mature meaning. As adults, we may use some words fluently in one context of discourse, but may not be able to think of them when they are needed in another context. Such context-boundness in the adult reflects the operation of contextual cues as aids in the retrieval of words from memory. In contrast, the context-boundness of the first level results from a conceptual limitation. The child does not automatically conceive of words as independent of the specific contexts of their use.

Relation Between Comprehension and Production in Level 1   In the first period of word use the difference between the number of words children understand and the number they produce is very large. In the Snyder et al. (1981) study the mean number of words the children understood was 45 and the mean number they produced was 11. Differences of similar magnitude were reported by Benedict (1979). This is a much larger advantage of comprehension over production than is normal for older speakers and is probably due to the child's difficulty in controlling the fine articulatory movements necessary for speech production, as well as to the greater ease of training comprehension than production.

In mature speakers the production vocabulary is a subset of the comprehension vocabulary. This is so because both in comprehension and in production mature speakers draw on a common store of word knowledge. But children functioning on the first level do not *know* words; they merely use them as vocal stimuli and vocal responses. There is, therefore, no reason why there should be any relation between the vocal stimuli they respond to and the vocal responses they produce. That is, the words that young children produce may differ from the words that they comprehend. In fact, in Level 1 one can speak of comprehension only in an analogous sense, which is why I put this term in quotes when I first introduced it here.

Toward the Symbolic Use of Words   As described, the child's initial use of words is characteristically not symbolic. Because the word is not conceived of as a symbol for a class of referents, but as part of the situation in which it occurs, there is little free, productive generalization of words. However, not all words are contextually restricted, and even those that are restricted are not totally restricted to fixed situations. There is some generalization. Allison, for instance, generalized *dog* to different dogs in the summer-resort context. Wendy produced the waving and banging gestures in response to her mother's utterances spoken in the home setting. Would she have made the same response if the words were uttered in a different setting or by someone other than her mother, assuming one could have properly motivated her under such circumstances? We do not know the answer to this question. But Wendy did demonstrate considerable flexibility on the response side. For instance, she was able to improvise her "make bangbang" routine; when there was no spoon in front of her she used her hands. Even more innovative was her response to "make peekaboo." Her standard procedure was to cover her face with a diaper, peek out, and smile. On one testing occasion when there was no diaper in front of her, Wendy initially looked puzzled but then took hold of a bowl and went through the usual routine.

No less important for symbolic development than the measure of flexibility that exists even on the first level is the interest that children show in the use of sounds for representational purposes. A couple of examples from Piaget's children (Piaget, 1951/1962) should help to elaborate on this point. At 1;2(25), Jacqueline "saw a lamp which hung from the ceiling swaying. She at once swayed her body, saying '*bim bam*'" (p. 64). Jacqueline was impressed with the lamp swaying and took notice of this event by the nonvocal gesture and the vocal expression that resembled it. There is thus representation here, but it is nonsymbolic because the signifier derives from the signified and bears a resemblance to it. Similarly, Laurent (Piaget, 1951/1962) used a vocalization interchangeably with nonvocal gestures to represent matchbox opening:

> At 1;0(10) T. [Laurent] was looking at a box of matches which I was holding on its end and alternately opening and closing. Showing great delight, he watched with great attention, and imitated the box in three ways. 1. He opened and closed his right hand, keeping his eyes on the box. 2. He said "*tff, tff*" to reproduce the sound the box made. 3. He reacted like L. at 1;4(0) by opening and closing his mouth. (p. 66)

The symbolization and decontextualization of words occur gradually. On the basis of a study by a Russian investigator, Luria (1982) described how the words of a child between the ages of 6 months and 2 years became gradually independent of their contexts:

In the early stages, the child acquired the object reference of the word only if he/she was placed in a certain position (e.g., in a lying position), if the word was pronounced by a certain person (e.g., by his/her mother), if the word was accompanied by a specific gesture, and if the word was pronounced with a certain intonation. If all these conditions were present, the child turned its gaze toward the object and stretched a hand toward it. If any of these features was absent, the word lost its object reference and the child did not respond to it. Hence, if a child of 6 or 7 months was lying down and heard his/her mother's voice naming an object, the child responded by turning its gaze toward the object. However, the child failed to respond if any of these conditions were changed (e.g., if the child was in a sitting position).

During the next stage, the child's position (e.g., lying or sitting) was no longer important for retaining the object reference of the word, but the identity of the speaker, the intonation of the voice, and the gesture accompanying the utterance continued to have a decisive influence. If the word "cat" was pronounced by the mother, the child turned his/her gaze toward it. However, if the same word was uttered by the father, the child did not respond in the same way.

At later stages, the identity of the speaker ceased to be an important factor in evoking a response to a word, but the child retained the object reference only when the utterance was accompanied by a pointing gesture or if it was included in a practical setting (especially in a play situation). At this stage, word comprehension is not yet separated from gestures or actions. It is only sometime during the second half of this period, or by the end of the child's second year, that the word is completely emancipated from these attendant conditions and acquires its stable object reference. (pp. 46-47)

As the child comes gradually to appreciate the symbolic potential of words, the earlier sign words do not remain unaffected. They are likely either to take on symbolic status or else to drop out. Attrition or "mortality" of early words has been noted by several investigators (see Bloom, 1973, ch. 4; Leopold, 1939/1970, pp. 159-160, 171-177). For instance, at 11 months Wendy no longer responded to "make bangbang," and when Allison started referring to dogs again, she used another word (*bow-wow*), not *dog* which she had used in the country situation. The mortality of sign words is not surprising. Sign words are tied to specific situational contexts as stimuli and responses, and when the contexts change, the words tend to disappear. The mortality of sign words is reminiscent of the ready extinguishability of conditioned responses, discussed in Chapter 2. (Leopold, 1939/1970, pp. 171-177, offered several other possible reasons for the instability of early words.)

Second Level: Words Used as Personal Symbols

In the analysis of Stage 6 in the previous chapter, I described advanced sensorimotor forms of representation. The verbal representations to be examined in the present section resemble in character the sensorimotor representation of Stage 6. In sensorimotor representation there are no external criteria of correctness. We saw in the previous chapter that at the advanced sensorimotor stage the child constructs signifiers that broadly resemble the signified (e.g., Lucienne opened her mouth to represent matchbox opening). But the choice of particular representations is subjective. Thus, Lucienne could have opened her hand rather than her mouth to represent the matchbox situation, as her brother Laurent did under similar circumstances at the same age.

At the sensorimotor level children feel free to choose different forms of representation at will. Their notion of what representation is derives from the world of action. There is no single "right" way to get hold of something physically. Anything that works for the individual in a given situation is right. The thing desired may be gotten hold of by grasping it with one hand, with both hands, by pulling a string, or whatever. Why, then, should mental grasping be confined to a particular, arbitrary procedure?!

Initially, children approach vocal representation in a way similar to that of sensorimotor representation. They do not seem to realize that language is a system of arbitrary symbols, governed by social conventions regarding both form and content. That is, mature speakers know that the phonetic forms of words and the referents to which they apply are determined by the language of the society, not by the individual speaker. Children in the beginning stages of language have yet to internalize this knowledge. There are normally enough indications in children's environments to impress on them eventually the social nature of language. But children at the present level are in the process of achieving this appreciation, and their approach to vocal representation is governed by personal, subjective considerations, rather than social, objective considerations. This approach to word use is elaborated on in the following subsections.

Diffuse Extension of Word Use   The child's subjective view of language is reflected in diffuse extension of words. At the first level word use is rather confined. At the second level children extend words quite freely, but in different ways than more mature speakers. When adults hear a new word they view it as applying to some essential aspect of the referent and generalize its application to other referents that exhibit these essential characteristics. Their conception of what the essential characteristics are in a given case may not coincide with those of the language, but they know that they have to operate under some externally imposed constraints on word generalization. They know that the range of generalization of word use is not by individual choice, but by social convention. In contrast, the child emerging from the world of subjective sensorimotor behavior is not yet sensitive to externally imposed standards of word extension. As a consequence the different word applications lack direction, and they appear labile and amorphous. A couple of examples can be given to exemplify this point. Piaget (1951/1962) describes Jacqueline's use of *tch tch* as follows:

At 1;1(0) J. used the conventional onomatopoeic sound "*tch tch*" to indicate a train passing her window, and repeated it each time a train passed, probably after the suggestion had first been made to her. But she afterwards said "*tch tch*" in two quite distinct types of situation. On the one hand, she used it indiscriminately for any vehicles she saw out of another window, cars, carriages and even a man walking, at 1;1(4). At about 1;1(6) and on the following days any noise from the street, as well as trains, produced *tch tch*. But on the other hand, when I played bo-peep, appearing and disappearing without speaking, J. at 1;1(4) also said "*tch tch*" probably by analogy with the sudden appearance and disappearance of the trains. (p. 216)

In this example there is extension of the use of *tch tch* from the initial instance to new instances. What seems to characterize this extension is that it lacks a consistent direction. Jacqueline appears to have extended *tch tch* in two directions: to moving and disappearing objects (including people) and to noisy things.

Bloom (1973, p. 73) cites an example of a 1-year-old French-speaking child whose extensions moved in multiple directions. This child used *nenin* (breast) to ask to be nursed, when he wanted a biscuit, in reference to a red button, eye in a picture, and his mother's face in a photograph. The child seems to have extended the word use on the basis of sustenance, color, shape, and co-occurrence (mother's face).

These types of extensions occur because at this level children do not use words to categorize objects and events as adults do, but rather as subjective associations. We see further examples of this tendency in the next subsection.

Personal Extensions   Word usages that appear confused from an external point of view sometimes become meaningful when considered from the child's own subjective perspective. Werner and Kaplan (1963) discuss the use of *door* by an 11-month-old girl. She used the word not only with respect to doors but also in relation to a cork and to the food tray of her highchair. Werner and Kaplan (1963) suggest that she defined the word as referring to: "obstacle standing in her way of getting out of, or at, something" (p. 118).

The use of *bow-wow* by Jacqueline (Piaget, 1951/1962) also seemed to have a unifying theme on the personal level:

At about 1;1(20) she said "*bow-wow*" to indicate dogs. At 1;1(29) she pointed from her balcony at the landlord's dog in the garden and said "*bow-wow*." The same day, a few hours later, she made the same sound as she pointed to the geometrical pattern on a rug (a horizontal line crossed by three vertical lines). At 1;2(1), on seeing a horse from her balcony, she looked at it attentively and finally said "*bow-wow*." Same reaction an hour later at the sight of two horses. At 1;2(3) an open pram which a woman was pushing and in which the baby was clearly visible, produced "*bow-wow*" (this too was seen from her balcony). At 1;2(4) she said "*bow-wow*" at the sight of hens, and at 1;2(8) at the sight of dogs, horses, prams and cyclists, "*tch tch*" being apparently reserved for cars and trains. At 1;2(12) "*bow-wow*" referred to everything seen from her balcony: animals, cars, the owner of the house (whose dog had first been called "*bow-wow*") and people in general. At 1;2(15) the term was applied to the trucks railway porters were pulling, a long way from the house. At 1;3(7) it again referred to the pattern on the rug. Finally, after 1;4 "*bow-wow*" seemed to be definitely reserved for dogs. (p. 216)

Jacqueline thus extended *bow-wow* from dogs not only to a particular rug which may have resembled dogs in shape or on which a dog may have sat, but also to a variety of other things seen *by her* from the same vantage point she had seen dogs from. There may be other explanations for Jacqueline's use of *bow-wow*—as well as for the other anecdotes described under Level 2—but whatever the explanation, the overriding point remains that she used this utterance in a personal rather than social-conventional manner.

A general comment is in order at this point. I have used the term "extension" in describing children's word usages at the second level. But strictly speaking, this term is appropriate only from the observer's point of view, not from the child's point of view. As Leopold (1949/1970a) has noted: "The term 'extension of meaning' is fitting only from the point of view of the standard language. Genetically, 'lack of limitation of meaning' would be a more adequate description" (p. 140). Leopold also offered "transfer of meaning" as a possible description of the process. What Leopold is saying is that when children use words in free and socially undisciplined ways it is because their word boundaries are vague and poorly defined.

Makeshift Uses   Leopold (1949/1970a, p. 123) suggested that because their word boundaries are hazy and indistinct, children feel no compunction about using words in makeshift ways to compensate for their limited vocabularies. He cites earlier writers who recognized "word poverty" as one of the contributors to nonstandard word uses. Current investigators have also come to recognize that unconventional word uses could be due to children's need to "stretch" their limited vocabularies (e.g., E. V. Clark, 1978). There is empirical support for the makeshift idea in Barrett's (1978) systematic analysis of the unconventional word uses of Hildegard Leopold. Barrett based the analysis on the information provided by Hildegard's father (Leopold, 1939/1970, 1947/1970, 1949/1970a, 1949/1970b) in his detailed four-volume account of her language, especially up to the age of 2. Analyzing Leopold's records Barrett found 20 words whose meaning Hildegard stretched beyond the standard limits. In 19 of these there was no more appropriate word in Hildegard's vocabulary at the time of the extended usage. For instance, at 12 months Hildegard used *Papa* not only for her father but for her mother as well. *Mama* appeared in her vocabulary only at 15 months. At 14 months Hildegard used *Papa* for any man. The appropriate word for man (in German, *Mann*) appeared only at 17 months. (Hildegard was exposed at home to both English and German, and she used both languages.)

Makeshift uses of words when they occur in the speech of foreigners merely reflect their need to communicate with limited lexical resources. But in the case of young children, makeshift uses seem also to be a symptom of their vague definitions of words. The fact that Hildegard persisted in calling her mother *Papa* over a 3-month period suggests that she felt little discomfort in extending the word in this way.

Words as Comments For adults words spoken in isolation, especially nouns, usually have a **naming function**. One is, therefore, inclined to interpret the child's single-word utterances as having the same function. But the early words of children sometimes make more sense if interpreted as serving the function of commenting and comparing rather than naming and categorizing.

Consider, for example, the following observation Piaget (1951/1962) made of Laurent: "At 1;2(23) he said '*daddy*' to J. who held out her arms to him like his father. The same day he used '*daddy*' in reference to a male visitor and to a peasant who was lighting his pipe (though he never referred to him thus in the usual way)" (p. 217). These uses of *daddy* appear strange indeed if interpreted as ordinary naming activities. But Laurent seems to be commenting here rather than naming. Seeing his sister raise her arms in a way typical of their father reminds him of the father, and he utters *daddy* to say something like, "You remind me of daddy when you do this." Or seeing a peasant smoking a pipe like his father, he utters *daddy* to comment, "Oh, you smoke a pipe like my father." By using the same word for his father, his sister in a particular pose, and a peasant smoking a pipe, Laurent is not placing them all in the same category for the simple reason that he does not have categories. He merely relates the sister and the peasant to the father.

In an insightful discussion, studded with interesting examples, Lewis (1936/1975, pp. 205-209) makes the point that is the theme of this subsection, namely, that early in their careers as speakers, children do not use words as names, but as subjective devices to relate their experiences to one another. Lewis reports, for instance, that a boy in the age range of 13-15 months used his word for father, *baba*, in relation to a variety of things associated with the father, including the father's trousers, the father's lap (on which he wanted to sit), and the sound of a car horn. The connection of the sound to the father apparently was that the father had repaired the doorbell a short time ago. Lewis (1936/1975) concluded that the naming function develops gradually: "Instead . . . of saying that the name of an object becomes extended to refer to other objects, it is much truer to say that the wide application of a word leads to its becoming the name of one or a group of objects" (p. 209).

Leopold (1949/1970a) approached early words in a similar fashion. He discusses, for instance, Hildegard's uses of *ball*. She learned the word first at 12 months and used it with respect to her toy balls. At 16 months she used it in relation to a balloon and a ball of yarn. At 20 months she said *ball* when she saw the dome of an observatory. Leopold (1949/1970a) comments:

She undoubtedly did not mistake it [the dome] for a ball to play with. I also refuse to interpret the designation as the result of an intellectual operation of the type: "This object is approximately spherical as my balls are; therefore it should be named the same." The process is undoubtedly more primitive: the shape recalled that of the balls, and this recollection brought up the word *Ball*. It could be paraphrased: "When I see this object, I am reminded of my ball." (p. 128)

One of the other examples that Leopold discusses concerns the application of the German *Wauwau* by Hildegard when she was 15-16 months. Leopold notes that she used it in relation to a picture of a man wearing fur. He comments that "her reaction to it did not mean that she took it for the picture of a dog, but that the shaggy furs brought dog's fur to her mind" (Leopold, 1949/1970a, p. 130).

Recent writers have also drawn attention to such associative uses. In a study to be discussed later, Rescorla (1980) referred to them as "analogical" extensions. Nelson, Rescorla, Gruendel, and Benedict (1978) also commented on what they called the "comparison" function of early words. They cited the case of Eva Bowerman, 18 months, who applied the word *moon* "first to the real moon and subsequently to such diverse referents as a half-grapefruit seen from below, flat shiny green leaves, lemon slices, mounted steer horns, a chrome dishwasher dial, hangnails, etc." (p. 967). Nelson et al. remarked that they did not think that Eva was "claiming that the grapefruit is a moon; rather there is something moonlike about it" (p. 965).

In some cases children may show awareness of their analogical uses, as in the following example Horgan (1981) gave of her daughter:

At 1;4 when Kelly had a vocabulary of less than 20 words, she learned the word *shoe*. Several days later, she put her foot through the armhole of a nightgown, saying *Shoe*, accompanied by shrieks of laughter. Later that day, she put her foot into a tennis ball can, saying *Shoe* and laughing. It is hard for me to believe that this is a case of overgeneralizing the word *shoe* based on its function. She was telling a joke. It was as though she was saying 'Look, a shoe is something you put on your foot; a nightgown is NOT something you usually put on your foot, but I did!' (p. 218)

In these examples children express in single words, meanings that mature speakers express in full sentences. (Such word uses are sometimes referred to as "holophrastic" utterances.) It would be a mistake, however, to attribute knowledge of sentences to children who use words in this way. Jespersen (1922/1964) made the point very cogently:

When we say that such a word [*up*] means what we should express by a whole sentence ["I want to get up"], this does not amount to saying that the child's 'Up' *is* a sentence, or a sentence-word, as many of those who have written about these questions have said. We might just as well assert that clapping our hands is a sentence, because it expresses the same idea (or the same frame of mind) that is other-

wise expressed by the whole sentence 'This is splendid.' The word 'sentence' presupposes a certain grammatical structure, which is wanting in the child's utterance.
(p. 134)

Conclusions and Prospects   In Level 1 words were locked into particular
contexts and enjoyed only limited extendability. In Level 2 there is wide and free
extension of word usage. But the extensions are based on personal and subjective
considerations, being very much in the realm of sensorimotor functioning where
children class different objects in terms of their own dispositions and reactions.
Subjective extension is by its very nature dependent on the whims of the subject
and, as a result, is unsystematic and fluid.

Piaget (1951/1962) has described this level of functioning in the following
words:

> The concept implies a fixed definition, corresponding to a stable convention which
> gives the verbal sign its meaning. The meanings of words do not constantly
> change, because the classes and the relations they denote involve a conceptual defi-
> nition determined once for all by the social group. But the meaning of a term such
> as "bow-wow" in the case of J. changed in a few days from dogs to cars and even
> to men. The method by which one object is related to another is therefore different
> in the case of the true concept from that of the intermediary schema of this level. In
> the case of the concept, there is inclusion of an object in a class and of one class in
> another, whereas in a schema such as "bow-wow" and the others, there is merely a
> subjective feeling of kinship between the related objects. (p. 220)

The immature character of the child's early word meanings derives, according
to Piaget (1951/1962, pp. 237-244), from fundamental lacks in cognitive functioning, which will continue for the next few years. A radical change in the underlying meanings of the child's words should therefore not be expected at the
third level. The progress marked by the third level lies in greater correspondence
of children's word extensions to the extensions of adults in their environment. It
lies in the realization that words are conventional names. Even though the conceptual underpinnings of words remain primitive, the attainment of the naming
function in and of itself constitutes a significant accomplishment.

The child's attainment of the naming function gains clearer significance when
compared to the resistance chimpanzees have shown to the learning of names. As
part of a long-term project to teach an artificially designed language to
chimpanzees—communicating with them by means of a computer-linked keyboard and CRT screen—Rumbaugh and Savage-Rumbaugh (1978) tried to teach
them the naming function. Even though the investigators expended considerable
efforts and used sophisticated methods, their attempt did not meet with success:

> Performance was invariably erratic, being extremely high on some days and dis-
> couragingly low on others. The animals also evidenced negative attitudes toward

and complete disinterest in this type of training. If, however, the words to be learned were allowed to connect with environmental occurrences in a direct, perceivable, and functional manner, learning proceeded rapidly and performance was stable. (p. 126)

As an example, Rumbaugh and Savage-Rumbaugh (1978) report that: "Attempts to teach 'key' by holding one up as an exemplar and encouraging, by various means, the chimpanzee to name it, might go on for weeks or longer to little avail. If, however, one links 'keyness' to the operations of opening doors of consequence, then the word is learned in a matter of hours" (p. 127). Thus, the chimpanzees learned words readily as action-inducing signs but had a total disinterest in learning words as naming symbols. The apathy of chimpanzees stands in stark contrast to the intense interest of children in the learning of names, a topic which I explore in the next section.

Third Level: Words Become Socialized Symbols

Children operating on the second level have not yet fully recognized and accepted the social-objective character of language. We consider them to have reached the third level when they have grasped the social principle of word use, namely, that words are labels for socially defined classes of objects and events. This achievement is reflected in more systematic and productive extension of words and in accelerated growth of vocabulary. While in the first half of their second year, children are groping to discover what words are all about, when they approach their second birthdays, they have grasped the unique character of words as symbols and go confidently about the task of acquiring them. This is the time when children may tire their caregivers by constantly asking for the names of things (e.g., *What's this?*). They eagerly utter the words they hear and explore their uses.

In the second half of the second year children usually increase their vocabularies at a rapid rate. This phenomenon is referred to as the vocabulary **growth-spurt**. One study (conducted in 1926 and summarized by McCarthy, 1954, p. 533) sought to determine the number of words children knew at different ages by questioning them about pictures in an attempt to elicit from them words they might be expected to know. The study found that there was an average increase of only 19 words (from 3 to 22) in the first 6 months of the second year, but an increase of 96 words in the following 3-month period (from 18 months to 21 months) and an increase of 154 words in the subsequent 3-month period.

More recently, Benedict (1979) followed eight children from the ages of 9-10 months to 19-24 months. She found that the children acquired the first 20 to 30 words slowly, but once they reached this level, the growth of vocabulary was rapid. Similar results were obtained in a study of five children by McCune-Nicolich (1981), to be described more fully at the end of this chapter. Figure 4.1

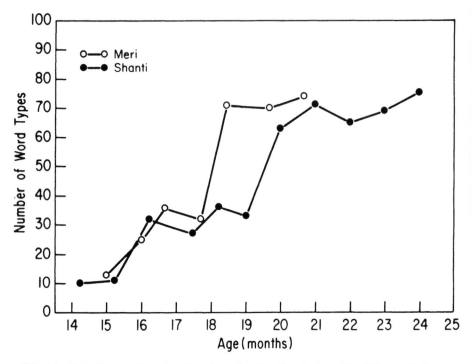

FIG. 4.1   Rate of increase in number of words as a function of age for two of the children studied by McCune-Nicolich (1981).

shows the number of different words produced by two of the children in McCune-Nicolich's study at different ages. It can be seen in the figure that there was a growth spurt for both children. The growth spurt occurred for one child between 18 and 19 months and for the other child between 19 and 20 months. The three other children also manifested growth spurts. The five children as a group jumped from a mean of 31 words at the mean age of 1;8(7) to a mean of 69 a month later.

Finally, it must be noted that although increased overt verbal output seems to coincide for many children with the emergence of the naming function and interest in learning words, this is not the case for all children. Some children may know many words but use only few of them. Stern (1924/1975) has remarked that: "Both changes [interest in word acquisition and increase in number of words used] may be active in varying degree, and do not necessarily occur at exactly the same time, since the words acquired by constant enquiry may lie hidden in the child's consciousness for a more or less lengthy time before they are used" (p. 162).

Level 3 and Sensorimotor Development   It would seem that the vocabulary growth-spurt should typically occur after the child has achieved full object permanence. It is only when objects become totally separated from the actions and contexts in which they are involved and thus have gained independent status that they can be represented via independent vehicles (i.e., word symbols). It is only then that objects and actions can be represented distinctly by separate words.

A study by Corrigan (1978) provides support for this postulated dependence of lexical development on prerequisite cognitive development. Corrigan studied three children longitudinally over a period of 18 months, beginning when the children's ages ranged from 9 months to 11 months. She recorded the children's vocabularies in 30-minute sessions at 3-week intervals. She also tested them for object permanence. Using a refined scale of object permanence, which divides Piaget's Stages 4 to 6 into 21 steps, Corrigan found that the growth of the children's vocabularies accelerated in the time period when they attained the highest levels of object permanence. This effect was clearest for her most talkative subject, John, who reached the highest stage of object permanence at the session that took place when he was 1;8(16). At this session John produced a total of 78 words, which was 37 more than he had produced in the immediately preceding session. The largest increase between any two previous consecutive sessions was 16.

The synchrony between achievement of full object permanence and rise in vocabulary is impressive, especially when one considers that the number of words uttered at any one short period of time, such as a 30-minute testing session, is a function not only of cognitive capacity but also of need and interest. Corrigan (1978, 1979) herself reached less positive conclusions about the relation between cognitive and linguistic development, but this is because she expected a narrow and rigid relation and did not make allowances for the complex vicissitudes of development. One should not expect two related capacities to appear exactly within the same narrow time span. It must be recognized that at the time children are working on developing their capacity in one area, they may not have enough mental resources left for other areas. Thus, although both object permanence and the symbolic use of words depend on internal representation, they need not become manifest at the same moment in time. In addition, in any one testing session a child may not exhibit the words he or she knows. Given these considerations and the small number of subjects in the Corrigan study, I am impressed by her finding that the vocabulary growth-spurt and the attainment of full object permanence appeared within weeks of one another and not discouraged by her finding that they did not appear in exactly the same testing sessions.

Once children have recognized the naming function of words, they are ready for the serious task of word learning. In the following subsections, I discuss what words children learn and how they learn them.

Comprehension and Production   As is well known, children (as well as adults) understand more words than they can produce. The reason for this is that one needs to know less in order to understand a word than to produce it. First, under normal circumstances one can be aided by contextual cues in comprehending the meanings of words. Second, to recognize the meaning of a word it is often sufficient to know only some aspects of it. For instance, children may recognize *throat* on the basis of its vowel and final consonant, but be unable to produce the word because they do not remember the other sounds or cannot articulate them.

However, the gap between production and comprehension narrows with the growth of vocabulary. Goldin-Meadow, Seligman, and Gelman (1976) conducted an experiment to compare comprehension and production. Their subjects were 12 children from middle-class families. One was 14 months old and the remainder ranged in age between 21 and 26 months. In the comprehension task the children were asked to point to body parts or toys, or to act out certain commands such as "Lie down." In the production task the children had to respond to questions such as "What's this?" and "What am I doing?" All the children obtained higher scores in the comprehension task than in the production task. But an important finding not brought out by the authors was that the gap between the two tasks was smaller for the children with larger vocabularies.

The inverse relation between the size of the gap between comprehension and production and the size of vocabulary becomes clearly evident when one relates the comprehension-production gap to the children's total vocabulary scores (i.e., their combined scores on the comprehension and production tasks). For instance, Melissa, 21 months, had a score of 36 in the comprehension task and 5 in the production task, or a ratio of 7.2:1 of comprehension to production. Her total vocabulary score of 41 was the lowest of all 12 subjects in the study. By contrast, Lee, 26 months, had a comprehension score of 82 and a production score of 68, or a ratio of 1.2:1. His total vocabulary score of 150 words was the highest.

For the group of 12 subjects as a whole there was a negative relation between the size of vocabulary scores and the magnitude of the comprehension-production ratios. This is shown statistically by a correlation of $-.72$ ($p < .01$) between total vocabulary scores and comprehension-production ratios. These findings indicate that with the growth of vocabulary the difference between comprehension and production becomes narrower. Children who are at home with the naming principle and are acquiring words as items of knowledge are normally able to demonstrate their word knowledge even under the more demanding requirements of production.

Deviation of Children's Word Usages from Standard Usages   At the third level children have realized that words are conventional labels for referents, not free, personal associations. However, although their word extensions are now more systematic, there are still deviations from standard usage. The deviations are due to a variety of factors, including children's limited experiences with words, their level of mental development, and their individual interests. In the paragraphs that follow I describe deviations that seem to be due to one or more of these factors.

The learning of the precise referential domain of a word depends on exposure to positive and negative examples of the word's use. Because of their limited experiences, children may initially form a different hypothesis concerning the meaning range of a word than has been ordained for that word by the language they are learning. For example, my son Shimon, 22 months, applied *handle* to the cords used to pull blinds up and down. This is a logical use of *handle*, although English happens not to sanction it. At the same age Shimon used *petza*, the Hebrew equivalent of *bruise*, to refer to a speck of dirt on a cake. He apparently interpreted *petza* broadly in the sense of 'blemish'.

In his discussion of Hildegard's word uses Leopold (1949/1970a) emphasized that her deviations from standard usage were "caused not only by the lack of experience on the part of the child, but also . . . by the arbitrary and accidental practices of the standard language" (p. 120). He points out, for instance, that Hildegard used a single word to refer to a handkerchief, a towel, and a napkin. Such usage would have corresponded to standard usage in German (*Tuch*), but in English it was an **overextension**. Obviously, children learning language have no a priori way of knowing what words in their particular language have broad ranges of meaning and what words have narrow ranges. They have to discover this by speaking and listening.

According to our analysis, then, the third level is distinguished not by the absence of nonstandard extensions, but by their consistency and plausibility. This analysis can find support in a study by Rescorla (1980), who followed six children from the age of 12 months to 16-18 months when their speaking vocabularies reached a minimum of 75 words. In this study 33% of the words uttered by the children were overextended one or more times. There was, however, a difference between the overextensions of the children in the beginning of the study when they were 12 months old, and their overextensions at the end of the study when they were 16-18 months old. At the early age 60% of the overextensions were of the subjective kind that would be classified as Level 2; at the later ages 70% were of the objective kind belonging to Level 3. The latter involved class-based extensions, like using *daddy* for men other than the father.

Rescorla's findings concern the transition from second-level to third-level overextensions. Brooks-Gunn and Lewis (1979) studied older children, and their findings afford a view of both the rise and fall of third-level overextensions. In this study 12 children in each of the ages of 15, 18, 21, and 24 months viewed projected photographs of their fathers, their mothers, unfamiliar children, and unfamiliar male and female adults. The experimenter encouraged the children to name the photographs by asking, "Who's that?"

Of interest here is the overextension of *daddy*. The results show that at no age was the word overextended to the pictures of children, indicating that the subjects took the word to refer to an adult. There was overextension of *daddy* to mothers and to strange adults, and, as can be seen in the following tabulation, the frequency of occurrence of this type of overextension was not equally distributed

THE FAMILY CIRCUS®   By Bil Keane

"Mommy! You've got bikini shoes, too!"

	15 mo.	18 mo.	21 mo.	24 mo.
Number of correct usages (CU)	8	14	18	19
Number of overextensions (OE)	0	13	7	3
Ratio of OE to CU	0	0.93	0.39	0.16

at the four ages studied. At 15 months there were no overextensions. We assume that at this age the children functioned on Level 2 and used *daddy* for their own fathers and for things and actions associated with them. Overextension reaches a peak at 18 months when, we assume, the children have reached Level 3 functioning and they extend words on a class-sharing basis. Overextensions have declined sharply by 21 months and have almost completely disappeared by 24 months. Once children become sensitized to the social factor in word use, it does not take them long to discover through interaction with mature speakers the range of application of a word such as *daddy*.

Another study suggests that even when children overextend words, they have some sense that the standard referent is the preferable one. Fremgen and Fay (1980) investigated the overextensions of 16 middle- and upper-middle-class children with a mean age of 20 months. They found that children who overextended words in a task requiring them to name every picture in a sequence responded with perfect accuracy in a task calling for the choice of a picture (from among four) for a given name. For instance, the same children who would call a cat *dog* when asked to name pictures, would pick out the picture of a dog, not a cat, when asked where the dog was. Apparently, they felt that although they could call a cat *dog* when they had to produce a label for every picture, the label *dog* was more appropriate for dogs than for cats and would therefore not use it for cats when presented with a choice. It stands to reason that children would distinguish objects (e.g., dogs) for which they heard a particular name (e.g., *dog*) from objects (e.g., cats) for which they did not hear that name.

Fremgen and Fay interpreted their results as showing that there are no overextensions in comprehension. This is a hazardous conclusion because the production and comprehension tasks were not fully matched (e.g., different types of objects were used in the two tasks). This methodological problem, however, is not relevant to my interpretation. I would claim that even in a production task, a child is not as likely to apply a word to an ''overextended'' object as to a target object. Thus, to continue with the example, I would claim that if the children had been shown a number of dog and cat pictures and not been forced to name all of them, they would have responded with *dog* more often to the dog pictures than to the cat pictures. I make this prediction because I expect children to be able to distinguish the core class of objects to which the name was given from other objects later attracted to it on the basis of similarity.

The discussion in the preceding paragraphs concerned deviations that involved overextended word uses. **Overrestricted** uses also occur, although they are harder to detect. Each instance of overrestriction corresponds to standard usage; the deviation is in the absence of certain instances, and absences do not impose themselves on the observer. Leopold (1949/1970a, pp. 150-153), however, noted the phenomenon of overrestriction in the speech of Hildegard. More recently, Bowerman (1976) reported that her younger daughter, Eva, 14-19 months, overrestricted the same word, *off*, that her older daughter Christy overextended. Eva restricted the use of *off* to removal of clothes or other objects from her body or other people's bodies. Christy, on the other hand, broadened the sense of *off*. According to Bowerman (1976) she used it not only to refer to standard ''off'' situations, such as those involving the removal of clothes, the taking off of lids, and getting off high places, but also to refer to ''non-'off' situations involving separation, such as pulling cups *apart*, *opening* hinged or sliding boxes, *unfolding* newspapers, and so on'' (p. 117).

It is hard to speculate as to why two children in the same family would form different hypotheses concerning the meaning of words, but presumably this has something to do with their individual interests and predilections. Leopold (1949/1970a, p. 128) also commented on the role of personal interests. He noted, for instance, that at 23 months Hildegard referred to marbles as *balls*, but she had a separate word for beads because of her interest in jewelry.

Differences between toddlers' meanings of words and adult meanings are, of course, also due to differences in mental capacity. Leopold (1949/1970a, pp. 126-127) describes Hildegard's groping for the meaning of *tick-tock* in the course of the second year. The idea of a time-keeping device was, of course, too advanced for her. She, therefore, applied *tick-tock* to things that resemble clocks in appearance: to round things and to things having dial-type faces. At 24 months Shimon used the generic *broken* in cases where *torn* was more appropriate. The distinction between separations involving cloth or paper and separations involving rigid objects was too subtle for him at that age.

Cognitive limitations are likely to be evident in particular in children's use of adjectives. Toddlers are not fully ready to isolate one attribute out of the totality of attributes making up an object, as one has to do to understand the meaning of adjectives. They may, therefore, interpret adjectives as concrete nouns or as action verbs. Thus, for the toddler *hot* may mean 'stove' or 'don't touch!' and *hungry* may mean 'food'. The adult observer is not likely to become aware that the child understands these words in an idiosyncratic way until the child comes out with something like, *I want hungry.*

What Kinds of Words Are Learned Early?   Children's early vocabularies contain words that pertain to things and actions that are of immediate pertinence to their lives (see Clark, 1979; Stern, 1924/1975, p. 164). In a study of the first 50-word vocabularies of 18 children in the age range of 1 to 2 years, Nelson (1973) found that the bulk of the early words (64%) referred to the "thing world" (i.e., to referents designated by concrete nouns in adult language). The nouns that were found to be prevalent designated people and objects that have a meaningful place in children's lives, including family members, toys, food items, parts of the body, and items of clothing. After nouns, the next highest percentage of words (19%) was for actions (e.g., *go, up, look*) and for states (e.g., *all gone*). Adjectives made up only 6% of these vocabularies. This compares with an estimate of over 12% for 6½-year-olds (see McCarthy, 1954, p. 560).

Articulatory factors also contribute to the selection of words. Children may sometimes avoid words that they find difficult to articulate. Leopold (1947/1970, pp. 267-268) suggested, for instance, that Hildegard avoided certain words (e.g., *radio*) because of difficulties in their pronunciation. Leopold also observed that ease of articulation helped determine Hildegard's choice between English and German words of equivalent meaning. Ferguson (1979, p. 195) refers to a similar basis of selection by a French-English bilingual child.

Phonetic considerations also seem to explain some findings obtained by Shoshana Goldman in a study of her twin sons (carried out as part of her dissertation work, under my direction). Goldman found that in the middle of their second year the boys did not pick up the word *dish*, even though it was regularly used at mealtimes. But they immediately adopted *bowl* when the word was substituted for *dish*. Similarly, at that time they did not use *Yoseph*, the name of one of them, despite their constant exposure to it, but when *Daudi* was introduced in place of *Yoseph*, they took to it right away. These children apparently avoided the articulatorily difficult words *dish* and *Yoseph*. At an older age children sometimes show that they are conscious of their phonetic difficulties. Thus, when it was suggested to Amahl, 26 months, that he say the word that sounds like *sip* for the thing that goes in the water (Smith, 1973, pp. 136-137), he responded: *No. I can only say "sip."* Amahl could not articulate the *sh* sound and avoided words that contained this sound.

Ferguson (1978) suggests that at the initial stages of speech development, children may restrict their lexical acquisitions to words exemplifying certain phonetic patterns. One child, for instance, may prefer words of the CVCV (consonant-vowel-consonant-vowel) shape that end in the *i* sound, such as *doggie* and *mommy*. Another child may like CV words, such as *see* and *hi*.

In this subsection I made reference to cognitive, personal, and phonetic considerations as determinants of the child's choice of vocabulary items. These comments notwithstanding, it is appropriate to echo here Leopold's note of humility. At the conclusion of his careful and extensive study of Hildegard's word uses, Leopold (1939/1970, pp. 168-169) commented on various gaps in her vocabulary that he could not account for. Children's abilities, life circumstances, and interests are no doubt relevant to explaining what words they do and do not acquire. But it is not easy to ascertain these factors independently of their vocabularies.

In the discussion so far, children's word uses have been described in terms of their conformity or nonconformity to adult uses. Such an approach is justified because children strive to discover and approximate the standard usages of their community. But this approach is one-sided because it does not sufficiently emphasize the child's constructive part in the process of word learning. The next subsection seeks to correct this imbalance.

Construction of Words and Meanings   Children do not passively absorb word meanings from their environment. Rather, they actively make up words and create meanings for words they hear. There is a report (Werner & Kaplan, 1963, p. 116) of a 26-month-old girl who, after she had used a single name for milk for some time, began to use two distinct names: one (*mimi*) for milk drunk out of a bottle and the other (*te*) for milk drunk out of a cup. The girl thus invented a distinction not present in the language she was learning.

Also, children do not acquire individual words in isolation, but as part of a system. Werner and Kaplan (1963, p. 116) have summarized, on the basis of information provided by Leopold (1949/1970a), Hildegard's changing organization of words in the domain of cakes and sweets (see Table 4.1). It can be seen that the field initially covered by a single word became gradually differentiated into four subfields.

TABLE 4.1
An Example of Semantic Restructuring by Hildegard

Age	Word	Referent(s)
18 mo.	titi	cookie, cake, candy, cherry, cracker
19 mo.	titi	cookie, cake, candy, cherry
	gaga	cracker
21 mo.	titi	cookie
	gaga	cracker
	geg	cake, candy, cherry
22 mo.	tutis	cookie
	gag	cracker
	geg	cake
	da:i	candy, cherry (: indicates vowel lengthening)

Note: Adapted from Werner and Kaplan (1963, p. 116).

In connection with this discussion of the child's constructive approach to word learning, it is appropriate to quote the comment Ricks (1979) made after he pointed out the difficulty in really knowing on what bases children make their early extensions:

What seems more important than the criteria adopted is the likelihood that the child's brain is not simply editing its sensory impressions and sifting out regularities, but is actively scanning the variety of impressions it receives, on the lookout, as it were, for categories which it is continuously in the process of establishing and modifying. Such a scanning process seems very likely in the child, if only to account for his zeal, for his early and vital capacity to anticipate, for the constantly changing criteria that he uses to categorise, and for the obvious self-generated quality of his early categories and labels. It is as if the growing child's brain is 'imposing' an order which it is constantly checking and adjusting. An executive conceptualising role is developing which converts the child from one who simply sees to one who looks and from one who hears to one who listens. (pp. 266-267)

Some Examples from Later Years   Thus far the discussion has concentrated on the characteristics of lexical processes during the second and third years of life. In the following paragraphs I take a brief look at children's word usages in later years.

At 37 months my son Shimon used *spill* not only to express its standard meaning but also to express the meaning of *pour*. Thus, asking to have juice poured into his cup, he said: *Spill it like this.* At the same age he overextended the use of *tall* into the domain of *high*, producing: *This sleeve is not pulled up tall enough.* At 35 months my daughter Miriam used *drink* in the sense of putting food directly from a container into her mouth, without the intermediary of hands or cutlery. This was indicated by her application of *drink* to cereal and crackers eaten directly off the plate. Both Shimon and Miriam, at the age of 3-4 years, used *bought* in relation to books *brought* from the library. The difference between a library card and a charge card or green pieces of paper did not appear very significant to them. The phonetic similarity between *bought* and *brought* further discouraged the exploration of potential differences in meaning between the words.

THE FAMILY CIRCUS
By Bill Keane

"Mommy's going to dress a letter. Wanna watch her do it?"

Bowerman (1978) provided examples of her daughters' gropings toward new understanding of certain verbs in their third to fifth years. Thus, for instance, they occasionally interchanged the uses of *put* and *give,* producing such sentences as: *Can I go put it to her?* (meaning 'Can I go and give her the juice?'), and *Give some ice in here, Mommy.*

The girls' confusion was about the restrictions governing the choice of recipient for these verbs. Both *put* and *give* concern the movement of an object to a new location. The difference is that *give* requires an active recipient (i.e., one that can take), whereas *put* requires a passive destination (which is usually inanimate, but could also be animate as in "Put the blanket on him" or "Put the money in her hand"). It is not surprising that at preschool age, the girls had difficulty sorting these things out.

Interestingly, Bowerman reports that when the girls first learned *put* and *give,* they used them correctly. It is possible that initially they used these words primarily with respect to the recipients they had heard them used with, perhaps forming only low-level generalizations. For instance, they may have generalized *put* from *tables* to *chairs* and to other familiar household pieces of furniture, and they may have generalized *give* from *mother* to *father* and to other familiar individuals. On this level there is little possibility of error. But later on they attempted to form higher level generalizations and to relate the words to one another, and because of the subtlety of the distinctions, confusion arose.

The occurrence of later incorrect semantic usage following earlier correct usage reported by Bowerman resembles the phenomenon, encountered in a preceding section, of a period of overextension following a period of predominantly correct usage. These developmental sequences in the lexical domain parallel a well-attested phenomenon in morphological development (to be discussed in Chapter 9). It has been widely observed that irregular nouns and verbs are initially inflected correctly (e.g., *feet* and *went*), but later are regularized (e.g., *foots* and *goed*). This developmental sequence in morphology is interpreted to mean that children initially learn inflections individually for each noun and verb. On this level of memory of individual items, there is no possibility of overregularization. In the next step children induce rules, and this is when mistakes occur on items that are exceptions to the rules. Similarly, in the semantic domain children seem to make mistakes when they attempt to coordinate the uses of different words and to reach higher order generalizations.

Nominal Realism   I have said that at the third level children begin to appreciate the social-conventional nature of words. This should not be construed to mean that children also appreciate the arbitrary nature of words. Piaget (1929/1979, chap. 2) has shown that until the early school years the child's view of words is dominated, to a greater or lesser extent, by "nominal realism." That is, children think of words as appropriate to and somehow inherent in the things that they label. They do not conceive of words as arbitrarily assigned by people. Nominal realism does not, however, preclude social sensitivity concerning the meanings of words. Although children believe words to be inherent in things, they also believe in the omniscience of their elders and depend on adults to tell them which words belong to which things.

Summary   At the first level of word meaning children use words nonsymbolically, tying them to specific contexts. At the second level children recognize the symbolic nature of words, but they use them subjectively as personal symbols, rather than as conventional symbols. At the third level, children grasp the social nature of words and begin to learn what the social conventions are concerning the extensions of the words they are acquiring. While in the process of discovering the conventional extensions of words, children's usages occasionally differ from standard usages. But these differences are in regard to specifics, not in the character of the extensions.

THE FUNCTIONS OF EARLY WORDS

In the previous section I discussed the kinds of meanings associated with children's words at different levels of development. In the present section I turn to the functions of early words. The functions of words may be different at the three levels of development that have been outlined. But such specific information is not available at present, and we have to deal globally with the entire initial period of word acquisition, particularly the period between 15 and 24 months.

Traditionally, two broad classes of language functions have been recognized: the **cognitive function**—to name, indicate, describe, and comment; and the **instrumental function**—to request, reject, manipulate, and express desires. This distinction played a prominent role in the behavioristic analysis of language proposed by Skinner (1957). In Skinner's analysis an utterance exhibiting the cognitive function was labeled a "tact" (derived from *contact*) and one exhibiting the instrumental function a "mand" (from *demand*). Halliday (1975) referred to the cognitive function as the "mathetic" function and to the instrumental function as the "pragmatic" function.

Relative Incidence of Instrumental and Cognitive Word Uses

Several investigators have found that words are used for cognitive purposes before they are used for instrumental purposes. In their study of two children, Greenfield and Smith (1976) concluded that: "children ask for specific people or objects only after the naming function . . . is firmly established" (p. 104). For instance, Matthew said *door* while looking at a picture of a door at 1;3(5), but he did not use it instrumentally until 2 months later when he was asking to have the refrigerator door opened for him (Greenfield & Smith, 1976, pp. 89 & 107). Matthew thus used *door* for a cognitive purpose before he used it for an instrumental purpose. In a study of his son Nigel, Halliday (1975) reached a conclusion similar to that of Greenfield and Smith: "For Nigel, the main functional impetus behind the move into the lexical mode is, very distinctly, that of learning about his environment. Most of the new vocabulary is used, at first, solely in the context of observation and recall" (p. 43).

Why do instrumental uses lag behind cognitive uses? For some of the cases one possible explanation might be that instrumental uses require a relatively more abstract representation. In naming and commenting activities the object to which the word relates is present to the senses. Its internal representation thus has external support. But in the case of requests for absent objects, the object has to be represented internally and the word has to be triggered without external cues. This would seem to call for a more autonomous internal representation, thus explaining the later appearance of requests. This explanation would not account, however, for cases in which children ask for things they see. I have observed that even after children freely name food items, they do not regularly use food words when they want something from the table at mealtime. Rather, they sometimes fall back on earlier nonlinguistic ways (e.g., reaching and whining) for making their desires known. The later appearance of such requests may be due to emotional reasons. The drive and excitement involved in such situations reduce children's mental control and leave them with the more automatic forms of behavior (see Greenfield & Smith, 1976, p. 159).

A similar point was made by Lewis (1936/1975, pp. 158-159). A child he observed said *cake* at 16 months when he was offered a roll and when he was eating one; but he did not use the word when a roll was out of reach and he wanted it to be given to him. Instead, he uttered something like *e e e* and showed other signs of impatience. Lewis comments that the child concentrated his attention on securing the desired food and was thereby prevented from using the appropriate word.

In the preceding paragraphs I have discussed the use of the same words for purposes of referring and requesting, and the point was made that the cognitive-referential function appears before the instrumental-request function. The requests considered involved names of specific objects. Children also employ general request terms, and these appear quite early and contemporaneously with cognitive uses of words. Greenfield and Smith (1976, pp. 91-103) report that both their subjects used *mommy* (and variants of it) as a generalized request term. For instance, in the week between 1;0(15) and 1;0(22), Matthew was heard calling *mama* once as he was whining and reaching for a glass of orange juice, and again while whining as he stopped rocking in his rocking chair and wanted to be taken out. The use of *mommy* for requests probably derives from the mother's role as an obliging caregiver. Piaget (1951/1962, pp. 216-217) relates that one of his daughters started at 1;6(13) to use *panana* as a general request term. This word referred to her grandfather who was particularly accommodating, and she used it to ask for things even in his absence.

Not only request terms based on address forms but also "purer" request terms can be found in children's early vocabularies. Bloom (1973), for instance, reported that: "The word 'up' was first used by Allison [1;4(21)] as a REQUEST to be taken out of her high chair (which involved picking her up). Within a few days after initial use, Allison commented 'up' when she got up or climbed up herself, when other people got up, when she picked up objects or pulled people up" (p. 88).

It thus appears that children use either general or specialized request terms relatively early. Any individual child uses only a few request terms, and they become so automatic that he or she can use them even under conditions of emotional stress. Content words, however, because they are more specific and not exclusively associated with request contexts, require an element of choice and decision making in their use. As a consequence, they are less readily available in stressful situations.

Such disruptive effects of stress are not restricted to language. Barker, Dembo, and Lewin (1943) found that the level of play behavior of children between 25 and 61 months deteriorated when frustration was introduced into the play situation. The rule is that the less automatic a behavior the more susceptible it is to interruption by emotional factors. In infancy the disruptive effects of stress can be quite pervasive. Escalona (1968) discussed the "generalized primitivization of behavior" (p. 242), which occurs in infancy as a result of stress produced by hunger or fatigue.

Individual Differences in the Relative Use of Different Word Classes

Nelson (1973) used a distinction similar to that between cognitive and instrumental functions as a dimension of individual differences. In her study of the first 50-word vocabularies, described earlier, she noticed that some children had relatively few words for expressing personal-social feelings and desires (e.g., *ouch*, *want*) and relatively many nouns, whereas other children had relatively more personal-social words and relatively fewer nouns. Nelson attached considerable weight to these differences and considered the vocabularies of the children in the first group as relatively more "referential" and those in the latter group as relatively more "expressive." It must be stressed, however, that all children had more referential words than expressive words. Even the children considered by Nelson as expressive had five times as many nouns as personal-social words (see Nelson, 1973, Table 6). Moreover, the differences between the two groups seem to be localized. Of the seven measures of linguistic development examined, the two groups differed only on two (see Nelson, 1973, Table 10).

It thus appears that although the distinction between "referential" and "expressive" speech is relevant to a description of different types of early vocabularies, its ramifications seem limited. There are undoubtedly other individual differences in the content and form of children's early language (see Horgan, 1980), but we have little systematic knowledge on this topic at present.

Final Comment

My discussion of the functions of early words concentrated on the comparison between the cognitive-referential function and the instrumental-expressive function. This emphasis reflects the preoccupations found in the available literature. But in concluding this section we should not forget that children use words for other purposes as well. Sometimes children utter words for no external motive at all. Just as children like to play with new toys, so they like to play with new words and will utter them, appropriately or inappropriately, for no other reason than the joy inherent in speaking and hearing words. Children also produce words to display their knowledge for admiring adults or to test whether their usage of the words corresponds to that expected by adults. As has been stressed by Karmiloff-Smith (1979) and others (see Sinclair, Jarvella, & Levelt, 1978), when children are in the process of acquiring language, they have a direct interest in it and display a fascination with its inner workings. In the words of Karmiloff-Smith (1979): "It may well be that language is a *privileged* problem-space for children between 2 and 8 years, and only much later does it become perhaps *solely* the representational tool of intelligence" (p. 17).

PROCESSES OF WORD LEARNING

In the discussion so far I have concentrated on what children know about words and how they use them at different levels of development. Our attention now turns to the process of acquisition, to the factors that contribute to lexical growth. The first section is concerned with parental contributions to lexical development, the second with the child's constructive role in the learning process, and the third with general constraints on lexical knowledge.

Parental Contributions to Lexical Development

Mothers and other caregivers engage in a variety of behaviors that have obvious relevance to the child's lexical development. For convenience of exposition these can be divided into direct tutoring behaviors and less direct behaviors.

Direct Lexical Tutoring   A common type of early lexical instruction is **deictic tutoring**. It involves marking off a particular object by pointing to it, gazing at it, touching it, or handing it over, and at the same time naming it. This form of naming is traditionally referred to in the philosophy of language as "ostensive definition" and is distinguished from the explanation of words through the medium of other words. Deictic tutoring has been recognized for a long time as important for lexical development (e.g., Latif, 1934), but it has not received careful analysis until recently.

Ninio and Bruner (1978) analyzed the details of the deictic tutoring procedure in the picture-book reading situation. Their subjects were an English middle-class mother and her first-born son, Richard, when he was between 8 and 18 months. Ninio and Bruner found that they could analyze the interaction between the mother and Richard into five sequential components. Not all five components were present at every reading episode, but when present, they occurred in a regular order. A typical episode with all five components present looked like this:

1. Turning to a picture, the mother would say something like "Look!" to get Richard's attention.
2. Richard would oblige by pointing to the picture or by focusing his gaze on it.
3. The mother would then say something like, "What's that?" or "What are those?" to induce Richard to provide the label for the picture.
4. Richard would respond by producing some kind of vocalization.
5. His mother would then provide feedback and a label by saying something like, "Yes, it's an x."

The label was at the core of the mother's verbalizations. She produced it about three times as frequently as she did the attention-getting vocative, the query, or the feedback, and it was always strongly stressed. In many instances the mother provided a label without accompanying feedback. These presumably occurred when Richard did not vocalize or when the mother was not inclined to interpret his vocalizations. When feedback did occur it was mostly positive; only 18% of the feedback was negative (i.e., "No, it's not an x."). One should not infer from this that Richard gave correct labels in the cases in which the mother responded positively. Mothers often use positive verbalizations to encourage their children to speak. They also make generous allowances for their children and are willing to interpret even remote approximations as correct.

This is a case of a particular mother (English, white, middle class) interacting with a particular child (a first-born son). Not all mothers have the interest or the skill to teach vocabulary to children in the book-reading situation or in other situations (see Ninio, 1980b). But mothers who are concerned with advancing their children's language often follow simple routinized procedures, not only in book reading but in other contexts as well, as we see later. Now we can return to the topic of book reading and consider how mothers adjust their reading styles to children of different ages.

Murphy (1978) studied maternal behavior in the book-reading situation as a function of the age of the children. The children's ages were 9, 14, 20, and 24 months, and eight mother-child pairs were tested at each age level. The subjects were classified as belonging to working-class and lower-middle-class families. Murphy's findings suggest that the mothers used age-appropriate methods of lexical tutoring. The mothers of the 9-month-old infants engaged in little direct tutoring, apparently recognizing that infants at this age are not yet ready for the serious study of words. By contrast, the mothers of the 14-month-olds focused a great deal of attention on teaching their children the names of objects. When pointing to a picture they tended to call out its name. In fact, the pointing-and-naming technique was at a peak at 14 months. By 20 months this technique had declined sharply, and its place was taken by a more sophisticated technique, which reached a peak at 24 months. Mothers using this new technique did not simply provide their children with a name of a picture, but first questioned them to find out if they knew it. While pointing to a picture they asked questions about it (e.g., "What's that in the picture?"). These questions were sometimes quite specific (e.g., "What sound does it make?" "Where are the doggie's ears?"). The mothers of the older children apparently realized that their children knew enough language to be able to benefit from this type of testing method of deictic tutoring.

Play is another situation in which deictic tutoring takes place. Messer (1978) studied the activities of mothers and children (aged 11, 14, and 24 months) in the joint-play situation. He found that maternal reference to a toy coincided with its manipulation by child or mother. Reference was particularly likely when the manipulation involved joint attention, such as in cases when the mother brought a toy and held it in front of her child.

In a subsequent study with children of the same ages, Messer (1980) further elaborated on the techniques mothers use to help their children identify the referents of the words provided. The typical mother in the study tended to produce a name when the child began to play with a new toy and then repeated the name or made pronominal reference to it several times in succession. The mother-child interactions were organized in episodes in which the referent word was the unifying, recurrent theme. For example, Messer (1980) reports the following sequence produced by one of the mothers: "Oh, there's a super car. You like cars, don't you? It's a car. What are you going to do with it? Are you going to make it go?" (p. 35).

Lexical tutoring is, of course, not restricted to the joint-play or book-reading situations. Throughout the day attentive parents take advantage of opportunities to isolate referents and to name them. Parents constantly address to their children such comments as: "Look, Johnny, there is an airplane up in the sky." "Here's Lucy coming." "What's the boy doing? He's jumping." "Here, take the ball."

As would be expected, deictic naming benefits the child's acquisition of vocabulary. In a study to be described more fully in Chapter 7, Newport, Gleitman, and Gleitman (1977) investigated the relation between the linguistic development of 15 girls in the age range of 12-27 months and their mothers' speech. They found a correlation of .62 between the tendency of mothers to use deictic naming and the size of the girls' vocabularies. The benefit of deictic naming resides in the explicitness of the correspondence between name and referent. By gesturing as she utters the name, the mother increases the salience of the object and makes it conspicuous for the child (see Quine, 1973, p. 42). Because the gesture identifies a particular object, the child knows what the referent of the moment is and can readily infer that the name spoken at the time belongs to that referent.

In a study of mothers' naming statements to children between the ages of 1;5 and 1;10, Ninio (1980a) found that the mothers adjusted their speech in ways designed to assure that the children understood what the referents of the names were. Thus, when referring to objects in their entirety, they would use general forms of expression, such as: "This is a ____ (e.g., car)." "Look at the ____ (e.g., doggie)." But when referring to parts of objects, they would use more restrictive expressions, such as: "Where're the girl's shoes?" "Look at the lovely doll. Where's the doll's nose?" "Here's a car. Here're the car's wheels."

Investigators have in recent years emphasized that deictic and other forms of early language learning are prepared for by mother-infant interactions in infancy. Through interaction in situations such as play, feeding, and dressing, mothers (or other caregivers) and infants develop a facility in monitoring one another's focus of interest. Even a casual observer of a caring mother with her infant cannot fail to notice the coordination of their gaze orientations. Mother and infant look intently at each other, and each turns to look at an object that is being observed by the other. Bruner (1978) has succinctly summarized the contribution of mother-infant interaction in the following words: "What has been mastered is a *procedure* for homing in on the attentional locus of another: learning where to look in order to be tuned to another's attention" (p. 30). Effective deictic learning—and language learning in general—presupposes the availability of this kind of procedure.

The period of infancy makes another, more general contribution to the process of early language learning. It affords an opportunity for mother and infant to develop the kind of intimate, mutual sensitivity that makes them understand one another with minimal dependence on language. Such a background of intimate acquaintance helps reduce the incidence of nonunderstanding and misunderstanding that would otherwise mar the linguistic interchanges between mother and child at a time when the child's knowledge of language is still very primitive. In fact, to avoid frustration, young children show greater interest in talking with their mothers and with others intimately involved in their lives than with strangers.

The experience of rewarding and joyful early language lays the basis for a continuing interest in language and communication, and because so much is learned from others through language, this experience provides the foundation for healthy social and cognitive development in general (see White et al., 1979).

Indirect Teaching of Words   In addition to the direct instruction about the meanings of words that children receive in such contexts as book reading and play, they also receive indirect instruction. Particularly useful are the running commentaries that caregivers provide for their own and their children's ongoing behavior. A hypothetical example should help clarify how this kind of input can help the child work out word-referent mappings.

A mother dressing her son might say, "Let's put on your shirt" as she picks up a shirt to put it on her toddler. Later in the same dressing situation she might say, "Let's put on your pants" as she prepares to do this. The two nonverbal acts are substantially alike except for the focus on the shirt in one and on the pants in the other. The two corresponding linguistic expressions are also alike except for the words *shirt* and *pants*. Information can thus be isolated to connect *shirt* with shirt and *pants* with pants. The child may not note the connection when it first occurs, but he is more likely to do so when the situation is repeated and the correlation recurs. He may then form a hypothesis as to what *shirt* is a name for and what *pants* is a name for. Inasmuch as I am assuming that he will form the correct hypothesis, he will obtain confirming evidence in other situations. An example of a confirming situation might be one in which the mother is putting away clean laundry and providing a running commentary on what she is doing. Thus, when handling her son's shirt, she might say, "Now, we'll fold your shirt," and when handling his pants, she might say, "Now, we'll fold your pants."

Ferrier (1978) emphasized the important role in word acquisition played by the mother's production of repetitive and predictable utterances in routine contexts. The "monotonous regularity" of the mother's speech helps the child form connections between verbal and nonverbal entities. Some of the connections the child infers initially may be erroneous. Ferrier gives the following example. In the period before 16 months her daughter had the habit of uttering an unconventional sound as she was pulling at drawers and doors. On such occasions the mother would ask, "Do you want to look?" Subsequently, the child adopted the last word of the mother's question to express a demand for drawers and doors to be opened. Errors of this sort are of little consequence, because they get readily corrected in the course of the child's interaction with the mother and other mature speakers. The important thing is that the child has a source model from whom to learn, the proper relation with the tutor to be able to learn with relative ease, and the interest to do so.

The Child's Role in Lexical Development

The instructional activities of parents serve an important function by providing children with clear lexical information. But it is the children who use this information to construct their vocabulary systems. Moreover, children do not wait for pertinent information to come their way. They actively seek out information in a variety of ways. Quite commonly, children ask questions (sometimes incessantly) about the names of things (e.g., *What's this?*). They also invite parents to read to them, as in the following report (Drucker, 1975) about a 16-month-old boy: "John brings a book to his mother and sits by her as they look at the pages. Each time John sees a new page, he points to the object, says 'da?' with a questioning inflection, and mother labels it" (p. 503).

Children also seek out verbal information in less obvious ways. In a study of the use of *why* by a girl, Dusty, in the age range of 18 to 31 months, Blank (1975) found that in the initial period of 18 to 25 months, Dusty used the question word not to elicit explanations, but rather to get sufficient feedback to figure out its meaning.

Drucker (1975) observed that some common language-teaching games are actually instigated by children:

> The children will all, for example, begin by poking or pointing at doll's eyes, opening and closing the lids if the dolls are built that way. When adults notice this behavior, they usually begin to join in, providing labels and then asking the child, "Show me the dolly's eyes," nose, etc. Eventually, when the child has sufficient speech, the game changes to "What is this part?," with the parent pointing and the child asked to label. (p. 507)

Children's behavior and their parents' behavior are in continuous reciprocal interaction. Inquisitive children seek out linguistic information and encourage their parents to provide it. Parental responsiveness and stimulation in turn reward children's curiosity and open up for them new vistas for exploration.

General Constraints on Lexical Knowledge

Parents and other caregivers no doubt play a critical role in children's acquisition of vocabulary by providing them with appropriate information on appropriate occasions. Children on their part encourage their parents to provide the information, and they utilize it in constructive ways. In addition, there are general **constraints** on word meaning under which both parent and child, tutor and learner, operate. I turn to these now.

Quine (1973, p. 42) has argued that the fact that children's word meanings gradually approximate adult word meanings suggests that there is substantial agreement in their similarity standards. The precise nature of the similarity standards and their origins are at present unclear, but some suggestions are available. Quine (1973, p. 54; see also Chomsky, 1965, pp. 29 & 201) has suggested that humans are innately "body-minded," that is, they have a natural predisposition to assign names to entities that function as integral units. For instance, children do not associate the word *hat* with the head cover plus the top part of the head on which it rests, because these are separate bodies. "Bodies" are privileged as nameable entities because their parts move together and share a common fate. Thus, according to Quine (1973): "The similarity that links the many presentations of Mama for us under the one name is not just static visual similarity, but a similarity that depends also on continuity of deformation and displacement" (p. 53).

Another constraint that children seem to operate under is to give primacy to the functions of objects in the generalization of their names (Nelson, 1977). Thus, it seems that the reason children do not generalize words on the basis of color (Clark, 1973) is that similarly colored objects do not serve similar functions.

There is experimental evidence in a study by Daehler and O'Connor (1980) on the role of functional similarity in children's implicit classification of objects. In this experiment children were first familiarized with objects (or pictures of objects) and were then exposed to the familiarized objects and to novel objects. The experimenter measured the children's looking times to the familiarized and to the novel objects. The novel objects were selected to resemble the familiarized objects in one of two ways: in shape (e.g., yellow pencil [familiarized] and white straw [novel]) or in functional status (e.g., plain gold ring [familiarized] and pink child's ring [novel]).

The results indicate that in both the shape condition and the functional condition, children aged 19 to 31 months looked longer at the novel objects than at the familiarized objects. But the difference was smaller for the functionally related items than for the shape-related items, suggesting that the functionally related items were perceived as more similar to the familiarized items. Because it is impossible to equate the *degree* of physical and functional similarity and because the functionally similar items were also physically similar, as is normally the case, it cannot be concluded from these results that function is more important than shape. But it does seem reasonable to conclude that similarity of function enhanced the children's subjective feeling of similarity.

LEXICAL DEVELOPMENT IN BROADER CONTEXT

The focus of this chapter is on children's learning of words during the second and third year. Many other developments take place in this period. In particular, children learn other aspects of language aside from vocabulary, their thinking is developing, and they are being socialized into the ways of their culture. This part places lexical development in the context of these other developments.

Lexical Development and Cognitive Functioning

Words as symbols are labels for groupings of objects. (I include under "objects" also people, events, qualities, ideas, and so forth for simplicity of exposition.) By labeling an object the child is placing it in a class with other objects. Even proper names (e.g., *John* and *Mommy*, in the sense of "my Mommy") are class names because the individual named does not look exactly alike at different times and under different circumstances.

Classification is a basic and ubiquitous process. There is evidence that at the end of the first year children already manifest implicit sorting of objects into classes. Thus, Starkey (1981) prepared eight sets of objects, each set containing four objects from one class and four from another class. For example, one of his sets contained four "people" figurines and four oval shapes made of Masonite. He placed one set at a time in front of 6-, 9-, and 12-month-old infants, arranging the eight objects randomly. Starkey found that the 9- and 12-month-olds tended to touch and manipulate the objects of one class first and then the objects of the other class. There was little mixing between classes. By contrast, the 6-month-olds did not show this kind of "sorting" behavior. No tests of sensorimotor development were given to the subjects in this study, but the ages suggest that the infants in the youngest group were below the fourth stage and the infants in the two older groups were in the fourth stage or beyond it. We have seen in the previous chapter that the fourth stage is when representation begins to take root. This is therefore when children can be expected to show an ability to sort objects into different representational classes. At the ages of 9-12 months the classes are defined not in symbolic terms, but in sensorimotor terms. We assume, therefore, that the different objects belonging to the same class elicited similar sensorimotor schemes that were different from the sensorimotor schemes elicited by the objects in the contrasting class.

During the second year classification becomes more purposeful and more sophisticated. But even at the third level classification is still qualitatively different from the classification of older children. This is not obvious on cursory observation. As we have seen, the word uses of the third level tend to conform to adult uses, and even when they do not, it is normally a matter of difference in the specific range of the extensions, not in their quality. Because of the conformity of usage, it is tempting to attribute to younger children underlying meanings similar to those of older children. However, this temptation must be resisted. Piaget (1951/1962, pp. 221-244) has argued that the underlying meaning system of children in their second and third years of life and even later is far from having mature quality. The extension that the child makes of a word to a new object is on the basis of direct similarity between the new object and an original object. According to Piaget (1951/1962) it is an "assimilation of the particular to the particular" (p. 235). For the child a class is "a kind of typical individual reproduced in several copies" (p. 226). The child has some internal representation of a prototype, possibly through mental imagery, and it is to the prototype that different objects are attracted by virtue of similarity.

We saw in Chapter 2 that the prototype also occupies a significant position in adult thinking. But for adults the prototype serves as the best or fullest exemplar of a conceptual category that has an independent psychological reality. In contrast, children's prototypes are determined on the basis of circumstances of occurrence; it may be the first item to which the label was given, it may be the most common object in their environment, and so forth. Other instances are directly linked to the prototype and to one another to form the referent class of the word. To capture the immature character of the young child's classes, Piaget referred to them as **preconcepts**.

I have discussed the child's word meanings in the framework of Piaget's theory. But other theorists have reached similar conclusions. In particular, the Russian psychologist Vygotsky (1934/1962) characterized the child's classes as being "complexes" rather than concepts. In a complex the bonds linking one member to another are concrete and direct. Vygotsky (1934/1962) commented that: "Word meanings as perceived by the child refer to the same objects the adult has in mind, which ensures understanding between child and adult, but . . . the child thinks the same thing in a different way, by means of different mental operations" (p. 69).

Luria (1982, chaps. 2-3), Vygotsky's student, elaborated on this approach. He highlighted the distinction between **referential meaning** (which he refers to as "object reference") and **conceptual meaning** (which he refers to simply as "meaning"). Knowledge of referential meaning consists of being able to assign words correctly to objects. Knowledge of conceptual meaning entails an appreciation of the essential properties characterizing the objects named by words and a sensitivity to the hierarchical organization of the meanings underlying words. Luria pointed out that even after the referential meanings of words stabilize, their conceptual meanings continue to develop as the child's cognition develops.

Luria (1982) exemplified the difference between referential meaning and conceptual meaning by an analysis of the conceptual meaning of *dog*: "Thus, if the word 'dog' has the same object reference for a child at the age of 3 years as it does for a child 7 years of age, or a university student, this does not mean that it has the same meaning at each of these stages of development" (p. 50). For the young child the conceptual meaning of *dog* is an unorganized conglomerate, consisting of a variety of affective and practical reactions. It is a playmate, a creature that obeys its master, barks, fights with cats, and so forth. For the mature speaker, however, *dog* is an internally organized entity that is part of a hierarchical structure, such as the one depicted in Figure 4.2.

The point concerning the coincidence of the referents of the child and the adult and the noncoincidence of their meanings, which I have elaborated through the work of Piaget, Vygotsky, and Luria, can be made in terms of the distinction developed in philosophy between the intensional and extensional aspects of meaning (see, e.g., Putnam, 1975). "Intension" refers to the definition of a term, to the concept associated with it; and "extension" refers to the range of instances to which it can be applied. A favorite example philosophers use to bring out this difference is the pair of expressions "a creature with a heart" and "a creature with a kidney." Because, as far as is known, every creature that has a heart also has a kidney, the extensions of these two terms are identical, whereas their intensions obviously differ. But one need not resort to esoteric examples. It is very common to find that individuals who differ in the intensions of their words converge on common extensions. Blind individuals have of necessity different concepts associated with their words, but they are able to communicate with sighted individuals because of the overlap of extensions. It has been observed that not all colorblind individuals are aware of their disability because they make normal color classifications on the basis of such redundant cues as brightness, shape, size, and context (Hebb, 1966, p. 31).

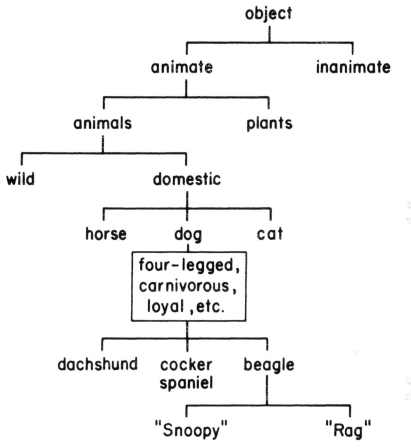

FIG. 4.2   An organized, hierarchical representation of *dog* (adapted from Luria, 1982, p. 52).

Returning now to children, what I am suggesting is that by the third level they have achieved a reasonably good correspondence between their extensions and the standard extensions of their linguistic community. But it will be a long time before they acquire the intensional meanings of their models.

There is broad-based evidence for the foregoing characterization of early word meanings in Piaget's work on conservation, correspondence, and class inclusion (Piaget, 1952/1965). This research shows that up to school age, children's thinking is global, nonanalytic, and nonhierarchical. There is also more direct research on the classificatory behavior of preschool children, showing it to be holistic, nonanalytic. Thus, Smith and Kemler (1977) presented children with three paper forms at a time and asked them to put together the two that belonged together. The forms differed in size and brightness. Kindergarten children

(5-year-olds) put forms together on the basis of global similarity, in contrast to older children (11-year-olds) who put them together on the basis of commonality of specific characteristics. For instance, a young child would put a 1-inch white square together with a ½-inch light gray square, but an older child would put a 1-inch white square together with a 1-inch black square.

The perceptive reader may ask at this point: If young children have vague and imprecise concepts associated with their words, how are they able to delimit accurately the referential applications of their words? The answer is that the referential usages of words are to some extent independent of their intensional meanings (see Anisfeld, 1968). In everyday-life naming practices there are normally enough incidental cues to yield correct word applications. Thus, a child may simply remember that the liquid that originates in faucets and can be found in lakes is called *water*. Children, or adults for that matter, need to know little else to be usually correct in their usage of *water*. Similarly, all a child may know about *refrigerator* is that it is something in which food items such as butter and milk are kept cold. Under normal circumstances this meaning assures correct usage. An adult observer is not likely to become suspicious that the child has a different meaning associated with *refrigerator* until the child refuses to use the word for a cabinet in a hospital in which blood is stored.

Implicit in the preceding discussion is a distinction between attributes defining concepts and cues or criteria guiding the labeling of objects. Until the early school years, children remain primarily concerned with criteria for labeling objects. They do not seem to appreciate the existence of attributes as distinct from labeling cues. We have seen that in their application of words at the first two levels, children use cues that may be irrelevant from an adult point of view. Through observation and feedback, they learn which cues produce acceptable word usages and which do not. For many objects in the environment there are redundant classification cues, and it is not surprising that by and large children at the third level are able to pick out one or another of the "working" cues. But the achievement of reasonable conformity in word usage does not reflect corresponding achievement in conceptual understanding.

There has been some criticism of the Piagetian-Vygotskian approach to early word meaning, which I have adopted here. However, I believe that the criticisms stem from a failure to distinguish between behavioral commonalities tying objects to one another by virtue of shared experiences and categorical classification based on the conceptualization of objects as belonging together. This point can best be clarified by reference to a specific experiment (Ross, 1980). Ross studied three groups of children between the ages of 12 and 24 months. The children were first shown 10 instances of one of several categories of objects, for 30 seconds each. For example, one category was food, and each child was shown (one at a time) 10 toy items of food (e.g., a toy loaf of bread) and was induced to view and manipulate them. After this exposure series, a pair of new items was shown: One was from the exposed category, with the item itself being new (e.g., a toy apple), and the other was from a new category (e.g., a toy chair). Ross found that the children looked at least twice as long at the new-category items as at the old-category items. In the example given, the children viewed chair for an average of about 17 seconds and apple for about 8 seconds. There were no differences among the three age groups.

These findings suggest that the children became satiated with looking at the same kinds of items and were ready for something new. Because both items in a pair were new and the only difference between them was that one belonged to an old category and the other to a new category, Ross concludes that the children must have had conventional categories, such as food, contrary to the views of Piaget and Vygotsky. But this is an overinterpretation. No one would deny that even young children have a sense of class belongingness. The question concerns the basis of this sense of belongingness. The argument I have developed here is that for the young child the basis is preconceptual, nonanalytic. For the young child food may be something one eats when one is hungry, or something mommy calls "food." Ross' failure to obtain age differences, which she finds surprising, is consistent with this interpretation, for even 12-month-old infants are capable of memory and sensorimotor representation.

Because the child's primitive categorical notions yield classificatory behaviors that overlap with those yielded by more mature notions, observers will not normally notice that the child's notion is different unless they specifically probe to find out. Investigators have indeed begun to probe (see Anglin, 1977, chap. 5; White, 1982). Thus, White presented children in the age range of 3-5 years with slides of various items belonging to six categories and asked them to indicate for each item whether it belonged to the designated category (e.g., a child would be shown a slide of peas and asked, "Is this food?"). White found that the children readily agreed to place typical items in the categories offered them, but were less willing to do so for atypical items. Thus, although 95% of the children agreed that meat and peas were foods, only 35% agreed that ketchup was a food. Similarly, 100% of the children accepted shirt as an item of clothing, but only 35% accepted mitten as an item of clothing. White presents evidence suggesting that these differential categorization tendencies are attributable to maternal naming practices. Mothers were found less likely to label atypical instances with the category name than typical instances. Whatever the explanation, this experiment shows that the bases of categorization of young children are different from those of more mature individuals.

Lexical Learning and the Direction of Thinking

The learning of words plays a central role in the child's intellectual development. The labels children pick up through interaction with their tutors provide hypotheses concerning the socially relevant groupings of objects, hypotheses which children are only too eager to test and explore. In fact, in teaching words to children, caregivers provide lessons in classification, and supply children with a framework that they can use to interpret and organize their own experiences.

In a study of children between the ages of 1 and 3, raised at home and in high-quality day care facilities, Carew (1980) found that:

> Language stimulation (the kind that is informative and designed to help the child master language skills) provided by caregivers when the child is between 12 and 30 months may supply the essential foundation and impetus to the child's intellectual development as measured by traditional pre-school-level IQ tests . . . . [Such stimulation] empower[s] him to play the role of his own teacher and architect of his intelligence in his independent activities at this age. (pp. 42-43)

One of the mothers in Carew's (1980) study said the following to her daughter as she was playing with toy animals: "See, this is a cow, this is a lamb, and this is a lion. They are all animals" (p. 73). The girl did not immediately acquire the concept of animal, but she got an inkling that there was something there to be discovered. Curiosity and natural experiences gradually do the rest.

A striking example of the directive role of words was observed by Shoshana Goldman in her twin boys in the middle of their second year. To the surprise of their parents, the boys responded unenthusiastically to a tyke bike that was given them. But their attitude changed radically, when after about a week, the bike was referred to as *car*. Their interest in it rose dramatically; riding it became their favorite activity. The label *car* put their plaything into a class of socially valued objects. In children, as in adults, even motor activities gain their significance from social sanction, which is mediated through language. I turn to the social context of word learning next.

Lexical Development and the Socialization of the Child

The learning of words, and of language in general, is an intensely social affair. Language is a system of *social* symbols. It is learned from people and for communicating with people. In learning words children are learning a social system of classification. I have emphasized one of the factors motivating the learning of vocabulary between the ages of 2 and 3, namely, children's desire to understand the world around them and to develop a representation of it. Another factor is their need to participate in the social group in which they live. Toddlers learn language to be like other members of their community and to be able to communicate with them.

Toddlers' absorption in language learning seems to be part of their acute sensitivity and heightened interest in social norms (see Kagan, 1981). Toddlers manifest their social sensitivity not only in the learning of language but in other realms as well, particularly in their play behavior. One of the functions of toddler play seems to be to gain a better understanding of social roles. Through play with toy figures, toddlers act out the roles of father, mother, police officer, and so forth. Girls play with dolls—feeding them, dressing them—in order to understand their roles in relation to the roles of their mothers and to resolve conflicts in these relations (see Drucker, 1975).

Wolf and Gardner (1981) noted that role switching appears in play at about 18 months. For instance, in the peekaboo game children go from playing exclusively the stylized role of the hider to playing alternately the hider role and the seeker role. Through this behavior children demonstrate that they separate roles from role enactments.

Parents actively encourage their children to fulfill their social responsibilities. Thus, Schachter (1979) found that a category of maternal utterances designated as "controls, restricts-commands" constituted about 30% of the speech of middle-class (both white and black) mothers to their 28-month-old children. For disadvantaged black mothers the figure was 54%. Included in this category were refusals to grant requests and utterances telling children that they are getting messy, that they should or should not be doing something, and so on. Mothers also imparted social norms in noncontrol modes of speech (e.g., in the context of teaching) or in response to an inquiry from the child. The middle-class mothers used the noncontrol mode more than the disadvantaged mothers.

The main agenda of toddlerhood, both from the point of view of the parent and the child, seems to be the socialization of the child. Language learning is an integral part of this process.

Lexical Development and the Emergence of Syntax

The relation between lexical and syntactic development has not been studied directly, but data reported by McCune-Nicolich (1981, Table 3), in a study concerned with other matters, are very revealing on this point. McCune-Nicolich studied five children longitudinally over periods ranging from 7 to 11 months. In the beginning of the study, the children ranged in age from 14 to 19 months. Their speech was recorded in 30-minute play sessions held at about monthly intervals. McCune-Nicolich reports the number of word types produced by the children and the mean length of their utterances (**MLU**; length was counted, roughly speaking, in word units) in each session.

Examination of McCune-Nicolich's data shows a clear relation between growth of vocabulary and development of syntax. During the initial 4-6 months of testing, the children's MLU stayed very close to the 1.0 level (i.e., their utterances consisted of single words); they had virtually no sentences. In this period their vocabularies showed only minimal growth (reaching the level of 23-37 words). Then came a sudden explosion in vocabulary growth, when the vocabulary of each child doubled in the course of 1 month. Syntax began to develop soon after; the children's MLUs reached the level of 1.31-1.84 within a month or two after the lexical explosion. During this initial period of syntactic develop-

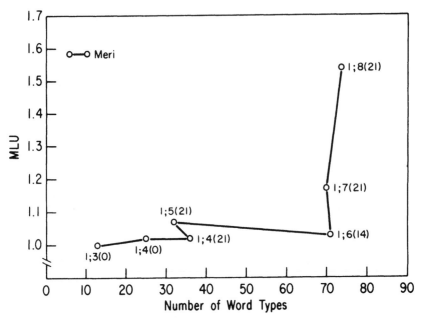

FIG. 4.3 Rate of increase in MLU for Meri, one of the children studied by McCune-Nicolich (1981), as a function of number of words in her vocabulary.

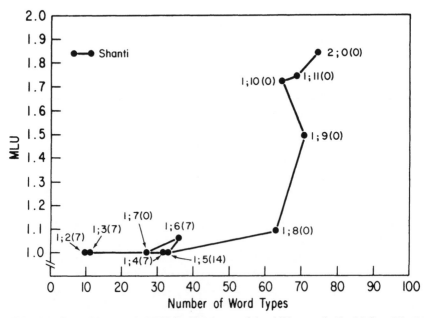

FIG. 4.4 Rate of increase in MLU for Shanti, one of the children studied by McCune-Nicolich (1981), as a function of number of words in her vocabulary.

ment, vocabulary growth came to a virtual standstill; the largest increase in vocabulary during the 2 months following the explosion was 4 words.

This pattern of relations between vocabulary and syntax is displayed in Figures 4.3 and 4.4 for two of McCune-Nicolich's subjects, Meri and Shanti. As can be seen in Figure 4.3, Meri's MLU stayed around 1.0 during five testing sessions over a 3½-month period, from 1;3(0) to 1;6(14). In the session that took place at 1;6(14), Meri's vocabulary leaped to 70 words from the 30 in the previous session only 3 weeks earlier. Her MLU started rising in the session, at 1;7(21), that followed the vocabulary explosion, and continued to rise in the next and final session, at 1;8(21). During this period of rapid syntactic development, in which Meri's MLU rose from 1.0 to 1.6, her vocabulary did not advance at all, staying at the 70-word mark. The pattern was similar for Shanti (Fig. 4.4) and for the other three children.

My interpretation of these results is that with the attainment of the naming function, as reflected in the rapid increase in vocabulary, children cross the threshold into language and become ready to acquire syntax. When they begin to acquire syntax, children become absorbed (for a while) in this novel, exciting task and ignore vocabulary acquisition. The following chapters explore in detail the characteristics of early syntactic development.

II

EARLY SYNTAX

5 Aspects of Syntax

An essential property of language is that it provides the means for expressing indefinitely many thoughts and for reacting appropriately in an indefinite range of new situations.

Noam Chomsky

By their second birthday many children have begun to construct sentences. In some respects their sentences resemble those of mature speakers, but in other respects they differ. To facilitate a reasonably sophisticated analysis in the following chapters of the peculiarities of children's early sentences, the present chapter outlines the essential characteristics of mature sentences.

The study of the structure of sentences is the province of the science of linguistics and comes under the heading of **syntax**. The term **grammar** is used in a narrow sense synonymously with syntax. It is also used broadly by linguists to refer to the overall theory of language they construct, which includes other components of language in addition to syntax.

The sentence is the center of language and the focus of its productivity. The sounds and words an individual utters are drawn from a limited, previously acquired repertoire. Sentences, however, are different. They are constructed, not reproduced from memory. There is no limit to the number of sentences one can construct, and hence no limit to the variety of ideas that can be expressed in language. In a real sense sounds and words exist to be used in sentences. This chapter is concerned with two aspects of sentences: their meanings and their structural forms.

THE MEANINGS OF SENTENCES

Individual words have lexical meanings. But when they are brought together in sentences, they give rise to **propositional meanings** (also referred to as *syntactic*, *sentential*, *relational*, and *compositional meanings*). The meaning relations expressed in sentences can be defined in different ways, which are sketched briefly in the following sections.

The Propositional Meaning of Sentences

It has been traditional to distinguish between the subject of a sentence and its predicate. Typically, the subject is the noun phrase (NP) that stands in a causal relation to the predicate, which is the verb phrase (VP). (An NP is a phrase that has a noun as its core; a VP is a phrase that has a verb as its core.) In sentences 1 and 2 *The campers* and *Albert Einstein* are the subjects, and the remaining parts the predicates:

1. The campers went on a hike.
2. Albert Einstein developed the theory of relativity.

The relation of the predicate to the subject constitutes the propositional meaning of the sentence.

The meaning relations in a sentence can also be expressed in terms of topic and comment. The topic of the sentence is what the sentence is about, and the comment is what is said about the topic. In English the subject is often the topic and the predicate the comment. But this is not always so. Consider sentence 3:

3. That man I recognize.

Here the topic is *That man*, and the comment is *I recognize*, but the subject is *I*, and the predicate *recognize that man*. The relation of topic-comment to subject-predicate is even more tenuous in some non-European languages.

Role Functions Expressed in Sentences

A major aspect of sentential meaning involves the assignment of **role**, or **case**, **functions** to NPs (see Brown, 1973, pp. 132-138; Fillmore, 1968). One of the clearest and most common cases is that of **agent**. Agents are NPs that have some responsibility for the action described by the verb. The initial NPs in 1 and 2 are agents. Some additional examples of agents can be seen in sentences 4-9, where the agent NPs are italicized:

4. *The boy* hit the ball.
5. *The baby* cried.
6. *Computers* check income tax returns.
7. *The guests* came late.
8. *The dog* chased the cat away.
9. The bill was signed by *the President.*

A distinction is often made between NPs that have a potency of their own (usually those that refer to animate beings), for which the term *agent* is reserved, and those that do not (usually inanimate things), which are called **instruments**. The italicized NPs in sentences 10-12 are instruments:

10. *The ball* hit the boy.
11. *The heavy snow* broke the tree branches.
12. The dentist cleaned his teeth with *dental floss.*

Agents and instruments are the typical subjects of sentences.

Both the agent and instrument NPs are in a sense responsible for the action of the verb. They contrast with NPs that result from the action of the verb or are affected by it. Although some distinctions can be made within the category of object NPs—also along the lines of animateness-inanimateness—these are not pursued here; all roles of this type may be considered as fulfilling the **objective** role. Some examples of NPs that serve the objective role are given in sentences 13-18:

13. John built *the house.*
14. John opened *the door.*
15. *The door* opened.
16. John recalled *the flood.*
17. Bill met *John.*
18. John spit on *the floor.*

I have distinguished so far between NPs that stand in an antecedent relation to the verb and those that stand in a consequent relation to it. In addition, there are NPs whose role in the sentence is that of **attributant**, as in sentences 19-20, or **possessor**, as in 21-23:

19. *John* is smart.
20. *John* is a musician.
21. The scarf belongs to *Joan.*
22. *Joan* owns a yacht.
23. *The baby* already has two teeth.

The Informational Structure of Sentences

The preceding sections analyzed the content of sentences in terms of role functions, subject-predicate, and topic-comment. Sentences also structure informational content into **new-given** or **asserted-presupposed**. In constructing sentences speakers can distinguish between background information presupposed to be known by the addressee and new information presently focused on. For instance, sentence 24 presupposes that someone saved the girl and asserts that John was the saver:

24. It is John who saved the girl.

The focus on new information is achieved in this case through the choice of the cleft sentence frame ("It is . . ."). In a declarative frame an element can be made focal by uttering it with heavier stress than is required by the sentential structure, as in 25:

25. JOHN saved the girl.

Any part of a sentence can be focused on through phonetic emphasis of this kind, which linguists refer to as "contrastive stress." When a declarative sentence is produced with a noncontrastive, normal stress pattern, it is usually presuppositionally neutral. That is, no part of the sentence is presupposed in that case; the entire message is new. (For further elaboration of the issues discussed here and for reference sources, see Chafe, 1976, and Klenbort & Anisfeld, 1974.)

THE STRUCTURE OF SENTENCES

A sentence is an ordered sequence of linguistic forms: Syllable follows syllable, word follows word, and phrase follows phrase. Language forces the expression of simultaneous content in a sequence of temporally ordered forms. A scene observed in one glance, when described linguistically, has to be analyzed into components and synthesized into an ordered sequence of linguistic forms. The person who reports sentence 26 did not see a series of four ordered percepts (the thief, wore, dark, and glasses):

26. The thief wore dark glasses.

He or she saw a single simultaneous percept, but was forced by language to break it down into components and string them out in order. Both the selection of content units and their organization into sentences are to a greater or lesser extent subject to arbitrary linguistic conventions, which I examine in the next two sections.

Selection of Linguistic Units

Linguistic determination of the components of sentences can be seen in two areas: in the direction language gives concerning what information is to be included in a sentence and in the fitting of information into part-of-speech classes.

Selection of Information   Although speakers normally feel that the information they include in their sentences is determined by what they want to say, this is not entirely true. Language regulates the informational content of sentences by requiring the specification of certain information and by making lexical and grammatical resources more readily available for the expression of some information and less readily available for the expression of other information.

Whorf (1940/1956) compares the expression of the same message in English and in Shawnee (an American Indian language) to show that the two languages differ in their "isolates of meaning" (p. 208). The message that English would express in sentence 27, is expressed in Shawnee in sentence 28:

27. I clean it (gun) with the ramrod.
28. nipekwalakha. 'I (ni) dry space (pekw) interior of hole (alak) by motion of tool (h) it (a).'

Thus, English relates the action (*clean*) performed on the gun to such actions as laundering clothes, washing hands, and sweeping floors, whereas Shawnee emphasizes the dry nature of the action. English does not concern itself with the particular shape of the thing cleaned, but Shawnee does (*interior of hole*). English, on the other hand, is more specific than Shawnee concerning the instrument used.

It is possible to convey in English all the information that is conveyed in Shawnee, as I have just done. Presumably, it is also possible to convey in Shawnee all the information conveyed in English. But what is expressible in one language in a simple and direct way has to be expressed in an awkward and roundabout way in the other language.

Sapir (1921, pp. 82-94) highlighted differences among languages in their informational requirements by analyzing how the content expressed in English sentence 29 would be expressed in other languages.

29. The farmer kills the duckling.

English does not require the speaker to indicate in the sentence the position of the farmer in relation to the speaker, nor the ownership of the duckling. But

Kwakiutl (an American Indian language) makes it obligatory for the speaker to provide both types of information. It should be further noted that the farmer and the duckling are marked in 29 as definite and singular. One cannot utter an English sentence without committing oneself as to the specificity (*the*) or nonspecificity (*a*) of the noun and as to its singularity or plurality. But in Chinese, both number and definiteness of reference are optional. Thus, one could say in Chinese the equivalent of *Farmer kills duckling*, leaving vague whether farmer and duckling are presumed known or unknown to the hearer and whether there was one or more than one of either of them. Definiteness and plurality can be expressed in Chinese, but they are not required and cannot be as readily expressed as in English.

Thus, every language determines how simply a particular piece of information can be expressed and whether it is obligatory or optional. In this way languages constrain what their speakers say.

Parts of Speech   Linguistic structuring of the world of experience can be seen clearly in the part-of-speech classification of words. The parts of speech capture distinctions present in the reality outside language (see Bolinger, 1975, p. 149; Brown, 1958, p. 248; Gleason, 1961, p. 94). The traditional, semantic definitions of parts of speech are, in fact, based on these distinctions. The world is populated with substantive entities—people, animals, objects, and places—providing the basis for the traditional definition of nouns as names of people, places, and things. The substantives participate in passing states and events—they run, sleep, can be lived in, or sat on—providing the basis for the traditional definition of verbs as names of actions and states. Nouns and verbs may have different qualities, which are expressed by adjectives and adverbs, respectively.

The traditional, semantic definitions are, however, not quite adequate (see, e.g., Bolinger, 1975, pp. 142-156; Gleason, 1961, chap. 8). In what way, for instance, are *height* and *happiness* more "things" than *high* and *happy*? *Height* refers to the same concept as *high,* and *happiness* to the same concept as *happy.* The choice between the two words that refer to the same concept depends on the particular sentential context involved. Consider sentences 30 and 31:

30. The dresser is 4 feet high.
31. The height of the dresser is 4 feet.

The vertical extension of the dresser is the same in 30 as in 31, even though it is expressed in 30 by *high* and in 31 by *height*. The choice between them depends on whether the sentence requires an adjective or a noun. In addition, the part-of-speech classes themselves are not clearly distinct in the traditional, semantic definitions. Verbs describe actions (e.g., *run*) and states (*rest*), but states are also described by adjectives (*quiet*).

Such considerations suggest that part-of-speech classes cannot be adequately defined solely in terms of the referential characteristics of words. Their status and functions in the language also have to be taken into account. Linguists have, in fact, developed structural definitions based on distributional criteria. Thus, they define nouns in English as words that can be preceded by articles (*a*, *the*) and other determiners (e.g., *this*, *that*, *my*, *some*, etc.) and are inflected for possession and plurality. Similarly, English verbs are defined as words that are inflected for tense and third person.

These criteria result in varying degrees of membership in the part-of-speech classes. For instance, *boy* has a high degree of nounness. It can be preceded by a variety of determiners (e.g., *the boy*, *my boy*, *every boy*, etc.), and it can be inflected for plurality (*boys*) and possession (*the boy's*). By contrast, *dirt*, *rice*, and *John* pass some noun criteria, but not all; therefore, they are nouns to a lesser degree.

Membership in part-of-speech classes is thus similar to membership in other natural human categories, which as we have seen in Chapter 2 is a matter of gradation. Ross (1974, pp. 111-120) has presented linguistic evidence in support of the argument that grammatical classes and grammatical rules, in general, function in a scalar more-or-less fashion, not in a discrete all-or-none fashion.

Words that are members of one part of speech can be made to function in another part of speech by attaching to them special identifiers to mark them as members of the target part of speech. Thus, the adjective *high*, can be made into a noun by appending the *-t* sound to make *height*, and into a verb by further appending the syllable *-en* to make *heighten*. (I am ignoring the change of *i* to *ei* because the analysis is in terms of sound characteristics, and the sound characteristics of the vowel remain the same in all three forms.) Bolinger (1975) considers the possibility of changing words from one part of speech to another as evidence for the validity of the part-of-speech classes: "The best evidence of all for the reality of classes is the fact that languages have ways of converting words from one class to another: *danger*, noun; *dangerous*, adjective; *dangerously*, adverb; *to endanger*, verb" (p. 146).

When a word functions as a member of a particular part of speech, it takes on shades of the semantic characteristics of the prototypical members of that category. Thus, *height* seems to be more thinglike than *high*, although both words refer to the same concept.

Languages differ in their part-of-speech assignment of words. Whorf (1940/1956), for instance, noted that Hopi (an American Indian language) considers events of temporary duration, such as lightning, wave, flame, and pulsation, as verbs, not as nouns.

Languages may differ in their part-of-speech assignment of individual words, but they all share the basic part-of-speech classes. The noun and verb classes, in particular, are fundamental. In the words of Sapir (1921):

It is well to remember that speech consists of a series of propositions. There must be something to talk about and something must be said about this subject of discourse once it is selected. This distinction is of such fundamental importance that the vast majority of languages have emphasized it by creating some sort of formal barrier between the two terms of the proposition. The subject of discourse is a noun. As the most common subject of discourse is either a person or a thing, the noun clusters about concrete concepts of that order. As the thing predicated of a subject is generally an activity in the widest sense of the word, a passage from one moment of existence to another, the form which has been set aside for the business of predicating, in other words, the verb, clusters about concepts of activity. No language wholly fails to distinguish noun and verb, though in particular cases the nature of the distinction may be an elusive one. (p. 119)

To summarize, parts of speech have a semantic basis; that is, there is a basis in human perception of reality for making the distinctions that the part-of-speech classes make. But language does not simply appropriate part-of-speech classes from the outside. Rather, it incorporates them into its system, giving them formal character and definition. Parts of speech relate to the real world, but they function as integral components of the language system.

Sentential Structuring of Content

Sentences organize words into coherent structures by sequencing them in order, by requiring that they be articulated in a unified fashion, and by adding various structural markers (i.e., tense markers, prepositions, articles, and the like). I discuss here the first two organizing devices; the third will be taken up in the next chapter and in Chapter 9.

Word Order   We saw in the previous section that language determines, to some extent, the units of information that are included in a sentence and the part-of-speech form that these units take. Linguistic imposition is much more glaring with respect to syntactic order. Order is a linguistic dictate. Much of what one says has no temporal valence, but speech is a temporal event, and arbitrary order has, therefore, to be imposed (Lashley, 1951).

Being arbitrary, the structure of sentences might be expected to differ across languages, as it does. Learners of foreign languages know that they have to pay attention to the order of elements in the sentence. For instance, in English the adjective precedes the noun, but in French it follows the noun (e.g., *white paper*, *papier blanc*). Neither of the two orders is any more natural than the other; the paper and its whiteness coexist. Their separation and ordering is a linguistic requirement.

Variability in sentential word order across languages is, however, within confined limits. Greenberg (1963) noted that of the six possible orders of subject (S), verb (V), and object (O), only SVO, SOV, and VSO "normally occur as dominant orders. The three which do not occur at all, or at least are excessively rare, are VOS, OSV, and OVS. These all have in common that the object precedes the subject'' (p. 61). On the basis of this observation, Greenberg (1963) formulated the following universal generalization: ''In declarative sentences with nominal subject and object, the dominant order is almost always one in which the subject precedes the object'' (p. 61).

Why do languages prefer to put the subject before the object? It may be that because the subject is often the agent instigating the action of the verb, it is conceived as being logically prior to the object which is the recipient or the result of the action. For instance, in sentence 32 one senses that the subject (*John*) is somehow prior to the object (*Bill*):

32. John hit Bill.

There is, of course, the passive voice, which puts the object first as in 33, but the passive is used very infrequently and for special purposes (see Svartvik, 1966):

33. Bill was hit by John.

In no language does the passive represent the dominant order.

There is a problem, however, with the attribution of subject-object ordering to the intuitive impression that the subject is logically prior. It is possible that the sense of priority is a consequence of sentential ordering rather than its cause. In any event, whether or not the subject-object ordering is natural or arbitrary, many of the other order requirements in every language are arbitrary.

Order is a major tool for the expression of sentential meaning. Languages differ in their reliance on order, but as Sapir (1921) noted: ''Order asserts itself in every language as the most fundamental of relating principles'' (p. 116). English is one of the languages that depends heavily on order. For instance, in English declarative sentences the subject and object are indicated by their place before and after the verb, respectively. Some languages mark the subject and object with case suffixes and allow their positions to vary more freely. For instance, in the Polish sentence in 34 the *-a* suffixed to *Josef* marks it as the object. *Josef* can therefore precede the verb as in 35 and still remain the object:

34. Rachel lubi ('loves') Josefa.
35. Rachel Josefa lubi.

Languages differ in the extent of their dependence on word order for the expression of relational meanings. But in no language is word order entirely free.

Prosodic Patterning   In addition to being structured on the level of word order, sentences are also structured prosodically. **Prosody** refers to the overall sound characteristics of sentences. Prosodic patterning is seen in the relatively fluent transition from one word to the other, in the unified intonational contour, and in the distribution of phonetic stress.

Intonation refers to the pitch changes that occur as a sentence is spoken. There are two basic intonation patterns: rising intonation, characteristic of interrogative sentences, and falling intonation, characteristic of declarative sentences.

Phonetic stress refers to the relative emphasis that syllables receive as a consequence of different amounts of air being pushed through from the lungs. It has been traditional in English linguistics to distinguish three levels of stress, but Ladefoged (1982, pp. 105-108) has questioned the validity of assuming more than a dichotomous distinction between stressed and unstressed syllables. Because there is little research on developmental aspects of stress, we do not need to enter into this discussion. It is sufficient for our purposes to distinguish between stressed and unstressed syllables, as does Ladefoged. Stress is marked by an upper line in front of the stressed syllable (e.g., 'emphasis, em'phatic).

Stress allows speakers to highlight some elements in a sentence relative to others to achieve their communicative intentions. But there are also linguistic requirements concerning stress distribution. In particular, stress depends on syntactic status. Take adjective-noun combinations in English. Stress falls on the noun if the combination constitutes a noun phrase, (e.g., black 'bird, 'any bird that is black'; high 'chair, 'any chair that is high'), but on the adjective if the combination is a compound noun (e.g., 'blackbird, 'a particular kind of bird'; 'highchair, 'an infant chair'). Syntactic conditioning of stress can also be seen in differences in the placement of stress in words that function both as nouns and as verbs (e.g., 'permit, 'a license', per'mit, 'to allow'). Beyond these obvious aspects of syntactic conditioning of phonetic stress, there are deeper, more sophisticated aspects (see Chomsky & Halle, 1968, chap. 3), but it is beyond the scope of this book to discuss them.

In this part of the chapter I touched on some aspects of the structure of sentences. We saw that unsegmented, holistic content when expressed linguistically is forced into segmental, serial form. I also discussed the ordering requirements imposed by sentences and their prosodic patterns. In the next part I introduce a more formal approach to the analysis of the structure of sentences.

ELEMENTS OF THE GENERATIVE
TRANSFORMATIONAL THEORY OF SYNTAX

Over two decades ago Noam Chomsky (1957) introduced a new approach to the study of sentences called "Generative Transformational Grammar." Chomsky's theory (see also Chomsky, 1965; for a general introduction, see Akmajian & Heny, 1975) has attracted many adherents and has gained dominance in linguistics. Chomsky has also had a profound influence on the study of language by psychologists. In the next three sections I distill the main ideas of the theory that help shed light on the nature of sentences.

Tree Diagrams

The tree diagram, depicting the structure of sentences, has become the trademark of transformational theory. Figure 5.1 presents a sample tree diagram for sentence 36:

36. The dog bit the boy.

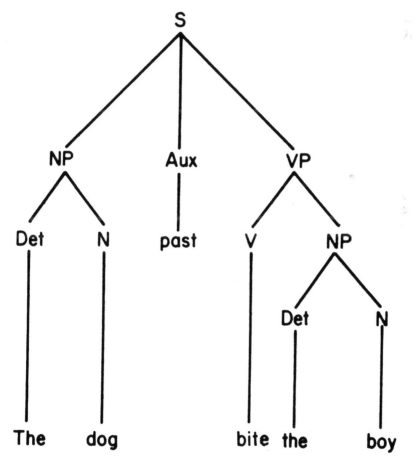

FIG. 5.1 Tree diagram for the sentence *The dog bit the boy*. S = Sentence; NP = Noun Phrase; Aux = Auxiliary; VP = Verb Phrase; Det = articles, demonstratives (*this, these, that, those*), and other noun-specifying forms; N = Noun; V = Verb.

The tree diagram represents a conception of the nature of sentences. On top is the single node S, reflecting the unity of the sentence as a semantic and structural entity. Although the sentence is realized in the flow of speech as a sequence of words, it is not constructed word by word. The entire sentence is preplanned, and its parts are intercoordinated even before the first word is uttered. The sentence is an integrated, cohesive whole. The singleness of the original S node also represents the simultaneity of the ideas expressed in speech.

The S node branches out into three nodes, NP, Aux, and VP. This means that a sentence is defined as consisting of three components: an NP, an Aux, and a VP. The Aux contains information concerning the form of the verb. In the present case it specifies the tense of the verb *bite*, indicating that it is used in the past tense. The relation of the VP to the NP gives the sentence its propositional character. The NP functions as the subject of the sentence and the VP as its predicate. The NP and VP are characterized on the third level. The NP is composed of an article plus noun and the VP of a verb plus an NP. This second NP is specified on the fourth level. The branches end up at the part-of-speech nodes where words are inserted.

The tree diagram characterizes the sentence as a hierarchical structure in which each level is defined by the level immediately below it. One of the implications of the hierarchical structure of sentences is that constituents have a measure of internal autonomy. Thus, the initial NP and final NP in sentence 36 can be expanded as in 37 without altering the constellation of relations in the sentence:

37. The ferocious dog belonging to the people who bought the new house bit the little boy whose parents are Irish.

Phrase-Structure Rules

The structure depicted graphically in the tree diagram can also be expressed by means of rules, called **phrase-structure** (PS) or **rewrite rules**. The rules can be formulated in the following general way to cover a variety of English sentence types, not just the type represented by 36:

PS1. S → NP Aux VP
PS2. NP → Det N
   Det(erminers): the, a, these, my, their, etc.
PS3. Aux → Tense (Modal auxiliary) (have en) (be ing)
   Modal auxiliaries: can, could, will, would, shall, and should.
PS4. VP → V (NP) (PP)   PP = Prepositional Phrase
   VP → V Adj

The arrow is to be interpreted as indicating that the category on the left is to be rewritten or realized as the category or categories on the right. Informally, PS1 means that a sentence is made up of an NP, an Aux, and a VP, and PS2 means that an NP is composed of a Det followed by an N. The parentheses in PS3 and PS4 indicate optional choices. Thus, PS3 means that every sentence is marked for tense, but sentences may also include a modal auxiliary as in 38, a "have en" (participial) form as in 39, a "be ing" (gerundive) form as in 40, or all three as in 41.

38. John *should* eat.
39. John *has* eat*en* already.
40. John *is* eat*ing* now.
41. John *could have been* eat*ing* for half an hour.

PS4 offers two alternative ways to construct a VP: one on the first line and the other on the second line. Sentence 42 is an example of a construction that realizes the first line of PS4 without any options.

42. The boy slept.
    NP   V

Sentences 43-45 exhibit examples of the different options on the first line of PS4, and sentence 46 exemplifies the second line.

43. The drunk drove (the car).
    NP   V   (NP)
44. The drunk drove (the car) (off the road).
    NP   V   (NP)   (PP)
45. The drunk drove (off the road).
    NP   V   (PP)
46. The boy is clever.
    NP   V Adj

Transformational Rules

In addition to characterizing explicitly the structure of sentences, generative transformational grammar has also revealed relations among different sentential structures. It has shown that a variety of phenomena fall into place if the structure of sentences is analyzed on two levels: a **deep-structure** or **base-structure** level, represented by the PS rules, and a **surface-structure** level. The deep structure defines the basic relations in the sentence, and the surface structure describes its manifest outer form.

Compare, for instance, the passive sentence 47 with the corresponding active sentence 36, which I have previously analyzed:

36. The dog bit the boy.
47. The boy was bitten by the dog.

The semantic relations are the same in both sentences. *The dog* is the agent in both sentences, and *the boy* the object. But they differ in their surface form.

In the transformational analysis active and passive sentences are considered to have the same underlying base structure, such as the one depicted in Figure 5.1 and expressed in the corresponding PS rules. But passive sentences are derived from the base structure less directly than active sentences, because they involve a passive transformation. The passive transformation can be stated as follows:

TR1. NP_1 Aux V NP_2 $\Rightarrow$ NP_2 Aux be en V by NP_1

In this rule the subscripts have no inherent meaning; they are used merely to distinguish the two NPs from one another. (Double-line arrows are used in transformational rules to distinguish them from PS rules.) What TR1 means is that a sentence analyzable as having the structure "NP_1 Aux V NP_2" can be converted into a sentence having the structure "NP_2 Aux be en V by NP_1."

Numerous other transformational rules have been formulated for English and other languages. They all have in common a central characteristic, namely, that they are **structure dependent** (see Chomsky, 1968, pp. 51-52). That is, the entities on which transformational rules operate are structurally defined components (such as NP and VP) of base structures. There are no rules in any language that allow a speaker to convert one sentence into another by taking particular *words* from one position and putting them into another position. Thus, although the rule that converts 36 to 47 could be formulated in terms of an interchange of the first two words with the last two words, instead of the interchange of NP_1 with NP_2, this word-based, structure-*in*dependent rule would have little generality. It would fail to yield an acceptable passive sentence even if only one word were added to one of the noun phrases in the active sentence in 36. Clearly, structure-independent rules are totally alien to language.

Generative transformational theory attempts to formulate an explicit system of rules that when put into operation would produce only grammatical sentences, no ungrammatical sentences. That is, the grammar aims to be sufficiently detailed and explicit so that when set into operation it will be able to generate sentences. However, no claims are made about how individuals generate or comprehend sentences; all that is being claimed is that knowledge of grammar is somehow involved.

FORM AND MEANING

We have looked in this chapter at the sentence in terms of the structure it has and the meanings it expresses. In normal use of language, meaning and form coexist; speakers produce sentences of particular form to convey particular meanings.

But the structural properties of sentences have independent psychological reality. Chomsky (1957) made this point by noting that people can evaluate the grammatical status of sentences independently of their semantic status. As an example he (Chomsky, 1957) offered sentence 48, which is fully grammatical, yet expresses unusual, deviant meaning.

48. Colorless green ideas sleep furiously. (p. 15)

Experimental research supports Chomsky's position concerning the autonomy of syntactic structure. For instance, Miller and Isard (1963) constructed three types of sentences: normal meaningful sentences, exemplified in 49; grammatical but semantically anomalous sentences, exemplified in 50; and ungrammatical sentences, exemplified in 51.

49. Hunters shoot elephants between the eyes.
50. Hunters simplify motorists across the hive.
51. From hunters house motorists the carry.

Miller and Isard recorded a sample of the three types of sentences on magnetic tape and played them to college students. The students had to "shadow" the sentences (i.e., to repeat each word immediately after it was heard). The results show that the subjects were able to shadow accurately 89% of the normal sentences and 79% of the anomalous sentences, but only 56% of the ungrammatical sentences. By doing so much better on the anomalous sentences than on the ungrammatical sentences, the subjects demonstrated that they were sensitive to sentential structure, even when the sentences conveyed little meaning.

Epstein (1961) found that even sequences of nonsense words were easier to memorize when they were grammatically structured than when they were not. Thus, 52 was remembered better than 53:

52. A vapy koobs desaked the citar molently um glox nerfs.
53. A vap koob desak the citar molent um glox nerf.

These experimental findings indicate that mature speakers have a grammatical sense that they can demonstrate in a variety of tasks. In the following chapters we see how children acquire the rules of language and develop a grammatical sense.

6

The Characteristics of Early Sentences

It seems that a basic expectation which the child brings to the task of grammatical development is that the order of elements in an utterance can be related to underlying semantic relations.

Dan Slobin

After a period characterized by single-word utterances, children enter the syntactic stage and begin to produce sentences as they approach their second birthday. First they produce two-word sentences and then longer sentences. The lag between the single-word stage and the syntactic stage seems to be quite short. In the study of five children by McCune-Nicolich (1981), already referred to in Chapter 4, there was a lag of about a month or two between the vocabulary spurt and the appearance of sentences. Halliday (1975) also found that his son Nigel started to produce syntactic speech "four weeks after the first major excursion into vocabulary" (p. 46). He was then 19 months old.

A sentence is a structured, cohesive entity. Its words follow one another in fluent succession. It has word-order regularity, and it has integrating patterns of stress and intonation. A sentence is also a unified whole on the level of meaning. In a sentence the individual meanings of words interact with one another to give rise to composite relational meanings. This chapter concentrates on the description of the semantic and structural aspects of early sentences. But before turning to these topics, we need to consider the criteria by which one can judge that a child has entered the syntactic stage.

THE INDICATORS OF SYNTACTIC PRODUCTIVITY

When children produce syntactic sequences of words, this does not necessarily indicate that they have constructed them on their own. They may be repeating by rote something heard from others. To be granted syntactic knowledge, children have to show evidence of syntactic productivity. Verbalization of an inventory of syntactic utterances is not enough.

The attribution of syntactic productivity to children is a matter of judgment based on a variety of indicators. The conformity of different utterances to a clear pattern is one of the indicators of syntactic construction. For instance, the corpus of utterances of a boy, Andrew, 1;7(15)-1;11(15), studied by Braine (1976, p. 7), consisted of 12 two-word utterances with *more* as one of the words. In all but 1 of the 12 utterances *more* was the first word, suggesting the operation of an order rule. Although possible, it is unlikely that the apparent pattern resulted co-incidentally from Andrew's happening to have heard and remembered each of the 12 utterances independently. The likelihood that a particular pattern reflects a psychologically real operation on the part of the child is increased by the presence of other patterns in his speech. It is highly improbable that the speech of a child will exhibit a variety of patterns by mere chance. In the case of Andrew, his sentences in general fell into clear patterns.

The appearance of utterances of a particular pattern at a high rate in a short period of time lends further credence to the inference that the pattern is functional for the child. A case in point is another child, Kendall, 1;11, who in the course of 1½ hours of recording over a 2-day period produced 41 actor-action utterances (Braine, 1976, p. 19). In 39 out of the 41 utterances the actor came first (e.g., *Kendall fix it.*) The profuse occurrence of a particular type of utterance suggests that the child has recently acquired this pattern and is rehearsing or exercising it, much the way children behave with respect to recently acquired sensorimotor schemes or new words.

One's confidence that utterances conforming to a particular pattern were constructed by the child rather than remembered by rote is increased by the presence of utterances not likely to have been heard from adults. Thus, Andrew uttered *more car* (meaning 'Drive around some more') and *more high* ('There is more up there'), bolstering the conclusion that he had a productive rule for constructing two-word sentences with *more* as the first word (Braine, 1976, p. 8).

Statistical evidence for the operation of syntactic patterns can be found by an examination of the rate of increase of sentences in a child's speech. Figure 6.1 plots the number of sentences produced at different ages by one of four children studied by Bloom, Lightbown, and Hood (1975) and by one of two children studied by Greenfield and Smith (1976). The graph shows that after a period of slow increase in sentence production, there is a period of accelerated growth around

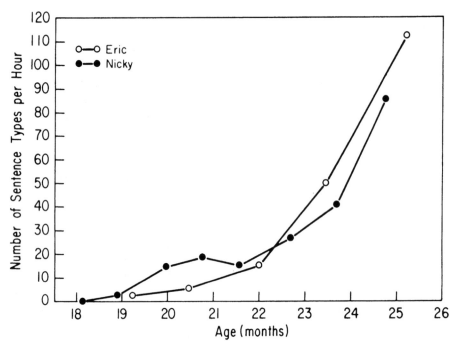

FIG. 6.1   Rate of increase of sentences as a function of age for two children. The data for Eric are from Bloom et al. (1975, p. 7), and for Nicky from Greenfield and Smith (1976, p. 38).

the second birthday. This general trend also holds for the other children in these studies for whom data are available at the relevant ages. There is no reason to believe that the ability to remember sentences heard from others improves that dramatically toward the end of the second year. Rather, the sentence growth-spurt seems more likely attributable to the acquisition of productive syntactic patterns.

Figure 6.1 depicts the progression in the number of sentences that children produce. A similar trend can be seen in terms of the increase of MLU from one word to two and more words (Bloom et al., 1975, p. 7; Brown, 1973, p. 55). At first, MLU increases slowly. This is the stage when children are groping for syntax. Their speech consists predominantly of single-word utterances with occasional sentences occurring here and there. After that begins a period of accelerated growth, when children acquire productive patterns and put them to use in their speech.

A third statistical indicator of syntactic productivity can be found in the token/type ratios of sentences. Figure 6.1 is based on number of sentence types (i.e., number of different sentences). So, for instance, a child who in a given time period said *this cup* three times received a score of 1 in the type count. Bloom et al. also present a token count alongside the type count for the four children they studied. In the token count *this cup* would be entered as 3. Token/type ratios can be calculated from these data. These ratios give an indication of the extent to which the child tends to produce new sentences or to repeat old ones. A high ratio means that some sentences are repeated over and over, whereas a low ratio (minimum 1) means that a variety of different sentences are produced. The ratios for the four children in the Bloom et al. investigation were initially close to 2, but they declined by the end of the observation period and began to approach 1. For instance, at 1;7(14), Gia produced 100 sentence tokens that consisted of 55 sentence types, yielding a token/type ratio of 1.82. In the last observation period, at the age of 2;1(14), she produced 1071 tokens and 842 types, yielding a ratio of 1.27. That is, at the end Gia was less likely to repeat sentences verbatim than she was at the beginning. The lower the token/type ratio, the greater one's confidence that the children are not merely repeating sentences that they have heard, but rather producing novel sentences on their own.

In the foregoing discussion sentence memory and sentence construction were treated as if they were incompatible alternatives. This was done for purposes of clarity of exposition. In fact, however, not only is there no sharp dichotomy between the two, but it seems likely that they interact in the acquisition of syntax. For children to be able to induce a pattern, they need to have relevant sentences exemplifying the pattern. Hence, there is the need to remember syntactic sequences heard. Even after children are able to construct sentences, they undoubtedly also produce prefabricated sequences. Adults also incorporate memorized sequences (e.g., idioms and habitual phrases) into their sentences.

A caveat is in order here. For convenience of expression I have used the term "rule" to refer to children's sentential patterns. It is unlikely, however, that children formulate the patterns they induce in terms of abstract rules, the way linguists formulate the rules of adult language. It is more likely, given the child's cognitive level at the beginning of syntax, that some memorized sentences serve as prototypes on the basis of which new sentences are generated. Thus, it is suggested that memorized sentences provide the material for the formulation of sentential patterns and for the resulting productivity (see Schlesinger, 1982, for a related point of view).

The granting of a sentential pattern to a child does not necessitate the assumption that all the sentences that conform to the pattern are new creations by the child. Knowledge of a pattern makes it much easier for the child to remember sentences that can be assimilated by the pattern. It is a well-established conclusion in the psychology of memory that material that can be assimilated by a structure is retained much better than material that has to be memorized by rote. The discovery of a pattern gives the child not only a vehicle for the creation of new sentences but also a very valuable tool for remembering sentences heard.

In conclusion, even though there are no hard and fast criteria to indicate when a child has attained syntactic productivity, its emergence is usually unmistakable. Syntactic productivity is marked primarily by the appearance of large numbers of sentences exhibiting specific patterns. Before the emergence of productive syntax, children retain specific sentences they hear, and these serve as a data base for the identification of patterns and the emergent productivity.

Because sentences express meaning relations by structuring linguistic entities (words and phrases), a theory of children's syntactic knowledge would specify how they map particular semantic relations into particular structural forms. However, it is not possible at present to provide such a complete account. What I can do instead is discuss some of the information that forms the basis upon which such an account will ultimately be built. The first section that follows sketches the semantic relations children express in their early sentences. The second gives an overview of the communicative functions for which young children use their sentences. The third section discusses in a general way some aspects of the structure of early sentences.

THE MEANINGS EXPRESSED IN EARLY SENTENCES

The present section reviews the six most prominent semantic relations expressed in children's first sentences. My groupings are, in general, similar to those used by other writers. It must be noted that the classification is descriptive, not explanatory. It provides an economical way of reporting observations. But we do not know to what extent these categories are functional for children.

Demonstrative Naming

In utterances falling into this category, children draw attention to particular objects and name them. The first word points out an object, and the second assigns it a name. The pointing words commonly used by children include *this*, *that*, *here*, and *a*. Table 6.1 gives some examples of demonstrative naming sentences.

Demonstrative naming is one of the most prevalent and common of the early syntactic relations. In a summary of the studies of the early language of 18 children, involving five languages, Brown (1973) found that only one child (one of two Samoan children) did not produce demonstrative naming sentences. In a study of 12 American children in the age range of 1;7(14)-2;1(14), Starr (1975) found that 40% of the sentences she recorded fell into this category (which she refers to as "nominative"). The percentages for different children ranged from 24% to 77%.

However, calculations I have done on the data provided by Bloom et al. (1975, p. 15) show that demonstrative naming (which they call "existence") sentences ranged from 5% to 7% (mean = 6%) for the four children that they studied, who were in the same age range as the children in the Starr study. It appears likely that the difference between the two studies is attributable to the

TABLE 6.1
Examples of Demonstrative Naming Sentences

Utterance	Child, Age, Context (and Source)
a record	Gia, 1;11(21), pointing to record (BLH, 53).
dis a jacket	Gia, 2;1(18), holding up jacket (BLH, 53).
a daddy	Peter, 2;1(0), taking out toy daddy from box (BLH, 70).
this is daddy	Peter, 2;1(0), showing toy daddy to visitor (BLH, 70).
here flower	David, 1;9 (B, 43).
there moon	Embla (Swedish girl), 1;10-2;1 (B, 49).
that teaspoon	Odi (Israeli girl), 1;11-2;2 (B, 40).
see juice	Eric, 2;1(7), looking at juice inside opened refrigerator (BLH, 47).
that dogs	Kathryn, 1;10(21), looking at picture of dogs (BLH, 61).
that's a train	Kathryn, 1;10(21), observing visitor assembling train (BLH, 61).

Note: Sources are abbreviated as follows: B = Braine (1976); BLH = Bloom et al. (1975). Page number follows source.

fact that Starr restricted her analysis to two-word sentences, thus tapping the very beginning of syntax, whereas the data of Bloom et al. covered not only two-word sentences but longer ones as well, and thus included syntactic development beyond the initial stage. An internal analysis of the Bloom et al. results shows indeed that demonstrative naming was common in the initial observations and gradually declined. A comparison of the incidence of demonstrative naming in the first and last observations for individual children brings out this point quite clearly: Eric, 30% and 6%; Gia, 23% and 3%; Peter, 20% and 7%. The only exception was Kathryn (4% and 7%), but the observations reported for her begin at a more advanced stage (as reflected in her MLU) than for the other children.

Demonstrative naming is thus a transitory phenomenon characteristic of the very beginning of syntax. In fact, it seems to be a continuation on the syntactic level of the preoccupations of children in the single-word stage. We have seen in Chapter 4 that in the advanced single-word level the predominant use of words is for purposes of identifying and classifying objects and events. Demonstrative naming sentences seem to have a similar purpose.

There is evidence that children use demonstrative naming utterances for cognitive rather than instrumental purposes. Bloom et al. give contextual information alongside each utterance, which facilitates a clear interpretation of the child's meaning and intent. The sample in the demonstrative naming category contains a total of 87 utterances. None of these utterances involved an instrumental purpose. They were uttered in the context of the child's pointing to something, holding it, or picking it up, not in the context of trying to get something or asking for it.

Werner and Kaplan (1963, pp. 160-162) have also seen the prevalence of demonstrative naming utterances (which they refer to as "judgments of identification" or "identifying predications") as providing support for the view that language develops primarily as a cognitive, rather than as a pragmatic, tool. They see the high frequency of demonstrative naming utterances as reflecting children's "tremendous interest and delight" in the naming activity. Children enjoy the naming activity because it is at the core of their grasp of the world. They do not merely attach labels to already formed classes of objects. Rather, the act of naming is part and parcel of the process of classification. By assigning the same name to different objects, children show that they consider them equivalent despite their differences.

Another perspective on the reasons for the wide occurrence of demonstrative naming sentences comes from the recognition that the child is not only a language user but also a language learner. In demonstrative naming utterances children are exercising the words they have learned, testing the range of their applicability, or proudly displaying their knowledge for admiring observers.

The style of parental speech to children may contribute to the prevalence of demonstrative naming. Brown (1973, p. 189) has drawn attention to the fact that parents often ask children questions such as "What's that?" to which the expected answer is, for instance, *a book*. Snow (1977) reports a study of the speech of nine Dutch mothers to their daughters, 1;11-2;11, while playing with them or reading them books. She found that naming constituted a substantial portion of the mothers' speech to their daughters. First, 36% of all maternal single-word utterances involved nomination (i.e., the calling out of the name of some object). Second, of the mothers' two-word utterances, 13% were of the demonstrative naming type, and an additional 11% were demonstrative naming questions (e.g., "What is that?").

My conclusion is that demonstrative naming utterances are common in the very beginning of syntax because they reflect children's interest in classifying and naming objects. This interest is actively encouraged by parents.

Werner and Kaplan see demonstrative naming as constituting the "first inroads" into the construction of propositional relations. Demonstrative naming sentences are indeed the most primitive of sentences. A sentence interrelates different entities. In the case of demonstrative naming, however, there is no real interrelation. Here the demonstrative word points to a particular object and the word following it assigns the object a name. Demonstrative naming utterances are, however, sentences on the structural level, because they exhibit word-order patterning, fluency, and prosodic integration.

Attribution

This category includes sentences in which objects are qualified and specified. Most attributive sentences consist of what in adult language are adjective-noun combinations. Examples may be seen in Table 6.2. The impression one gets from reading reports of children's early language is that the attributes that children commonly use in their first sentences concern size, color, and state of clean-

TABLE 6.2
Examples of Attributive Sentences

Utterance	Child, Age, Context (and Source)
red car	Eric, 1;10(0), taking out toy truck from bag (BLH, 43).
that's yellow one	Eric, 1;11 (21), holding a yellow disc (BLH, 43).
big bottle	Gia, 1;11(21), carrying a bottle (BLH, 52).
this a blue one	Gia, 2;1(14), putting brush in blue paint (BLH, 52).
funny man	Kathryn, 1;9(0), picking up wooden peg man (BLH, 60).
that a funny man	Kathryn, 1;10(21), pointing to picture in magazine (BLH, 60).
broken train	Kathryn, 1;10(21), observing that train cars are unhooked (BLH, 60).
three trucks	Peter, 1;10(14), playing with train cars (BLH, 69).
two cars	Peter, 1;11(14), removing from bag toy car and truck that he has never seen before (BLH, 69).

Note: The initials BLH refer to Bloom et al. (1975). Page number follows source.

liness. This is not surprising because these attributes are perceptually prominent and occur frequently in speech to children.

The attribution category has not been defined in the same way by all investigators. I have included numerical designations (e.g., the last two examples in Table 6.2) under attribution, following the practice of Bloom et al. (1975). Braine (1976), however, placed numerical utterances in the recurrence category (to be described later). The grouping of sentences into categories is, of course, to some extent arbitrary. I have chosen to include numerical utterances in the attribution category because such utterances reveal children's appreciation of class membership, a cognitive process similar to that involved in other types of attributive sentences.

Attribution is not nearly as common in early syntax as demonstrative naming, but it occurs frequently enough to have been identified by many observers (e.g., Bloom et al., 1975; Braine, 1976; Brown, 1973, p. 197; Werner & Kaplan, 1963, pp. 166-168). In the Starr (1975) study attributives constituted 11% of the multiword utterances examined, and in the Bloom et al. study they constituted 9%. Attribution would appear to be one step beyond demonstrative naming with respect to the cognitive classification that it implies. In demonstrative naming, objects are treated as unanalyzed wholes, but in attribution, there is a distinction between objects and properties associated with them (see Werner and Kaplan, 1963, p. 166). Attribution becomes possible only when the child sufficiently separates a property of an object from the object itself to assign them different labels. The separated entities are then brought into relation in the attributive sentence.

From children's attributive sentences one can learn something about their definitions of object classes. In an attributive sentence children use an attribute to distinguish one object within a class of objects from other objects in that class. They thereby reveal that that attribute does not distinguish the class as a whole from other classes. When Johnny says *red car* he uses a color term to designate a particular car and to distinguish it from other cars, and thus implies that color is not part of his definition of *car*. Even though every actual car has a color, the general class of cars is sufficiently removed from the specific instances to be colorless.

Caution must be exercised in drawing inferences about children's notions of classes from utterances that have an attributive form. There is a basis for the type of inference discussed in the preceding paragraph only when the child uses different qualifiers with the same name to distinguish different objects. When only a single qualifier is encountered with a particular name, this may mean that the qualifier plus the name function as an indissoluble whole, having for the child the status of a single word. This is even more likely to be the case when the child does not use the object name by itself without qualifiers. For example, a child was observed who used *school bus* but not *bus* by itself nor with any other qualifier. For her, *school bus* functioned as a single word, having more or less the same range of meaning as *bus* has for adults.

In conclusion, I have viewed attributive sentences as part of children's attempts to sort out and to make sense of the world around them. From this point of view attribution continues in more refined form the function reflected in demonstrative naming. When children's language develops to the point that they are able to produce longer sentences, they sometimes embed attributive components in demonstrative frames. For instance, Kathryn produced *funny man* at 1;9, and 7 weeks later, *that a funny man*.

Possession

Utterances in this category consist of a human possessor and a possessed object. Possessives constituted 6% of the multiword utterances examined in both the Bloom et al. study and the Starr study. Some examples may be seen in Table 6.3.

I have separated possessive sentences from attributive sentences, as has been the common practice in recent years. Werner and Kaplan (1963, p. 167), on the other hand, group them together. Both practices can be defended on a priori grounds. It could be argued that attribution and possession belong together because they both qualify objects. But it could also be argued that they should be separated because they entail different kinds of qualification. Clearly, what is needed is evidence concerning how the two types of relations function for children. A study by Wieman (1976) concerning phonetic stress, which is described later in this chapter, suggests that attribution and possession have different status for children. In Wieman's study children stressed the second words in attributive sentences and the first words in possessive sentences. This finding provides a rationale for separating possessive sentences from attributive sentences.

It is not known what young children's idea of possession is: whether it has some sense of ownership, habitual use, or priority of use (Brown, 1973, pp.

TABLE 6.3
Examples of Possessive Sentences

Utterance	Child, Age, Context or Gloss (and Source)
Lois scarf	Gia, 1;10(7), taking Lois' scarf (BLH, 56).
Kevin Snoopy	Gia, 1;10(7), in answer to question: Whose Snoopy is that? (BLH, 56).
mommy sock	Kathryn, 1;9(0), has pair of mommy's socks (BLH, 65).
my pen	Peter, 2;0(7), whimpering and reaching for his pen (BLH, 72).
daddy car	Jonathan, 2;0, 'Daddy's car' (B, 34).
this Nina	Jonathan, 2;0, 'This is Nina's' (B, 34).
dis a my chair	Gia, 2;1(14), pointing out that visitor was sitting on her chair (BLH, 56).
that daddy paper	Kathryn, 1;10(21), pointing to newspaper (BLH, 65).

Note: Sources are abbreviated as follows: B = Braine (1976); BLH = Bloom et al. (1975). Page number follows source.

195-197). All that can be said at present is that in possessive utterances the child expresses some special association between a person and an object. It must be noted that the identification of possessive utterances is more heavily dependent on context than the identification of other categories, because the possessive marker 's is characteristically missing in the early utterances. The last two entries in Table 6.3 show that in later stages of syntactic development, possessive sequences may be included as components in demonstrative sentences.

Action

Characteristically, action sentences contain an action term and at least one other term (see Table 6.4), but occasionally, the action term may be missing, the action being implicit (example 9 in Table 6.4). Because actions combine in rich ways with other terms, this category has been subject to a variety of subcategorizations. Brown (1973, pp. 193-195) listed four types of action sentences: actor-action (examples 1-4 in Table 6.4), action-object (examples 5-8), actor-object (example 9), and action-location (example 10). Bloom et al. (1975) combine the first three into a single action category, which includes also actor-action-object sentences (example 11). In addition to action-location, Bloom et al. also have a locative action category for actions that involve movement of things or people from one place to another (examples 12-13). Actor-action and action-object constructions are by far the most common (Brown, 1973, p. 174; Bloom et al., 1975, p. 15). In the Starr (1975) study these two constructions constituted 16% of the total number of two-word utterances.

Action sentences generally increase in prevalence with the growth of syntactic competence. In the Bloom et al. study the increases in action sentences (as they define the category) from the first session in which there was a substantial number of sentences to the final session, 3-6 months later, were: for Eric, from 18%

TABLE 6.4
Examples of Action Sentences

Utterance	Child, Age, Context (and Source)
1. Gia push	Gia, 1;11(21), pushing cart (BLH, 50).
2. mommy push	Kathryn, 1;9(0), asking her mother to push animal form into board (BLH, 59).
3. mother opens	Seppo (Finish boy), 1;11-2;2 (B, 23).
4. chick flies	Seppo (Finish boy), 1;11-2;2 (B, 23).
5. build house	Gia, 1;11 (21), describing what she is doing: building a house out of blocks (BLH, 50).
6. fix that	Peter, 1;11(7), putting train car together (BLH, 68).
7. give me cream	Odi (Israeli girl), 1;11-2;2 (B, 40).
8. take off jacket	Embla (Swedish girl), 1;10-2;1 (B, 53).
9. Gia bike	Gia, 1;10(7), as she was getting onto her bike (BLH, 10).
10. walking street	Eric, 2;1(7), looking out window at man walking (BLH, 42).
11. Gia ride bike	Gia, 1;10(7), telling what she was about to do (BLH, 50).
12. tape on there	Peter, 2;0(7), putting masking tape on toy (BLH, 11).
13. I get down	Peter, 2;0(7), is about to get off piano bench (BLH, 11).

Note: Sources are abbreviated as follows: B = Braine (1976); BLH = Bloom et al. (1975). Page number follows source.

to 20%; for Gia, from 6% to 32%; for Peter, from 10% to 17%. The fourth child, Kathryn, had 24% action sentences at the beginning and end of the observations. But, as I have mentioned in explanation of Kathryn's atypical demonstrative naming behavior, she was already advanced in syntactic functioning at the beginning of the study.

In action sentences, as in the previous three types of sentences, children reveal their conception of the world around them. We have seen that in demonstrative naming, attribution, and possession sentences children manifest their attempts to organize the world of things. In demonstrative naming sentences children classify objects; in attributive sentences they explore the tolerance of variation within object classes; and in possessive sentences they manifest an interest in the relation of objects to people. In action sentences children manifest similar cognitive concerns with respect to the world of action. Here, they express the independence of actions from actors and from objects. Thus, different individuals can push and different things can be pushed. In this way children explore the relations among actions, people, and objects.

The categories of demonstrative naming, attribution, possession, and action cover the most common relations expressed in early syntax. These categories accounted for some 75% of the two-word sentences that the 12 children in the Starr study produced. But other categories of relations have also been noted by various investigators. Two of these that highlight some general characteristics of early syntax are described in the following subsections.

TABLE 6.5
Examples of Recurrence Sentences

Utterance	Child, Age, Context (and Source)
more clown	Gia, 1;8(14), taking out a second clown (BLH, 57).
more cookie	Peter, 1;11(21), requesting an additional cookie (BLH, 73).
another one	Eric, 1;11(21), commenting that he is eating another piece of pineapple (BLH, 47).
do again	Gia, 1;10(7), stacking blocks again after she had made tower and knocked it over (BLH, 57).
more read dat	Gia, 1;10(7), asking to be read more from a book (BLH, 57).
another piece of a clay	Eric, 2;1(7), handing another piece of clay to adult (BLH, 48).

Note: The initials BLH refer to Bloom et al. (1975). Page number follows source.

Recurrence

In recurrence sentences children comment on or request the recurrence of a particular thing or event (see Table 6.5). A recurrence sentence consists of a word indicating recurrence plus another word referring to the thing or event that recurs. The most common recurrence word is *more*, which for the child covers in addition to its standard meaning also the meanings of *again* and *another*.

In Chapter 4 I emphasized the predominance of the cognitive function over the instrumental function in early language. Of all the semantic relations, recurrence would seem most naturally suited for the expression of instrumental goals. It was, therefore, of interest to examine the functions of recurrence sentences. What I found was that even in the recurrence category, the cognitive function predominates. For the four children studied by Bloom et al. (1975, pp. 41-74), the ratios of comments (i.e., a cognitive function) to requests (i.e., an instrumental function) were: 27:1, 32:6, 25:5, and 32:2. That is, the children used recurrence sentences much more often to give expression to their observations than to ask for goods and services.

Negation

Early negative sentences typically express the nonpresence or disappearance of something desired or expected or the inability, impermissibility, or unwillingness to engage in some activity. A sample of negative sentences can be seen in Table 6.6. The negative term in sentences, as in single-word utterances, is usually *no*.

A distinction has been drawn (Bloom, 1970; Brown, 1973, pp. 191-192) between negative sentences in which children comment on the nonexistence of something (first example in Table 6.6) and those in which they reject something (last example). Analyzing the incidence of nonexistence and rejection in single-

TABLE 6.6
Examples of Negation Sentences

Utterance	Child, Age, Context (and Source)
no more	Eric, 1;10(0), looking for more beads but can't find any (BLH, 46).
no more airplane	Eric, 1;10(0), a few minutes after he heard an airplane (BLH, 46).
no play matches	Gia, 2;1(14), taking out matches from box (BLH, 55).
can't reach it	Gia, 2;1(14), whining as she is trying to reach dish of pretzels (BLH, 55).
no bib	Eric, 2;1(7), squirming away as his mother tries to put bib on him (BLH, 46).

Note: The initials BLH refer to Bloom et al. (1975). Page number follows source.

word and multiword utterances, Bloom (1970, p. 187) found that nonexistence was expressed more often by the use of sentences than by the use of *no* alone, whereas rejection was expressed more often by the use of *no* alone than by the use of sentences.

Bloom (1970, p. 219) suggested that when children refuse something, the thing is present, and an isolated *no* is sufficient to communicate their intent. By contrast, in the expression of nonexistence the object negated is not present, and without its mention the negative word would often not communicate clearly the child's intent. This explanation seems plausible. There is no evidence, however, that children reaching their second birthday are as sensitive to the communicative needs of the listener as this explanation would require them to be. An alternative, or additional, explanation might be that in the rejection situation the child is too emotionally involved to be able to mobilize the cognitive resources required for sentence construction. We saw in Chapter 4 that in the single-word stage, children may regress to nonverbal means of communication under the stress of need and desire. It is now suggested that at the stage of beginning syntax, children may regress to the single-word stage under similar circumstances.

Conclusion

I have described six types of semantic relations children express in the first syntactic period and analyzed the cognitive processes involved in them. These six are commonly found in observational studies of children at the beginning of syntax. But there are wide individual differences among children in the extent of use of different semantic relations.

SOME REMARKS ON FUNCTION

In this chapter and in Chapter 4 a distinction has been made between cognitive and instrumental uses of language. It must be pointed out now that both functions have a social-communicative character. In instrumental speech children use people as means to achieve desired ends. In cognitive speech they use people as sounding boards to tell about their experiences, perceptions, memories, and so on, often expecting feedback or praise.

It is true that children sometimes talk to themselves, but even such speech is often modeled on communicative exchanges, as when a child conducts a conversation with an imaginary listener. The most systematic and richest account of speech of a child in the absence of an interlocutor is the report of Ruth Weir (1962). Weir recorded the presleep soliloquies of her son Anthony, 2;4-2;6, after he was put to bed and was alone in his room. Weir (1962) says the following about Anthony's behavior: "The nature of the soliloquies is not monologue *in abstracto* but dialogue with imaginary interlocutors or the child's assuming both roles in the exchange" (p. 23).

This point is well exemplified in the following sample (Weir, 1962) of Anthony's speech:

1. Daddy.
2. Cobbers crossed the street (said twice).
3. Cobbers always cross the street (said twice).
4. Look at Kitty.
5. Come here Kitty.
6. Make it all gone.
7. That's the boy. (p. 134)

Anthony begins by addressing his father (1). Then he reports to his father on their dog Cobbers in two utterances (2 and 3), each repeated for emphasis. In 4 Anthony continues addressing his father; now about the cat. In 5 he addresses the cat. Then in 6 Anthony addresses himself, reproducing a sentence he has heard many times at mealtime as a request for him to finish his food. In this case Anthony functions in a dual role: as a parent and as himself. Anthony takes on the same roles in 7, where he reproduces the typical praise he received when he complied with the request in 6. We thus have here a clear dialogue with the child acting both as speaker and as addressee. Anthony was older and his language was more advanced than that of the children we have studied in this chapter. However, it is reasonable to assume that younger children also carry over to their soliloquies patterns of speech that they experienced in real-life interactions with other people.

So far I have discussed the functions of children's own speech. In this paragraph I report a study that investigated children's perception of the function of the speech of others, in particular, their perception of the function of questions addressed to them. Studying children in the age range of 19 to 34 months (mean = 27 months), Shatz (1978) found that her subjects interpreted questions addressed to them as requests for action. For instance, in response to the question, "Can you talk on the telephone?" they would run over to the telephone. This is not surprising, because questions addressed to children often do have a directive intent. What is more interesting is Shatz's finding that the tendency to respond to questions with action can be largely undone through appropriate context. For instance, children who, prior to being asked the foregoing question, were engaged in a conversation in which they were asked questions that had to be answered verbally (e.g., "Who talks on the telephone in your house?" and "Can mommy talk on the telephone?"), gave many more informational yes/no responses than children who were not given this kind of contextual preparation. Thus, by the third year children are able to respond to questions with information, not just action.

THE FORM OF EARLY SENTENCES

Sentences are organized entities: They exhibit word-order regularity and prosodic patterning. The following two subsections examine these characteristics in children's early sentences. The third subsection considers the brevity of children's sentences and their omission of components obligatory in adult sentences.

Word Order

One of the best established findings in the study of syntactic development is that normal word order is acquired early. Summarizing the observations of early syntax in twelve American children, Brown (1973) stated: "The violations of normal order are triflingly few" (p. 156). In a study of seven American children, Ramer (1976) found that the percentage of utterances in which word order constraints were not observed did not exceed 3.8 for any child, and for some it was as low as 0. This is a very impressive record.

Word-order regularity has also been found for children speaking languages other than English (see Brown, 1973, p. 157; Miller, 1976/1979). In languages that allow variable word order (e.g., Finnish, Hebrew, Russian), children follow one of the orders, usually the dominant order. Children thus seem to impose on themselves greater constraints than their language requires. This may reflect their striving to maximize regularity and may be the syntactic equivalent of the over-regularization in morphology, referred to in Chapter 4 and discussed fully in Chapter 9. Slobin (1973) was so impressed with the cross-linguistic evidence for order regularities that he formulated a universal principle of language acquisition stating that children pay attention to the order of words in the input language and follow that order in their own speech. It is clear that the word-order principle appears early in the course of language development, but it is less clear in what ways children formulate the word-order regularities that they discover.

Schlesinger (1974) has taken the position that children's sentence-formation rules are in terms of broad semantic categories of the sort that I discussed in the second section of this chapter. According to this approach, children have a rule that positions the demonstrative word first and the name second. They have rules that position the attribute first and the attributant second, the possessor first and the possessed second, the actor first and the action second, and so on.

In contrast to Schlesinger, Braine (1976) argues for a narrower, "limited-scope formulae" approach to early syntax, in particular, to the two-word combinations that usher in the syntactic stage. To exemplify Braine's approach and to make concrete the difficulty in choosing among competing approaches, consider the sentences involving primarily attribution and possession presented in Table 6.7. These sentences were recorded by Braine for his son Jonathan over a period of 2 months, from 1;11 to 2;0. It is evident that Jonathan had word-order regularities. Thus, adjectives precede nouns, and possessors precede their possessions. But how is one to formulate such regularities in a way that is functional for the child? Braine prefers narrow, lexically based formulations. Thus, he assumes that Jonathan had separate rules positioning *hot* first, *more* first, *daddy* first, and so on.

TABLE 6.7
Some of the Sentences Produced by Jonathan at 23 and 24 Months

23 months			
big ball	little ball	more ball	other ball
big plane	little plane	more plane	
big stick	little stick	more stick	
big blue	little blue	more blue	
big duck	little duck	more duck	
big lamb	little lamb		
big bread	little bread		
big rock	little rock		
big book		more book	other book
big car	little key	more juice	other banana
big sock		more catch	other shoe
big chicken		more dice	
big dog		more bee	
big tower			
hot stick			
hot pipe			
hot light			
	red car	blue car	green car
	red block	blue block	
		blue ball wool	green light
clean diaper	hurt toe	old carrot	

24 months			
big boy	little boy	more boy	
big banana	little banana		
big light	little light		
big shell	little shell		
big bird	little bird		

(Continued)

TABLE 6.7 (*Continued*)

	23 months		
big step	little step		
big tobacco	little tobacco		
big balloon	little hat	more glass	other door
big hot	little duck	more raisins	other pin
big juice	little ham	more shovel	other hand
big pants	little water	more "O"	old stick
big lion	little wet	more boy	old cookie
big jump	little split		old apple
big water	little hurt		
two bread	daddy bread[a]		
two car	daddy car		
one daddy car			
two door	daddy door		
two daddy door			
two plane	daddy coffee		
two ducks	daddy hat		
two fly	daddy chair		
two daddy	daddy eat[b]		
two mommy	daddy butter		
two shoe		Andrew shoe	
two diaper		Elliot diaper	
two stick			
two spoon			
two bird			
two pipe			
two cup			
two tobacco			
two raisins			
two squirrel			
	daddy book	mommy book	Andrew book
	daddy cookie	Elliot cookie	
	daddy tea	mommy tea	
	daddy shell	mommy shell	
	daddy butter	mommy butter	
	juice daddy[c]		
	daddy juice[c]	Elliot juice	
		mommy mouth	
		Elliot boat	

Note: This table is based on Tables 7 and 8 in Braine (1976).

[a]The utterances in this column and in the one to its right from here down have the possessive sense (i.e., daddy's bread).

[b]daddy's food.

[c]Braine (1976, p. 33) suggests that the second utterance, which occurred immediately after the first, may constitute a self-correction.

In some specific cases Braine is willing to assume that a child operates on slightly more general entities than words. Thus, he assumes that Jonathan did not have two separate rules positioning *big* first and *little* first, but a single size-first rule. Braine grants Jonathan a size rule because of two considerations. First, the adjectives *big* and *little* are close semantically; and second, as can be seen in Table 6.7, there was considerable overlap between the words that were combined with them. Braine also notes that Jonathan often produced *big* and *little* utterances one after the other (e.g., *big stick, little stick*).

In deciding on the separation or amalgamation of constructions, Braine considers the chronology of the appearance of utterances in addition to semantic commonality and distributional overlap. If different types of utterances appear at the same time in a child's development, they are likely to be part of the same rule. Further, in deciding on the rules for any one child, Braine also considers what kinds of rules are indicated for other children. Of all the considerations semantic commonality is for Braine the most important and constitutes a necessary condition, although not a sufficient condition, for the amalgamation of different constructions.

It must be pointed out that in Braine's formulation, words enter into the child's rules not as formal linguistic entities but as meaning-bearing entities. Thus, it is not *hot* as a word that is positioned first, but *hot* as a meaning category. The difference between the word-as-form and the word-as-meaning has no practical implications in cases where there is one-to-one correspondence between form and meaning. But the difference becomes relevant when two or more words are associated with the same meaning or when different meanings are associated with the same word.

A clear example of the latter case can be found in the record of Jonathan's speech (Braine, 1976, pp. 37-39). Between 2;1 and 2;2, he produced sentences in which *here/there* came first (e.g., *here milk, there cereal*) as well as sentences in which they came second (e.g., *bounce here, jam there, hot there*). Braine notes that when *here/there* came first, the words following them were only nouns, whereas when *here/there* came second, the words preceding them were adjectives and verbs in addition to nouns. He suggests that there was a semantic difference between the two *here/there*s. The utterances in which *here/there* came first were demonstrative naming utterances, and *here/there* had a pointing function. On the other hand, the *here/there* that occurred in second position had locative senses. Braine thus assumes that Jonathan functioned with two *here/there* rules, one placing the demonstrative *here/there* in the first position, and the other placing the locative *here/there* in the second position.

Both Schlesinger and Braine advocate a semantic approach to early syntax. They differ in that Braine favors narrow, word-level categories, whereas Schlesinger favors broader categories. Bowerman (1976, pp. 156-161) represents yet a third approach to early syntax. She agrees that some children do indeed start the acquisition of syntax with narrow, lexically based rules as outlined by Braine but claims (Bowerman, 1976) that other children operate from the start with formal syntactic categories (e.g., subject, object, modifier) that are "independent of any particular semantic content" (p. 158).

Bowerman's conclusions are based primarily on the chronological order of appearance of different constructions. She believes, for instance, that her daughter Christy operated at the beginning of her entry into the syntactic stage with a "noun + modifier" sentence-construction rule, because she started to produce within a few days a variety of utterances having the noun first and the modifier second (e.g., *daddy hot, bottle all gone, that wet*). By contrast, Bowerman attributes to her other daughter Eva narrower rules within the noun-modifier domain, because the appearance of different constructions was spread out over a longer time span. According to Bowerman Eva stayed with the narrow, lexical rules for 2½ months and then shifted directly to the formal syntactic rules of Christy's variety.

Bowerman's theory that children start out with formal syntactic categories or approach them directly and swiftly is intriguing. However, the evidence concerning the coacquisition of different constructions that she cites in support of her theory is unconvincing, because it can be accounted for by the broader semantic categories that Schlesinger has postulated. Moreover, it is hard to see how one would obtain evidence that would unequivocally indicate the operation of meaning-independent syntactic classes. In the case of mature speakers the evidence for such classes comes from their ability to place words and phrases in sentential positions on the basis of formal characteristics. For instance, adults place in the subject position of English sentences not only such bona fide agents as *the baby* and *John* (e.g., "The baby is crying," "John is playing") but also such syntactically derived nouns and noun phrases as *laziness* and *the construction of the auditorium* (e.g., "Laziness is debilitating," "The construction of the auditorium is delayed"). Young children, however, do not produce sentences of the latter kind, making it difficult to determine whether they have syntactic classes that do not coincide with semantic classes. Note that *laziness* and *the construction of the auditorium* are marked as noun phrases (and subjects) by *-ness* and *the*, respectively, and it is the very absence of such markers that characterizes early syntax. It seems unreasonable to attribute to the child formal syntactic classes before the appearance of formal syntactic markers.

To summarize, the three theories I have outlined differ in how broad they consider the child's sentence-construction categories to be at the beginning of syntax. Braine opts for narrow, word-level categories, Schlesinger prefers broader, but still semantic categories, and Bowerman favors syntactic categories. There is at present no clear evidence to enable one to choose among these different approaches. But perhaps we do not have to choose.

If instead of taking the concepts of Braine, Schlesinger, and Bowerman as describing the same point in the child's syntactic development, we view them as describing different points, a coherent framework for a theory of syntactic development can be constructed in a way that is consistent with the Piagetian approach of this book. We assume that children start the process of syntactic acquisition with the narrow, word-level classes of Braine. Then, they proceed through the broader classes of Schlesinger and ultimately reach the syntactic classes of Bowerman. The processes of assimilation and accommodation can account for this progression as well as they do for other developmental progressions. Maratsos (1981) has presented an approach to the development of syntax along these lines. Following Maratsos, I now elaborate somewhat on this approach.

Imagine a child named Suzie who initially constructs the pattern *boy walk* by hearing such utterances as "See, the boy's walking to school." This pattern functions like any other scheme. Suzie enjoys practicing it and playing with it, and she is sensitized to notice utterances potentially assimilable by it. Therefore, when she hears "See, the girl's walking to school," she assimilates it to the *boy walk* pattern and, through the process of accommodation, generalizes the pattern to "child + *walk*." In a similar fashion Suzie generalizes "child" to "human" and "*walk*" to "move" to form the rule "human + move." Later, she generalizes the rule to "animate + action" to take account of such utterances as "The dog is running," and "The man is digging." Utterances such as "The bus is going fast," and "The elevator is moving slowly" bring about further generalization of the rule to "actor + action." In addition, utterances such as "The baby is sleeping," "Robin likes apples," and "Johnny wants to go home" lead to the generalization of "actor" to "agent" and of "action" to "predicate."

At some point in the process Suzie will become sensitive to purely linguistic considerations and incorporate in the rule utterances such as "The dress fits you well," in which *the dress* is not an agent in any sense. When this happens the category "subject" will replace "agent" in the rule. Suzie will also learn to define other syntactically relevant classes (e.g., object, modifier, noun phrase, etc.) in purely linguistic terms.

I put Suzie through a simplified progression of learning to construct two-word sentences of the subject-predicate type. There is little doubt that the actual process of language acquisition is enormously more complicated and subtle than the sketch I provided. Children are exposed to a variety of utterances, not just those fitting a particular pattern, and they are learning simultaneously a variety of patterns and interrelating them to construct sentences longer than two words. The amazing thing is that children acquire syntax so smoothly and with such relative ease. I take up some suggestions as to why this is so in the next chapter.

Prosodic Patterning

Children exhibit not only word-order patterning but prosodic patterning as well. I discuss here two main aspects of prosody: phonetic stress and intonation.

Stress Distribution in Early Sentences   Wieman (1976) has produced evidence showing that even in the two-word stage, children exhibit stress-placement regularity. Wieman's study was based on an analysis of the two-word utterances found in a recording of about one hour of the speech of each of five children aged 21 to 29 months. All but a few of the sentences recorded were characterized by differential stress on the two words. An analysis of the stress distribution between the two words showed considerable regularity.

There were 23 sentences containing a verb and a locative, and in all, the locative element was stressed (e.g., *play mu'seum, coming 'up*). Wieman notes that for expressions containing verbs and locatives, there was greater regularity in stress distribution than in word order. The locative did not always appear in second position, but it was always stressed (e.g., *'here goes* and *goes 'here*). Wieman further reports that in 26 of 27 verb-object sentences the object was the element stressed. In adjective-noun constructions the stress was on the noun in 63 of the 78 cases. In possessive constructions the stress was on the possessor in 27 of the 28 cases (e.g., *'my boot, 'rabbit house*).

Wieman interpreted his findings in terms of the "new-given" distinction of sentential information. He suggests that his subjects emphasized the new information by placing phonetic stress on it, leaving the old information unstressed. The problem with this interpretation is that Wieman did not determine independently what information was new and what information was old. Instead, he offered examples of exceptions as evidence for his explanation. One child produced 20 adjective-noun sentences. In 16 the noun was stressed; in 4 the adjective. The four exceptions involved cases where the noun had been uttered first by itself immediately preceding its incorporation into the sentence (e.g., *'man, 'blue man; 'ball, 'nice ball, 'orange ball*). When placed in the sentence the noun was therefore already "old" and undeserving of emphasis. In another case cited by Wieman, a child produced 10 noun-locative sentences. In 8 the stress was on the locative, and in 2 it was on the noun. The 2 exceptions involved answers to questions where the locative was already present in the question. For instance, a mother asked, "What's in the street?" and her son answered *'fire truck street*.

Wieman's study is ground breaking, and his conclusions seem plausible. However, one wishes he had presented his findings more fully and systematically to allow an independent examination. The results that he did present permit an alternative explanation. It seems that in all cases except for the possessive constructions and the exceptions mentioned specifically, the children placed primary stress on the final word in the sentence. This is exactly the pattern of normal stress in English, and the children may have extracted this simple regularity from the speech around them. It may very well be that the exceptions noted by Wieman were due to a desire to emphasize a particular element, as he has claimed. But it does not follow that all the stress placements of his subjects reflect this motivation. According to this interpretation children's early stress patterns are similar to adult patterns. For adults there is normal stress assignment, and there is contrastive stress, which by virtue of its deviation from the normal pattern carries a message of emphasis.

Intonation in Early Sentences   Children are sensitive to differences in intonation even before the linguistic stage. Thus, Morse (1972) found that young infants could discriminate between a syllable produced with rising intonation and one produced with falling intonation. Adults on their part tend to exaggerate intonational differences in their speech to infants and toddlers (Blount and Padgug, 1977). It has also been observed that children produce rising and falling intonational patterns even before the syntactic stage. But it is not clear when they begin to associate different meanings with different intonations (Menyuk, 1971, pp. 61-62). Weir (1962, p. 28-29) reported that her son Anthony correctly imitated the rising and falling intonations of words and sentences from about the age of 1 year, but the different intonations were not associated with different meanings even at 2½ years.

However, Halliday (1975) reported an early use of intonation to distinguish different functions. He found that beginning at 1;7(2) and continuing for a couple of months, Nigel used the rising and falling intonational patterns for distinct functions. The rising tone was characteristically used in sentences that had an instrumental (or in Halliday's terms, a pragmatic) function; the falling tone was used for sentences that had a cognitive (or in Halliday's terms, a mathetic) function. In instrumental sentences Nigel asked for goods and services from the people he addressed. The rising tone is used in standard English for asking questions (i.e., it indicates that a response is expected). Nigel also used the rising tone to obtain a response, except that he normally expected a nonverbal response. In cognitive sentences, on the other hand, Nigel expressed his interpretation of his social and physical environment. Table 6.8 gives some examples of the two intonation patterns that Nigel used.

TABLE 6.8

Examples of Sentences Expressing Instrumental and Cognitive Functions Produced by Nigel, 1;7(14)-1;10(14)

Instrumental Expressions	Gloss
chuffa stúck	Calling for help in freeing toy train.
find fóryou	Asking for help in finding something (foryou = for me).
more grávy	Asking for more gravy.
that sóng	Requesting that a particular song just sung be sung again.

Cognitive Expressions	Gloss
molasses nòse	Commenting that he has molasses on his nose.
big bàll	Frequent expression on occasion of playing with ball.
little bàll	Frequent expression on occasion of playing with ball.
Mummy boòk	'Mummy's book' (i.e., a book without pictures).
Anna say go awaỳ Nila	Reporting what Anna said (Nila = Nigel).

Note: Sentences expressing instrumental functions were spoken with a rising intonation, and those expressing cognitive functions were spoken with a falling intonation. The source for these utterances is Halliday (1975, pp. 95-103).

Incompleteness of Early Sentences

In reading the sentences given as examples so far in this chapter, you must have noticed that they are brief and incomplete. Among the components left out, two types can be distinguished: (1) components that are present in some sentences but omitted from other sentences; (2) elements that are more-or-less totally absent. These omissions and absences are discussed separately.

Omissions in Early Sentences   Transcripts of early speech give the impression that if different sentences produced by a child at a particular time were put together, one would obtain adultlike, fully formed sentences. For instance, children produce few subject-verb-object sentences in their early syntax, but they do produce a sizable number of subject-verb and verb-object sentences. Thus, children have the notions of subject, verb, and object (on whatever level and in whatever form), but they do not include all of them in the same sentence. For instance, Kathryn, 1;9-1;10, said *Mommy push* when she wanted her mother to push an animal piece into a puzzle board, but she said *do it*, not *Lois do it*, when she wanted Lois to assemble pieces of a slide (Bloom et al., 1975, p. 59).

It thus appears that children produce incomplete sentences even when they have the words and the relational notions required for completeness. The difficulty seems to be in combining different constituents into a single sentence. A sentence is a product of coordination and planning. After the words of a sentence have been primed internally, they have to be processed for word order and prosodic pattern. Naturally, the larger the number of components, the more difficult the internal processing. There is thus a cognitive constraint on length.

What determines what children do and do not include in any one particular sentence? The same question can be asked about adult sentences as well, for no sentence is ever as complete as it potentially could be. What adults say depends on what information they want to communicate and what they think their listeners already know. It may be assumed that the same factors—the speaker's own interests and the needs of the listener—operate in children's choices as well, except that young children are much less concerned and knowledgeable about the background information of the listener.

It must be noted that even in the initial syntactic period, when children still produce many single-word utterances and their MLU is just approaching 2, they occasionally utter sentences up to 5-7 words long (Brown, 1973, p. 56). One may conjecture that the longer sentences concern content that is very familiar and whose expression is well practiced. Three factors would facilitate the construction of longer sentences in such cases. First, in talking about familiar topics children require less cognitive effort for the content, and they can therefore concentrate their energies on the process of sentence construction. Second, construction of longer sentences is facilitated by the presence of practiced word sequences, which function as prefabricated components. This is quite common in adult speech. Thus, for instance, in this book the phrase "word order" does not have to be put together every time it is used; its evocation is almost as automatic as that of a single word. Third, in addition to content familiarity and word-sequence familiarity, sentence-frame familiarity can also be assumed to aid in the construction of longer sentences. It would seem that a well-practiced structure, by reducing the burden of syntactic processing, would allow for the construction of longer sentences.

The foregoing suggestions were introduced on the basis of a purely theoretical analysis. However, some anecdotal evidence can be adduced in their support. Bloom et al. (1975, p. 60) give a sample of ten attribution sentences for Kathryn, 1;11(3). Seven of these were composed of two words, two were composed of three words, and one was composed of four words. The four-word sentence was *that a funny man*, which Kathryn uttered as she was pointing to a picture in a magazine. The sequence *funny man* occurs two times in the sample for the period between 1;9(0) and 1;10(3), and two-word sentences with *funny* as the first word occur two more times. In the same period Kathryn also produced five sentences that had the same pattern as the four-word sentence (i.e., *that a man*, *that a lamb*, *that a mirror*, *that a chine*, and *that's a mommy*). It thus appears that the four-word sentence involved a favorite topic, used familiar words, and had a well-practiced syntactic pattern.

Another example comes from Gia (Bloom et al., 1975, pp. 50-58). The fullest sentences for Gia in the last observation session, at 2;1(2), were: *You read this book, I read this book, I wanta read it, I want my book, Lois sit a couch read a book*. Gia thus exhibited the highest level of syntactic functioning on the topic of reading books. This was indeed a favorite topic of Gia during the entire time in which she was studied. The following sentences are found in the sample of sentences preceding the ones cited: *more, see book; read a book; a read dat book; this a nice book; Gia book; my library book; Gia library book; mommy book; more read; more read dat*. It would seem that Gia was relatively more articulate in a topical area in which she had considerable interest and practice.

Whereas factors that reduce the cognitive demands of sentence production increase length, factors that increase cognitive demands reduce length. Thus, Leonard and Schwartz (1978) found that when children's attention shifted to a new focus, the length of their utterances declined. Leonard and Schwartz obtained this finding in a study that examined 21 samples of speech of eight children. The children's ages ranged between 16 and 26 months in the beginning of the study and between 22 and 32 months at the end of the study. The MLUs of the 21 samples ranged from 1.20 to 1.91. Analyzing the occurrence of the same words in single-word and multiword utterances, Leonard and Schwartz found that the children were more likely to speak in single-word utterances than in multiword utterances when their focus of attention changed, and they were more likely to speak in multiword utterances when their focus of attention remained unchanged. This result can be clearly seen in the following tabulation:

	Focus of Attention	
Mean Number of	Changed	Unchanged
Single-word utterances	10.25	5.75
Multiword utterances	3.50	12.50

Leonard and Schwartz found that after the children made an initial single-word response, they frequently (in 56% of the cases, to be exact) went on to expand it to a longer utterance. For instance, while reaching for a toy, Greer suddenly noticed dirt on her finger and responded by holding it up to the adult observer and saying *dirt*. After she uttered *dirt*, she went on immediately to expand it to *dirt on finger*. This type of speech, in which children follow up less complete speech by more complete speech, is analyzed systematically in the next chapter. The point of this study for the present purposes is that the attentional demands of the new focus of attention interfere with children's ability to construct utterances of the length they are capable of under more favorable circumstances.

Absences in Early Sentences   In the previous subsection I discussed elements that children leave out from *particular* sentences because of the difficulty they have in constructing longer sentences. Here I take up entities that children in the early syntactic stage do not seem to use altogether. ˈ

Brown (1973, pp. 74–90) has provided a summary and systematic analysis of entities usually missing from early sentences. He has characterized early speech as "telegraphic" because, like telegrams, it tends to leave out function words, or functors, and to retain content words. Content words are words (e.g., nouns and verbs) that have referential substance. Function words are words that connect and relate words in a sentence to one another or modulate their meanings (e.g., prepositions such as *on* and *in* and the articles *a*, *the*). Brown has defined the category of functors broadly to include also pronouns, the copula (*be* and its different forms), verbal auxiliaries (e.g., *will*, *have*), and various inflectional suffixes (e.g., plural -*s*, possessive -'*s*, progressive -*ing*, past -*ed*).

Why are functors missing in early speech? Some of them have little communicative utility for the child, and in the competition for the limited space in sentences, they tend to yield to other more pertinent information. This is not to say, however, that children do not need some functors, sometimes, for communicative understanding. The following observation I made of my daughter Rachel shows what difficulties can arise from the absence of the preposition *on*. After hearing her older sister being asked, "Do you want egg on your muffin?" Rachel, 1;11(16), said *I want my muffin*. When she saw her parent's puzzled face, because she did have a muffin, she added, *like Shimi*. Shimi, her brother, had an egg on his muffin, and she obviously wanted the same. But such incidents do not occur frequently enough to force on children the need to include functors in their early speech.

Another factor that could account for the absence of functors concerns the difficulty of the meanings associated with them. The meanings of pronouns, for instance, change from speaker to speaker and from situation to situation. Thus, a person who is "you" when I speak becomes "I" when he speaks. This variability would make it more difficult for children to acquire pronouns. Similarly, prepositions are often associated with a bewildering variety of different uses. Thus, *on* has not only the spatial sense as in *on the table*, but also other, hard-to-define senses as in *on time, on the phone*, and so on. Other considerations concerning the absence of functors are taken up in Chapter 10 when I discuss inflections. It must be noted, however, at this point that some children use some function words (i.e., *a, this, that*) even in their earliest sentences.

CONCLUSION

In this chapter we saw children enter into the syntactic stage and we examined the structural and semantic characteristics of their early sentences. In acquiring syntax children demonstrate the attainment of the word-order principle, namely, that new, relational meanings can be composed by ordering words in relation to one another. Earlier the child had acquired the lexical principle of semantic expression, namely, that things can be referred to by means of verbal labels. These two principles provide the foundation for the child's mature use of language. In the next chapter I discuss the precursors to syntax and other issues pertaining to its acquisition.

7

The Emergence and Early Development of Syntax

At the end of the second year, Hildegard still spoke haltingly, uttering each word separately, or at best small groups of words. The incipient sentence had not yet become a free-flowing stream, but was still a succession of ripples.

Werner E. Leopold

The previous chapter described the characteristics of children's early sentences. The present chapter considers factors that anticipate the emergence of syntax and facilitate its development. I start in the first section with a discussion of the cognitive basis of syntax. The second section describes some practices children engage in, seemingly to overcome deficiencies in their knowledge of syntax or to advance its mastery. The third section examines the role of social influences in the development of syntax. The concluding section offers a general discussion of how syntax is acquired.

THE COGNITIVE BASIS OF SYNTAX

The construction of sentences involves analysis and synthesis. The situation to be described has to be first analyzed into components and then synthesized and integrated into a unified sentential structure. Thus, actor-action sentences entail first an explicit differentiation between activities and actors responsible for them and then a propositional connection between the two. Similarly, in attribute-object sentences a particular property of an object is first explicitly separated away from the entirety of the object, and the two are then brought together in a propositional relation.

Werner and Kaplan (1963, pp. 138-144) adopted a similar approach to early sentences. They emphasize that in sentences children represent in a more differentiated and precise way what in the single-word stage was represented globally and imprecisely. Werner and Kaplan point out that in the single-word stage, children would use a particular word (e.g., *milk*) both to refer to an object and to request it. Their intentions had to be inferred from extralinguistic clues. In contrast, in the syntactic stage children can explicitly mark their intentions by means of additional words (e.g., *see milk* and *gimme milk*).

Werner and Kaplan further suggest that sentences presuppose and help advance the development of the distinction between things and actions. They exemplify this point by an analysis of the use of motion and vehicle words by Hildegard Leopold. At the age of 1;5-1;7, Hildegard used the words *auto, choo-choo*, and *hai-hai* synonymously (with, perhaps, only a difference in emphasis) to refer to the total situation that included both vehicle and motion. But at the age of 1;8-1;10, she delimited *auto* to vehicles and *choo-choo* and *hai-hai* to movement.

Aside from requiring differentiation and coordination, sentence construction also calls for a higher degree of detachment of representation from reality than is involved in the symbolic use of single words. We saw in Chapter 3 that in early infancy there is no genuine representation, internal holding being merely a byproduct of instrumental action. Gradually, the child becomes capable of autonomous representation and ready for symbolic use of words. But symbolic representation, although necessary, is not sufficient for sentence construction. Words as symbols relate to external entities (i.e., their referents), but to become components of a sentence, they have to relate to one another. They have to cease being mere designators and have to become members of the language system. A child who produces sentences must see words both as referential symbols (i.e., names) and as sentential constituents.

At the time that children develop the ability to organize words into sentences, they also evidence increased planning and organization in other domains as well. Kagan (1981) commented on the changes in play that he observed in six children whom he followed from 17 to 27 months:

One of the most striking changes in the child's play over the 10 months of observation was the increased duration of an episode of play. At 17 months the epochs of play that involved a particular object or theme lasted 10 to 15 seconds and were usually followed by an act that was theoretically independent of the one that preceded it. Subject L at 18½ months began the play session by closing a box. About 10 seconds later she put a toy telephone to her face, then gave a doll to the observer, and then pointed to the doll's feet. Each act seemed, on the surface, to be psychologically unrelated to its predecessor. But at 27 months L began the play session by picking up a doll and played with it for 12 minutes. She covered the doll, then picked it up and said, "Baby ready to get up," hugged the doll, covered it again, woke it, looked for an additional blanket, told the mother, "Don't touch her," declared again, "She's ready to get up," changed her diaper, played with the doll's eyes, took the cover off, and asked rhetorically, "Maybe she like a story?" Then she said, "Where's my story?" meaning, "Where is my storybook?" . . . Such temporally extended sequences with one object and variations on the sleeping theme rarely occurred at 17 months. (p. 138)

It seems clear that this type of planful play calls for a high-level capacity of internal representation, just as sentence construction does. But it is not known to what extent the forms of representation involved in the different domains are related. My own feeling is that language is basic, serving as an internal code that facilitates planning and coordination of nonverbal behavior.

Although children acquire syntax naturally and smoothly, they do not acquire it effortlessly. Some of the ways children grope to acquire syntax are described in the next section.

COMPENSATORY AND LEARNING STRATEGIES

Before the emergence of syntax and during its initial stage, children engage in a variety of practices that seem designed to compensate for their meager knowledge of syntax or to aid in its mastery. These practices will be reviewed in the following subsections.

Word Sequences

There is a gradual transition from single-word speech to syntactic speech. One of the transitional phenomena that has been identified is the **word sequence**. A word sequence has less semantic and structural cohesion than a genuine sentence, but more than a succession of isolated words. Word sequences vary in the extent of their semantic and structural cohesion. I discuss the semantic aspect first.

Some sequences merely have a common theme, whereas others seem to express propositions of the kind expressed in sentences. An example of a sequence exhibiting low-level semantic cohesion is one that involves the successive naming of different objects, as in the case Bloom (1973, p. 43) reported for her daughter, Allison. Looking at a man dressed in a coat sitting with a suitcase beside him, Allison said *man/chair/coat/suitcase*. Another example is found in Greenfield and Smith (1976, p. 148). One of their subjects, Nicky, 1;8(19), called out *daddy/mommy/daddy* as he was touching articles of clothing in a closet and identifying their owners. In contrast to such primitive thematic sequences there are relational sequences that seem to express propositional content. Examples of relational sequences have been gathered in Table 7.1 from different sources.

TABLE 7.1
Examples of Relational Sequences

Sequence	Child, Age, Interpretation (and Source)
Mama?/mit?	Hildegard, 1;8, 'Will you, Mother, come along with me to put me to bed?' (L, 25).
mit?/Papa?	Hildegard, 1;8, 'Will you, Father, come along with me to put me to bed?' (L, 25).
Marion?/Dodo?/away!	Hildegard, 1;6, 'Where are Marion and Dodo? They are away' (L, 26).
Marion/Joey/away	Hildegard, 1;6, 'Marion and Joey are away' (L, 37).
build/house	Hildegard, 1;9, indicating that she wants to build a house (L, 24).
Mommy/shovel	Nicky, 1;6, indicating to his mother that he wants the shovel (GS, 93).
fan/on	Nicky, 1;6, first named the fan as a request for it to be turned on, and when it wasn't he added *on* (GS, 123).
bear/trolley	Nicky, 1;9, saying that his bear was left in the trolley (GS, 152).
mouth/bread/no mouth	Nicky, 1;9, 'Mommy put bread in her mouth, I don't want bread in my mouth' (GS, 99).
train/train/bump	Richard, 1;9, 'The train bumped' (CA, 572).
cow/moo	Richard, 1;9, imitating the sounds of cows (CA, 572).
beep/beep/trucks	Richard, 1;9, imitating the sounds of trucks (CA, 572).
Daddy/peach/cut	Allison, 1;6, asking father to cut peach (B, 41).
cook/baby	Allison, 1;7, describing what baby is doing (B, 41).
car/see	Eric, 1;7, saying that he saw cars as he was looking out the window (B, 40).

Note: Sources are abbreviated as follows: B = Bloom (1973); CA = Carlson and Anisfeld (1969); GS = Greenfield and Smith (1976); L = Leopold (1949/1970a). Page number follows source.

Word sequences, even the advanced relational ones, are not sentences, because they do not obey word-order constraints, and they allow longer time intervals between successive words. It has also been suggested that the words in a sequence lack a unifying intonational contour. For instance, Hildegard uttered each of the two words in the first entry in Table 7.1 with a rising, questioning intonation. In a sentence the two words would have been uttered with a single intonational contour, rising at the end.

The earliest discussion of word sequences that I have come across is by Guillaume (1927/1973), who referred to them as "pseudosentences." He emphasized that in this type of utterance the child responds individually to each stimulus with an appropriate word. It is the stimuli that are brought into relation with one another, rather than the words. In discussing the sequences produced by Hildegard, Leopold (1949/1970a, pp. 24-26 & 37) commented that each of the sequences was essentially a series of two or three one-word utterances, rather than one double-word or triple-word sentence. Commenting on relational sequences, Carlson and Anisfeld (1969) suggested that children produce relational sequences when they have the semantic ability to propositionize but lack the syntactic ability to construct sentences. In the production of a sentence words cannot be uttered as they come to mind. They have to be held in check, ordered, and assigned prosodic structure before they are produced. Further, the speaker has to accomplish these syntactic operations while at the same time attending to the semantic content of the utterance. Relational sequences reduce the structural burden and allow children to express propositional content even when they cannot structure the content syntactically.

The investigators whose work I have discussed so far based their conclusions concerning the structure of word sequences on their own perception of what their subjects said. Branigan (1979) introduced instrumental measurements into the study of the characteristics of word sequences. His data came from recordings of three boys at biweekly play sessions lasting 30 to 45 minutes. The boys' ages ranged from 17 to 19 months at the beginning of the study, and they were observed for 3½ to 5 months.

Branigan classified the children's utterances into three categories: a series of isolated words, sequences, and sentences. His classification was based on the length of the pauses between successive words. If the pauses did not exceed 400 milliseconds (msec), the utterance was classified as a sentence. If the pauses ranged between 400 and 1100 msec, the utterance was classified as a sequence; and if they exceeded 1100 msec, the utterance was classified as a series of isolated words. Branigan found that individual words were pronounced at different rates depending on the type of utterance. The more cohesive the utterance, the faster the articulation. Thus, the duration of monosyllabic words was 552 msec in isolated-word utterances, 403 msec in sequences, and 285 msec in sentences. There were similar differences for multisyllabic words. Thus, the increased fluency as one proceeds from isolated words to word sequences to sentences is reflected not only in reduction of interword pauses but also in faster articulation of the words themselves. The more cohesive an utterance, the shorter its interword pauses, and the more compressed its words.

Branigan also measured instrumentally the intonational patterns of the three types of utterances. Contrary to the conclusions of previous investigators, Branigan found that in sequences the terminal contour tended to fall on the last word, just as it does in sentences. To reconcile these divergent reports, I assume that some sequences have a unified intonational pattern, and others do not. There are undoubtedly different kinds of sequences differing not only in the extent of intonational integration but also in length of pauses and, as I have already pointed out, in degree of semantic unity.

In a study of a Hawaiian girl, Brenda, 1;0(2)-2;0(12), Scollon (1976, 1979) identified a type of sequence in which an adult query intervenes between the child's successive words, as in the following example (Scollon, 1979):

Brenda: hiding.
Adult: Hiding? What's hiding?
Brenda: balloon. (p. 221)

Brenda's response *balloon* answered the query and clarified the intent of her initial utterance.

What the different types of sequences share is that they are presyntactic. They serve as a transition between single words and sentences. There is statistical evidence regarding the transitional status of sequences. Greenfield and Smith (1976, pp. 38-39) presented information on the frequency of words, sequences (of all kinds), and sentences for their two subjects, at different ages. The information for one of their subjects is depicted in Figure 7.1. The other subject showed a similar pattern. It may be seen in the figure that in the course of the last three trimesters of the second year, the relative frequency of single words decreased, that of sentences increased, and that of sequences first increased and then decreased. Sequences apparently serve a bridging function to ease the transition between the single-word level and the sentential level.

The phenomenon of word sequences can help explain the experimental findings of Sachs and Truswell (1978) concerning comprehension of sentences. Sachs and Truswell gave children in the age range of 1;4 to 2;0 minimally contrasting sentential instructions (e.g., *kiss horsey*, *kiss teddy*, and *kiss ball*). Some

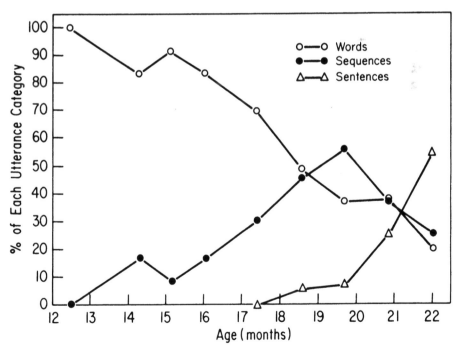

FIG. 7.1   Percentage of single words, sequences, and sentences as a function of age for one of the children, Matthew, studied by Greenfield and Smith (1976, p. 39).

of the sentences asked the children to perform unusual actions (e.g., *tickle shoe*). Sachs and Truswell found that the children responded correctly to 58% of the two-word instructions given them.

Because the children had to analyze the relational meanings of the requests in order to respond correctly, Sachs and Truswell concluded that the children demonstrated early syntactic ability in a comprehension task. One may, however, question this conclusion because the task given the subjects required little structural syntactic knowledge. To respond correctly the children had to be able to compute the semantic relations between the two words in the utterances they heard, but they did not need to know how to order the words and how to integrate them prosodically. The children in the Sachs and Truswell study thus had to be able to function on the level of relational sequences, but not on the level of sentences. Sachs and Truswell imply that the children did not yet produce two-word sentences. They do not, however, consider whether the children did produce sequences. To demonstrate that in a comprehension task children respond to the syntactic aspects of sentences, one would have to show, in a properly controlled experiment, that they are at least sensitive to word order (i.e., that they react differently to such pairs as *hit Mary* and *Mary hit*, and *kiss teddy* and *teddy kiss*). This kind of sensitivity to word order was not demonstrated in the Sachs and Truswell experiment.

The general point I am trying to make is that comprehension of sentences normally requires only semantic knowledge, whereas production of sentences requires both semantic and syntactic knowledge. Sentence comprehension is, therefore, more justifiably comparable to sequence production than to sentence production.

I have described in this subsection the phenomenon of word sequences, which appears at the threshold of syntax. Word sequences gradually diminish in frequency as syntax develops. But they are sometimes replaced by a parallel phenomenon on the level of phrases. The next subsection takes note of this phenomenon.

Phrase Sequences

The practice of nonsyntactic sequencing of elements appears not only on the level of single words but also on the level of phrases. Observation indicates that children produce sequences of interrelated phrases and short sentences that more mature speakers would integrate into a single comprehensive sentence. Table 7.2 gives some examples from observations I made of my daughter Rachel. Some of Rachel's **phrase sequences** reflect her train of thought. Thus, in item 3 in the table Rachel comments on things as she observes them. Similarly, in item 6 she lists the pieces of outerwear she normally put on in the winter when she went out. In other instances Rachel uttered phrase sequences because she was not able to

TABLE 7.2
Examples of Phrase Sequences Produced by Rachel, 1;10(3)-1;11(11)

Utterance	Context and Interpretation
1. I want cereal/that kind.	
2. I want napkin/hand/wipe hand/ and mouth.	'I want a napkin to wipe hand and mouth'.
3. man/see man/man coat/hat/ other doggie.	Looking out the window, Rachel is reporting what she sees.
4. I sleeping/blanket on.	'I am sleeping with a blanket on me'.
5. I need napkin/wipe myself/ I wipe myself.	
6. where man go?	Mother responded: "To Russia." Father asked: "You want to go to Russia?"
yes/put coat on/hat too/ snow pants/get coat.	This episode occurred in February when Rachel was accustomed to putting on these articles of clothing when she went out.
7. tastes good/in my mouth	Said it as she was eating grated apple.
8. yes/with salt on it/ with myself.	In response to the question: "You want cucumber?" Meant to say: 'I will put salt on it by myself'.

construct longer, more complex sentences. The fuller version of item 2, for example, would contain a "to-complement" clause (i.e., "I want a napkin to wipe hand and mouth"). At this point Rachel did not have structures of this complexity.

Fragmentary speech of the type presented in Table 7.2 does not persist for long. In the case of Rachel it disappeared after her second birthday. But children speak in short, simple sentences for many years. Learning to integrate clauses into complex sentences continues, of course, well into the school years.

In word and phrase sequences children produce a sequence of elements, which they leave as a sequence without combining the elements into a full sentence. In the next subsection we encounter a similar style, but with the difference that after the words or phrases are uttered as a sequence, they are integrated into a comprehensive sentence.

Gradual Assembly of Sentences

It has been observed that during the initial period of active growth of syntax, children sometimes put together sentences in a piecemeal fashion. For example, my daughter Miriam, 2;2(10), said, *hat/clown hat/that Shimi's/that Shimi's clown hat*. Miriam could not yet construct a sentence such as the final one all at once and therefore assembled it gradually. She first uttered a sequence and then made it into a sentence. In this case, all the components were first produced in isolation before they were combined in the sentence. There are also cases where one or more of the components are not uttered by themselves but only in the full sentence. We can see examples of this sort in the studies of the gradual-assembly style to which I now turn.

General Observations   Braine (1971, pp. 16-18) noted that in the recordings he made of the speech of children in the age range of 24 to 30 months, 30%-40% of the utterances were what he called "replacement sequences," that is, sequences of increasingly more elaborate utterances spoken in succession in the same context. Some of the examples Braine gives are reproduced in Table 7.3. It may be seen in the table that most of the replacing utterances fill in information missing in the beginning of the replaced utterances. It is noteworthy that the subject is often the element omitted from the initial utterance and then supplied in the replacement sentence.

How can we account for the occurrence of replacement sequences? It appears that the terminal expanded forms were too difficult for the children to construct all at once. The terminal forms were, however, within the children's reach, so that they were able to assemble them gradually. But this interpretation by itself would not explain why the subject in particular tended to be left out from the initial utterances. A supplementary explanation would be that the predicates carry the comment, the new information, which the child is eager to get out. The

TABLE 7.3
Examples of Gradually Assembled Sentences
Reported by Braine (1971) for Three Children

Steven (2;1-2;2)

Stevie byebye car. Mommy take Stevie byebye car.
Stevie soldier up. Make Stevie soldier up, Mommy.
Want more. Some more. Want some more.
Fall. Stick fall.
Go nursery. Lucy go nursery.
Push Stevie. Betty push Stevie.

Jonathan (2;2-2;3)

Car on machine. Big car on machine.
Noise. Noise car.
Stand up. Cat stand up. Cat stand up table.
Hot. Meat hot.
Back there. Wheel back there.
On table. Wine on table.

Andrew (2;3)

Plug in. Andrew plug in.
Off. Radio off.
All wet. This shoe all wet.

---

subject or topic is initially ignored because it is taken for granted. After children express the important predicative information, they are relieved of the communicative urge and attend to the grammatical requirement of speaking in complete sentences that include subjects.

Although the predicate is commonly the element singled out in the initial utterance, there are reports of the subject being treated in the same manner. For instance, a child studied by Bowerman (1973, p. 182) said, *Lisa/Lisa/Lisa write*, apparently to highlight the subject. Here, the emphasis of the subject is also reflected in its repetition.

The explanation for replacement sequences in terms of emphasis that I am offering is speculative, because there is no independent evidence in the reports examined as to what the children considered important and wanted to highlight. However, this explanation accords well with the view that children's language is predicative. Foremost among the writers holding this view is Vygotsky (1934/1962) who argued that children's language resembles the language of intimate friends and the language of question answering. In such interchanges speakers include in their sentences only new information, omitting information already known by their listeners, even though it is required from a strictly grammatical point of view. Because the subject of the sentence is often known to the listener, it tends to be omitted.

More recently, Bates (1976, chap. 6) proposed that two Italian children she studied had a word-order rule that placed the comment in the first position in the sentence and the topic in the second position. She adds that this ordering was: "probably an automatic extension of an earlier strategy at the one-word stage, in which the child simply talked about the element that seized his attention" (Bates, 1976, p. 210). Although the evidence Bates presents in favor of her suggestion is not very strong, the idea is interesting. Taken in conjunction with Braine's findings, Bates' observation suggests the possibility that in languages such as Italian, where sentential word order is flexible, children may prefer word orders that accommodate their urge to express the new information first, whereas in languages such as English, where word order is more constrained, they may accomplish the same end independently of sentential word order, as in the replacement strategy described. A closer look at a strategy of "unloading" urgent information first is provided under the next heading.

Rachel's Strategy   The observations to be reported here span a period of 3½ months, starting when the subject, Rachel, was 1;8(15) and ending when she was 2;0. The study began when Rachel exhibited an upsurge in her verbal activity. Although Rachel had produced one-word and two-word utterances prior to the initiation of the study, the quantity and variety of her output had been rather limited.

Rachel's utterances were recorded at meals and other convenient times by her father (the author) or mother. Intensive recording began when the phenomenon of gradual assembly was first observed. Rachel's utterances were taken down in English orthography. Verbal and nonverbal context pertinent to the interpretation of the material was also noted.

Rachel's gradual-assembly style lasted 7 weeks, from 1;8(15) to 1;10(7). Some examples representing this style are given in the first section of Table 7.4. As can be seen, Rachel would first produce a short utterance, and immediately thereafter, a longer, expanded utterance that included the initial short utterance. Occasionally, she would produce three increasingly more elaborated utterances. The initial utterances were invariably positioned at the end of the final utterances. In the largest number of cases (34) the initial utterances consisted merely of a noun, but there were also instances of initial utterances consisting of two words, which constituted a noun phrase or a verb phrase.

I would like to suggest that the reason for Rachel's gradual sentence-formation style was a difficulty in holding back communicative impulses. The initial utterances appear to carry more information than any other element of comparable length in the expanded utterances. Rachel would thus first express the essence of her message, and only after she "unloaded" herself of the communicative urge would she turn to a syntactic clarification of her intention. The

TABLE 7.4

Examples of Gradually Assembled and Fully Formed Sentenced
Produced by Rachel, 1;8(15)-1;10(7)

Gradually Assembled Sentences

Cracker. More cracker.
Dish. Gimme dish.
Popobook. Where popobook? (popobook = pocketbook)
Coffee. That coffee.
Train. I made train.
Aba. I want some pom Aba. ('I want some egg from Aba')
Glasses. I found glasses.
Juice. Give dolly juice.
That cheese. I want that cheese.
My book. Here my book.
Hold it. Let me hold it.
Drop it. I drop it.
Roni. Open roni. I open roni. (roni = macaroni, open = take apart)
More. Some more. I want some more.

Fully Formed Sentences

I already eat it.
I have two pencil.
I want some of this.
I don't want it.
I want go.
Aba binished. (binished = finished)

fact that Rachel went on to produce the elaborated utterances suggests that she was dissatisfied with the incomplete utterances, because they did not measure up to her standards of proper speech. At the age under consideration, Rachel was, in fact, capable of better performance than she demonstrated in the gradual-style utterances. The second section in Table 7.4 gives examples of advanced sentences, which Rachel produced full-blown without preceding them with partial utterances. Rachel produced these advanced sentences when she seemed to be in a relaxed, unpressured state.

Rachel's gradual style thus seems to be due, at least in part, to the tendency discussed in Chapters 4 and 6 for performance to deteriorate under conditions of excessive emotion. Under such conditions the child cannot fully mobilize the mental resources necessary for sentence construction. As children's knowledge of syntax becomes firmer and more automatic, the interfering effects of emotions decrease. It should be noted, however, that even adults do not speak as well as they can when upset or excited. The production of complex sentences requires fine control and coordination, which an individual may not be able to exercise when distracted or preoccupied. Particularly clear cases of emotional lowering of linguistic performance occur in situations where there is external danger or urgency. Thus, on seeing a dog approach, Rachel, 2;1(26), called out, *coming/ coming me* ('Coming toward me'). (Rachel had ambivalent feelings toward dogs at that age.) But after gaining the security of a parent's protection, she said playfully, *hi doggie, I got something for you.* This fuller, grammatical utterance was more in line with the normal level of her utterances at that time. Adults, too, shout ''Fire!'' not, ''There is a fire here!''

The gradual-assembly style observed in Rachel and in Braine's subjects occurred in the context of their daily activities and in interaction with other people. It seems to have resulted from the tension between the children's developing respect for syntax and their inability to inhibit communicative urges. I describe next a similar style that occurred in different circumstances and seemed to reflect metalinguistic interests.

Anthony's Soliloquies Many young children have the habit of talking to themselves. Weir (1962) listened in on one type of such speech. She recorded and analyzed the solitary monologues of her son Anthony, 2;4-2;6, when he was left alone in his room for the night. In this situation Anthony produced imaginary conversations with familiar individuals as well as statements directed to no one in particular. The types of constructions that Weir recorded are exemplified in Table 7.5.

Anthony's ''buildups,'' in which he would produce part of a sentence and then go on to complete it, are similar to the gradual constructions of the children discussed above. I attributed the gradual constructions of the other children to their lack of sufficient syntactic control to plan an entire sentence internally, especially when eager to say something pressing. Anthony was, however, older

TABLE 7.5
Sequential Utterances Produced by Anthony, 2;4-2;6

Buildups

Daddy. Daddy bucket please. (p. 80)
Donkey. Fix the donkey. (p. 80)
Block. Yellow block. Look at all the yellow block. (p. 82)
Sit down. Sit down on the blanket. (p. 82)

Breakdowns

Anthony jump out again. Anthony jump. (p. 82)
Another big bottle. Big bottle. (p. 82)
Was that from that? Was that? That from that? (p. 82)

Substitutions

What color? What color blanket? What color mop? What color glass? (p. 109)
Take the money. Take it. (p. 110)
There is the light. Where is the light? Here is the light. (p. 112)

Phrase Sequences

Look at those pineapple/in a pretty box. (p. 83)
Bobo's goes/to the bathroom/clean off. (p. 83)
Anthony take the/take the book. (p. 83)

Note: The utterances in this table are from Weir (1962).

and linguistically more advanced, and he produced his buildups in a relaxed state, free of the pressures of practical interaction. He was certainly able to form the terminal sentences all at once, as is evident from the numerous sentences he produced fully formed from the start. His ability to produce full-blown sentences is also reflected in the "breakdown" constructions exemplified in Table 7.5. Breakdowns are constructions in which Anthony first produced the full sentence and then analyzed it into components.

Weir (1962, p. 109) saw Anthony's behavior as reflecting metalinguistic interests. That is, Anthony was manipulating language to reflect on it and to try to understand its workings. This interest is perhaps most clearly evident in the substitution exercises in the third section of Table 7.5. Here, Anthony seems to be selecting sentence frames and consciously making word substitutions in them. In a foreword to Weir's book Roman Jakobson noted that Anthony's exercises were reminiscent of drills for foreign language students. Anthony also showed an interest in the phonetic aspects of language and engaged in sound play, as in *Babette, back here, wet*. Occasionally, Anthony would express his awareness of what he was doing, as when he said after a counting rehearsal: *Anthony counting, good boy you.*

In Anthony's breakdowns and buildups one or more components were isolated from a sentence, which was actually produced either before or after the production of the components. Anthony also exhibited constructions, termed "completions" by Weir, in which he would produce the components but not integrate them into a sentence. Anthony's completions are similar to Rachel's phrase sequences discussed earlier. To bring out this similarity, I labeled them "Phrase Sequences" in Table 7.5. It should be noted, however, that even though there is a formal similarity between Anthony's and Rachel's phrase sequences, the two differ in function. Rachel's phrase sequences were interpreted as reflecting train of thought characteristics or deficiency in syntactic control, whereas Anthony's phrase sequences seem to reflect metalinguistic interests (i.e., attempts to identify sentence constituents).

The syntactic strategies described so far involved meaningful elements (words or phrases). The next subsection describes a strategy that involves meaningless elements.

Structural Juxtaposition with Dummy Forms

In relational word sequences semantic relations are expressed, but the words are not integrated syntactically. Here, I consider the reverse phenomenon: syntactic juxtaposition without propositional content.

Bloom (1973, pp. 33-39) was the first to notice this phenomenon. During a 3-week period in her 17th month, Allison produced multiword utterances with a meaningless form *widə* as one of the elements (e.g., *Mama widə,* where the symbol ə represents the English vowel that sounds like the second *e* in *enemy*). The utterances with *widə* were syntactically cohesive: There was no intervening pause between the components, and there was terminal intonation at the end of the utterance. In virtually all cases *widə* was the last word in the utterance. It seems that Allison invented *widə* to use as a place holder in the practice of sentence construction. In this way she could concentrate on the structural aspects of sentences without having to divert cognitive energies to matters of content and wording.

The syntactic status of *widə* is supported by evidence showing that Allison used it extensively in juxtaposition with other words but rarely in isolation. Of 272 single-word utterances produced by Allison, 1;4(3), in a 40-minute recording session, only two were *widə*. In contrast, *widə* was one of the elements in 65 out of the 78 multiword utterances she produced in that session. Furthermore, in the majority of cases the other element with which *widə* entered into construction also appeared to be meaningless and/or easy to articulate. In 31 of the 65 multiword utterances *widə* was preceded just by the vowel ə, and in 9 utterances by *uh, oh,* or both. Bloom also noted that Allison used with *widə* only 6 of the 30 words she had in her vocabulary at that time. This further suggests that the *widə* utterances were used for practice, not for communication. It seems that Allison employed empty forms in constructing sentences so as not to have to concern herself with meaning while concentrating on the mechanics of syntax. When learning how to drive a car, one is not at the same time trying to get somewhere!

A later study (Dore, Franklin, Miller, & Ramer, 1976) also reported the use of dummy forms. Two children were observed in this study: one (A) from 12 to 19 months and the other (B) from 16 to 24 months. Their speech was videotaped in 1-hour sessions held at monthly intervals. Dore et al. give the results for the initial testing session (Session 1), for the middle session (4), and for the final session (8). There was no syntactic speech of any kind during Session 1. In Sessions 4 and 8 there were both meaningful syntactic utterances and syntactic utterances that conjoined dummy forms with English words. Unlike Allison, who used a single dummy form, these children used several dummy forms consisting of meaningless vowels or syllables.

The number of dummy-utterance types and meaningful-utterance types (i.e., the number of *different* constructions in the two categories) in Sessions 4 and 8 is tabulated in Table 7.6 for the two children. This tabulation shows that although the number of meaningful sentences quintupled (for child A) or tripled (for child B) in the 4 months between Session 4 and Session 8, the number of dummy utterances stayed about the same. These results are consistent with the results of Bloom in suggesting that the dummy-construction phenomenon serves as a temporary strategy in the acquisition of syntax. But it should be noted in relating the studies of Bloom and Dore et al. that the subjects in these studies used the dummy-construction strategy differently. Allison used her dummy constructions

TABLE 7.6
Frequency of Dummy and Meaningful Utterance Types in
the Speech of Two Children

	Child A	
	Number of Dummy Utterances	*Number of Meaningful Utterances*
Session 4	11	6
Session 8	13	31
	Child B	
	Number of Dummy Utterances	*Number of Meaningful Utterances*
Session 4	21	24
Session 8	18	79

Note: These two children were studied by Dore et al. (1976).

heavily over a short period of time (3 weeks), whereas the subjects of Dore et al. used them more sparingly over a longer period (at least 4 months).

Another study (Ramer, 1976) found individual differences in the extent of use of dummy constructions. Ramer followed seven children for varying periods of time, from before the onset of syntax until they reached the point when 20% of their utterances had a subject-verb-complement structure (e.g., *Lisa eat fast*). The ages of the children at the beginning of the study were between 15 and 20 months and at the end between 19 and 27 months. Ramer found that the incidence of dummy constructions for her subjects ranged from 0% to 64%. She suggested that children who acquire syntax slowly are more heavily dependent on dummy forms than children who acquire syntax more rapidly. This is a reasonable hypothesis, but the evidence Ramer presented in its favor is not statistically significant.

Finally, Leonard (1975) reported the use of a dummy form by a 3-year-old girl whose language was inadequate for her age. She used the dummy *goking* as a generalized verb form, producing "actor + *goking*" constructions. Examples of her use of *goking* and of other verbs are given in Table 7.7. It is noteworthy that *goking* was the only verb Leonard's subject used in sentences. With meaningful verbs she produced only sequences, no sentences. Apparently, the extra mental effort involved in the processing of meaningful verbs left little mental energy for the construction of sentences. Aside from *goking* sentences, the only other type of sentence the child produced involved demonstrative naming. We saw in Chapter 6 that demonstrative naming sentences express no semantic relation. It thus appears that Leonard's subject could integrate words syntactically only when no propositional content was involved. She could not at the same time propositionize and construct sentences.

The dummy constructions that I have described seem to reflect a strategy of learning the mechanics of syntax without having to attend at the same time to semantic content. This complements the strategy of gradual sentence assembly where the child's interest is in the expression of semantic content. The two strate-

TABLE 7.7
Examples of the Use of *Goking* by a Linguistically Delayed 3-Year-Old Girl

Adult's Prompt (and Context)	Child's Response
1. What is happening in here?	it goking.
(Questioner asked as he was pointing to a picture of a lighted fireplace.)	
What is it doing?	burning.
What's happening?	it goking.
2. Tell me about this picture.	mommy/washing. Her goking.
(Picture showed a woman washing her feet.)	
What?	mommy goking.

Note: Case reported by Leonard (1975).

gies have been reported independently, for different children. It is not known what determines whether a particular child will use either of the strategies or both. The dummy-formation strategy appears to be less common than the gradual assembly strategy.

The strategies described are the ones that have been specifically identified in recent writings. Observation suggests that children employ a variety of other ways to cope with syntactic inadequacies and to grope for syntactic mastery. The following subsection takes note of some of these ways.

Other Ways of Coping and Groping

I noted earlier that the gradual-assembly style indicates that the standards children have of what sentences should be like exceed what they are able to produce without the aid of external manipulation. Gradual assembly is really a specific form of self-correction, and there are other forms. Snyder (1914) reported some self-corrections for a boy she observed in the age range of 2;5-2;8. The largest number of his self-corrections involved adding or changing a noun modifier (e.g., *All gone tail . . . Pony tail all gone*; *Dat water . . . Dat dirty water*; *I want throw dat ol . . . dat big stone way*).

Children also reveal their groping for higher levels of performance in occasional slow and deliberate articulation of difficult sentences. For instance, our subject, Rachel, whose gradual-assembly constructions were described earlier, produced at the age of 1;10(21) the sentence: *Look how nice I did*. She articulated the words slowly and deliberately. This was indeed a difficult sentence for Rachel, because it contains a subsidiary clause within the main clause. Rachel's normal sentences at that age were shorter and simpler.

Children's gropings to produce fuller sentences are also reflected in hesitations. Here are some examples from Rachel at the age of 1;11(18)-2;0(12). Her hesitations were marked by nonfinal intonation before the pause and facial expression indicating uneasiness and effortful groping:

1. *I am going to get paper out . . . by myself.*
2. *Mommy go . . . with me.* Rachel wanted to say, 'When Mommy goes out, I'll go with her', but she became tongue-tied by the complexity of the expression.
3. *Miriam not . . . not down.* Here the pause is due to the search for the last word.
4. Rachel's sister was going upstairs on her brother's (Shimi) back. Rachel positioned herself to go up on her father's back and said, *like Shimi*. Then realizing that what she had said wasn't quite right, she attempted again *like . . .* , but could not get it. Her father then suggested, "Like Miriam on Shimi's back?" Rachel responded with a relieved *yeah*, and added, *piggyback ride.*

These examples reveal Rachel's attempts to give linguistic expression to her thoughts and her implicit awareness of the inadequacy of her attempts.

In the period around her second birthday there were also other indications of Rachel's increasing awareness of language. For instance, she would occasionally introduce an account of something she had experienced with, *I tell you something.* She would also directly "hold up" her utterances with pride as in: *hi Miriam, I say "hi Miriam."* Rachel reflected not only on her language but also on her nonverbal behaviors, as in: *Aba, I am eating now.*

MOTHER-CHILD INTERACTION AND THE ACQUISITION OF SYNTAX

The previous section focused on the child's own strategies of learning syntax. In this section the focus shifts to the child in interaction with others, particularly the mother. The first subsection is concerned with the preverbal period of infancy, and later subsections with the verbal period of postinfancy.

Prelinguistic Mother-Infant Interaction and the Acquisition of Syntax

Some investigators have sought to find foreshadowings of syntax in early patterns of interaction between mother and infant. As this work progresses, investigators are becoming more cautious about the relation of mother-infant interaction to syntax. The present subsection reviews a range of positions on this issue.

Bates (1976) was perhaps the most extreme in arguing for a relation between syntax and prelinguistic communicative interaction. Her views are based on the observation of three Italian girls over a period of 8 months. Their ages at the inception of the investigation were 2, 6, and 12 months. Among other things, Bates attempts to trace the emergence of imperative and declarative sentences to prelinguistic origins. An examination of these two points should suffice to represent her approach.

In imperative sentences speakers use others as mediators in the achievement of their goals. The use of imperative sentences, therefore, presupposes the ability to separate means from ends. In agreement with Piaget's findings discussed in Chapter 3, Bates reports that her subjects used adults to obtain desired goals only after they reached the fifth stage of sensorimotor development. (Only two of her subjects reached this stage by the end of the study.) Typically in the fifth stage, when a child could not obtain a goal on her own, she would turn away from it and make her request known to the attending adult through gestures and vocalizations.

Bates gives an example from one of her subjects, Carlotta, 1;1(2). Sitting outside the kitchen Carlotta called her mother with *ha*. When the mother appeared,

Carlotta looked toward the kitchen. The mother interpreted this gesture to mean that Carlotta wanted to be taken to the kitchen, and she obliged her. When in the kitchen, Carlotta expressed her request to be given water by pointing to the sink. After the mother poured her a glass of water, Carlotta showed clear signs of satisfaction.

Bates notes that prior to Stage 5 her subjects did not seek adult assistance when they wanted to obtain something. They would try themselves to obtain the desired object, and when their efforts failed, they would give up in frustration. Bates points out that even before Stage 5 her subjects engaged in social interaction with familiar adults and sought contact with them through smiling, cooing, and touching. It is just that they did not think of using adults as intermediary agents.

So far there is little to object to in Bates' revealing analysis. But she seems to be stretching the point when she calls the assistance-seeking prelinguistic behaviors "protoimperatives." It is certainly true that children would not use imperatives unless they had the idea that they can use others to achieve their goals. But in what way do linguistic imperatives grow out of prelinguistic assistance-seeking behaviors?!

Bates' analysis of declaratives seems no less problematic. First, she assumes that in declaratives (i.e., labeling utterances) children use objects as a means to obtain the attention of people. She further assumes that pointing gestures and acts of showing and giving are precursors of declaratives, and she calls them "protodeclaratives." However, her basic assumption that declaratives have social contact as their primary motivation seems questionable. The evidence reviewed in Chapters 4 and 6 suggests that such utterances reflect children's interpretations of reality and their attempts to learn the names of objects. Children undoubtedly use language as well as a variety of other means to get attention, but there is no evidence that language develops primarily for this purpose.

Bruner (1978) was also interested in showing the continuity of language with prelinguistic communicative development. But he advocated a more cautious approach, rejecting "inappropriate reductionism," presumably of the kind espoused by Bates. Bruner sees the interactions between infants and mothers as providing useful background experiences on which linguistic interaction can build. In various joint-action routines, such as those involving giving and taking, children learn to assume different roles in relation to other individuals, a skill necessary for linguistic interaction. Also, through their preverbal interaction mothers and children develop specialized communicative formats that facilitate their mutual interpretation of each other's intent. They also develop strategies for joint focus of attention on particular objects. These skills too, Bruner argues, should serve the mother and child well in the tutorial episodes of language learning.

Bruner reviews studies showing the strategies mothers employ to direct the attention of their infants to a particular object and to refocus it when it wanders away from that object. Mothers do such things as shake the object, touch it, or put it in the baby's direct line of vision. Bruner suggests that such cooperative relations should provide mother and child with a helpful background for the interaction involved in language learning. Because they have developed mutual sensitivities, mother and child will be able to understand one another more easily despite the immaturity of the child's linguistic knowledge. More specifically, because children have learned how to "read" the mother's signals, they will be able to interpret her utterances with the aid of the nonlinguistic cues she provides concerning her intentions. This will make it easier for them to discover how language codes reality.

Dore (1978) is even more cognizant than Bruner of the difficulty in specifying the nature of the connection between seemingly parallel prelinguistic and linguistic behaviors. He states: "It is perfectly conceivable that the human infant, like other species, could continue using a communicative system of signals without ever creating a grammar whose structure is independent of communicative and other cognitive systems" (pp. 94-95).

In conclusion, it appears reasonable to assume that healthy mother-infant interactional experiences prepare the child to become an efficient and interested communicator and language learner. But there is little evidence that specific aspects of syntax are prefigured in prelinguistic behavior. Children learn syntax, and other aspects of language, through *verbal* interaction with more mature speakers. The following subsections consider some of the maternal behaviors that might potentially facilitate this learning.

Verbal Interaction Between Mothers and Children

Language is learned in the context of verbal interaction between children and people in their environment, normally and particularly their parents. What are the characteristics of this interaction and how does it affect the acquisition of syntax? Most of the research in this area has been concerned with the characterization of the speech that mothers and other caregivers address to children rather than with the relation between maternal speech and children's linguistic development (see review by Snow, 1977). But the latter issue is beginning to be investigated, and I review some results that have been reported on this point.

Newport, Gleitman, and Gleitman (1977) studied the speech of 15 mother-daughter dyads. Their results are based on two 2-hour sessions, 6 months apart. The girls were 12 to 27 months old in the beginning of the study. Cross (1977) investigated 16 mother-child dyads, including 10 girls and 6 boys. Their ages ranged from 19 to 32 months. The children in the Cross study were selected on the basis of various indications that their language development, as well as that of their siblings, was advanced. The Cross study is based on an analysis of 1 hour of recording of the interaction between mother and child.

Both studies found that the mothers spoke to their children in short sentences. The MLU of the mothers' speech to their children was 4.2 in the Newport et al. study and 4.8 in the Cross study. The children's MLU was 1.65 in the Newport et al. study (first session) and 2.2 in the Cross study where the children were older. By comparison, Newport et al. report that the MLU of the mothers' speech to the experimenter was 11.94. The finding that the sentences addressed to young children are short has been well established in other studies as well. Even 4-year-olds were found to direct shorter sentences to 2-year-olds than to peers or adults (Shatz & Gelman, 1973).

Newport et al. further report that the mothers' speech to their children was more intelligible than their speech to adults. Whereas 9% of the mothers' speech to the experimenter could not be transcribed, only 4% of their speech to the children could not be transcribed. Another reflection of the careful articulation that mothers use in speaking to children can be seen in the finding of Newport et al. that 5% of the mothers' speech to the experimenter contained disfluencies (slips of tongue, etc.), but their speech to the children contained virtually no disfluencies. Mothers, of course, also speak more slowly and use simpler words when addressing children (see Snow & Ferguson, 1977).

Another characteristic of mothers' speech is that it concerns the child's ongoing activities and immediate interests. Thus, 73% of the utterances that the mothers addressed to their children in the Cross study concerned the situation in which the children were involved at the time or objects that were present in the immediate environment. The mothers not only talked about matters that their children were involved in, but they also tended to say things that followed up on what the children had said, producing expansions, extensions, and imitations. In an "expansion" the mother fills in the missing words as she echoes the child's utterance; in an "extension" the mother continues a thought started by the child; and in an "imitation" she simply repeats all or part of what the child had said. It seems clear, then, that the speech of the mothers was guided by their children's activities and utterances.

The speech of mothers to children is thus characterized by simplicity and immediate pertinence. Even though mothers do not consciously speak this way in order to teach syntax, they nevertheless contribute to the acquisition of syntax by making it easier for their children to understand what is said to them. As Macnamara (1972) has stressed, a basic condition for learning syntax is that children readily understand the sentences spoken to them without much reliance on syntax. It is only when children know the meanings of sentences independently of syntax that they are able to discover how these meanings are encoded syntactically. The characteristics of maternal speech that have been described seem to meet this requirement. Because a mother's speech relates to what is on the child's mind at the moment, the child needs only a hint—a word here and there—to understand what she is saying. In this way the child is able to find out which syntactic structures express which propositional meanings. Mothers thus facilitate the acquisition of syntax indirectly by making themselves easily understood. In contrast to vocabulary, there is little direct, intentional teaching of syntax.

One additional aspect of the findings of Newport et al. and Cross deserves comment because it relates to an issue that has received considerable attention in the literature. Brown and his co-workers (Brown, 1973, p. 105; Brown, Cazden, & Bellugi, 1969) were the first to draw attention to the expansion phenomenon mentioned earlier. They reported having heard such exchanges as the following:

Child: Eve lunch.
Mother: Eve is having lunch.
Child: Throw daddy.
Mother: Throw it to daddy.

Brown noted that 30% of the "telegraphic" utterances of two of the children (aged 18 and 27 months) that they studied were expanded by the mothers. In the Cross study expansions accounted for 18% of the utterances of the 16 mothers studied.

Brown reported that the mothers' expansions were produced with varied intonations. Some of the expansions were produced with a declarative intonation, sounding like the mother was offering a correct syntactic gloss for her child's utterance. In other cases there was a questioning tone, which sounded like the mother was asking the child whether she understood him or her correctly.

Both Cross and Newport et al. correlated the number of the mothers' expansions with the children's MLU levels. Cross found a negative correlation (approximately $-.60, p < .05$), whereas Newport et al. found a positive correlation ($.88, p < .001$). It may be suggested speculatively that in the Cross study, where the group as a whole was older and more advanced, the children at the higher levels of MLU did not require expansion. Expansion was thus associated in the Cross study with relatively lower levels of performance, hence the negative correlation. In the Newport et al. study, on the other hand, the children in the low end were so low (at the one-word stage) that they probably did not invite expansion. Expansion was thus associated in the Newport et al. study with relatively high performance, hence the positive correlation. These results therefore seem to say more about when mothers are likely to expand than about the effects of their expansions on their children's syntax.

A subsequent study by Cross (1978) with middle-class Australian children in the age range of 19 to 33 months does seem to show some positive effects of expansion on children's syntactic development. It found that the speech of mothers of children whose language was "accelerated" contained more expansions than the speech of mothers of children whose linguistic development was "normal." The children in the two groups were matched in pairs for level of linguistic competence as indicated by MLU (which ranged from 1.5 to 2.5) and by a test involving sentence comprehension. There were eight children in each of the two groups. The children in the two groups differed only in age: Those designated "accelerated" were 5 to 10 months younger than those designated "normal." The finding that the accelerated children were exposed to more expansions suggests that well-timed maternal corrective speech plays a facilitating role in children's acquisition of syntax. Cross also found that the mothers of the accelerated children introduced fewer semantically new utterances than the mothers of the normal children. In other words the mothers of the accelerated children allowed themselves to be guided by their children's interests. It is noteworthy that purely syntactic measures of the types of sentences produced by the mothers did not differentiate the two groups.

In conclusion, it seems reasonable to assume that no one method of guidance is indispensable for the acquisition of syntax. What would seem more important than method is an attentive caregiver who is sensitive to the needs of the child at different levels of development and adjusts his or her speech and other behaviors in appropriate ways. The sensitive mother will speak to the child on matters the child is interested in at the moment, making her utterances highly redundant with the information available to the child in the nonverbal context.

I have concentrated so far in this section on the child's comprehension of the mother's utterances. But the other side of the interaction, the mother's comprehension of the child's utterances, is no less important. Early speech is hard to understand without knowledge of the child, his or her interests, and experiences. As we have seen, children's speech is syntactically incomplete. It is also phonetically distorted in relation to adult speech. The child we observed (Rachel) had some of the following versions of English words: *boo* ('spoon', 'book'), *hia* ('here') *goak* ('coat'), *kuck* ('sock'), *roni* ('macaroni'), *bik* ('fix').

What makes it possible for mothers to understand their children's utterances and to respond to them meaningfully is their familiarity with their children's particular "dialects" and intimate knowledge of their daily lives and activities. This point can be exemplified by citing a couple of examples from my observations of Rachel at the age of 20 to 21 months:

1. Rachel pulled her father to a cupboard and said *keyo*. The father opened the cupboard and gave Rachel the crayons that were there, and she was satisfied. Only someone who knew what was in the cupboard and what Rachel might have wanted at the moment could have interpreted correctly this incomplete and distorted utterance.
2. Sitting in the kitchen in her highchair, Rachel said: *turtle/broke turtle/ cupboard/my cupboard*. Her mother interpreted this sequence to mean that Rachel saw the bottom part of her broken toy turtle on the windowsill, which reminded her that the other part was in the cupboard. Again, comprehension was made possible by the mother's familiarity with the minutiae of Rachel's life.

Comprehension of children's early speech is also aided by their tendency to talk about their ongoing activities. The contextual information helps the listener understand what the child intended in his or her fragmentary or distorted utterance. For instance, sitting at the breakfast table Rachel called out *momee*. Because she was looking in the direction of the egg plate, this utterance was interpreted as meaning *more me* ('give me some more egg'). In another context the same utterance might have meant 'mommy' or 'money'.

It seems reasonable to assume that parental comprehension of children's speech plays a role in facilitating linguistic progress. Parents who are responsive to their children's utterances encourage them to talk and to communicate linguistically. It is clear, however, that even the best intentioned parents do not understand everything their child says. Such occasional failures, when they come on the background of positive attitudes and generally successful communication, may in fact have a beneficial effect by forcing on the child a realization of the needs of the listener. We encounter examples demonstrating this point in a later subsection on dialogue. But a few examples can be given right here from the records of Rachel's speech when she was 21 months old:

1. Rachel asked for a pretzel and was given one. After a short while, she called out *two*. When there was no reaction, Rachel amplified her request with, *I want two/I want two*.
2. On another occasion Rachel said *more* after salt was sprinkled on her egg. When no action resulted, she added, *more salt*.
3. Rachel, sitting at the breakfast table, observed that her sister, who was not in the room, left milk in her cup. She called out, *drink your milk*, and seeing that her call did not bring her sister to the table, added, *come and drink your milk, Miriam*.

In all three cases Rachel expanded and clarified her initial utterances when she was not responded to or not understood.

The message of this subsection is simple and common-sensical. Progress in the mastery of syntax, and of language in general, is facilitated by the high contextual redundancy in which mother-child communication normally takes place, by the sharing of daily experiences, and by a mutual desire to understand and to be understood.

Imitation

In the previous subsection I discussed the phenomenon of expansion, which is essentially a form of imitation (plus correction) of children by parents. Children, of course, also imitate their parents, and the value of this imitation to language development has received considerable attention in the literature (see Snow,

1981). I now discuss one of the studies in this area to highlight some of the issues involved.

Bloom, Hood, and Lightbown (1974) analyzed the imitations of six children who at the beginning of the study were between the ages of 1;4(21) and 2;1(0). The children were followed for 1½ to 5½ months. At the beginning of the observations their MLUs were close to 1 (i.e., they spoke mainly in single-word utterances); at the end their MLUs were close to 2 (i.e., they already had considerable syntactic speech).

Bloom et al. defined imitation as a repetition of the model's utterance that was separated from it by no more than five child utterances. In fact, most of the imitations studied turned out to be immediate repetitions. The clearest finding was that the children differed in their tendency to imitate. Two children imitated very little; at most observation points less than 10% of their utterances were imitations. For another child imitations ranged from 15%-17%. For the remaining three children imitations exceeded 27% at virtually all points.

There was, however, no correlation between the tendency to imitate and syntactic development. The children who imitated less were as advanced syntactically (in terms of their MLUs) as those who imitated more. These results suggest that imitation is not necessary for the acquisition of syntax and are consistent with the conclusion of Ervin (1964) who stated categorically: "There is not a shred of evidence supporting a view that progress toward adult norms of grammar arises merely from practice in overt imitation of adult sentences" (p. 172). Bloom et al. themselves concluded that for some of the children imitation served as an aid in the acquisition of syntax. But the evidence they based this conclusion on is very tentative.

The preceding discussion was concerned with children's spontaneous imitations. There is also directed imitation, which is initiated by parents. Western parents use directed imitation primarily to instruct their children in the correct pronunciation of words (e.g., "Can you say _____ ?") and to instill in them proper manners (e.g., "Say 'thank you' ").

In a study in Papua, New Guinea, in 1975-1977, Schieffelin (1979) found that the Kaluli people (population: 1200) have institutionalized directed imitation and use it broadly for the purpose of linguistic socialization of their children. The Kaluli have a term, *elema*, that they append to an utterance addressed to a child to have the child repeat it to the speaker or say it to another person. *Elema* means 'say like this/that'. Through observation of three Kaluli children in their third year, Schieffelin found that Kaluli caregivers used *elema* mainly to teach children how to interact verbally with others; for example, how to make requests and how to obtain information. Here are a couple of instances:

1. Wanu, 2;2(21), offered a flashlight to his mother saying, *mother/over there*. The mother corrected him saying, "You take, *elema*." Wanu re-

peated, saying *you take it*. Now that Wanu stated the request in the normative form, his mother accepted the flashlight from him.

2. Wanu, 2;2(21), dropped a pentop and couldn't find it. The mother directed
   him to ask an older cousin to give it to him. She said, "give that, *elema*."
   Wanu obeyed and said to his cousin, *give that*.

I have introduced *elema* as an imitation-based method of linguistic socialization. But it must be pointed out that the relative effectiveness of this method in
comparison with other methods of linguistic socialization is not known.

Dialogue

In this subsection I examine the information available in mother-child dialogue
for enhancing the development of syntax and other aspects of language. I must
emphasize at the outset that I am trying to determine the potential there is in
dialogue for learning syntax. It is not known to what extent children actually
make use of the opportunities provided by dialogue.

Table 7.8 brings together examples of dialogue. In items 1 and 2 in the table
Matthew first utters a single word, and because it is a single word, its intent is
ambiguous. The mother offers a possible interpretation in the form of a question,
asking, in effect, whether her interpretation is correct or not. Matthew then responds, confirming the mother's interpretation in 1 and offering a different one in
2. Such interchanges have the potential of bringing to children's attention the
need for fuller (i.e., sentential) expression of their intentions.

In more advanced dialogues one can see how the child benefits from parental
reactions right then and there. In items 3-5 we see how Nigel alters his initial
utterances to take account of parental queries. In 3 he expands an initial object
phrase into a full sentence as a consequence of a question by his father. In 4 the
mother's response tells Nigel that the word *table* by itself leads to misunderstanding and he supplies a modifier. In 5 a parent's questions lead Nigel to elaborate
his initial utterances and, indeed, to compose an entire story.

In the first two examples of Rachel's dialogue in Table 7.8 we see how failure
of parental understanding (in 6) and parental misunderstanding (in 7) induce her
to clarify her initial utterances. In 8 Rachel is the one who misunderstands her
mother, because she had a restricted sense of *change*. The mother's clarification
may have alerted Rachel to this problem and provided the basis for derestricting
the meaning of *change*. In 9 we see how Rachel takes advantage of her father's
suggestion and corrects her initial utterance, in fact, improving on the father's
expression.

Through conversations with others, children learn not only about the subtle-
ties of language and the usefulness of speaking in full sentences, but also about
the external world. Item 10 is an example showing how Rachel learned that

TABLE 7.8

Examples of Early Dialogue

Child's Utterance, Other Behavior, Interpretation, and Age	Parental Utterance
Matthew	
1. After blowing out match, says *Again*. *Yeah*, 1;7(21). (p. 155)	You want to blow it again?
2. Uttered *Gone*. *Birdie*, referring to a pet canary who died that day, 1;6(3). (p. 110)	Are the people gone?
Nigel, 1;7(14)-1;9	
3. *Big noise.* *Drill make big noise.* (p. 99)	Who made a big noise?
4. *Put bemax down on table.* *Nila table.* (Nila table = Nigel table, i.e., 'my table') (p. 97)	It is on the table.
5. Returning home from visit to zoo, reports: *Try eat lid.*	What tried to eat the lid?
Goat . . . man said no . . . goat try eat lid . . . man said no. Later in the day said spontaneously: *Goat try eat lid . . . man said no.*	
Goat shouldn't eat lid . . . (shaking head to gesture *not*) *good for it.*	Why did the man say no?
Goat try eat lid . . . man said no . . . goat shouldn't eat lid . . . (shaking head) *good for it.* (p. 112)	The goat shouldn't eat the lid; it is not good for it.
Rachel	
6. *Shimi doesn't want to.* *Get chair. Shimi doesn't want to get chair,* 1;9(23).	What?
7. *Money . . . money.* *Take off mitten.* (It turned out that Rachel intended to make the observation that she had pennies stuck in her mitten.), 1;9(23).	I am not giving you any money.
8. *I not have BM,* 2;1(26).	I'm going upstairs to get changed. I am not going to change you; I am going to change my shirt.
9. *Jeffrey came home.* *Jeffrey came to my house,* 2;1(26).	Jeffrey came to our home.
10. Looking out the window on a March day, said *It snowing.* *I think raining.* Pointing to window, responded *What this?* 2;0(28).	No. No. Steam on the window.

Note: Matthew's dialogues are from Greenfield and Smith (1976). Nigel's dialogues are from Halliday (1975). Page numbers in parentheses refer to these sources. Rachel's dialogues are our own observations.

180

things aren't always what they appear to be. In this case she demonstrated an ability to change her judgment as a result of negative feedback (''no'') and to express it more cautiously (*I think*).

Halliday (1975, pp. 48-51) has emphasized that dialogue helps children learn to appreciate the social nature of language. They learn to function in different and changing linguistic roles, including the roles of speaker and listener, questioner and respondent, requester and complier, and so forth. The different roles require different structurings of information and different linguistic expressions. Dialogue thus provides an effective way to learn about the structure of language and its uses in communication.

HOW SYNTAX IS ACQUIRED

Syntactic speech is part and parcel of propositional thought and higher intelligence. In an attempt to understand the emergence and development of syntax, I examined three topics in this chapter: the cognitive processes involved in sentence construction, the unique patterns of speech occurring at the beginning of syntax, and the characteristics of parent-child verbal interaction.

Sentence construction entails semantic integration, syntactic integration, and coordination between the two. The simultaneous engagement in these three levels of processing may be too taxing for young children. We have seen that children are not prevented by this difficulty from producing propositional ideas. When not able to integrate syntactically words that are semantically interrelated, children utter them as a word sequence. In complementary fashion children use meaningless forms in practicing syntactic patterns to eliminate the semantic load.

The interactional speech between children and mothers was also examined to discover what it might contribute to syntactic development. Imitation and dialogue provide opportunities for learning about language and communication. But it is not known to what extent and how children utilize these modes of interaction.

The characteristics of maternal speech were also studied. It was found that mothers speak to children in short, clearly intelligible sentences, and most importantly, they talk to them on familiar here-and-now matters that children are interested in and can readily understand with only slight dependence on the linguistic message. Mothers' understanding of children's speech is facilitated by similar factors. Even though children's speech is phonetically distorted and semantically ambiguous, mothers are able to understand it because it relates to the children's momentary activities and interests and because mothers know their children's preoccupations and ''dialects.''

The discussion in the present chapter and in previous chapters makes one point abundantly clear, namely, that children take the initiative in the process of language learning. They invent learning strategies, adopt compensatory practices, detect regularities, and formulate rules. In a word, children do not absorb language; they construct it. But we do not know much about how they do it.

In school learning it is normally the case that the more advanced the subject matter, the more demanding are the procedures for its acquisition. That is why one wonders how it is that something as complex as syntax is acquired so rapidly with no designed instruction. Chomsky (1965, 1975) has forcefully formulated and sharpened this question. Looking beyond the initial stage of syntactic development Chomsky stressed that the syntactic knowledge that human beings ultimately possess contains certain universal characteristics that could not have been induced by processes of generalization from linguistic information available to language learners.

To account for how syntax is nevertheless acquired Chomsky has proposed the nativist hypothesis, which claims that children bring to the task of language learning a priori notions concerning its structure. Children, according to Chomsky, are not only able to induce linguistic regularities, such as word order patterns, but they are inclined to formulate these regularities in particular ways. In his view children do not have to discover empirically that language consists of sounds, words, and sentences and that it is organized by grammatical transformations that are structure dependent. They "know" all of this and much more as an innate given. Chomsky does not deny, of course, that exposure to language under the appropriate conditions is necessary for language development, but he feels that linguistic exposure is needed only to determine specific details (i.e., what particular sounds, words, and sentence types the language has), not its general design, which is common to all languages and is genetically prescribed. Chomsky naturally also recognizes the existence of individual differences in linguistic competence, and these he would attribute to biological variation and environmental influences. But he is more impressed by the fact that all normal members of the human species acquire the intricate system of language "on relatively slight exposure and without specific training" (Chomsky, 1975, p. 4) than by individual variability in linguistic skill.

Chomsky views language as a mental organ not very different from the physical organs of the body. The form of language, like the forms of the hands and eyes, is biologically determined. Social and linguistic experiences, like nourishment and exercise for the hands and eyes, have an effect on the language that develops but do not determine its essential character. Language resembles physical organs in yet another way. Just as an individual's knowledge and understanding of the anatomy and physiology of a particular organ is not relevant to its healthy functioning, so in language, especially in the domains of syntax and phonology, conscious knowledge of the concepts and rules is not necessary for proper functioning. Unless they are students of linguistics, most adults have little awareness of the principles of syntax. They are nevertheless guided by them.

With respect to children in the beginning stages of syntax, we saw in the previous chapter that they have to be granted at least implicit knowledge of such concepts as actor, action, and object, and of rules for their combination. Explicit conscious understanding of such concepts and rules could hardly be expected even in the early school grades. Implicit use of syntactic rules is thus independent of the capacity to grasp them on the conscious level. The separation of implicit use from conscious knowledge does not hold for all cognitive domains. Thus, it seems that one could not advance very far in the use of arithmetic operations without some explicit knowledge of what is involved. The separation of implicit use from explicit knowledge that occurs for the grammatical aspects of language is consistent with the idea of language as a biological organ.

Chomsky's nativist hypothesis has evolved over the years. Initially, his nativist hypothesis (Chomsky, 1965) encompassed all aspects of language. However, in a recent book Chomsky (1980c) adopts a "modular" approach, distinguishing among different modules or components of language in his application of the nativist hypothesis. He now restricts his nativist hypothesis to the grammatical or "computational" aspects of language (i.e., to aspects of language that are governed by internal, sophisticated rules). The computational domains of language include primarily syntax and phonology and are distinguished from the domain of reference and meaning, in which the innate basis is not as profound. This distinction makes intuitive sense. As we have seen in the previous two chapters, the classes involved in sentence construction are rather subtle and abstract. In contrast, I argued in Chapter 4 that the referential classes that children operate with are conceptually quite primitive. This kind of difference would be accounted for by Chomsky's assumption that the domain of syntax is more thoroughly structured by innate factors than is the domain of meaning.

Taking an approach related to Chomsky's modular position, Curtiss (1981) has argued that syntax and semantics draw on independent abilities. She based her argument on cases where there is a strikingly uneven development of syntactic competence on one hand and semantic-cognitive competence on the other. In particular, Curtiss draws attention to the observation that mentally retarded individuals, who by definition achieve low-level facility in the semantic-cognitive domain, achieve fairly high facility in the syntactic domain.

Curtiss cites the case of Marta, who, when tested at 16, had an IQ of 44. Marta had difficulty attending to cognitive tasks, performing at the level of sensorimotor Stage 6 (i.e., at the level reached by normal children at about 18 months). By contrast, Curtiss (1981) reports that Marta's: "syntactic and morphological abilities are richly developed. . . . she easily performs sentence-repetition tasks, correcting minor phonological, syntactic, and morphological errors presented to her" (pp. 24-25). Her sentences were well formed but often confusing or meaningless. For instance, to the question, "How many nights did you stay there?" she replied, *Oh, about four out of one*. Perfectly grammatical, but semantically anomalous!

This profile of abilities contrasts with that developed by a severely abused and deprived girl referred to as Genie (Curtiss, 1977). Genie was isolated by her parents in a bare, dark room from the age of 20 months to 13 years. Her movements were restricted, and she was exposed to very little speech. After her discovery she was given an intensive training program. At the age of 20 Genie reached the concrete operational stage in a variety of tasks. (The concrete operational stage is normally reached at the age of 7-8.) Genie's vocabulary was large and sophisticated. But some of the formal aspects of her syntax were on the level of a 2-year-old. Although her sentences were fairly long and rich in meaning, they were primitive in structure, exhibiting low-level "telegraphese." Genie produced, for instance, such sentences as: *I like hear music ice cream truck* and *think about Mama love Genie.* Curtiss (1981) concluded the comparison between Genie and Marta with the following statement:

> Marta's profile contrasts . . . sharply with Genie's. . . . Marta's speech is fluent, abundant, and richly structured; Genie's speech is belabored and agrammatic. Marta's speech is usually inappropriate and confusing both in and out of context. Genie's speech is always appropriate and usually clear in meaning in and out of context. Marta has severe attentional and conceptual deficits, causing her to perform poorly or fail to grasp almost all tasks. Genie has far superior attentional and conceptual abilities enabling her to perform most tasks easily and well. (pp. 25-26)

The dissociation between the development of syntactic and semantic knowledge found in cases such as Genie and Marta supports the modular view of language acquisition.

As you may have gathered from the discussion in this chapter and in Chapter 6, I side with Chomsky in assuming that the learning of syntax is guided by prior constraints on the structure of sentences. On the other hand, I have also proposed a Piagetian assimilation-accommodation approach to the learning of syntax. Despite the appearance of opposition between these two approaches (see Piattelli-Palmarini, 1980), I see them as perfectly compatible. The differences that appear between Chomsky and Piaget are due to their very different foci of investigation and are not, in my view, inherent in their theories.

Chomsky focused his studies on the inherent nature of language and uncovered deep universal principles of organization. The depth and complexity of linguistic rules and their structural similarity across languages led Chomsky to the conclusion that an organism not preprogrammed with some general principles of organization could not acquire human language. Piaget, on the other hand, focused his work on a detailed analysis of the development of human knowledge. He was impressed by its slow, gradual growth, and formulated principles of learning to account for it.

Although unconcerned about learning processes, Chomsky could not deny that specific sentential patterns are learned and that the processes of learning language may not be different from the learning processes in other domains of human knowledge. Piaget, on the other hand, would have readily acknowledged that the acquisition of language, as the acquisition of other aspects of knowledge, is guided by genetic constraints. After all, the sensorimotor schemes and the logical structures that children develop are uniquely human. A domestic animal and a child exposed to the same environment will learn through the same processes of assimilation-accommodation, but what they will acquire will be vastly different.

The only real disagreement between Piaget and Chomsky concerns the question of whether the underlying constraints are specific to language—or even only to some aspects of it, on the modular view—or constitute a special case of more general, higher order cognitive constraints. Chomsky (1980a, 1980b, 1980c) now advocates the former view, whereas Piaget (1980) leans to the latter view. Although Chomsky's position seems to me to have considerable merit, it seems prudent to keep an open mind on the issue until we know more about both language and cognition. Chomsky (1965) himself had earlier advocated such a course: "It is an important problem for psychology to determine to what extent other aspects of cognition share properties of language acquisition and language use, and to attempt, in this way, to develop a richer and more comprehensive theory of mind" (p. 207).

In conclusion, there is little doubt that the predisposition for the acquisition of syntax includes constraints on what will ultimately be learned. That much is indicated by the fact that all normal children acquire language with relative ease and end up with similar products. But at present we do not know much about the specific nature of these constraints.

III

THE DEVELOPMENT OF
SPEECH AND MORPHOLOGY

8 The Nature of Speech

In Part I of the book I traced the child's acquisition of the capacity to use words in a referential-symbolic way in conformity with societal usages. In Part II I examined the child's acquisition of the next level of linguistic symbolism: syntax. In this part I analyze a still more advanced aspect of language, morphology (e.g., the use of the plural and the past tense). I also trace in this part the development of the capacity to perceive and to articulate the sounds of speech.

This part has three chapters. The present chapter describes the nature of speech and its functioning in mature speakers. Chapter 9 deals with the acquisition of morphology, and Chapter 10 analyzes the acquisition of speech.

Speech consists of a sequence of sound segments arranged to form syllables, words, phrases, and sentences. The prosodic integration of words into phrases and sentences was discussed in Chapter 5. Here I concentrate on the analysis of segments and their integration into syllables and words.

THE SEGMENTS OF SPEECH

The sounds of speech are characteristically produced in the expiratory part of the breathing cycle. Events occurring during the passage of the air from the lungs to the outside account for the differences among sounds. This section explains how the different sound segments are produced.

Phoneticians, the specialists studying the sounds of speech, have developed symbols to identify the various sound segments found in human languages. The phonetic notation uses the letters of the Roman alphabet with supplementation as necessary. To mark letters as representing sounds, they are enclosed either in slashes / / or brackets [ ]. The difference between the two is explained later.

TABLE 8.1
Phonetic Symbols

Consonants		Vowels	
symbol	example	symbol	example
p	*p*it, *sp*it	i	h*e*, m*ea*t
b	*b*it, ta*b*	I	b*i*d, s*i*t
m	*m*itt, s*m*all	e	b*ai*t, *eigh*t
t	*t*ip, s*t*ill	ɛ	b*e*t, *e*xact
d	*d*ip, ri*d*e	æ	b*a*d, b*a*t
n	*n*ip, pi*n*	u	wh*o*, b*oo*t
k	*k*in, s*ch*ool	U	p*u*t, f*oo*t
g	*g*ive, bi*g*	ʌ	b*u*t, *u*tter
ŋ	si*ng*, thi*n*k	ə	*a*bout, *e*nemy
f	*f*it, rou*gh*	o	b*oa*t, g*o*
v	*v*at, di*v*e	ɔ	b*ough*t, s*aw*
s	*s*it, p*s*ychology	a	p*o*t, f*a*ther
z	*z*ip, rou*s*e	:	Following a vowel indicates
θ	*th*igh, e*th*er		lengthening of the vowel,
ð	*th*y, ei*th*er		compare, for example, [bæ:d]
š	*sh*ip, ra*ti*o		(*bad*) and [bæt] (*bat*).
ž	plea*s*ure, vi*si*on	*Liquids and Semivowels*	
č	*ch*ip, ri*ch*		
ǰ	*j*oy, *g*yp	l	*l*id, fi*ll*
		r	*r*ip, ca*r*
		y	*y*es, bu*y*
		w	*w*e, q*u*ick
		h	*h*igh, w*h*o

You may get acquainted with the phonetic notation by examining the symbols for English sounds given in Table 8.1.

The fundamental distinction in all languages is between **vowels** and **consonants**. Vowels are produced by allowing the airstream to pass in a relatively uninhibited fashion. In the case of consonants greater obstruction is put in the way of the airstream. In addition to vowels and consonants there are sounds that cannot be clearly classified as belonging to either category. Included in this borderline group are **liquids** (i.e., /l/ and /r/) and **semivowels** or **glides** (i.e., /y/, /w/, and /h/). In what follows I first describe vowels in a general way and then turn to a more detailed discussion of consonants, because consonants more clearly reveal the nature of human speech.

Vowels

As has been noted, vowels are produced in the course of free expulsion of air. The differences among vowels are determined primarily by the position of the tongue in the mouth during expulsion. The vowel is the nucleus of the syllable and the carrier of pitch and inflection. It can be readily manipulated: lengthened, shortened, clipped, drawled, and so forth. It is for this reason that dialectal and individual differences in speech are especially evident in vowels. Indeed, as Bronstein (1960) wrote: "The vowel is the voice of language" (p. 133). Vowels blend into one another, and their boundaries are not as distinct as the boundaries of consonants (Ladefoged, 1982, p. 72). I want to draw your attention to one particular vowel, the **schwa**, /ə/. The schwa is the most common vowel of unstressed syllables in English (e.g., the *o* and the *a* in *inconceivable* are pronounced as schwas). Articles, prepositions, and other "little" words (e.g., *a, the, but, can*) are typically enunciated with a schwa in fluent sentential speech, unless they are stressed. Other vowels are reduced to schwa when stress shifts away from them. Thus, in "comp*e*te" the italicized letter is enunciated as /i/, but in "comp*e*tition" the same letter becomes an /ə/. In the alternation an*a*lysis-an*a*lytic an /æ/ changes to /ə/, and in the alternation s*o*lid-s*o*lidify an /a/ changes to /ə/.

Consonants

Consonants differ from one another in terms of three characteristics: place of articulation, manner of articulation, and voicing. These three aspects of articulation are discussed in turn in the three subsections that follow. Table 8.2 provides an analysis of the English consonants in terms of these articulatory characteristics. Please refer to this table and to Figure 8.1, which depicts the vocal organs, as you read along.

TABLE 8.2
Classification of English Consonants

Manner of Articulation	Place of Articulation					
	Bilabial	Labiodental	Dental	Alveolar	Palatal	Velar
Stops	p b			t d		k g
Fricatives		f v	θ ð	s z	š ž	
Affricates					č ǰ	
Nasals	m			n		ŋ

Definition of the Places of Articulation

Bilabial: Articulated by bringing the two lips together.
Labiodental: Articulated by bringing the lower lip against the upper teeth.
Dental: Articulated by placing the tip of the tongue against the upper teeth.
Alveolar: Articulated by bringing the tip of the tongue against the alveolar ridge.
Palatal: Articulated by bringing the front of the tongue against the hard palate.
Velar: Articulated by bringing the back of the tongue against the velum, or soft palate.

Note: Under each heading the entry on the left is voiceless, on the right voiced.

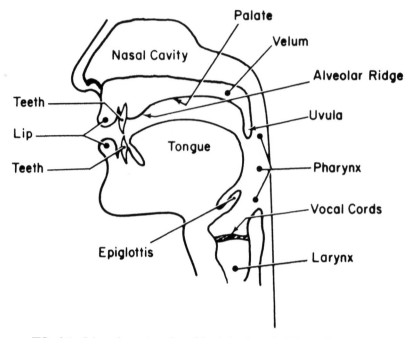

FIG. 8.1   Schematic cross section of head showing principle speech organs.

Place of Articulation   The primary obstruction to the free flow of the airstream can occur in different places in the oral cavity, resulting in different consonants. You can get a sense of differences in place of articulation by attending to your production of /p/, /f/, /θ/, /s/, /š/, and /k/. Each successive sound is produced by an obstruction farther back in the oral cavity. To produce /p/ the two lips are brought together. In the production of /f/ the obstruction is created by moving the lower lip toward the upper teeth. Behind the /f/ is the /θ/, which is articulated by bringing the tip of the tongue toward the upper teeth. Next in the direction to the back of the mouth is the /s/. It is produced by moving the tip of the tongue toward the alveolar ridge. Next comes the /š/, for which the front of the tongue moves toward the hard palate. Still farther back is the /k/, in the production of which the back of the tongue makes contact with the velum.

Manner of Articulation   Another aspect of articulation that determines what sound is going to be produced is the type of passage afforded to the airstream. Manner of articulation divides consonants into two broad classes: **stops** and **fricatives**. In the production of stops (e.g., /p/ and /t/) the airflow is brought to a complete halt by total closure at the point of articulation. The air is then released abruptly. By contrast, in the production of fricatives (e.g., /f/ and /s/) the blockage is such that air is allowed to flow out continuously through the constricted passage. A third class of consonants, the **affricates** (i.e., /č/ and /ǰ/), combines characteristics of stops and fricatives. The production begins with a complete closure as in stops but is then followed by a gradual expulsion as in fricatives. In fact, each of the two affricates can be thought of as a stop plus a fricative, /č/ = /t/ + /š/ and /ǰ/ = /d/ + /ž/.

In the production of stops, fricatives, and affricates, the air is released solely through the mouth, because the speaker blocks the passage to the nasal cavity by raising the velum. When the speaker lowers the velum, air can pass through both the mouth and the nose. In this case the sounds produced are **nasal**. There are three nasal consonants in English: /m/, /n/, and /ŋ/.

Voicing There is a third aspect of articulation that contributes to distinguishing consonants from one another, namely, voicing. Some consonants are indistinguishable with respect to place and manner of articulation but differ with respect to voicing. When the vocal cords are close together as the air passes through them in the production of a sound, they vibrate, giving the sound a **voiced** quality. When the vocal cords are apart, they do not vibrate, and the sound has a **voiceless** quality. Thus, for instance, both /s/ and /z/ are alveolar fricatives. They differ only in regard to voicing, with /s/ being voiceless and /z/ voiced. You should be able to hear the difference clearly by saying *ssss* and *zzzz*.

Lisker and Abramson (1964, 1967) developed a quantitative measure of voicing for stops occurring in the initial position in words. What they measured was **voice onset time (VOT)**, which is defined as the time between the release of the closure and the beginning of vocal cord vibration. Lisker and Abramson found that VOT was shorter for voiced stops than for voiceless stops. Thus, in a study of the VOT characteristics of some 400 words spoken in isolation by four speakers of English, they found that the average VOT for the voiceless /p/ was 58 milliseconds (msec),whereas the VOT for its voiced counterpart /b/ was bimodally distributed at much lower levels. It is to be noted that Lisker and Abramson (1967) found that the differences between voiced and voiceless stops were less sharp in running speech. Lisker and Abramson also found that the magnitudes of VOT depended on what sounds followed the stop and whether it was in a stressed or unstressed syllable. Subsequent research substantiated the original findings of Lisker and Abramson and added additional factors to the list of those that determine the magnitude of VOT (see, e.g., Menyuk & Klatt, 1975). In all follow-up investigations the basic finding that voiced stops have shorter VOTs than voiceless stops held up consistently. Generalizing broadly, one could say that VOTs of 30 msec or less are associated with voiced stops and VOTs of more than that with voiceless stops.

So far I have discussed the use of VOT to distinguish voiced from voiceless sounds. There is a language, Kikuyu, spoken in Kenya, that distinguishes prevoiced from voiced sounds, instead of voiced from voiceless sounds (Streeter,

1976). A prevoiced sound is one in which vocal cord vibration precedes the release of air, and it is noted by a negative VOT value.

Distinctive Features

In recent years the distinctive-features approach to the analysis of sounds has gained prevalence. This analysis is not fundamentally different from the analysis by place of articulation, manner of articulation, and voicing, which I have just outlined, but it is more formal and stresses more explicitly the notion that sound segments are not unitary entities, but rather composites of independent characteristics. In the distinctive-features framework a sound segment is defined as a bundle of simultaneously occurring distinctive features (Jakobson, Fant, & Halle, 1963, p. 3). The distinctive-features approach has been influential in developmentally relevant research, and it is therefore important for us to take note of it. Table 8.3 presents a distinctive-features characterization of English consonants. The consonants are marked in the table as having a positive or negative value on each feature.

TABLE 8.3
Distinctive Feature Composition of English Consonants

	p	b	f	v	m	t	d	θ	ð	n	s	z	č	ǰ	š	ž	k	g	ŋ
Anterior	+	+	+	+	+	+	+	+	+	+	+	+	−	−	−	−	−	−	−
Coronal	−	−	−	−	−	+	+	+	+	+	+	+	+	+	+	+	−	−	−
Voice	−	+	−	+	+	−	+	−	+	+	−	+	−	+	−	+	−	+	+
Continuant	−	−	+	+	−	−	−	+	+	−	+	+	−	−	+	+	−	−	−
Nasal	−	−	−	−	+	−	−	−	−	+	−	−	−	−	−	−	−	−	+
Strident	−	−	+	+	−	−	−	−	−	−	+	+	+	+	+	+	−	−	−

Characterization of features

Anterior: Sound articulated at or forward of the alveolar ridge (+) or back of it (−).
Coronal: Sound articulated at the center of the mouth (+) or at the periphery (−).
Voice: Vocal cords vibrate (+) or do not vibrate (−) during articulation of sound.
Continuant: Sound produced with uninterrupted (+) or interrupted (−) expiration of the airstream
   through the oral cavity.
Nasal: Articulation characterized by the release of the airstream, wholly or partly, through the nasal
   cavity (+) or only through the oral cavity (−).
Strident: Articulation characterized by relatively greater (+) or lesser (−) noisiness.

Note: The information presented here is based on Chomsky and Halle (1968, particularly pp. 176-177, 293-329). I have included only the major features relevant to describing English consonants.

PHONETIC AND PHONOLOGICAL ANALYSES

In my analysis of sounds in the preceding section, the emphasis was on aspects of articulation that are distinctive (i.e., that help distinguish one word from another). But speech sounds also have nondistinctive characteristics. For instance, in English there is a difference in articulation between the /p/ in *pin* and the /p/ in *spin* and between the /k/ in *kin* and and the /k/ in *skin*. But this difference is not used in English to distinguish words from one another; it is nondistinctive. However, there are languages (e.g., Thai) in which the difference is distinctive (see Ladefoged, 1982, pp. 130-134).

Another example of differences between languages in what is distinctive and nondistinctive concerns [r] and [l] (Jakobson, 1978, p. 31). In English the two constitute different sounds that can be used to distinguish one word from another (e.g., *ray* and *lay*). In Korean, however, the two belong to a single sound category, whose articulation is conditioned by its position in the word. It is articulated as *l* in initial position and as *r* in final position. This accounts for such mispronunciations by Koreans learning English as *lound* for *round*, *ser* for *sell*, and *lure* for *rule*.

An analysis of speech sounds that takes into account their distinctive (i.e., phonemic) roles in a particular language is called a **phonological analysis**, and the sound segments identified in this kind of analysis are called **phonemes**. An analysis that takes into account nondistinctive (i.e., nonphonemic) details as well is called a **phonetic analysis**, and the sound segments identified in this kind of analysis are called **phones**. Phonemes are enclosed in / / and phones in [ ]. The different phonetic variants of a phoneme are its **allophones**. Thus, for instance, in Korean [r] and [l] are allophones of a single phoneme. A phonetic transcription can be carried out by a trained phonetician without reference to the sound system of the particular language being transcribed. A phonological transcription, on the other hand, seeks to identify individual sounds in terms of the unique framework of the language being studied.

SPEECH AS A SYSTEM OF RELATIONS

Linguists hold firmly to the view that on the phonological level the identity of speech units is defined as much by their relations to one another as by their physical characteristics. As Hockett (1958) put it:

> The phonological system of language is . . . not so much "a set of sounds" as it is a *network of differences between sounds*. In this frame of reference, the elements of a phonological system cannot be defined positively in terms of what they "are," but only negatively in terms of what they are *not*, what they *contrast* with. While it

is true, and not irrelevant, that English *p* is a "voiceless bilabial stop," it is much more important that *p* is *different* from certain other elements. (pp. 24-25)

One of the earliest and most articulate exponents of phonology as a functional-psychological system was Edward Sapir. In his first article on the topic, Sapir (1925/1957) emphasized that the sounds of language form a self-contained system and that they can be defined only in relation to one another. It follows from the conception of speech as a system of relations that two individuals may differ in the absolute values of their sounds, but they will be speaking the same language, if they maintain the same patterns of relations. As a concrete example Sapir considers the articulation of the fricatives /θ/, /s/, and /š/. As we saw earlier, they differ in that each successive sound is produced farther back in the mouth. Sapir suggests that the /š/ of individual B may actually correspond in place of articulation to individual A's /s/, as in the display that follows, but it will be perceived as a /š/ because in B's articulation it is articulated farther back than /s/.

A:	θ		s	š
B:	θ	s	š	

The absolute points of articulation of particular sounds are not as important—within limits—as the relations among them.

Sapir further suggested that the perceived similarity between sounds is determined just as much by their similarity in linguistic functioning as by their articulatory or acoustic similarity. He indicated that in English the phonemes in the pairs /s/-/z/ and /θ/-/ð/ are felt to be closer to one another than the phonemes in the pairs /p/-/b/ or /k/-/g/, although in all four pairs the objective difference is similar (i.e., the first item is voiceless and the second voiced). Sapir based this suggestion on the fact that the phonemes in the first two pairs are functionally closer to one another than in the second two pairs. Thus, /θ/ changes to /ð/ when a noun changes to a verb, as in the pronunciation of the *th* in the pairs *breath-to breathe, mouth-to mouth*. There is an even closer functional relation between /s/ and /z/. Not only do they alternate in the noun-verb conversion (e.g., *house-to house)* but they also alternate as plural markers. Note the pronunciation of the final letter *s* in *caps, fats,* and *backs* versus its pronunciation in *cabs, fads,* and *bags.* Following the voiceless /p/, /t/, and /k/ the letter *s* is rendered /s/, but following the voiced /b/, /d/, and /g/ it is rendered /z/.

Sapir's views concerning the importance of functional relations in the subjective similarity between sounds were apparently based on personal intuitions. There is now, however, empirical evidence in support of his position. Research was conducted (Anisfeld & Gordon, 1968) in which first-, second-, and fourth-grade children, and college students were given artificial singular nouns and were requested to choose between two alternative plurals, neither of which contained the correct plural ending, which in all cases was /z/. For instance, subjects were offered the singular *dar* and asked to choose between *darb* and *darch*, or between *darb* and *darth* as a plural.

Of the sounds offered for comparison, the subjects showed a clear preference for sounds that shared with the plural marker /z/ (as well as with /s/) either the feature +strident (i.e., /č/ and /ǰ/), +continuant (i.e., /θ/), or both (i.e., /f/, /v/, and /š/). (For instance, subjects tended to choose *darch* over *darb* as a plural for *dar*.) These two features are critical in the identification of the plural markers, because they distinguish them from the other major inflection in English, past tense, which is served by /t/ and /d/. As can be seen in Table 8.3, /s/ and /z/ differ from /t/ and /d/ only with respect to the features strident and continuant. Thus, it appears that when they had to identify sounds most similar to /z/, the subjects selected those that shared with it features that distinguish it from other sounds that perform an analogous (i.e., inflectional) function. They did not choose on the basis of the number of features separating the substitute sounds from /z/. Thus, for instance, both /č/ and /b/ differ from /z/ in three features. But the subjects preferred /č/ words (e.g., *darch*) over /b/ words (e.g., *darb*), because /č/ shares with /z/ the feature +strident. What mattered was the functional weight of the features, not their number.

The functional similarity between any two sounds is, of course, language specific. For instance, although /s/ and /z/ alternate in English, they do not in Hebrew. On the other hand, there are alternations in Hebrew that do not occur in English. Thus, /b/-/v/ and /p/-/f/ alternate in Hebrew (e.g., *beit hasefer* = the school, l'*v*eit hasefer = to the school; *p*i = my mouth, b'*f*i = in my mouth), but not in English. An informal experiment I conducted suggests that individuals take functional relations into account when judging the similarity of sounds. Thus, for instance, English-Hebrew bilinguals considered /b/ to be more similar to /p/ than to /v/ in English, but more similar to /v/ than to /p/ in Hebrew.

Sapir (1933/1951) further emphasized that the perception of individual words is influenced by their relation to other words in the language. To make this point Sapir relates the following anecdote. When he was working on the Indian language Sarcee in Alberta, Canada, his informant insisted that the two words *dini* ('this one') and *dini* ('it makes sound'), which to the phonetically skilled investigator sounded like homonyms, were actually different. However, the informant could not pinpoint the difference. After some probing he said that the second *dini* sounded like it had /t/ at the end. He admitted, however, that listening carefully to the word, he himself could not hear a /t/. It turned out that although the second *dini* did not have a /t/ in its root form, it did have /t/ when a vowel suffix was added to it. Thus, when /i/ ('the one who') is added to *dini*, the form becomes *diniti* ('the one who makes sound'). The other *dini* ('this one') is not altered in this way under suffixation. It thus appears that although there was actually no /t/ in the form given to the informant, he heard a /t/, because there was a /t/ in his internal representation of the word.

Sapir's point is that in listening to speech people do not respond to each word in its own terms, but take into account the place of the word in relation to other words. Experimental support for Sapir's position can be found in a study (Anisfeld, 1969) in which college students were given made-up verbs and asked to indicate for each one which of two derived adjectival forms offered them was more appropriate. The verbs ended either in /t/ (e.g., *yermit*) or in /d/ (e.g., *garlude*). According to English adjectivization rules the proper adjectives for these verbs would be *yermissive* and *garlusive* on the pattern of English verbs of similar form (e.g., *permit-permissive* and *intrude-intrusive*, respectively). The process of converting verbs of this form into adjectives involves changing the /t/ or /d/ to an /s/ and appending to it the adjectival marker /iv/. Both the /t/ verbs and the /d/ verbs thus have the same final form when they are converted into adjectives. However, because it originates in the voiced /d/, the /s/ for the /d/ verbs was hypothesized to appear to listeners to have a more voiced quality (i.e., sound more like a /z/) than the /s/ for the /t/ verbs.

In the experiment that tested this hypothesis the subjects were presented orally with a series of artificial verbs of the /t/ form and of the /d/ form, and for each verb they were given two adjectival forms, neither of which was correct, and asked to choose the better of the two. In the alternative adjectival forms given the subjects, the correct /s/ was substituted by /z/, /š/, /θ/, and /f/ to yield such forms as *yermizive, yermishive, yermithive,* and *yermifive.* For instance, subjects were asked whether *yermizive* or *yermishive* was a better adjective for *yermit* and whether *garluzive* or *garlushive* was a better adjective for *garlude.* The four substitute phonemes were compared with one another for the /t/ verbs and for the /d/ verbs. Our interest here is in the relative number of /z/ selections over the other three alternatives for the /t/ verbs and for the /d/ verbs. Because /z/ is the only sound of the four alternatives that is voiced, it was expected that it would be chosen significantly more often for the voiced /d/ verbs than for the voiceless /t/ verbs. This was, in fact, the case. Thus, even though the /z/ substituted for the same sound (/s/) in both cases, it seemed to the subjects relatively more appropriate for the /d/ forms than for the /t/ forms, presumably because of the carry-over of the voiced flavor from the verb forms. Thus, we see that in responding to the adjectival forms, the subjects took into consideration the verbal origins of these forms.

The message of this section is that in their psychological functioning the sounds of speech constitute a system of subtle and intricate relations. Other facets of the intricacy of the speech system are explored in the following sections.

THE COMBINATION OF PHONEMES

The preceding sections described the properties of phonemes as isolated entities. This section discusses the interaction of phonemes with one another when they are combined in the flow of speech. When phonemes are brought together in words, they have to adjust to one another. Under the pressure of mutual adjust-ment, neighboring sounds sometimes change to resemble one another in their articulatory characteristics. This type of change is called **assimilation** in linguis-tics (see Bronstein, 1960, pp. 209-215; Fromkin & Rodman, 1978, pp. 118-119). For instance, adjacent sounds tend to have the same voicing character-istics. Thus, compare the pronunciations of the *th* in *worth* and *worthy*. In the first word the *th* is pronounced as a /θ/, a voiceless dental fricative, but in the second word it changes to a /ð/, a voiced dental fricative, in anticipation of the voiced vowel. More common is adjustment in the opposite direction, from voiced to voiceless. Compare the pronunciation of the *s* in *news* and in *newspa-per*. In the first case it is pronounced as a /z/, but in the second it is pronounced as a /s/ under the influence of the voiceless /p/. There is also assimilation on the basis of place of articulation. Thus, the alveolar /n/ of the negative prefix *in-* (as in *inadequate, insufficient*) changes to the bilabial /m/ before bilabial stops (e.g., *impossible, imbalance*).

Assimilation obviously serves to smooth the transition between one sound and the next. Without close intercoordination of sounds, speech production could not be as fast as it is—about nine phonemes per second (see Liberman, 1982). Other, more subtle, aspects of intercoordination in speech production are incorporated into the next section.

SPEECH PERCEPTION

In order to assess what people do in the listening process, it is essential to know what kind of physical information arrives at their ears. Fortunately, a device called the sound **spectograph** provides detailed information on the acoustic char-acteristics of human speech. As speech is fed into the spectograph it makes a pen trace a visual display that represents the essential characteristics of the input. This display is called a sound **spectogram**, an example of which is given in Fig-ure 8.2.

Two striking points emerge when spectograms are examined in relation to what human listeners hear (see Liberman, 1970). First, speech is heard as a se-quence of discrete sound segments, but in sound spectograms there is typically a continuous flow with no indication of sound boundaries. Second, sounds that the human ear perceives as the same may have radically different qualities on the spectogram. For instance, it has been found that the spectographic cues for the initial consonant in the syllables /di/ and /du/ are very different. Yet human lis-teners hear them as one and the same sound. The difference becomes strikingly apparent to the human ear when the part of the tape corresponding to the vowel is excised. When this is done, the remaining parts, which correspond to the two consonants, sound very different in the two syllables.

The obvious question arises as to why the speaker's intention to produce a certain consonant results in varied acoustic signals. The answer is that speakers

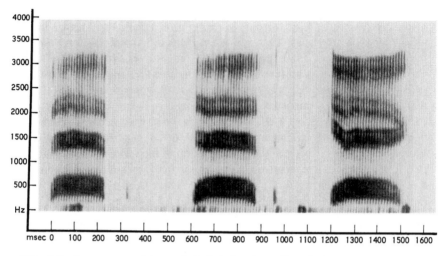

FIG. 8.2   A spectogram of the words *bad, dad,* and *gag* (From Ladefoged, 1982, p. 182).

execute their intention to produce a particular consonant differently in conjunction with one vowel than in conjunction with another vowel. The muscular adjustments in the production of /d/ before /i/ differ from the muscular adjustments
in the production of /d/ before /u/. One of the main differences between the vowels /i/ and /u/ is in the position of the highest part of the tongue. For /i/ the highest
part of the tongue is in the front of the mouth, whereas for /u/ it is in the back.
Now, for the articulation of /d/ the tip of the tongue has to touch the alveolar
ridge. In order to produce the /d/ and the following vowel as a fast, smooth gesture, the tongue, in positioning itself for the /d/, anticipates the position it will
need to be in for the vowel. Thus, for /du/ the tongue will make contact with the
alveolar ridge farther back than for /di/. There are also likely to be differences in
the shape of the entire tongue. The reason, then, why the spectographic patterns
for the /d/ in /di/ and /du/ are different is that the /d/ is articulated differently in
the two cases.

  As another example consider the articulation of the /k/ in *key* (/ki/) and *caw*
(/kɔ/). Because the two /k/s are followed by different vowels, they are articulated
differently. Ladefoged (1982) writes: "The whole body of the tongue has to be
pulled up and forward for [i]. This action begins during the formation of the closure for /k/, which is consequently farther forward than the closure in the allophone of /k/ before /ɔ/" (p. 53).

  Implicit in the preceding discussion is also an answer to the question of why
sound spectograms do not show sound-segment boundaries. The reason is that
adjacent sounds are planned together and **coarticulated** (see Ladefoged, 1982,
pp. 52–56). Thus, the articulations of the /k/ and the /i/ in *key* overlap. The /i/ is

present during the articulation of the /k/, and the /k/ is present during the articulation of the /i/.

The overlapping in the articulation of sounds makes it possible for speakers to produce speech at a much faster rate than they would have been able to produce if they had to articulate each sound individually. But as Liberman (1979) has pointed out:

> These gains have a cost: there is no direct correspondence in segmentation between units of the message [i.e., the sounds the speaker intended to articulate] and units of the [acoustic] signal; also, the shape of the signal that carries the information for a given segment of the message will vary, often in apparently peculiar ways, depending on the nature of the other message segments that are simultaneously encoded with it. (p. 687)

Thus, the speaker's intention to produce a sequence of distinct individual sounds is executed on the level of articulatory production as a single articulatory amalgam (of syllabic length), in which the different segments overlap. This kind of articulation results in an acoustic signal in which the different sound segments are not represented distinctly in a direct manner. Yet, listeners, who rely on the acoustic signal, perceive what the speaker intended to say. They hear a sequence of individual segments, and they hear the same /k/ in *key* and *caw*, and the same /d/ in *di* and *du*. How does the listener recover from the acoustic signal the phonological information that the speaker intended to convey? The listener cannot simply take acoustic segments sequentially one after the other and identify the phonemes correlated with them. Few phonemes would be recovered in this manner. Rather, the listener must take a larger acoustic stretch (perhaps of syllabic length) and make inferences concerning its phonemic composition. Strictly speaking, the sounds the listener hears are not there to be picked out from the acoustic signal. Instead, the acoustic signal provides cues on the basis of which the listener can reconstruct the sounds. We should perhaps think of the listener as performing an analogous function to that of the chemist who is able to analyze out the individual elements that contributed to the making of a particular compound. Chemists can do this not because the elements retain their original appearances, but because they know what happens when particular elements are compounded with each other. Similarly, listeners are able to perceive the speech of their language because they know its rules and patterns.

The constructive view of speech perception sketched here is in accord with current interpretations of the perceptual process in general. If you find this view hard to accept (and most people do on first exposure), this is because we tend to think that what we perceive is fully out there in the physical world. But we have to recognize that our perceptions are a result of an interaction between the raw stimulus material and our previous knowledge and experience. We always assimilate stimuli through our internal structures and have no way of experiencing them in their raw physical form.

CONCLUSIONS

In this chapter I outlined the nature of the sound system of language and its functioning. Overriding the details presented is the point that speech is not an external, mechanical means for expressing meaning but a system of knowledge in its own right. We saw that speech is regulated by rules and patterns, by a grammar, just as syntax is. To function as speakers and listeners individuals must have not only an intact speech apparatus, but they also must have control of the grammar of speech. Chomsky (e.g., 1968) has, in fact, argued that the learning of phonology is subject to a "restrictive, universal schematism" of the same kind he has postulated for syntax (see Chapter 7). Liberman (1982) has promoted a related point of view on the basis of experimental evidence concerning speech perception.

9
Development of Morphology

Beginning with the age of two, every child becomes for a period of time a linguistic genius.

Kornei Chukovsky

In the previous chapters I dealt with the lexical meanings of words, with their syntactic status, and with their phonological structure. In the present chapter I examine the processes of word formation, which are studied by a branch of linguistics called **morphology**. This chapter consists of three sections. The first section briefly outlines the essential elements of morphology, and the last two sections discuss the acquisition of morphology by children.

NATURE OF MORPHOLOGICAL PROCESSES

The unit of analysis in morphology is the **morpheme**. Generally speaking, a morpheme is a minimal element of meaning. A word is composed of one or more morphemes. For example, *forget* consists of a single morpheme; *forgetful* has two, the stem morpheme *forget* and the adjectival marker *-ful*. An additional morpheme can be added to *forgetful* by prefixing it with the negative marker *un-* to make *unforgetful* or by suffixing it with the noun marker *-ness* to make *forgetfulness*. In this example morphemes having grammatical meanings (i.e., *-ful*, *un-*, and *-ness*) were added to a morpheme having referential meaning (i.e., *forget*) to form new words. New words can also be formed by compounding referential morphemes; for example, *pickpocket* is derived from the morphemes *pick* and *pocket*, and *sightsee* is derived from *sight* and *see*. The morphological processes described so far have traditionally been referred to by linguists as **derivational**, because they result in the derivational formation of new words.

Inflections constitute another aspect of morphology. The main inflections in English are pluralization, past tense, and possession. Thus, the plural morpheme -*s* is added to the stem *pupil* to make *pupils*, the past tense morpheme -*ed* is added to the stem verb *walk* to make *walked*, and the possessive morpheme -'*s* is added to the stem noun *mother* to make *mother's*.

Most of the morphological formations that we have discussed involve the affixation of morphological markers as prefixes, and suffixes to stem forms. The stem forms can be freely used by themselves and are therefore called **free morphemes**. The markers are called **bound morphemes**, because they have to be bound to stems; they cannot be used by themselves.

There is more to morphological processes than simply adding a bound morpheme to a free morpheme. Morphological markers often adjust their phonological shape to fit in with the characteristics of the stem forms, and the stem forms are also subject to change in the process. In other words, morphological processes are truly interactive.

Consider some examples of phonological changes in stem forms as a result of morphological processes. When *divide* is transformed to *division* the final /d/ changes to a /ž/, and the second *i* changes its pronunciation from a long vowel to a short vowel; the same happens in the conversion to nouns of other verbs of similar form (e.g., *deride-derision, decide-decision*). In some languages words may change drastically when they undergo morphological changes. Thus, someone who does not know Hebrew could hardly recognize that the words in the following pairs are related: *nafal* ('it fell')-*yipol* ('it will fall'), *naval* ('it wilted')-*yibol* ('it will wilt'). These alternations between past tense forms of verbs and future tense forms are not arbitrary—as is, for instance, the alternation between "he *went*" and "he will *go*" in English—but follow a rule that speakers of Hebrew have internalized.

The adaptation of morphological markers to the stems to which they are attached is well exemplified by the rules governing the formation of the regular plural and past tense in English. In writing, the plural is marked by -*s* or -*es*, and the past tense is marked by -*ed*. But the pronunciation of these letters differs depending on the final sound of the stem.

Consider the plural first. In *caps* the -*s* is rendered as /s/, but in *cabs* it is rendered as /z/. Similarly, the first words in the pairs *bets-beds* and *backs-bags* are pronounced with a /s/ and the second words with a /z/. What determines the choice is the voicing characteristic of the final sound of the singular noun. Nouns ending in voiceless sounds are pluralized by the addition of a /s/, and nouns ending in voiced sounds are pluralized by the addition of a /z/. Note also that /s/ and /z/ differ minimally in that /s/ is voiceless and /z/ is voiced. The choice of /s/ or /z/ as a plural is thus an example of voicing assimilation: the voiceless /s/ following voiceless sounds and the voiced /z/ following voiced sounds. The -*es*, pronounced as /əz/, is added to singulars ending in phonemes such as /s/, /z/, and /š/ (e.g., *bus*) after which /s/ and /z/ cannot be sounded.

The past tense formation rule parallels the pluralization rule. The *-ed* marker is pronounced as /t/ (which is voiceless) in verbs ending in voiceless sounds (e.g., *mopped*), and it is pronounced as /d/ (which is voiced) in verbs ending in voiced sounds (e.g., *mobbed*). When the *-ed* follows sounds after which /t/ and /d/ cannot be pronounced, namely, /t/ and /d/, it is rendered as /əd/ (e.g., *patted* and *added*).

The pluralization and past tense rules can be stated on a more abstract level (see Anisfeld & Gordon, 1968, and p. 197 above), but the statements given here are sufficient for the present purpose of showing that the phonological realization of a morpheme depends on the stem to which it is attached. The different variants of a given morpheme are referred to as its **allomorphs**. The plural morpheme thus has the regular allomorphs /s/, /z/, and /əz/, as well as irregular ones (e.g., /rən/ in *children*).

THE ACQUISITION OF INFLECTIONS

In the subsections that follow I first discuss general aspects of the acquisition of infectional morphology and then turn to a discussion of specific inflections.

Morphology After Syntax

One of the most reliable findings in the area of language development is that morphological processes appear in children's language after the emergence of syntax. MacWhinney (1976) suggested that in morphologically rich languages, such as Hungarian, children tend to begin to acquire morphology earlier than in languages whose morphology is more limited. But he emphasized that even in those languages, morphology never appears before syntax.

The developmental sequence of morphology after syntax is so general that Roger Brown (1973), the leading developmental psycholinguist, used it to identify two stages in the acquisition of grammar. Children enter the first stage when they begin to produce sentences, and they enter the second stage when they begin to use morphological devices.

Why does morphology emerge after syntax? Brown proposed several explanations. One of them was that the relational meanings expressed by syntactic devices, such as actor-action and attribution, are more essential than those expressed by morphological devices, such as pluralization and past tense. The latter do not encode independent meanings; they only modulate the meanings of other terms. Brown (1973) writes:

> The present progressive *-ing* indicates that a process named by a verb is in progress at the time of speaking, but temporarily so. The past inflection indicates that a proc-

ess named by a verb began and ended before the time of speaking. The plural in-flection indicates that the thing referred to by a noun exists in more than one in-stance. It does not seem possible to think of these tunings or modulations without the things and processes they tune whereas it does seem to be possible to conceive of the latter without the former. (p. 253)

The explanation in terms of the relative unimportance of inflections applies well to the plural, past tense, and progressive. But it does not hold for the posses-sive inflection. We saw in Chapter 6 that children do express the idea of posses-sion in sentences such as *Kendall chair*, *daddy book*, *my penny*, and *our car* (Braine, 1976, p. 15). Yet, the possessive marker -'s is totally absent in the samples of beginning syntax published for English-speaking children. The idea of possession is important, and young children do express it, but not morpholog-ically. Why not?

Brown (1973) offered an explanation for possession in terms of semantic re-dundancy: "The possessive inflection adds a usually redundant marker to such N + N constructions as *Adam chair* and does not modulate the sense at all" (p. 253). Some support for Brown's redundancy explanation can be found in chil-dren's selective use of the possessive marker when it begins to appear in their speech. Cazden (1968) examined the inflections of three children who were stud-ied longitudinally by a group of investigators at Harvard, headed by Roger Brown. Cazden found that in the age range of 18 to 33 months, the children in-cluded the possessive marker only in 11% of the utterances in which the pos-sessed noun was present (nonelliptic utterances), but they included it in 81% of the utterances in which the possessed noun was absent (elliptic utterances). For instance, a child who said *mommy girl* instead of *mommy's girl* said, correctly, *I shared daddy's* (i.e., daddy's ice cream). In the nonelliptic utterances the pos-sessive marker is superfluous, but in the elliptic utterances it is needed to clarify the meaning; in the example, it was needed to indicate that the ice cream was divided, not daddy.

There is a problem, however, with the redundancy explanation for posses-sion. The possessive marker is superfluous only because possession is already marked by word order, such that *mommy girl* means 'the girl belonging to mommy', and *girl mommy* means 'the mommy belonging to the girl'. But the fundamental question remains why children rely first on word order, not morpho-logical marking, to encode possession. Why don't they mark possession with the possessive morpheme, and allow themselves free word order? Concretely, why don't children use both *mommy's girl* and *girl mommy's* to mean 'the girl belong-ing to mommy,' and both *mommy girl's* and *girl's mommy* to mean 'the mommy belonging to the girl'? In fact, the morphological marker -'s has more to recom-mend it as a way to express possession than syntactic word order, because it is more reliable in adult English. Thus, the possessing entity may appear in English not only before the possessed entity but also after it (e.g., "The ball is Suzie's,"

"The blocks belong to Johnny"). Yet, children use syntactic order to express possession before they use the morphological marker. Why?

The question of why syntactic devices are used before morphological devices is not restricted to possession in English. It is even sharper in highly inflected languages. Russian, for instance, uses case endings to mark such fundamental relations as agent and object, and therefore allows relatively free word order. Yet Russian children first use syntactic order to express these relations and only later add the case markers (Slobin, 1966, p. 134). Why don't they use case endings from the start, instead of word order, to express these relations? It thus appears that the redundancy explanation, and semantic explanations in general, are not fully adequate to account for all cases of morphological lag.

An additional explanation for the lag in the appearance of English inflections was offered by Brown (1973, pp. 74-88) in terms of low perceptual salience. Inflections are characteristically brief, unstressed, and as I have indicated, variable in phonetic form. Inflections would, therefore, not attract the child's notice. It should also be added that inflections, being bound morphemes, require analysis and abstraction for their identification.

The perceptual explanation, however, also presents problems when applied to inflections, such as the possessive and case markers, which are expressed syntactically before they are expressed morphologically. In a sense the perceptual explanation begs the question. It is true that the possessive marker and case markers have low perceptual salience. But is their salience lower than that of word order? Obviously, salience is relative to what one is predisposed to notice. The question therefore remains why children notice and make use of word order before they notice and make use of inflections to express the same meanings. I do not have an answer to this fundamental question. It is possible that order is more basic in language, because it is essential not only in syntax but in phonology as well (e.g., to distinguish between *mitt* and *Tim*). Or it could be that there is a natural predisposition to be sensitive to order.

In summary, morphological devices appear in children's speech after the emergence of syntax. Why? This question has been discussed with respect to inflectional morphology, and two types of inflections were distinguished: inflections whose meanings are usually not expressed syntactically before the onset of morphology (e.g., the English plural, past tense, and present progressive), and inflections whose meanings are expressed syntactically before they are expressed morphologically (e.g., the possessive in English and case markers in Russian). Two explanations are available to account for the relatively late appearance of the first class of inflections. First, the meanings of these inflections are too subtle and relatively unimportant. Second, they are relatively inconspicuous as phonetic-perceptual forms. For either or both of these reasons the inflections of the first class do not attract the child's early attention and interest. With respect to the second class the explanation must lie in the primacy of word order, the reasons for which are not clear.

The Emergence of the Morphological Principle

It has been observed that once children begin to learn inflections, they acquire a variety of them within a relatively short period of time. In a summary of the extensive observations made by the Soviet linguist Aleksandr N. Gvozdev on his son Zhenya, Slobin (1966) noted: "All words are unmarked in Zhenya's speech until about 1,10 [1 year and 10 months] and then, in one month between 1,11 and 2,0, there is a sudden emergence of contrasting morphological elements in various grammatical categories" (p. 136). What this suggests is that in acquiring specific inflections, the child is also acquiring the morphological principle, namely, that meanings can be expressed through phonological modification of words. Once children have grasped this principle, they are ready for the productive acquisition of inflections.

Children sometimes display behavior reflecting some cognizance of the modulating uses of phonological modification even before they acquire any of the standard inflections in their language. Thus, Werner and Kaplan (1963) observed that children modified words for the purpose of expressing "some qualification of, or affective reaction to, an event" (p. 155). They cite a report of a French child who changed *papa* to *papal* and *papap* to indicate affection. Slobin (1973) also cites examples of children's inventive use of morphological modification to express modulations of meaning before the onset of standard morphology. For instance, a Czech boy "inserted extra syllables into adjectives in order to intensify their meanings" (p. 193).

Children have also been observed to use nonmorphological means to express morphological meanings before the onset of standard morphology. Thus, Richard, studied by Carlson and Anisfeld (1969), used *ree-roar* (from "one, two, three, four") to express plurality 1½ months before he began using the standard English plural for this purpose. For instance, at 21 months Richard said *ree-roar boy* when he saw his brother and a friend come down steps simultaneously, and he said *ree-roar car* when he saw several cars passing. At that time, apparently, Richard had not yet grasped the morphological principle, but he felt the need to express the notion of plurality, which he did through lexical means.

Order of Acquisition of Different Inflections

After children attain the morphological principle, they have the basis for the acquisition of specific morphological devices. The rate of acquisition of particular devices depends, however, on their individual characteristics. The present subsection compares the order of acquisition of different English inflections.

Brown (1973) examined thoroughly the order of acquisition of English inflections by the three children in the Harvard longitudinal study. From samples of spontaneous speech that were collected, Brown calculated when different inflections became established in the speech of his subjects. For a child to be credited with a morpheme, it had to appear in at least 90% of the contexts in which it was obligatory. For instance, a plural is required when reference is made to more than one item or when the noun is preceded by a numeral larger than 1. Using a similar approach to that of Brown, de Villiers and de Villiers (1973) conducted a cross-sectional study in which they recorded the spontaneous speech of 21 children in the age range of 16 to 40 months. The studies of Brown and of de Villiers and de Villiers, as well as other studies which Brown brought together, show that children tend to master the plural and present progressive markers before the possessive and past tense markers.

How is one to account for this order of acquisition? The possessive marker has the same allomorphs as the plural; and, as we have seen, the regular past tense marker parallels the plural marker in form. Why, then, are the past tense and possessive inflections acquired after the plural inflection? We also have to consider why the past tense is acquired after the present progressive.

It would seem that the past tense is acquired after the plural because the conceptual notion of past is more abstract than that of plurality. In fact, children do not seem to grasp fully the notion of past tense till after the age of 6. Bronckart and Sinclair (1973) asked French children between the ages of 3 and 8½ years to describe events they had just observed. One of their findings was that up to the age of 6, children described imperfective events (i.e., events that did not come to a conclusion) in the present tense, even though they took place prior to the time of description. For instance, after viewing a scene of a fish swimming in a basin, the younger subjects described the swimming in the present tense. In this experiment the children gave the descriptions 7 seconds after the cessation of the event. It would therefore be hazardous to generalize from these results about the description of events that took place in the more remote past. But the point stands that even children who are older than the 2- and 3-year-olds in the de Villiers and de Villiers and Brown studies do not use the past tense with the same meaning as more mature speakers.

Conceptual difficulty, though adequate to explain the delayed mastery of the past tense, cannot explain the delayed mastery of the possessive, because possessive relations are expressed syntactically even before the emergence of morphology. The syntactic expression of possession may, in fact, be responsible for the late appearance of possession in morphology. That is, children may be slow in acquiring the possessive marker because they already have means for expressing possession.

The early acquisition of the present progressive marker is difficult to explain, because it is not clear what meaning it has for young children. In adult English the present progressive designates a presently ongoing activity of relatively short duration and contrasts with the simple present, which is used to mark a habitual activity; compare, for example, "I am walking to work" and "I walk to work." Brown (1973, pp. 319-320) does not think that young children have a grasp of the habitual-ongoing contrast, because he did not find that they expressed the notion of habitual activity.

In trying to account for the order of acquisition of English inflections I have drawn on semantic considerations. Semantic factors have also been found to play a role in the acquisition of inflections in other languages. Thus, Slobin (1966) noted that in Russian: "Those classes whose reference is clearly concrete emerge first. The first morphological distinction is number, at 1,10, followed shortly by diminutive suffixing of nouns . . . [whereas] noun endings indicating abstract categories of quality and action continue to be added as late as seven" (pp. 141-142).

However, semantic factors alone are not sufficient to explain all aspects of morphological development. The formal complexity of the morphological rules also has to be taken into consideration. Slobin (1973) pointed out, for instance, that in Egyptian Arabic the plural "is the most difficult and latest aspect of language structure to be mastered" (p. 181). This stands in contrast to the situation in other languages where the plural is one of the earliest inflections to be acquired. Slobin attributes the late acquisition of the Egyptian plural to its great complexity.

As further support for the importance of formal characteristics, Slobin cites a study of two girls in northern Yugoslavia who spoke both Serbo-Croatian and Hungarian. Even before the age of 2 years, the girls used Hungarian markers to encode locative relations (e.g., the relations expressed in English by *into* and *out of*), but they did not develop Serbo-Croatian locative markers until much later. Slobin attributes the difference in rate of acquisition to the difference in complexity of the markers in the two languages. In Hungarian, locative markers are simply suffixed to the stems (e.g., *hajó* ['boat'], *hajóban* ['located in the boat'], *hajóból* ['moving out from inside of the boat']), whereas in Serbo-Croatian the rules are much more complicated.

Acquisition of Individual Inflections

So far I have discussed the acquisition of inflections in relation to syntax and in relation to one another. In this subsection I look more closely at the course of development of individual inflections: the plural, past tense, and present progressive.

Acquisition of the Plural Inflection   In the discussion of the acquisition of words and sentences in previous chapters, I noted a characteristic statistical trend. The rate of increase in the number of words and sentences that children produce is at first slow and then takes a sharp upward turn and grows at an accelerated rate. The growth spurts in vocabulary and syntax were interpreted as indicating that the child has grasped the naming principle and the order principle, respectively, and is applying them in his or her speech.

A spurt is evident in the development of morphology as well. Cazden (1968) provided data on the rate of production of plurals for the three children studied in

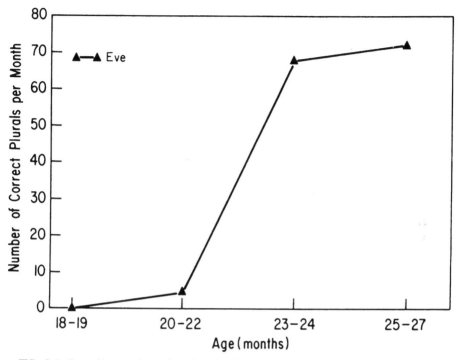

FIG. 9.1   Rate of increase in number of correct plurals as a function of age for one of the children studied by Cazden (1968, p. 436).

the Harvard project. Her data are based on 2 hours of recording of spontaneous speech every other week (Brown, 1973, p. 257). On the basis of Cazden's results, summarized in her Table 1, I plotted the rate of production of plurals for one of her subjects, Eve (Figure 9.1). The figure shows a very slow rate of growth of plurals in Eve's speech in the period of 18-22 months and a precipitous rise in the period of 23-24 months. The other two children showed similar spurts. I interpret the period of slow growth as a time when children simply repeat specific plurals that they have heard. The spurt occurs when they formulate a rule on the basis of the specific instances in their memory. Once children have formed a rule, they are no longer limited to the specific plurals they have heard; they can and do construct plurals on their own. This is when the growth spurt occurs.

The strongest evidence for the psychological reality of rules is provided by the phenomenon of **overregularization**. In the case of plurals overregularization occurs when a child attaches a regular plural marker to an irregular noun and says, for example, *mans* and *foots*. Because the child could not have heard these forms from adults, we can be certain that he or she is applying a pluralization rule. Cazden found that overregularization began to occur at the time of the abrupt increase in plurals. For instance, the records of Eve's speech show no overregularizations at all up to 22 months, but 15 overregularizations between 23 and 27 months.

Overregularization reflects the child's inclination to form rules of the broadest sweep and thus to reduce the burden of memory. Slobin (1973) formulated this inclination as a universal operating principle that guides children to avoid exceptions. The striving for general rules is clearly evident in the overgeneralization of the plural allomorph /əz/. At first children do not apply this allomorph to singular nouns that require it for pluralization. Rather, they use the same form both for the singular and the plural, for example, they say *one box-two box* and *one peach-two peach* even when they say *one ball-two balls*. (This occurs probably because the singulars requiring the /əz/ already sound like plurals, e.g., *box*, where the *x* is pronounced as /ks/, and *peach*, where the *ch* is pronounced as /č/, which is similar in sound to /s/.) But after a while children notice the /əz/ allomorph and begin to use it productively and to overgeneralize it. Ervin (1964) analyzed the spread of /əz/ in a report of naturalistic observations of 7 children and systematic testing of 24 children between the ages of 2 and 4. She described her testing procedure as follows: "We tested children systematically by showing them objects, first singly and then in pairs, and asking for a description. These tests were conducted at monthly intervals. Some of the things we asked about were familiar, such as 'boys' and 'oranges.' Others were new objects, called such things as *bik*, *pud*, or *bunge*" (Ervin, 1964, p. 174).

Ervin reports that when children began to use the /əz/ with appropriate nouns (e.g., *box-boxes*), they overgeneralized it to nouns requiring /s/ and /z/ plurals. This reflects the child's inclination to construct rules of the broadest applicability. Of course, the /əz/ allomorph could not completely overthrow the well-established /s/ and /z/ allomorphs, especially because they continued to be heard. What happened was that for a while the children used both the old forms and the new form, "vacillating unpredictably" between them; for example, sometimes they produced *foots* and sometimes *footes* as plurals of *foot*. Often, they superimposed the new form on the old and produced such plurals as *footses* and *handses*. It took them 2 months to learn when to use /s/ and /z/ and when to use /əz/.

There is also a report of overregularization of a plural marker in Hebrew (Levy, 1980). Hebrew is a gender language, making a distinction between masculine and feminine nouns. Singular nouns ending in /a/ or /t/ are feminine; all other nouns are masculine. Feminine nouns are pluralized by appending /ot/ to the singular, and masculine nouns are pluralized by appending /im/. There are additional complications, but these need not concern us here. Levy studied the acquisition of pluralization by her son Arnon between the ages of 22 and 32 months. She found that in the initial period, between 22 and 24 months, Arnon had only the masculine form, and he overgeneralized it to feminine nouns; for example, his plural for *simla* ('dress') was *simlaim* (correct plural: *smalot*). At 24 months he began using the feminine form for some classes of feminine singulars, and the process of gradual approximation to the standard rules of pluralization continued throughout the period of the study. Overregularization is generally widespread in children learning Hebrew (see Berman, 1981).

The child's urge to construct general rules is also evident in bilingual children. Our son Shimon was exposed to a limited amount of Hebrew, from his father, in addition to his native English. In the course of his acquisition of pluralization rules for the two languages, he experimented for about a week, in his 27th month, with forming English plurals on the pattern of the Hebrew masculine pattern /im/. He was heard saying, for instance, *boyim*, *pine conim*, and *wash clothim*. This attempt at an overarching plural for both languages could not last long because of the weight of evidence against it. But the fact that such an attempt was even made testifies to the child's passion for generalization and regularity.

Sorting out different languages and different allomorphs is not all there is to learn in the acquisition of pluralization. Even after children have formed a particular rule, they still must have practice in its application. Thus, Ervin (1964) found that there was an interval of 2 to 6 weeks or more between the time children were able to form plurals for familiar nouns and the time they were able to form plurals for analogous made-up nouns:

> Between the time when the child contrasted *block* and *blocks* and the time when he said that two things called *bik* were *biks*, there was a small but reliable gap of about two weeks. For *car* and *boy* and the analogous *kie*, the gap was about six weeks. For other words the gap was greater. In all cases—*pud*, *bik*, *kie*, *tass*, and *bunge*—the new contrast appeared later than the contrasts the children had heard. (pp. 174-175)

Other studies (e.g., Bryant & Anisfeld, 1969; Berko, 1958) have shown that children continue to have some difficulty with artificial nouns even up to the age of 6.

Brown (1973, pp. 289-293) offered several possible reasons for the lag between familiar nouns and synthetic nouns. One of them was that the extra mental effort required for the processing of a new form reduces the mental energy available for the application of a rule. Another possibility suggested by Brown is that some of the familiar plural nouns children produce may be recalled from memory rather than constructed anew (see also MacWhinney, 1975).

In conclusion, the learning of pluralization, as language learning in all spheres, proceeds in recurrent cycles of rule formation, consolidation-generalization, and revision. As soon as children have grasped the morphological principle and have some examples of plural formation, they form a pluralization rule and attempt to generalize and consolidate it. When counterevidence builds up, children revise their rule, and the cycle repeats until the rule gains maximal consistency with the evidence. As children grow older their pluralization rule becomes refined and integrated with other inflectional rules (Anisfeld & Gordon, 1968). They also gain increasingly greater facility in its application.

Acquisition of the Past Tense Inflection   Not as much research has been done on the English past tense as on the plural, but the evidence for overregularization is even clearer here because there are more irregular verbs than irregular nouns, and hence more opportunities for overregularization. Some examples are *make-maked*, *tell-telled*, *come-comed*, and *do-doed* (for additional examples, see Brown, 1973, pp. 325-326; Slobin, 1971, p. 221). Ervin (1964) made a striking observation about overregularization in the past tense: "I looked for the first case of extension of the regular past tense suffix which could not have been imitated— for instance *buyed*, *comed*, *doed*. The odd, and to me astonishing thing is that these extensions occurred in some cases before the child had produced *any* other regular past tense forms according to our sample" (p. 178).

Children overregularize because of their desire to introduce consistency and regularity into the language they are learning. They actively seek out regularity. Slobin (1971, p. 220) tabulated the verbs addressed to Eve (one of the Harvard subjects whom we encountered before) by adults in 49 hours of recorded speech, in the age range of 18 to 26 months. This tabulation reveals that Eve heard more irregular verbs (40) than regular verbs (30). In addition, the irregular verbs occurred much more frequently than the regular verbs; the average frequency of each of the irregular verbs was 7.3 and of each of the regular verbs 3.3. Yet, Eve formed a rule on the basis of the regular verbs and ignored the irregular verbs. This is because the regular verbs exhibit a pattern, and the irregular verbs do not; and Eve looked for patterns.

Acquisition of the Present Progressive   Brown (1973, pp. 315-328) noted in his comprehensive review of the acquisition of inflections that the progressive was the only inflection for which there were no reports of overregularization. That is, children were not heard saying *I wanting*, *I needing*. The question is why. Brown considered the possibility that the reason for the reported absence of overregularizations in the progressive is that the exclusion of some verbs from the progressive inflection was not an arbitrary matter, but a principled one. Verbs that take the progressive refer to processes, whereas verbs that do not take the progressive refer to states. By comparison, the verbs that take irregular past tense forms and the nouns that take irregular plural forms have no distinctive characteristics. However, Brown rejected this explanation on the grounds that young children are not likely to be sensitive to the subtle distinction between process and state. He suggested that perhaps children learn specifically which verbs are "*-ing*able" and which are not.

An alternative explanation might be that there simply are not enough potential verbs in the child's realm of interest for the overregularization tendency to become apparent. After all, even in cases for which overregularization has been reported, it occurs rather sparsely. In an examination of the 35 irregular past tense verbs produced by the 24 children in the study reported by Ervin (1964), Slobin (1971, p. 221) found that 13 were used correctly and not overregularized by any of the children; for the remaining 22, the incidence of overregularization ranged from 1 to 42. Because there are fewer potential candidates for overregularization of the progressive than of the past tense, the failure of observers to record instances of progressive overregularization may not indicate that the child does not have a progressive rule. In fact, there is evidence for the operation of a progressive rule in the occurrence of progressive forms in the Hebrew speech of an English-Hebrew bilingual child. Eight days before his third birthday Shimon was heard saying, *marbitzing* ('hitting'), *mitlabeshing* ('getting dressed'), and *lishkaving* ('lying down'). Because Shimon could not have heard these forms from others, it must be that he generalized the English progressive form to Hebrew words; that is, he was guided by a progressive rule.

Morphology is Learned as a Formal System   To become a mature language user one has to approach language as an independent system, not merely as a vehicle for the expression of meanings. In acquiring inflections children demonstrate this level of language appreciation. The choice of an allomorph for a given stem has nothing to do with its meaning; it is determined solely by its form. To form an English plural one appends /s/, /z/, or /əz/ to the singular depending on its final sound, not on its meaning.

Popova (1958/1973) has given an example where children follow the dictates of form at the expense of semantic considerations. She studied the noun-verb agreement in the speech of 55 Russian children between the ages of 1;10 and 3;6. In Russian, verbs have to agree with their subject nouns in gender. Generally, feminine nouns are marked by an -*a* suffix, and masculine nouns by the absence of a suffix, for example, *kubik* ('block', masc.), *kukla* ('doll', fem.). In addition, there are biologically masculine nouns that also have -*a* endings, for example, *papa* ('father'), *dyadya* ('uncle'), *dedushka* ('grandfather'). As in the noun, feminine gender is marked in the verb with an -*a* suffix (e.g., *ona upala*, 'she fell'), and masculine gender is unmarked (e.g., *on upal*, 'he fell'). All biologically masculine nouns, even those marked as feminine, require masculine verb forms. But Popova (1958/1973) found that: ''Children who have basically mastered correct agreement make errors with words such as *papa*, *dyadya*, *dedushka* . . . often using the feminine form of the past tense verb: '*Dyadya sidela na loshadke*'; '*Moy papa zabolela*'; and so on [Uncle was sitting (fem.) on the little horse; My father got sick (fem.)]'' (p. 273). This is not merely another example of overregularization, but rather evidence that children really appreciate the formal workings of language. When faced with a referential formulation of a generalization and a formal formulation, the children Popova studied chose the latter.

CHILDREN'S CREATIVITY

The child's linguistic creativity, which pervades all aspects of language, is clearest in the realm of morphology. Who could miss the overregularizations in inflectional morphology?! Equally striking are examples of overregularization

THE FAMILY CIRCUS

7-11

Copyright 1979
The Register and Tribune
Syndicate Inc

"If this one's a fork, is this one a 'THREEK'?"

and inventiveness in derivational morphology. For instance, in her fourth year Hildegard produced such common derivational overregularizations as *gooder* and *goodest* (Leopold, 1949/1970b, p. 57). Instances of derivational inventiveness, which I heard from a two-year-old child, are the following: *brooming* (for 'sweeping'), *knifer* (for 'screwdriver'), *chairdresser* (for his baby sitter who dressed him on a chair), *bird-man* (for a man on whom a bird landed), and *ladygement* (said in correction of his mother who ordered, "you have to obey the management here").

In an analysis of the types of innovative word-formations that children exhibit, Clark (1981) found that noun-noun compounding (e.g., *bird-man*) and derivation of verbs from nouns (e.g., *brooming*) were the most common patterns of innovation of English-speaking children.

The Russian poet Kornei Chukovsky (1959/1963) was so impressed with the creativity of children at the ages of 2 to 5 that he said:

> It is frightening to think what an enormous number of grammatical forms are poured over the poor head of the young child. And he, as if it were nothing at all, adjusts to this chaos, constantly sorting out into rubrics the disorderly elements of the words he hears, without noticing, as he does this, his gigantic effort. If an adult had to master so many grammatical rules within so short a time, his head would surely burst—a mass of rules mastered so lightly and so freely by the two-year-old "linguist." The labor he thus performs at this age is astonishing enough, but even more amazing and unparalleled is the ease with which he does it. (p. 10)

10 Development of Speech

Children's learning of the sound system of their language involves developmental processes of the same kind as are involved in the acquisition of vocabulary, syntax, and morphology. The main aim of the present chapter is to elucidate these processes.

Speech development can be divided into two periods: the **prelinguistic** or **prephonemic period**, till about the first birthday, and the **linguistic** or **phonemic period**, from then on. In the prelinguistic period children refine their perceptual sensitivities to speech sounds and gain practice in sound articulation, but in this period speech does not yet function as a phonemic system. Because speech as a phonemic system requires internal representation of phonemes and phoneme combinations, it cannot begin to develop until Stages 4-5 of the sensorimotor period when the representational capacity begins to emerge.

Moreover, as we saw in Chapter 8, linguistic speech is integrally connected to meaning, and it cannot be acquired independently of it. We saw that a particular class of sounds functions as a distinct speech entity, as a phoneme, in a particular language only if it is relevant to the differentiation of one word from another word in that language. It follows that children can acquire linguistic or phonemic speech only in conjunction with the acquisition of meaning. Without semantic anchor points they have no basis for grouping sounds into phonemic categories and for determining which sound differences are distinctive and which are not in the language they are learning. The only way a child, or any other language learner for that matter, can discover, for instance, that [l] and [r] fall into different phonemic categories in English is by hearing them distinguish words, such as *lip* and *rip*, that differ in meaning. As we saw in Chapter 4, the reference-making use of words begins around the first birthday, and this is when linguistic speech can also begin to develop. In the sections that follow, I first discuss the prelinguistic phase of speech development and then turn to the linguistic phase.

PRELINGUISTIC DISCRIMINATORY CAPACITIES AND VOCAL ACTIVITIES

This section concentrates on three areas: the ability of infants to discriminate perceptually between different sounds, the characteristics of infants' vocal activity, and the vocal interaction of infants with other people.

Discriminatory Capacities

For children to learn to speak they have to be perceptually sensitive to the parameters that distinguish sounds from one another. Considerable evidence has accumulated in recent years that even young infants can discriminate between sounds differing in various characteristics (for reviews, see Eimas & Tartter, 1979; Yeni-Komshian, Kavanagh, & Ferguson, 1980).

The type of method used in this research and the kind of results obtained can be exemplified through a description of the first, ground-breaking study in this area (Eimas, Siqueland, Jusczyk, & Vigorito, 1971). This study investigated the ability of 1- and 4-month-old infants to discriminate between a [b] and a [p]. You may recall that these bilabial stops differ only in regard to voicing, [b] being voiced and [p] voiceless. Eimas et al. employed the **habituation method**, which is based on the tendency of infants to seek arousing stimulation (auditory, as well as other) and to get bored (like the rest of us) with repeated exposure to the same stimulus. In the habituation method infants are presented with a particular stimulus until they show signs of losing interest in it; technically, until they habituate to it. At this point a new stimulus is introduced. If the infants regain interest (technically, dishabituate) when the nominally new stimulus is presented, one infers that they discriminate between the new stimulus and the old stimulus. In the Eimas et al. experiment the infants' habituation-dishabituation was rendered observable by making the presentation of the sounds contingent on their high-amplitude nonnutritive sucking. In this design, if the sucking rate rises upon presentation of the new stimulus, after it had waned in the course of the presentation of the previous stimulus, one can infer that the infant discriminates between the two stimuli. The sequence of steps followed in the Eimas et al. experiment can be seen in Table 10.1, which also summarizes the results for the 4-month-old infants. Eimas et al. have stated that "the results for the younger infants show very nearly the identical overall pattern of results seen with the older infants" (p. 305).

In the experimental procedure the sucking rate of each infant in the absence of any experimental stimulus was first determined. Following this baseline-

TABLE 10.1
Mean Number of Sucking Responses per Minute for the 4-Month-Old Infants in the Eimas et al.
Experiment

Baseline Phase	Experimental Phases			
	First Phase			Second Phase
	1st–3rd min.	4th min.	5th min.	1st–4th min.
	Phonemic-Change Condition			
no sound	ba (VOT = +20)	ba (VOT = +20)	ba (VOT = +20)	pa (VOT = +40)
no sound	pa (VOT = +40)	pa (VOT = +40)	pa (VOT = +40)	ba (VOT = +20)
26	53	39	34	48
	No-Change Condition			
no sound	ba (VOT = +20)	ba (VOT = +20)	ba (VOT = +20)	ba (VOT = +20)
no sound	pa (VOT = +40)	pa (VOT = +40)	pa (VOT = +40)	pa (VOT = +40)
24	53	36	30	22
	Nonphonemic-Change Condition			
no sound	ba (VOT = −20)	ba (VOT = −20)	ba (VOT = −20)	ba (VOT = 0)
no sound	pa (VOT = +60)	pa (VOT = +60)	pa (VOT = +60)	pa (VOT = +80)
26	61	43	35	32

Note: The results summarized in this table were read off graphs given by Eimas et al. (1971, p. 304) for the 4-month-old infants. The table was checked for accuracy by Dr. P. D. Eimas.

determination phase, infants were put through one of three conditions: the phonemic-change condition, the no-change condition, and the nonphonemic-change condition.

In the phonemic-change condition, there was a 5-minute period during which the infants were exposed either to the syllable [ba] or to the syllable [pa]. These syllables were prepared artificially by machine. In particular, the VOT for [ba] was +20 msec, and for [pa] +40 msec, these values being on the two sides of the phonemic boundary between [b] and [p]. The number of times the infants heard the [ba] or [pa] syllable during the 5-minute period was contingent on their rate of sucking. The more they sucked, the more they heard the syllable. The results show that during the first 3 minutes of the 5-minute phase, there was an increase in sucking rate as compared to the baseline level. The number of sucking responses rose from an average of 26 per minute during the baseline phase to an average of 53 per minute during the first 3 minutes. But after the initial 3 minutes, sucking rate began to decline and approach the baseline level. Evidently, after 3 minutes the infants lost interest in the sound; in other words, they habituated to the repeated stimulus ([ba] or [pa]). After the first 5-minute phase, the experimenter presented a new syllable for 4 minutes. The infants who heard the syllable [ba] in the first phase were now exposed to [pa], and vice versa. This change resulted in a rise of the average sucking rate to 48 responses per minute. Clearly, the infants noticed that a new sound was being presented, and their interest was reawakened; that is, they dishabituated.

A second condition was the no-change condition. The infants in this condition continued to be exposed to the same syllable during the 4 minutes that the infants in the phonemic-change condition heard a different syllable. The sucking rate of the no-change infants continued to decline during the 4-minute period, dropping to about baseline level.

The Eimas et al. experiment also included a nonphonemic-change condition in which the VOT difference between the first syllable and the second, posthabituation, stimulus was of the same magnitude as in the phonemic-change condition (i.e., 20 msec), but here both syllables were either within the range perceived by adults as [b] or within the range perceived as [p]. In the [b] range exposure, the initial stimulus had a −20 msec VOT, and the posthabituation stimulus had a 0 msec VOT; in the [p] range exposure the two values were +60 msec and +80 msec, respectively. The results show that the infants in the nonphonemic-change condition behaved like the no-change infants; that is, they did not increase their sucking rate after the introduction of the new stimulus.

The contrast between the results of the nonphonemic-change condition and those of the phonemic-change condition suggests that infants have a special perceptual sensitivity in the VOT area dividing voiceless sounds from voiced sounds. This type of differential sensitivity had previously been established for adults (e.g., Liberman, Harris, Hoffman, & Griffith, 1957). It is reasonable to assume that this sensitivity serves as the biological basis for the voiced-voiceless distinction.

The results of Eimas et al. were replicated by Trehub and Rabinovitch (1972) in an experiment with 4- to 17-week-old infants, which used naturally produced syllables ([ba]-[pa] and [da]-[ta]). Subsequently, investigators found that young infants can discriminate sounds not only on the basis of voicing but also on the basis of other phonologically relevant characteristics, such as place of articulation.

Furthermore, there is evidence that infants have less specialized discriminatory abilities than adults. For instance, Werker, Gilbert, Humphrey, and Tees (1981) found that 7-month-old American infants could discriminate between two Hindi sounds which to adult Americans sounded indiscriminable. Obviously, humans have the discriminatory capacity to acquire any speech system. But as they become socialized into a particular language, their discriminatory abilities seem to become dulled with respect to contrasts not distinctive in that language.

In sum, research in the last decade has shown infants to have impressive discriminatory abilities. Because these abilities can be detected as early as 1 month, it is reasonable to assume that they have a strong innate basis. The precise nature of these abilities is, however, unclear at present. This entire area is currently subject to lively research and discussion (see Aslin & Pisoni, 1980; Eilers, Gavin, & Wilson, 1980; Eimas & Tartter, 1979; Liberman, 1979; Trehub, Bull, & Schneider, 1981; Yeni-Komshian et al., 1980). One of the findings that has intrigued investigators is that chinchillas are also able to discriminate between voiced and voiceless stops, suggesting that at least some mammals share this auditory ability with humans.

Finally, a comment is in order about the relation between the discriminatory abilities of young infants and speech development. It is self-evident that in order to learn to speak the learner has to be sensitive to the sound differences that are functional in language, and the studies discussed do demonstrate that even young infants have at least some of these sensitivities. It would be a mistake, however, to jump to the conclusion that the infant has what it takes, even on the perceptual side, to learn to speak. We saw in Chapter 3 that young infants are able to tell faces apart and to remember them over long periods of time without having an attendant notion of the objective reality of faces (and of objects in general). Similarly, the ability to discriminate sounds does not imply representation of the sounds, much less a notion of their featural composition. For the adult observer looking at tasks such as that of Eimas et al., there is an old syllable /ba/, a new syllable /pa/, and a perception of difference between them. But infants, I am arguing, have no consciousness of sounds or of differences between them; they merely have an experience of auditory monotony when the first stimulus is repeated and an experience of auditory arousal when the second stimulus is introduced. The infants' discriminations are sensorimotor, not representational. Young infants respond to sounds as stimuli, not as entities of knowledge represented internally. The ability to represent sounds appears in the beginning of the second year with the emergence of the symbolic capacity.

Vocal Activity

In order to speak children have to be able not only to represent sounds internally but also to exercise control over the fine articulatory movements and coordinations that speech entails. The articulatory muscles have to develop to a point where they can function in the highly precise and finely tuned fashion required for speech. We can assume that prelinguistic vocalizations in infancy help in this development; therefore, they deserve our attention.

Crying and Cooing   The vocalizations occurring in the first 8 weeks can be separated into two categories (Stark, 1979). One category consists of vegetative sounds and includes burping, swallowing, spitting up, and the like. The other category consists of discomfort sounds and includes reflexive crying and fussing. Vegetative sounds are brief in duration and occur both during air inspiration and expiration. They contain both vowellike and consonantlike qualities. By comparison, crying occurs during expiration and is characterized by the predominance of vowellike sounds. It occurs in series consisting of vocalizations separated by silences. Each series may last up to 5 minutes. Fussing is similar to crying except that it occurs in series of much shorter duration.

Discomfort and vegetative sounds do not, of course, disappear after 8 weeks, but they decrease in frequency, and new forms of vocal activity appear. Wolff (1969) noted that: "the baby's non-cry vocalizations diversify rapidly between the sixth and eighth week" (p. 104).

The period between 9 and 20 weeks constitutes the second stage in the chronology of vocalizations. It is characterized by **cooing** and laughter; sustained laughter occurs at 16 weeks. Stark (1979) notes: "Cooing (comfort) sounds are produced in comfortable states usually in response to smiling and talking on the part of the mother" (p. 24). Cooing is richer in sound composition than either crying or vegetative sounds. It combines elements of both in a way that makes it closer to speech proper than the sounds of the preceding period. Like crying, cooing is produced during exhalation, and like vegetative sounds, it contains both vowellike and consonantlike sounds. The consonantlike sounds have the quality of back stops ([k] and [g]). According to Stark (1979): "When cooing sounds first emerge they are produced as single segments only, each one of about 500 msec in duration. Subsequently these segments enter into series with one another, series which may have as many as 3 to 10 segments within them" (p. 26).

Following the cooing period there is an extended period in which infants engage in babbling. Babbling continues the diversification of sounds begun in cooing. The main difference between the two is in function. Whereas cooing seems to have the function of expressing feelings of comfort, babbling is primarily sound play (see Lewis, 1936/1975, ch. 5; also Leopold, 1947/1970, pp. 138-142).

Babbling   The term **babbling** describes playful speech that is devoid of referential meaning. It is prominent in the second half of the first year. As referential speech begins to develop at the end of the first year, babbling begins to decline, but it continues to be present to a greater or lesser extent well into the second year.

Earlier writers (see Jakobson, 1941/1968) noted an interesting contrast. Whereas in the babbling period, children exhibit an "astonishing quantity and diversity of sound productions" (p. 21), when they begin to acquire meaningful speech, they have difficulty producing the very same sounds they manifested in babbling. Why? The answer is that there is a fundamental difference between spontaneous-impulsive productions and intentional-planned productions (see Jakobson, 1941/1968; Jespersen, 1922/1964, p. 106; Shvachkin, 1948/1973). In the course of activation of the articulatory muscles in babbling, any sound may be emitted by chance. But this is an entirely different matter from the willful production of a sound to specifications in a particular position in a word to express a particular meaning. The former is a sound; the latter is a phoneme, a unit represented in the speech system. Shvachkin (1948/1973) put it well: "A child in the prephonemic period of speech, in reality, does not pronounce the sounds expressed by him; they . . . 'pronounce themselves'; these are involuntarily pronounced sounds" (pp. 96-97). Guillaume (1926/1971) gave an interesting analogy to capture the involuntary character of infant babbling: "He plays with his voice like a novice musician who amuses himself by pounding on the keyboard, without being able to reproduce the sounds from the memory of their acoustic quality after moving his hand" (pp. 35-36). What Guillaume is saying is that the sounds produced in babbling do not result from intentions to produce sounds represented in memory; rather, they are merely an incidental byproduct of articulatory play.

There has been some empirical research on the relation between babbling and meaningful speech. Oller, Wieman, Doyle, and Ross (1976) analyzed the babbling of 10 children in the second half of their first year. The study found patterns of vocalization that were similar to the patterns reported for early meaningful speech. For instance, in early meaningful speech consonantal clusters (e.g., *play*, *sky*) are infrequent. Oller et al. found that consonantal clusters were also uncommon in the babbling of their subjects, occurring with a frequency of less than 8%. The reason for the low occurrence of consonantal clusters in meaningful speech and in babbling would seem to be that the articulation of uninterrupted clusters of consonants requires greater articulatory control than the articulation of consonants interspersed with vowels (Leopold, 1947/1970, pp. 127-137).

Oller et al. saw their results as contradicting the notion of discontinuity between babbling and meaningful speech, championed by Jakobson. But this is a mistaken interpretation. The claim of discontinuity concerns the psychological status of the sounds. The sounds of meaningful speech are manifestations of internally represented entities, whereas the sounds of prelinguistic babbling are merely the accidental results of vocal activity. But there is bound to be similarity on the level of articulation, because the same speech apparatus is used in babbling and in meaningful speech. Consonantal clusters are difficult to produce because of the fine coordination of articulatory movements that they require. This difficulty is bound to be reflected both in babbling and in meaningful speech.

Although babbling is distinct from speech proper, it does contribute to the acquisition of speech. Fry (1975, pp. 149-150) thought that babbling was beneficial in two ways. First, through babbling, children learn about the mechanism of speech, how to control it, and how to coordinate articulatory movements with breathing. Second, they learn about the relations between vocal-motor actions and auditory consequences, and gain experience in using auditory and kinesthetic feedback for the control of articulatory movements. It has been further proposed (Ferguson & Garnica, 1975) that: "The major achievement of the babbling period is the child's discovery of the sentence unit, characterized by the co-occurrence of an intonation contour with a string of speech sounds" (p. 168).

Vocalization in Interpersonal Context

So far I have examined infant vocalizations in terms of the speech-relevant capacities that they demonstrate or prepare for. Here I deal with speech not from a capacity point of view, but from a social point of view. I discuss separately the nature of speech to infants, infants' reactions to speech, their imitation of speech, and vocal communication.

Speech to Infants   Mothers and other caregivers have been observed to talk to infants from the moment they are born (Rheingold & Adams, 1980; for a description of the characteristics of talk to infants, see Kaye, 1980). Adult talk to infants is part of a complex of behaviors that derives from viewing the infant as a social being from the start. On the basis of extensive analyses of filmed interactions between mothers and infants in the ages of 2-3 months, Trevarthen (1979) described the "mirroring" and interpreting behaviors of the typical Western middle-class mother. The mothers reacted to their babies' behaviors by repeating them, faithfully or in exaggerated form, and interpreting them, often verbally. Anyone who has ever observed a mother in interaction with her baby will recognize such utterances as the following, cited by Trevarthen (1979): "Oh, what a big smile!" "Oh, really?" and "I'm *sure* you're right" (p. 340). Such interactions help create a communicative bond between mother and infant.

Aside from this general communicative value, speech to prelinguistic infants also serves a more specific function. We have seen that even neonates show sensitivity to and interest in speech sounds, and these keep increasing as they get older. Speech to infants no doubt enhances their interest and provides them with stimulating material that they can explore and become familiarized with on the sensorimotor level. The sensorimotor assimilations of and accommodations to speech refine infants' perceptions and prepare them for the learning of speech proper. Just as the sensorimotor exploration of objects lays the groundwork for object representation, so the sensorimotor exploration of speech lays the groundwork for speech representation.

It would also seem that parental speech to infants helps them develop cross-modal associations. Thus, Spelke and Owsley (1979) found that at 3½ months an infant will turn to look at either his/her father or mother depending on who spoke. This kind of association between sound and sight, which probably aids in the development of cross-modal coordination, depends on the exposure of infants to parental speech.

There are individual and social-class differences in the amount of speech to infants. Thus, Tulkin and Kagan (1972) found that American working-class mothers talked half as much to their 10-month-old daughters as middle-class mothers. It is noteworthy that the working-class mothers differed only minimally from the middle-class mothers in regard to amount of physical contact and nonverbal interaction with their babies.

Naturally, sensitive mothers adjust their speech, and other behaviors as well, to the infant's age. In a study of speech of mothers to 4-, 6-, and 8-month-old infants, Sherrod, Crawley, Petersen, and Bennett (1978) found that although directive speech (e.g., "Stand up," "Look") was common to the infants of all three ages, it was relatively more common to the oldest infants. Comments (e.g., "You're sleepy"), on the other hand, were uncommon altogether, but were relatively more frequent to the two younger groups of infants than to the oldest group. Evidently, mothers realize that the behavior of 8-month-old infants can be more readily directed than that of 4- and 6-month-old infants, and they adjust their speech accordingly. It is doubtful whether such adjustments in the preverbal period have any direct effect on language development. They do, however, reflect maternal interest and sensitivity, which as we saw in Chapters 4 and 7 play an important role in the child's learning of language in the verbal period proper.

Infant Reactions to Speech   Infants show social sensitivity to speech quite early. Common observation suggests that infants are soothed by gentle speech and relaxed to sleep by lullabies, especially when these come from their caregivers. An experimental study by Mills and Melhuish (1974) found that infants as young as 3 weeks showed a preference for the voices of their mothers over the voices of strange females. When presentation of the voices was made contingent on infant sucking, the infants sucked more to hear their mothers than to hear the strangers. The preferences of the infants were, of course, based on their ability to discriminate between the mother's voice and the stranger's voice. Although impressive, this kind of discriminatory capacity is not out of line with the infant's other discriminatory capacities reviewed earlier.

However, claims have been made about infant capacities that seem grossly exaggerated. I am particularly concerned about the wide acceptance of the claims made by Condon and Sander (1974a, 1974b). Condon and Sander (1974a) asserted: "As early as the first day of life, the human neonate moves in precise and sustained segments of movement that are synchronous with the articulated structure of adult speech" (p. 99). What is the evidence for this dramatic claim? Condon and Sander filmed the body movements of 16 1- to 14-day-old neonates as an adult was speaking in their presence. In the procedure used in the analysis of the films, a trained investigator listened to the speech on the sound track and with the aid of an acoustic sound reader marked on the film "the boundaries of speech segments, such as phones, syllables, and words" (Condon & Sander, 1974a, p. 99). He then viewed the films repeatedly in an attempt to identify configurations of gestures that were sustained for the same duration as one or another of the speech segments. The analysis of movements was very fine-grained. Distinctions such as the following were made: head moves right (left), head moves right slightly, and head moves right very slightly; head moves down, head moves down slightly, and head moves down very slightly; left elbow extends, left elbow extends fast, left elbow extends very fast, left elbow extends slightly, and left elbow extends very slightly.

Condon and Sander (1974a) report on the synchrony between "units" of movements and units of speech for two infants, stating that similar results were obtained for the remaining 14 infants. For one of the two infants there was agreement between the units of movement and the units of speech in 93% of the frames analyzed, and for the other the agreement was 87%. However, there was also 65% agreement between the gestures that one neonate produced without any exposure to speech and the speech spoken to another neonate. As there is no indication that the synchrony analysis was done blindly (i.e., without the analyzer knowing whether the speech and movements belonged to the same infant), the difference between 65% and 87%-93% could easily be due to analyzer bias. This is especially likely in view of the subjective nature of the analysis.

Moreover, one wishes the authors had provided evidence that they were able to score the movements of their subjects as finely as they did with a reasonable degree of reliability. They mention that there was high reliability in movement scoring in previous studies with adults. But surely it is misleading to generalize on this point from the precise and controlled movements of adults to the amorphous movements of neonates.

The case of Condon and Sander would have been more convincing had they identified the units of body movement and the units of speech independently of one another, and then predicted one from the other accurately. They did not even attempt to accomplish a feat of this sort. The subjective character of their technique is clearly stated (Condon, 1970): "The method that evolved is essentially similar to that of the ethologist who observes animal behavior for many hours, seeking for patterns and regularities. In the present case, films . . . were viewed over and over until regularities began to be seen" (p. 51).

Finally, it is hard to understand how neonates could have responded to speech in terms of sound segments and word units. Neither sound segments nor words are separated by boundaries in the acoustic signal. We hear sound segments and words because we know they are there and interpret the signal so as to detect them. But how could neonates do this? In addition to the methodological problems discussed, there is thus the logical difficulty of how infants could have responded to units of speech that they could not have perceived.

In view of the criticisms raised against the Condon and Sander work, it has to be concluded that the case for a synchronous relation between speech spoken to neonates and their movements has little objective support; it rests primarily on the subjective impressions of the investigators.

Imitation   During the first 6 months (i.e., in the first two sensorimotor stages), infants tend to increase the rate of their vocalizations when exposed to speech. This is an automatic type of response, there being no intention to imitate and no concern about correspondence to the model. Piaget (1951/1962) referred to these vocalizations as "vocal contagion" (p. 10) and considered them to be precursors of vocal imitation. In addition to the observations of Piaget and other diarists, there is other evidence in support of the existence of vocal contagion. A study of eight infants aged 3-4 months in spontaneous interaction with their mothers found that the infants were more likely to vocalize when the mothers spoke than when they were silent (Stern, Jaffe, Beebe, & Bennett, 1975).

Other studies suggest that whether the infant vocalizes or not in response to the vocalizations of others may depend on who the other is and on the context. For instance, Brown (1979) found that the voices of fathers elicited less vocalization in 4-month-old infants than either the voices of mothers or of male strangers but not less than those of female strangers. However, Brown's findings may be restricted to the artificial experimental situation she used. In her experiment each of the speakers had to utter the standard phrase: "Hello baby, how are you today?"

Taking the studies as a whole it may be concluded that speech addressed to infants has an effect on their rate of vocalization. However, we do not know at present the parameters of this effect, nor even under what conditions adult speech enhances or suppresses infant vocalization.

Although the first 6 months are characterized by imprecise, global imitation, occasional more-or-less exact reproductions of models can also be found, but they occur only sporadically and cannot be reliably elicited (Guillaume, 1926/1971, pp. 40-41; Piaget, 1951/1962, pp. 10-11). Piaget (1951/1962) notes that exact, differential imitation tends to occur more readily under circumstances of mutual imitation: "when the experimenter imitates the child at the very moment when he is uttering this or that particular sound" (p. 10). This is really a form of self-imitation, the model merely serving to reinforce the child's own repetitive vocalizations. Guillaume (1926/1971, pp. 36-37) thought of self-imitation in terms of mental inertia, it being easier to reactivate already excited neuromuscular processes than to activate new ones.

Although infants do not characteristically imitate individual sounds in the first 6 months, they do seem to imitate pitch levels. A recent study found that infants between the ages of 3 and 6 months were able to imitate selectively different levels of pitch (Kessen, Levine, & Wendrich, 1979).

Genuine imitation of sounds can be reliably elicited in the third sensorimotor stage (the third quarter of the first year). At this point the child's imitations are clearly deliberate, differential, and systematic. Stage 3 differs, however, from later stages. Only imitation of immediately heard sounds occurs (there is no delayed imitation), and imitation is restricted to sounds familiar to the child. Here is an example from Jacqueline (Piaget, 1951/1962) of Stage 3 vocal imitation:

At 0;6(25) J. invented a new sound by putting her tongue between her teeth. It was something like *pfs*. Her mother then made the same sound. J. was delighted and laughed as she repeated it in her turn. Then came a long period of mutual imitation.

J. said *pfs*, her mother imitated her, and J. watched her without moving her lips. Then when her mother stopped, J. began again, and so it went on. Later on, after remaining silent for some time, I myself said *pfs*. J. laughed and at once imitated me. There was the same reaction the next day, beginning in the morning (before she had herself spontaneously made the sound in question) and lasting throughout the day. (p. 19)

According to Piaget (1951/1962, p. 21), in the third stage children's motivation in imitating speech is to bring about the continuation of sounds that interest them. He emphasizes that at this stage children imitate sounds for the pleasure inherent in hearing them; the sounds imitated do not need to have any associations with meaning.

The increased interest in the third stage in the imitation of speech cannot but help advance the child's acquisition of speech. Through imitation, children learn to listen carefully to the utterances of others and to reproduce them. These perceptual and motor skills—which are also practiced in babbling—are essential for the acquisition of meaningful speech.

Vocal Communication   Imitation is a form of communication, but it is adult guided and it is usually noninstrumental. In the beginning of the second year children begin to use vocalizations for instrumental communicative purposes. Harding and Golinkoff (1979) have shown that this use of vocalization occurs at Stage 5 of sensorimotor development. In their experiment infants in the last quarter of the first year were tested to determine level of vocalization and stage of sensorimotor development. In the vocalization task the infants were confronted with a situation in which they could not obtain a desired goal without the mother's aid. In one of these a toy needed to be wound up, and in another a cookie was placed in a container that the infants could not open. The infants' vocalizations in this task were classified as intentional or nonintentional. Intention was inferred from the infants' nonverbal behavior accompanying vocalization. Thus, Suzie was considered to be vocalizing intentionally if, while vocalizing, she looked at the mother's hand, looked at the object, pointed to the object, or handed the object over to the mother.

The infants' stage of development in the realm of causality was also assessed using two Piaget-type tasks. For instance, in one task the experimenter abruptly pushed the infant's chair from behind. The infant was considered to be in Stage 5 if he or she actively searched for the cause of the movement by looking in front or behind. Harding and Golinkoff (1979) report: "No reaction, a startle response to the sudden movement but no search behavior, or the enactment of a 'procedure' . . . such as banging on the high chair, was scored as stage 4 behavior" (p. 36).

The results show that not one of the infants who were in Stage 4 in the causality tasks (there were 11 of them) vocalized intentionally, whereas 17 of 24 who were in Stage 5 did so. In this study vocalizing was defined globally to include "any vocal sound made by the infant, except uncontrollable crying, burping and sneezing"; the study was not concerned with linguistic speech. But children who recognize the social utility of vocalizing are ready to acquire the language of their community, as indeed they do. I turn now to a discussion of the acquisition of linguistic speech.

SPEECH DEVELOPMENT IN THE EARLY LINGUISTIC PERIOD

In the previous section I examined capacities and activities in infancy that prepare for the development of speech. Here I analyze the acquisition of speech proper.

Segments and Features

This subsection is concerned with the acquisition of individual sounds and the features composing them.

Jakobson's Theory   The most influential theory on the sequence of development of segmental speech units has been the one proposed by Jakobson (1941/1968). The fundamental point of his theory is that the child learns a series of oppositions rather than an inventory of individual sounds. The sequence of development of the oppositions is from the broadest to the narrowest, paralleling their relative importance in the languages of the world.

The first opposition the child acquires is between consonants and vowels. This is the broadest and most fundamental distinction in speech, and it is present in all human languages. Vowels allow relatively free passage of air, whereas consonants obstruct it to a greater or lesser degree. The consonants children tend to produce first are stops, whose articulation involves the greatest degree of airflow obstruction. Children produce, in particular, front stops ([p], [b], and [m]), which are relatively easy to articulate. The vowel common in early speech is the wide open [a]. Children thus begin the process of speech acquisition with the most extreme contrast on the vowel-consonant, open-closed dimension.

By saying that at first children have only the vowel-consonant opposition, Jakobson is claiming that only this difference is functional in their speech; that only this difference is phonemic. Children produce a variety of other sounds, but all of them are variants (allophones in the adult sense) of the vowel class or the consonant class. For the child at this first level of development, [papa], [mama], [baba], [tata], [dada], [kaka], and [gaga] are equivalent.

Gradually, differentiations develop within the vowel class and within the consonant class. The first consonantal contrast to develop is between oral and nasal stops, making possible such distinctions as those between [mama] and [papa]. At the oral-nasal stage [mama] and [nana] are equivalent, as are [papa] and [tata]. The second consonantal contrast is between labial and dental-alveolar stops (e.g., between [papa] and [tata] and between [mama] and [nana]). According to Jakobson (1941/1968): "These two oppositions [oral vs. nasal and labial vs. dental-alveolar] form the minimal consonantal system of the languages of the world. These are the only oppositions that cannot be lacking anywhere" (p. 48).

Jakobson further hypothesized that within a pair of opposing poles, one pole is more basic than the other. For example, in the opposition stops-fricatives, stops are more basic. Some linguists refer to the more basic term as **unmarked** and the less basic term as **marked** (see Anisfeld & Klenbort, 1973, for an exposition of the marked-unmarked distinction). As a rule, the presence, in child language or standard language, of the marked term presupposes the presence of the unmarked term, but not vice versa. Jakobson (1941/1968) wrote: "The acquisition of fricatives presupposes the acquisition of stops in child language; and in the linguistic systems of the world the former cannot exist unless the latter exist as well. Hence, there are no languages without stops, whereas [there are] a number of . . . languages in which fricatives are completely unknown" (p. 51). Jakobson notes further that children tend to mispronounce fricatives as their corresponding (in terms of place of articulation) stops, but not vice versa. Similarly, back consonants (marked) tend to be mispronounced as their corresponding (in terms of manner of articulation) front consonants (unmarked).

Jakobson's theory has introduced order into a field in which there were many scattered observations but no overall organizing framework (Leopold, 1953/1971). His fundamental insight—that speech development consists not in the learning of an inventory of sounds, but in the construction of a system of relations—captures the essence of the process of development not only in the area of speech but in other domains as well. Moreover, the particular hierarchy of development that he postulated generally accords well with available evidence (see Ferguson & Garnica, 1975).

However, it must be realized that Jakobson's theory is an idealization. As becomes apparent later in this exposition, there is much less uniformity across children and much more variation within children than his theory would suggest. In a study of 10 children between the ages of 1;4 to 1;10, whose vocabularies did not exceed 50 words, Leonard, Newhoff, and Mesalam (1980) found that pronunciations of sounds tended to be lexically bound. That is, a child may have articulated a particular sound successfully in one word but not in another word. Moreover, Leonard et al. also found some instability even in the pronunciation of the same word. For instance, one child articulated *bye-bye* differently in the same session, once as [baba] and once as [dayday].

Jakobson's theory can be accepted in probabilistic terms, not in absolute terms (see Macken, 1980). For instance, it can be predicted with some certainty that most children are likely to acquire some front consonants before acquiring any back consonants. But the statement that all children will acquire all front

consonants before all back consonants is contrary to fact. In this respect, phonological predictions are no different from any other psychological predictions.
They are all probabilistic.

Another criticism leveled against Jakobson's theory is that it is too one-sided
in considering functional contrast as the sole factor determining order of acquisition. As Leopold (1947/1970) so aptly stated: "I am not inclined to accept his
tenet that physiological difficulties play no part at all. The delayed acquisition of
the 'liquids,' for instance, can be explained just as well by their complex articulation as by the lack of contrast with other consonants, which is the consequence
of it" (p. 267). Empirical research has indeed begun in recent years to explore
the physiological factors that might be related to order of acquisition in various
domains of sound production (see, e.g., Cooper, 1977).

The foregoing points are not so much criticisms as amendments to the essentially correct emphasis of Jakobson. We saw in Chapter 8 that in the mature
speaker phonology operates as a structured system. Jakobson's paramount contribution lies in his proposal that phonology also develops as a system. As the
rest of this chapter demonstrates, the evidence for this position is overwhelming.

Children Construct Phonological Contrasts   When we hear young children
articulate words differently than we do, our spontaneous tendency is to consider
their articulations as no more than distortions of the correct pronunciations, but
this attitude fails to recognize children's constructive approach to the acquisition
of speech. It is true that sometimes children's deviant pronunciations are simply
mistakes due to inattentiveness or to faulty hearing of an unstressed syllable or
rapidly produced sound (Leopold, 1947/1970, pp. 268-269). But more characteristically, when carefully examined, children's speech reveals internal logic
and coherence. Jakobson (1941/1968) made this point by saying that children's
copying entails "a creative departure from the prototype" (p. 14). As an example he indicates that before they gain control of the [r], Russian children represent it in their speech by lengthening the vowel preceding it. For instance, they
would render *marka* ('mark') as something like [maːka]. Russian children thus
invent a vowel-length contrast that standard Russian does not have. In a thorough
and sophisticated study of the speech of his son Amahl between the ages of 26
months and 4 years, Smith (1973, p. 95) also found a functional use of vowel
length. Amahl, for instance, rendered "pink" as [bik] and "pig" as [biːk].

An example of construction in the domain of fricatives is provided by Carlson
and Anisfeld (1969) for a 25-month-old boy, Richard Carlson. Richard exhibited
pronunciations that at first glance seem like spiteful distortions of the speech of
his elders. He said, for instance, [bæf] for "bath" and [giθ] for "kiss," not
articulating the [θ] in the final position of "bath," where it did belong, and
articulating it in the final position of "kiss," where it did not belong. The most
striking example was "toothbrush" /tuθbrʌš/, which Richard articulated as
[duwfbəθ], rendering the [θ] of the target word as [f] and the [š] as [θ].

Richard's speech falls into place, however, when we consider it in terms of contrasts and relations in the fricative system. The English fricatives are distinguished from one another by place of articulation and voicing. We can disregard the voicing distinction because at this point it was not yet functional in Richard's speech. In terms of place of articulation the fricatives are ordered from the back of the mouth to the front as follows: [š ž] [s z] [θ ð] [f v]. (The two sounds bracketed together are articulated at the same point; they differ only in regard to voicing, which is not relevant to this analysis.) Because Richard had difficulty articulating sounds in the back of his mouth (a difficulty characteristic of young children), he was restricted to two points of articulation instead of the four in adult English. Given this restriction, Richard's fricative system as a *whole* corresponded very well to the adult system. Thus, Richard moved the two back pairs of sounds [š ž] and [s z] one step forward and rendered them as [θ ð]. The [θ ð] in turn were moved one step forward and articulated as [f v]. Inasmuch as this is the most forward point for fricatives, Richard's [f v] were also articulated here and corresponded to standard [f v]. The relation between the standard adult system and Richard's system can be displayed as follows:

Standard:	š ž		s z		θ ð		f v
Richard:					θ ð		f v

Thus, Richard's fricative system corresponded to the adult system in terms of patterns of relations, even though it was not faithful to the adult system on the level of rendition of specific sounds. A phenomenon similar to Richard's was reported for a 38-month-old boy by Smith (1973, p. 150).

Finally, a technically based investigation of the development of voicing reveals patterning not perceptible by the unaided adult ear (Macken & Barton, 1980). This study analyzed spectographically the VOTs of three pairs of voiceless-voiced stops, /p-b/, /t-d/, and /k-g/, produced by four children over an 8-month period, from about 1;6 to about 2;2. The children's utterances were recorded in biweekly sessions lasting 20-30 minutes. The analysis was restricted to the children's productions of the stops in the initial positions of words.

The VOT analysis revealed three phenomena concerning the voicing feature. First, at the younger ages the children articulated both the voiceless and the voiced stops with mean VOT values that were within the adult range for voiced stops (i.e., VOT < 30 msec). Second, at the older ages the VOT values for the voiceless stops increased and began to approximate adult values. These two findings confirm what had been known on the basis of unaided observation. In addition, Macken and Barton observed a phenomenon that had not been known before. Two of the four children they studied had, in some sessions, mean VOT values for the voiceless stops that were significantly higher than the values for the voiced stops, but both were within the adult range for voiced stops and, for this reason, indistinguishable by the adult ear. For instance, one of the children,

Tessa, produced her /d/s in Session 1 with a mean VOT of +2.40 (range: −21 to +14) and her /t/s with a mean VOT of +20.50 (range: +7 to +43). Even the trained linguists who studied Tessa's speech did not hear this difference. These findings raise the possibility that young children may have sound contrasts that adults do not hear. However, further experimental clarification of these results is needed, especially in view of the findings discussed earlier that infants do not discriminate between VOT differences that fall within the adult voiced and voiceless categories.

Word Structure

The previous subsection focused on the characteristics of individual sounds. The present subsection examines the phonetic structure of words.

Reduplication One of the best established phenomena in early speech is reduplication, the production of bisyllabic words in which the second syllable repeats the first wholly or partly. Examples of full reduplication are *wawa* (for 'water') and *haihai* ('ride'); examples of partial reduplication are *gogi* ('doggie') and *kekl* ('kettle'). Early reports of this phenomenon can be found in Jespersen (1922/1964, pp. 108-110), Leopold (1947/1970, pp. 213-226), and Lewis (1936/1975). In an examination of the first six words of 27 children, Lewis found that 46% were reduplicated. Languages have recognized children's fondness of reduplication and legitimized reduplicated words for talk with children (e.g., *choo-choo* and *mommy*). As Ferguson (1964) stated: "Reduplication can probably be regarded as a feature of baby talk throughout the world" (p. 109).

Children on their part seem to use reduplication to bring their speech closer to the speech of their community. Early investigators (Guillaume, 1926/1971, p. 36; Leopold, 1947/1970) noted that the words reduplicated by children tend to be more than one syllable long in standard language. Leopold (1947/1970) considered this characteristic part of the definition of reduplication: "It consists of the imitation of a standard two-syllable word by a two-syllable form, of which however only one, usually the stressed one, is evolved regularly from the model, whereas the other one is simple repetition" (p. 216). The association of reduplication with longer words suggests that children try to match the syllabic structure of words, even though they cannot fully reproduce their individual sounds.

An investigation by Schwartz, Leonard, Wilcox, and Folger (1980) provides statistical evidence for the matching hypothesis. Schwartz et al. selected, out of a group of 12 children, 6 who exhibited a high rate of reduplication. The reduplication for these children ranged from 20%-50%, as compared to a range of 3%-12% for the remaining 6 children. The reduplication count included both full and partial reduplications. Some examples from this study are: [mImI] ('banana'), [nɛkɛ] ('necklace'), and [kikə] ('chicken'). An analysis of the words the children produced in relation to the standard target words they attempted to produce revealed that only 9% of the monosyllabic targets were reduplicated, whereas 71% of the multisyllabic targets were reduplicated.

The production of bisyllabic words involves the integration of the component syllables into a cohesive whole. It would seem that a young child on the threshold of language would be able to manage this integration effort more readily if the additional syllable did not add to the effort involved in planning and producing individual sounds. Reduplication is a strategy that accomplishes just that and thereby reduces the total cognitive effort required for the production of bisyllabic words. According to this interpretation reduplication is a transitional strategy that should decline as the child gets older and more skilled at linguistic coordination in other aspects of language, such as sentence production. There is some support for this hypothesis in the Schwartz et al. study. Their descriptive data show that the group of high reduplicators was younger (mean age = 17.0 months) than the group of low reduplicators (mean age = 19.7 months). Also, the low reduplicators had begun to produce sentences (MLU = 1.13), whereas the high reduplicators had virtually no sentences at all (MLU = 1.03).

This interpretation of reduplication in terms of the cognitive effort involved in coordination can also find support in a study by Ramsay (1980) on the relation between the incidence of nonreduplicated multisyllabic words in children's speech and the acquisition of bimanual handedness. Bimanual handedness refers to the ability to hold an object with one hand and to manipulate it with the other. Ramsay found that an increase in multisyllabic words coincided with the achievement of bimanual handedness. This finding suggests that there may be some relation between the neurological development necessary for hand coordination and for speech coordination.

The Consonantal Structure of Words   One of the clearest characteristics of early speech is the rarity of consonantal clusters (i.e., of sequences of consonants without intervening vowels, as in the beginning of "*st*reet"). Children often represent in their speech only one of the consonants from a target consonant cluster, even when they are able to produce all the consonants in the cluster individually. This happens because the production of a sequence of consonants without intervening vowels requires fine articulatory control.

When replacing a consonantal cluster by a single consonant, children do not choose the consonant randomly. Smith (1973), for instance, found that in the case of Amahl, clusters that contained a stop were "almost invariably reduced to the stop alone" (p. 166). Leopold (1947/1970, p. 137) suggested that the general tendency is to retain the consonant easiest to articulate. To substantiate this suggestion more work will have to be done to determine the relative articulatory difficulty of different sounds for children.

Ingram (1974a) formulated a different kind of regularity in the use of consonants in words. His formulation is based on a systematic examination of the speech records of two children and of anecdotal evidence from other children.

One of the two children was a French-speaking, 17-month-old girl who lived in France at the end of the 19th century. Her speech record was available in a published source. The other was an English-speaking, 21-month-old boy who lived in California in the 1970s. Analyzing words that contain two consonants (not in a cluster), Ingram discovered a tendency for children to acquire words in which the second consonant was articulated farther back in the articulatory tract than the first before they acquired words in which the first consonant was farther back. For instance, *book*, in which the first consonant is articulated in the lip region and the second in the velar region, tends to appear in children's speech before *cup*, in which the order of consonants is reversed. Ingram also found that deformations of words were in the direction of conformity with the forward-backward ordering tendency. Thus, *animal* was rendered [mænu], reversing the [n-m] order of the target, and *cup* was rendered [pak], reversing the [k-p] order. A critical examination of Ingram's formulation indicated that it is fairly general, although by no means absolute for any children or universal for all children (Menn, 1975). In another publication Ingram (1974b) formulated other generalizations about early phonology.

Individual Words and Conformity to the System

The emphasis throughout the preceding exposition on patterns and regularities should not be interpreted to mean that all the utterances a child produces are governed by rules. In as complex a system as speech, which is in continuous flux and is dependent on the vagaries of exposure from others, there are bound to be items, at any given point in time, that are extrasystemic. Some words may be less advanced in their phonological characteristics than the system at the moment allows because they have become entrenched at an earlier level of development, whereas other words may be more advanced because of privileged exposure or special attraction. Even so, the sweeping influence of patterns is unmistakable. This point was highlighted by the two most sophisticated diarists in the area of phonology, Werner Leopold (1947/1970, p. 264) and Neilson Smith (1973, pp. 140-143).

Smith (1973) emphasized particularly the rapidity of change from one pattern to another: "Usually any change was spread over a period of several days or, rarely, weeks, with free variation between the old and the new form occurring first in a few words, then in a majority, and then again in just a few stragglers" (p. 140). An example should make this point more concrete. From 28 to 31 months Amahl consistently assimilated alveolar consonants to the velar consonants that followed them. For example, he articulated *dark* as [ga:k], changing the alveolar [d] to a [g], which is a velar stop, just like the [k] that comes after it, and he articulated *stuck* as [gʌk], dropping the initial [s] and changing the alveolar [t] to a velar [g]. Then over a period of some 6 weeks, Amahl gradually moved to full conformity to the adult pattern. First, a couple of words broke away from total conformity to the old pattern and appeared both in the old pattern and the new pattern; specifically, *doctor* was pronounced sometimes as [gɔktə] and sometimes as [dɔktə], and *choke* was pronounced sometimes as [ko:k] and sometimes as [to:k]. Next, in addition to words that appeared exclusively in the old pattern and words that appeared in both patterns, there were words that appeared exclusively in the new pattern (e.g., [tʌŋ] for *tongue*). In the third step in the process of changeover, the new pattern predominated. At this point, 22 words appeared exclusively in the new form, 1 in both the new and old forms, and 2 only in the old form. Finally, at the end of the 6-week period all words but one appeared exclusively in the new form.

This example illustrates two points. First, it demonstrates individual variation among words. Whereas some words led in the launching of the new pattern, others joined in only after it became established. Second, it brings to light the sweeping force of an emerging pattern. After a relatively short period the new pattern asserted its dominance and brought into line dissident words.

The extreme pressure for conformity exercised by a pattern is shown quite dramatically in an example provided by Leopold (1947/1970, pp. 33, 133, & 265). In the age range of 10-20 months Hildegard correctly pronounced the cluster [pr] in the word *pretty*, even though she generally reduced [pr]s and other consonantal clusters to single consonants. Leopold (1947/1970) notes that in this 10-month period Hildegard used *pretty* as a "vague emotive" (p. 265) and articulated it in a distinct, whispered fashion. But *pretty* "lost the r and voiced the p

THE FAMILY CIRCUS   **By Bill Keane**

"These are called place maps 'cause they show
you where your place is."

in agreement with the prevailing phonetic practice as soon as it became an attributive adjective'' (p. 265). At this time it also lost its whispered pronunciation and was spoken in the same way as other words. We see here that *pretty* was not subject to pressures for conformity as long as it stood outside the linguistic system (indicated by the whispered pronunciation and by the lack of distinct referent). But as soon as it joined the system, it had to give up the longstanding habit and fall into line. Such is the force of a pattern!

Speech in Imitation, Production, and Perception

So far the discussion of phonological development in the linguistic period was based on children's spontaneous productions. In this subsection I widen the base by analyzing children's phonological functioning in several behavioral domains.

Imitation   Sometime during their second or third year children's imitation of speech increases markedly. Typically, a child will echo the last word or phrase of someone else's utterance, as in the example Jespersen (1922/1964) gave from his son Frans, 1;9:

Father: Shall I carry you?
Frans: Carry you.
Father: Shall Mother carry Frans?
Frans: Carry Frans.
Father: The sky is so blue.
Frans: So boo.
Father: I shall take an umbrella.
Frans: Take rella. (p. 135)

Jespersen referred to this kind of incessant imitation as "echoism," and Guillaume (1926/1971, p. 34) referred to it as **echolalia.** Echolalia is a reflection of the child's intense interest in and preoccupation with the acquisition of language.

In such immediate imitations children sometimes exhibit sounds and sound sequences that they do not normally produce on their own. Weir (1966), for instance, reported the following exchange of her son Michael, 2;2, with her and his brother Anthony:

Michael: How about a coom?
Mother: You have a spoon.
Anthony: Why does he say coom?
Mother: I don't know.
Anthony: Mikey, can you say spoon?
Michael: Spoon. (p. 164)

Michael was thus able to imitate correctly a word that he distorted in his spontaneous speech.

Scollon (1976, p. 72) also noted that the imitations of his subject, Brenda,
were sometimes on a more advanced level than her spontaneous productions. For
instance, Brenda, 1;8(21), dropped the final [ŋ] in *hiding* in spontaneous production, but she produced it in immediate imitation. Higher level competence in immediate imitation than in spontaneous production was also demonstrated in an
experimental investigation by Leonard, Schwartz, Folger, and Wilcox (1978).
Immediate, echoic imitation reveals phonetic capacities that have not yet been
incorporated into the child's active-productive system of phonological
knowledge.

Perception   There have been persistent anecdotal reports of children being
able to hear differences between words that they pronounce as homonyms (see,
e.g., Leopold, 1947/1970, pp. 267-274). Jakobson (1941/1968), for instance,
refers to a 1-year-old Serbian boy who "distinguished faultlessly the words *tata*
and *kaka* when spoken to him" (p. 22), but in his own speech consistently used
tata for both words. It is hard, however, to draw definite conclusions from anecdotal reports because of the possibility that the child responded not to the difference between the words but to the difference between the contexts in which the
words were spoken.

A systematic comparison between performance in a production task and in a
perceptual task was reported by Edwards (1974) for children between the ages of
20 and 47 months. In the perceptual task pairs of artificial names that differed
minimally (e.g., *tup* and *dup*) were assigned to different objects. The child was
then asked, in requests using one or the other of the names, to do something with
one of the objects. Children who picked the correct objects at above chance level
must have heard a difference between the two names; that is, they must have
discriminated between the minimally contrasting sounds (in the example, between a [t] and a [d]). In the production task the children were asked to repeat the
same words, and their articulation of the minimally different sounds was noted.
Edwards found that in most comparisons children did better in the perceptual
task than in the production task. The most obvious interpretation of the difference between the perception and production tasks is that children hear differences that they have difficulty articulating.

The research discussed so far concerning children's discriminations was based
on their direct responses to words. Smith has used more subtle kinds of evidence
to support the claim that children discriminate perceptually between sounds that
are indistinguishable in their articulations. To get an idea of the approach Smith
uses, consider the following example (Smith, 1973, pp. 2, 20, 102, 145-146,
208, & Appendix C). At 26 months, Amahl produced a [w] both for standard /w/
and standard /f/ (e.g., [wɛt] for 'wet', [wiːt] for 'feet', [wit] for 'fish', and
[wæwə] for 'flower'). From these productions one would conclude that Amahl

did not distinguish between /w/ and /f/. But Smith argues that Amahl did distinguish perceptually between the two, even though he articulated them identically. Smith bases his argument on the fact that when the [f] began to appear in Amahl's speech 6 months later, it appeared only for adult /f/ words, not for adult /w/ words.

From examples such as these, Smith concludes that Amahl made finer perceptual distinctions than articulatory distinctions. Smith's line of evidence is innovative. But critical scrutiny suggests some problems. In particular, because Amahl continued to be exposed to words from adults, it is possible that his later differentiations (e.g., between /w/ and /f/) were due to contemporaneous experience rather than to earlier internal knowledge.

The discussion so far has concerned perceptual discriminations which the investigator infers from one type of behavior or another. I now turn to children's own awareness of perceptual differences.

The Fis Phenomenon   Children sometimes express displeasure when adults imitate their distorted pronunciations of words (e.g., Jespersen, 1922/1964, p. 110). Here is an example concerning the pronunciation of *fish* by a 3-year-old girl (Palermo, 1978):

Adult: What do you have in your bag?
Child: Candy fis. Would you like one?
Adult: Candy fis?
Child: No, fis.
Adult: I would love to have a fis.
Child: No, not fis, fis!
Adult: Oh, fish.
Child: Yes, fis. Here is one for you. (p. 96)

Similar observations have been recorded for other difficult sounds besides [š] (see Priestly, 1980), but it is convenient to focus our discussion on the *fish* example.

There are two aspects to the "fis phenomenon." First, the girl obviously heard some difference between the adult's normative rendition of the word (*fish*) and the adult's distorted rendition (*fis*). Second, she articulated the word in the distorted form but believed that her articulation corresponded to the normative form.

The girl obviously had difficulty articulating the palatal [š] and articulated it, one step forward in the mouth, as the alveolar [s]. But why did she hear herself distinguishing between [s] and [š]? There are two possible answers. First, it may be that she did articulate the two sounds somewhat differently, but the adult listener did not hear the difference because her articulations did not match his. This interpretation gains some plausibility from the voicing results of Macken and

THE FAMILY CIRCUS

By Bill Keane

"Know why PJ doesn't talk so good? I sink it's cause he's too yittle."

Barton discussed earlier. However, initial experimental attempts to have children listen to their own recorded speech to see if they hear differences in their speech not heard by adult listeners have produced conflicting results (see Priestly, 1980).

An alternative, and at present more plausible, explanation would be that the girl heard not what she said but what she intended to say. According to this interpretation the girl had a separate internal representation for [s] and for [š] but was able to articulate only the [s], not the [š], which is farther back in the articulatory tract.

Practice and Play

So far the discussion in this section concentrated on manifestations of children's knowledge of speech. I turn now to manifestations of children's interest in speech.

Children take an active part in the acquisition of speech and direct considerable effort to this task. One of the most detailed accounts of speech practice was provided by the Labovs (1978). Their description is based on close observation of their daughter Jessie over a span of 5 months from 1;3(15) to 1;8(15). During this period Jessie was so preoccupied with the words *cat* and *mama* that the

Labovs characterized it as "the *cat* and *mama* period." Of a total of 12,400 word tokens that were recorded for Jessie in this period, *cat* and *mama* accounted for 85%; *cat* contributing 5268 instances and *mama* 5255. According to the Labovs Jessie used these words so frequently not primarily because of interest in their referents, but because they served as useful vehicles for the discovery of the principles of phonological structure. The Labovs base this conclusion on the patterned variations in pronunciation to which Jessie subjected these words.

During this period, when Jessie concentrated on the workings of speech, she showed little interest in the acquisition of new sounds or new words. In fact, active attempts to teach Jessie new words were unsuccessful at this time. Jessie embarked on the acquisition of new words and sounds only after she acquired the mechanisms and general principles of speech production. This is reminiscent of the observation made at the end of Chapter 4 that when children begin to acquire syntax, the acquisition of vocabulary comes to a temporary standstill. Jessie's was an individual strategy, and it will not be known how common this type of strategy is until the speech of other children is analyzed in as minute detail as Jessie's was. But the interest she showed in the learning of speech is not unrepresentative of other children, although different children may exhibit their interest in different ways.

Just as children grope toward the correct construction of sentences (see Chap. 7), so they also grope toward correct rendition of words. Scollon (1976, pp. 54 & 66) reported some observations on this point from his subject, Brenda. Holding up a shoe, Brenda, 1;7(2), went through the sequence: š, šI, š, šIš, šu, šu?, šuš. About 2 months later, at 1;8(21), she worked on the correct pronunciation of *give,* saying in succession: gieuf, gief, giv.

A particularly precocious form of phonological sensitivity at a young age was reported by Horgan (1981) for her daughter Kelly. At 1;8, Kelly engaged in such phonetic-pattern games as the following: *cow go moo*; *mommy go mamoo*; *daddy go dadoo*; *ha ha.* As Kelly grew older her phonetic games became more sophisticated. Horgan (1981) reports: "For example, at 3;3 she began starting the last syllable of every content word with a [t] and stressing that syllable: *banana* became *banaTA,* dinner became *dinTER* . . . Her special way of talking was always accompanied by much giggling" (p. 219).

In her analysis of the presleep soliloquies of Anthony between the ages of 28 and 30 months (introduced in Chap. 7), Weir (1962) also found an interest in sounds. In one example, Weir shows how Anthony exercised the correct pronunciation of the first vowel in *berries.* He first pronounced it as [ɛ] and then rejected this pronunciation in favor of [æ]. Weir (1966) reported that her two other sons also showed metalinguistic interest in speech. For example, at 3 years David practiced his newly acquired [r] in the word *story.* He would first render the word with an [l] as he had done before, recognize that this pronunciation was wrong, and proceed to articulate it with an [r].

Jespersen (1922/1964) also noted that children practice sounds and sound combinations and "are proudly conscious of the happy results of their efforts" (p. 111). For instance, when Frans mastered the consonantal cluster *fl-*, at 2;11, he went around to his parents saying various words (in Danish) that began with this cluster and asking them whether they could pronounce them. Jespersen (1922/1964) reported that: "When asked whether he could say *blad*, he answered: 'No, not yet; Frans cannot say *b- lad*' (with a little interval between the *b* and the *l*)" (p. 111). And when 5 weeks later Frans could say *kl-*, he announced proudly "Frans can say *kla* so well" (p. 111).

Keenan (1974) recorded the interactions between her twin boys, 2;9, while they were still in bed early in the morning. She found that speech-play was quite common in this situation. The boys showed awareness (through laughter) that they were using speech in an out-of-the-ordinary fashion. Here is an example:

First boy: sha, batsh.
Second boy: bathi:, bi:shi:, badi:, bi:di, babi.
First boy: badi: (laughing).

The *social* speech-play of Keenan's twins reflected their unique relationship and special circumstance. It does not appear to be very common. Garvey (1977) investigated the speech-play of children between the ages of 3 and 5½ years. The children were observed during a 15-minute play session, playing either individually or with another child. Garvey (1977) found that the children did not engage one another in speech-play and concluded: "playing with sounds and noises appears to be primarily a private, solitary activity" (p. 33). Garvey's explanation is that under the pressures of social interaction children do not have the peace of mind for speech-play.

Garvey gives some interesting examples of individual speech-play. One boy was playing with a dune buggy. Then shortly after it was named for him, he dropped the buggy and began playing with the name. First, he changed the stress pattern from 'dune buggy to 'dune 'bu-'ggy, emphasizing all three syllables, not just the first one. Then, he changed *dune* to *june*, saying 'june 'june 'bu-'ggy.

In another example given by Garvey a 3-year-old girl entertained herself for the entire 15-minute period by taking apart and putting together the word *yesterday*. The first two lines of Garvey's (1977) report are reproduced here:
'yester 'yester 'yesterday.
'yesterday yes 'too. (p. 33)

In their speech-play children engage not only in the manipulation of the syllabic structure, the stress patterns, and the sounds of words but also in the production of special voice effects. Garvey observed children "talk funny" in squeaky or gruff voices to produce desired effects. In role playing they adjusted their voices to take on the qualities of the characters they attempted to enact.

Voice manipulation was also reported for a child younger than the subjects in Garvey's study (Carlson & Anisfeld, 1969):

> From the very first (21 months) there was a clear distinction between language meant to communicate with others and language which was not used primarily to elicit a response. The communicative speech was normally loud, there was eye contact or even physical contact with the addressee, and utterances were repeated almost identically until the addressee responded or until frustration or boredom overcame the child. Roughly 20 per cent of the child's utterances were communicative in the normal play situation, with mother or brother present, during the first 6 months of the study (21 to 27 months), although during certain activities, such as looking at a book with his mother, the percentage of response-eliciting speech was much higher. The chief characteristics of noncommunicative speech were variability in the repetitions and lack of focus on an addressee. Loudness tended to the extremes (whispering or shrieking), and the pitch patterns were sometimes deviant (squeaking, singing).
>
> Different styles of noncommunicative speech are reflected in the following three examples. At 31 months, after a discussion about the bath temperature with his brother, Richard said, "Is it too hot for me?" in a staccato rhythm which he had used since about 22 months. The question was directed at no one, and his action at the time was to play with a toy rather than to attempt to get out or to feel the water temperature. By 27 months he also had a joking tone of voice—lower in pitch, more forced, half-smiling—which became more common, especially when he was deliberately making a statement which was semantically deviant. For example, he said, "Mommy is John, and I'm Steven, and Geoffrey is Steven," using the names of some playmates. This tone was seldom used in imaginative play.
>
> One of the most striking noncommunicative speech styles, sometimes involving grammatical as well as phonological deviation, occurred at about 31 months, usually in situations in which he knew he would probably be forbidden to do what he was about to ask. The characteristics were fuzzy enunciation, very soft voice, and twisting of the head as he spoke. For example, at a stage at which he produced sentences such as "Now can I get out?" he asked to go into a forbidden room by pointing and saying, "Can me here?" in this strange soft voice. When asked, "What?" he repeated the question in the same way rather than in the normal voice one would expect if he were interested in the answer. (pp. 574-575)

The various anecdotes described here have shown how speech engages the interest of children and involves them in play and practice. Presumably, all these activities are somehow related to the learning of phonology and other aspects of language, although we do not know precisely how. It is also clear that different children approach speech in different ways. A preliminary attempt to systematize the different learning styles was made by Ferguson (1979), and we can look forward to productive research in this area in the coming years.

SUMMARY

The course of speech development can be divided into two periods: the prelinguistic period, until about 12 months, and the linguistic period, from then on. From the start, infants exhibit attentiveness to speech and a capacity to discriminate speech sounds on the basis of phonetically relevant characteristics. In the course of cooing, babbling, and imitation, infants develop articulatory skills and enhance their discriminatory abilities. Then, when the symbolic capacity begins to emerge at the start of the second year, they are ready to utilize what they have learned about speech perception and the mechanics of articulatory production to construct a linguistic system of speech. The sound system children construct is part and parcel of the language system as a whole. They develop sound categories on the basis of differences in word meanings and for the purpose of differentiating meanings.

Children take an active role in the process of building up a speech system: They listen carefully, and they play and experiment with sounds. A close examination of children's speech in the linguistic period shows that even young children treat speech not as an inventory of isolated sounds, but as a system of relations.

11 Summary and Integration

This book attempted to tell the story of how children construct for themselves the language of their community in the first 3 years of life. Authors typically begin the exposition of language development around the middle of the second year, when children start to produce interpretable words. But language development really begins before such overt signs are manifest. It begins at birth. First, exposure to speech and vocalization in the first year prepare the perceptual and vocal mechanisms for speech proper in the second year. Second, in the period of infancy children develop formats of interaction with their caregivers that facilitate the learning of language and its communicative use. Third, and critically, in infancy children develop the symbolic capacity, which is a prerequisite for the acquisition of language.

The emergence of symbolic-linguistic intelligence in the second year constitutes a true revolution in human development. But, like other successful revolutions, the groundwork has been laid in advance. The entire course of sensorimotor development can, in fact, be viewed as aimed at getting the child ready for symbols and language.

During the first 6 months of life, infants have no representational capacity; therefore, they have no way to store knowledge and little interest in acquiring it. All they remember are the residues of their sensations and actions, their sensorimotor schemes. Young infants have little voluntary control over their sensorimotor schemes. The schemes cannot be activated at will by the infant; they are evoked by internal and external stimuli. Gradually, sensorimotor schemes become capable of increasingly greater dissociation from stimulus contexts and they begin to serve as vehicles of representation. By the end of the first year there are normally clear signs that the infant has ceased being a sensorimotor creature and is becoming an information processor. Curiosity flourishes, exploratory activities become abundant, and there are the beginnings of make-believe play. Early make-believe play is only minimally symbolic, because the representational entities in the make-believe episodes are closely tied to sensorimotor action. Thus, when Suzie pretends to drink from a cup, she is not moving very far from a familiar instrumental sensorimotor scheme. The advance is in that she is using the scheme for a representational purpose.

The first manifestations of symbolic language also appear around the first birthday. During the first year, infants showed a great deal of interest in speech sounds, but the interest was focused on the pleasure inherent in hearing the sounds themselves. Now they begin to use speech referentially; they begin to make connections between sounds and meanings. But early words are limited symbolically; they are context bound. Gradually, children achieve an appreciation, in the second half of the second year, for the social-symbolic character of word meaning, and when this happens their vocabularies increase by leaps and bounds.

Productive syntax begins about a month or two after the vocabulary growth spurt. The use of syntax involves a higher level of symbolism than the use of single words, because in sentences words have to relate not only to external entities, but also to one another. Morphology develops after the onset of syntax, sometime during the third year.

The symbolic capacity is a prerequisite for language, but it does not determine its structure or course of development. That is, once children become symbolically ready for language, they acquire it in terms of its own inherent structure and dynamics. Language ushers in a new phenomenon not foreshadowed by preceding developments. I have emphasized, following Piaget, the continuity of language with earlier symbolic development, taking the position that language can emerge only after the symbolic capacity has been developed in infancy. But there is also discontinuity in the acquisition of language, particularly in the acquisition of its grammatical aspects: syntax, morphology, and phonology. Children develop the grammar of their language to a large extent independently of their achievements in other intellectual domains. Piaget did not appreciate the autonomy of language, because he focused on words and meanings and did not concern himself with the grammatical aspects of language. I side with Chomsky in assuming that the extent of linguistic autonomy is due to a specialized innate predisposition which unfolds without the necessary mediation of conscious intelligence.

Thus, one of the issues I have attempted to address in the book concerns the relation between the acquisition of language and the development of the symbolic capacity. Another theme I have tried to clarify relates to a fundamental distinction between skills and knowledge, which is often not fully appreciated. I have tried to make clear, for instance, that when infants distinguish an object they have seen before from an object they have not seen, this does not mean that they have knowledge and memory of the object as such. This kind of discrimination can be accomplished on the sensorimotor level. Similarly, it does not follow from the fact that young infants can discriminate between various speech sounds that they represent sounds internally.

The issue of skills versus knowledge does not concern the quality of performance, but rather the processes underlying it. Discrimination and recognition can be as good or better on the sensorimotor level as on the representational level. But they are accomplished in different ways. The transition from sensorimotor to representational intelligence consists not primarily in children being able to do things better, but in their becoming thinkers and not merely doers.

A third theme that is highlighted in the book concerns children's active role in the acquisition of language: their discovery of principles and formation of rules. We have seen over and over again that children's language in all its aspects has internal logic and coherence. This is perhaps clearest in the area of phonology where it has been shown that when children's distorted speech is examined in its own terms, it reveals clear patterning and regularity.

The child's discovery of principles and construction of rules is also evident in the shift from slow to accelerated growth, which is seen in the acquisition of vocabulary, syntax, and morphology. Thus, when one traces the acquisition of vocabulary, one sees at first small increases from week to week in the number of words uttered, and then an abrupt upturn in the rate of word acquisition. Likewise, after a period of small increments in the number of sentences, comes an explosion in syntactic productivity. A similar trend appears in the acquisition of inflections. During the slow periods, children seem to be groping to discover the operating principles, that is, that words are names, that word order can be used to express meaning, and that morphological changes can be used for semantic purposes. When a principle is discovered, it serves as a basis for the formation of generalizations and rules that can subserve a broad range of uses, thus explaining the emergent productivity. The capacity for the discovery of principles and the formation of rules has its roots in the fourth sensorimotor stage at the end of the first year, when children begin to be able to learn by inference.

By the age of 3 years the typical child has gained entry into all domains of language, including vocabulary, phonology, syntax, and morphology. There is a great deal of specific material that remains to be learned, but the child will now be learning as an insider on the basis of the foundations laid in the first 3 years. The laying of the foundations of language is not accomplished without effort and hard work, but children take naturally to the task and proceed enthusiastically and in a sure-footed manner.

Glossary

Accommodation (Piagetian) Modification of **schemes** as a result of the **assimilation** of new **stimuli**.

Actor The entity in a sentence that is responsible for the action described by the verb (e.g., *The man* in *The man cut the wood*).

Adjectivization Formation of adjectives from verbs (e.g., *decisive* from *decide*).

Affricate A speech sound that combines a **stop** and a **fricative** (e.g., the initial sound in *chair*).

Agent The entity in a sentence that is responsible for the action or state described by the verb (e.g., *The boy* in *The boy slept late*). The category of agent subsumes the category of **actor**.

Allophone See **Phoneme**.

Alternation A predictable variation in the pronunciation of a word stem (e.g., /gz/ and /kš/ alternate with each other in the pronunciation of "anxiety" and "anxious").

Arousal Sensory excitation. An individual is in a high arousal state when he or she is alert and highly responsive, and in a low arousal state when sleepy and less responsive.

Asserted information The information in a sentence that is being emphasized. For example, *the jewel* is the asserted information in the sentence, *It was the jewel that was stolen*. Contrasted with **Presupposed information**.

Assimilation (phonetic) Adjustment of adjacent sounds to one another.

Assimilation (Piagetian) Interpretation of objects and events, the transformation of **stimuli** into psychological experiences.

Associative learning See **Habitual-associative learning**.

Attributant The noun or noun phrase to which a quality is attributed. For example, in *green dress, dress* is the attributant, and in *The boy is smart, The boy* is the attributant.

Attribute An implicit characteristic of a concept (e.g., green is an attribute of grass), or an explicit characteristic qualifying a noun (e.g., *green* in *green dress*).

Attribution sentence An early two-word sentence in which a quality is attributed to an object (e.g., *red car*).

Babbling The production of meaningless syllables by babies for purposes of sound play.

Base structure See **Deep structure**.

Bound morpheme A **morpheme** that cannot occur by itself, it has to be bound to another morpheme (e.g., the noun marker *-ness,* as in *happiness*). Contrasted with **Free morpheme**.

Case The function of a noun phrase in a sentence (e.g., as **agent, instrument**, or **object**).

Categorization Implicit or explicit placement into **categories** or **classes**. Thus, verbal labeling involves categorization as does the sorting of objects into distinct piles.

Category See **Concept**.

Class A general term for a grouping of objects regardless of the basis of the grouping. See also **Concept, Preconcept**.

Classical conditioning A training procedure by which a response associated with one **stimulus**, the unconditioned stimulus (UCS), is caused to be elicited also by another stimulus, the conditioned stimulus (CS), through repeated presentation of the CS just before the UCS. The response conditioned to the CS can be extinguished by presenting it a number of times without the UCS.

Classification See **Categorization**.

Cognitive function The use of words and sentences for the purpose of expressing thoughts. Contrasted with **Instrumental function**.

Cognitive processes Mental operations that are responsible for behaviors in the domains of thinking, attention, perception, memory, and language.

Concept The internal representation that makes it possible for an individual to identify a **stimulus** not previously encountered. Thus, Suzie has a concept of tree if she is able to assign the label *tree* to a kind of tree she has not seen before.

Conceptual meaning The aspect of meaning that concerns the organization of the meanings of individual words into a hierarchical system of interrelated meanings. See also **Referential meaning**.

Conditioning See **Classical conditioning**.

Consonants Sounds of speech whose articulation involves some constriction in the way of the passage of the air through the mouth. See also **Vowels**.

Constituent (of a sentence) A cohesive part of a sentence. For example, in the sentence *The little girl wore a fleecy dress, The little girl* is a constituent, but *girl wore* is not.

Constraints Limits on the variability of a particular behavior or capacity.

Context-bound usage A low level of word meaning characteristic of young children who produce words and respond to words primarily in the contexts in which they originally encountered them.

Continuity (in development) Gradual advances in functioning where each advance grows out of and builds on the preceding one.

Cooing The spontaneous production of sounds by young infants as an expression of pleasure and well-being.

Correlation coefficient An index of the extent to which the scores of individuals on one variable (A) covary with their scores on another variable (B). Correlation coefficients can be positive or negative; they range from -1 to $+1$. Assume, for instance, that you computed the correlation between children's ages and their reading comprehension scores. You would expect to find that the older the child the higher would be his or her comprehension score. If your expectation is confirmed you would obtain a positive correlation of some magnitude, say .60. But if you computed a correlation between children's ages and the time it takes them to read a passage of text, you would expect a negative correlation, say $-.60$, because the older the child the faster he or she would be reading (i.e., the shorter his or her reading time). There are different types of correlation coefficients. The most common one is the Pearson Product Moment Correlation Coefficient, designated by r. A *partial correlation* is a correlation in which the correlation of variable A with C and of variable B with C was removed or partialed out from the correlation between A and B.

Cross-sectional study A study in which the effects of age are investigated by comparing the performance of children of different ages. See also **Longitudinal study**.

Cue An external, perceptible characteristic that aids in the classification of an object, sound, or event.

Decalage The temporal gap in children's attainment of the ability to succeed in different tasks that seem to involve the same basic mental capacities.

Decontextualization Broadening of the usage of words beyond their original contexts.

Deep structure The analysis of sentences—within the framework of **generative transformational grammar**—into hierarchically organized structural components in terms of the meaning relations that they express.

Deictic tutoring Teaching the meanings of words by referring (i.e., pointing, holding up, etc.) directly to the objects as they are named.

Demonstrative naming utterance An utterance containing a pointing word (e.g., *a, the*) and a label, as in *the dog*. Demonstrative naming utterances are children's earliest and most primitive **sentences**.

Derivational morphology An aspect of **morphology** that concerns the derivation of words of different part-of-speech forms from the same root (e.g., *danger, endanger, dangerously*).

Diary study A scientific investigation based on the frequent observations of a subject's behavior over a period of time, ranging from a few weeks to a few years.

Diffuse extension An early form of word use in which children extend the use of words from original **referents** to new referents in a fluid, unsystematic fashion, on the basis of personal attitudes and experiences. See also **Overextension**.

Discontinuity (in development) The sudden emergence of new forms of functioning that are not anticipated by preceding developments.

Discrimination Recognition (not necessarily conscious) that two **stimuli** are different.

Dishabituation Increase in responsiveness to a new **stimulus** after **habituation** to a previous stimulus.

Distinctive features Characteristics distinguishing speech sounds from one another.

Distributional criteria Criteria for the classification of words into part-of-speech classes based on the positions that words can occupy in sentences. For instance, *boy* and *weakness* are nouns because they can follow *the* in a sentence.

Echolalia Tendency to engage in frequent echoing of speech.

Encoding A form of **assimilation (Piagetian)** that entails some conscious awareness of the assimilatory process.

Expansion An utterance by an adult that corrects the syntax and attempts to clarify the meaning of a preceding **sentence** of a child by filling in missing elements, as in this exchange:
    Child: Daddy back.
    Adult: You want to go on Daddy's back?

Experimental study A scientific investigation in which the investigator observes the behavior of subjects under controlled conditions.

Extension 1: The **referential meaning** of a word. 2: Using a word beyond the original **referents** to which it was applied. 3: Maternal continuation of an utterance produced by a child.

Extinction Undoing the effects of **classical conditioning**.

Familiarity The feeling that one had a particular experience before without necessarily being conscious of the reasons for this feeling. See also **Recognition memory**.

Free morpheme A **morpheme** that can occur by itself. Words are free morphemes. Contrasted with **Bound morpheme**.

Fricatives Consonants in whose articulation the air flows out continuously through a narrowly constricted passage. The initial sound in *frame* is a fricative. See also **Stops**.

Function words Words that do not make reference but rather serve to connect other words in a sentence to one another (e.g., *the, on*). The term *functors* includes function words as well as **inflections**.

Functors See **Function words**.

Generative transformational grammar A formal theory of language, primarily of **syntax** and **phonology**, that has been developed by **linguists** under the leadership of Noam Chomsky. The theory distinguishes between **deep** and **surface structures** and formulates the rules to construct deep structures and to transform them into surface structures. The adjective *generative* means "explicit," emphasizing that the theory strives to be explicit in its formulations.

Gestural representation Representation of objects by means of gestures (e.g., Johnny putting a cup to his mouth for the purpose of identifying it). Gestural representation is related to **motor recognition** but implies more advanced and more systematic performance.

Given information See **Presupposed information**.

Grammar In the broad sense the term includes all the rule-governed aspects of language. In the narrow sense it is synonymous with **syntax**.

Grammatical meaning See **Syntactic meaning**.

Growth spurt A sudden developmental advance, evidenced in an abrupt increase in the occurrence of relevant behaviors.

Habitual-associative learning A type of learning that results in the formation of associations and habits. See also **Inferential learning**.

Habituation Reduced responsiveness to a **stimulus** due to overexposure.

Index Piaget's term for **indicator cue**.

Indicator cue A cue from which it can be inferred that equivalent behaviors experienced through different modalities are indeed equivalent.

Inferential learning A type of learning that involves the making of inferences and the acquisition of knowledge (as distinguished from the acquisition of habits). Infants are thought to become capable of inferential learning in the fourth quarter of the first year. See also **Habitual-associative learning**.

Inflections Particles added to words to modulate their meanings. English inflects words for tense, plurality, and possession.

Informant A native speaker of a language, usually an exotic language, from whom **linguists** obtain information about a language they do not speak.

Information processor A human being from the time, at about the age of 9 months, that he or she begins to engage in the acquisition and manipulation of information.

Instrument An inanimate entity in a sentence that is responsible for the action described by the verb (e.g., *The wind* in *The wind blew the leaves*). See also **Agent**.

Instrumental function The use of words and sentences to make requests and for other practical purposes. Contrasted with **Cognitive function**.

Intension The **conceptual meaning** of a word.

Interlocutor A participant in a conversation.

Intermodal coordination Coordination between the activities of different sensory modalities. For instance, Suzie shows coordination between vision and touch when she reaches directly and smoothly for an object she sees at a distance.

Intermodal coorientation The term used in this book for the tendency of activity in one sensory modality to give rise to activity in another modality in the same spatial orientation. Intermodal coorientation occurs soon after birth and is to be distinguished from **intermodal coordination**, which does not appear till several months later.

Intonation The changes in pitch that occur when sentences are spoken.

Invisible gesture A motor gesture that cannot be seen by its performer (e.g., tongue protrusion).

Kinesthetic sense ''A sense mediated by end organs located in muscles, tendons, and joints and stimulated by bodily movements and tensions.'' (Webster's Seventh New Collegiate Dictionary)

Lexical meaning The meanings of words in isolation, as in a dictionary. Contrasted with **Syntactic meaning**.

Linguist A scientist who investigates the structure of human languages.

Locative A term (e.g., *on, to*) designating a locational relation.

Longitudinal study A study in which the effects of age are investigated by comparing the performance of the same children at different ages. See also **Cross-sectional study**.

Magical efficacy A primitive form of causality, characteristic of young infants, that involves the indiscriminate reapplication of procedures that in the past were associated with pleasant experiences.

Manner of articulation The manner in which the airstream is allowed to pass through the oral cavity. This is one of the characteristics that distinguishes consonants from one another, mainly, **stops** from **fricatives**.

MLU (mean length of utterance) The length of an utterance in **morphemes**.

Morpheme The smallest linguistic form that has meaning. For example, the word *books* is composed of two morphemes: *book* and *s*.

Morphology The study of the formation of words from **morphemes**.

Motor recognition A form of object recognition that occurs in infancy in which the infant shows recognition of an object by acting out an abbreviated version of the action he or she habitually uses in its actual manipulation or by performing an action that resembles the action of the object. See also **Gestural representation**.

Multimodal object An object whose internal representation includes properties from different sensory modalities.

Multimodal representation An advanced form of sensorimotor representation that involves the construction of **multimodal objects**.

Naming function Mode of word learning and word use that is based on the realization that words are socially determined names for things, people, actions, etc.

Nasals Speech sounds, such as *m,* in whose articulation the air flows out through the nose as well as the mouth.

Naturalistic observation Observation of behavior occurring naturally without the observer's inducement or manipulation.

Neonate An infant in the first month of life.

New Information See **Asserted information.**

Noun phrase A phrase that has a noun as its core.

Object Often used broadly in the sense of **stimulus** to refer not just to things but also to people, sounds, events, etc.

Object (of a sentence) The noun or noun phrase in a sentence on which the verb operates. Thus, *a present* in *John gave a present* is an object.

Object permanence The notion that objects have an independent reality and continue to exist when one is not in sensory contact with them. See also **Search for vanished objects.**

Observational study A scientific study in which an investigator observes naturally occurring behaviors with minimal intervention on his or her part.

Overextension Extension of the use of a word in a more or less systematic way beyond its standard usage (e.g., the use of *dog* for four-legged animals). Distinguished in this book from **diffuse extension.** See also **Overrestriction.**

Overregularization The use of a regular inflection in cases where an irregular inflection is required (e.g., *mans* as a plural form of *man* and *goed* as a past-tense form of *go*).

Overrestriction Application of a word to a narrower range of **referents** than is allowed by standard usage (e.g., using *dog* to refer only to poodles). Distinguished in this book from **context-bound usage.** See also **Overextension.**

Paired-comparison technique A technique used to investigate the discriminatory capacities and memory of infants. In a paired-comparison test, Johnny might be shown a picture of a face for 1 minute, and 1 hour later be shown the same face again along with a new face. If he exhibits differential reactions to the two faces (e.g., gazes more at the new face), we can infer that he discriminates between the two faces and remembers the first face.

Partial correlation See **Correlation coefficient.**

Perception The process of identifying **stimuli.**

Perceptual identification Recognition of people and things for what they are.

Phone A distinct identifiable speech sound. See also **Phoneme.**

Phoneme A sound category in a particular language that functions to distinguish words from one another. For instance, the initial sound in *pin* is the phoneme /p/, and the initial sound in *bin* is the phoneme /b/. A particular phoneme may

may be realized as one **phone** or another depending on where in the word it occurs and what phoneme is adjacent to it. The different phones of the same phoneme are its *allophones*. For instance, the *p* in *pin* and the *p* in *spin* are articulated differently; they are different allophones of the phoneme /p/.

Phonemic period A period that begins around the first birthday when children start constructing **phonemes** and use phonemic differences to express differences in meaning.

Phonetic analysis An analysis, characteristically in the form of a written transcription, of speech on the level of detail of **phones**. See also **Phonological analysis**.

Phonetic stress The intensity with which a particular syllable is uttered relative to adjacent syllables. Syllables receiving relatively higher stress are referred to as *stressed* and those receiving relatively lower stress are referred to as *unstressed*.

Phonological analysis An analysis, characteristically in the form of a written transcription, of speech on the level of abstraction of **phonemes**. Such an analysis ignores details of sound not relevant to distinguishing words from one another in a particular language. See also **Phonetic analysis**.

Phonology The study of the sound systems of languages.

Phrase A **constituent** or potential constituent of a sentence.

Phrase sequence A series of structurally unintegrated phrases expressing the meaning of a sentence. One of the entities in a phrase sequence may be a short sentence.

Phrase structure rules The rules developed in the framework of **generative transformational grammar** to construct **deep structures**.

Place of articulation The place where the outflow of the airstream from the lungs is wholly or partly obstructed in the production of speech. This is one of the characteristics that distinguishes consonants from one another.

Possessor The noun or noun phrase to whom a possession is attributed. For example, in *John has a book* and *John's book, John* is the possessor, and in *The book has an appendix* and *The book's appendix, The book* is the possessor.

Preconcepts The primitive groupings of objects that young children associate with their words.

Prehension Activities of the hand, mainly grasping.

Prephonemic period The period in infancy in which children babble speech sounds but do not yet have **phonemes**.

Presupposed information The information in a sentence that is assumed by the speaker to be already known to the listener. For instance, in the sentence *It was the jewel that was stolen*, it is presupposed that something was stolen. Contrasted with **Asserted information**.

Pretend substitution The entity in make-believe play that is made to perform the function of something else in real life. For example, in pretending to sleep on her hand, Suzie makes the hand substitute for a pillow.

Pretense Short for *pretend play*.

Propositional meaning The meaning engendered when words are juxtaposed in sentences.

Propositional thinking Thinking that involves interrelations of the kind expressed in sentences.

Prosody Sound patterning. Sentential prosody is reflected in a unified intonational contour and fluent transition between words.

Recognition memory 1: Memory that entails the ability to distinguish things that were encountered before from those that are new. Infants have only this kind of memory, they have no recall memory (i.e., no ability to evoke experiences in their absence). 2: Ability to remember whether or not one encountered a particular item in a particular context (e.g., to judge whether a particular word was on a list of words one was asked to memorize). This type of contextual memory has not been studied with prelinguistic subjects.

Reduplication Production of bisyllabic words in which the second syllable repeats the first wholly or partly (e.g., *wawa* for 'water' and *kekl* for 'kettle').

Referent The entity to which a word refers. The referents of words change with development. For young children they are concrete things, but for mature speakers they are **concepts**. For instance, the mature referent of *table* is not a particular table or a collection of actual tables but the concept defining the essential properties of tables.

Referential meaning The aspect of meaning that concerns referral to objects, events, qualities, etc. See also **Conceptual meaning**.

Referential period This period begins around the first birthday when children start using words to refer to things and no longer use them primarily for the pleasure of hearing the sounds.

Relational meaning See **Propositional meaning**.

Reliability See **Test reliability**.

Representation Internal storage of information, typically in some abstract, symbolic form.

Representational capacity The capacity to represent information symbolically.

Role function See **Case**.

Schema See **Scheme**.

Scheme (Piagetian) A psychological structure. Used primarily to refer to the sensorimotor schemes of infants. Sensorimotor schemes are the psychological structures that are responsible for the regular, repeatable patterns of behavior exhibited by infants. See also **Sensorimotor mentation**.

Schwa The English vowel that sounds like the second *e* in *enemy*. Its phonetic symbol is ǝ.

Search for vanished objects A task invented by Piaget to test for **object permanence**. The task entails showing a desirable object to an infant and then hiding it. The object can be hidden in increasingly more complex ways, and the extent of the infant's attainment of object permanence is assessed by observing under what hiding conditions he or she will search for the object. Infants under 6 months typically do not search for the object even under the simplest conditions.

Semantic relations The meaning relations typically expressed in sentences.

Sensorimotor mentation The form of psychological functioning characteristic of infants that is based on the individual's sensory impressions of **stimuli** and motor reactions to them. In sensorimotor mentation people and objects are not retained as independently existing entities, only as stimuli that elicit particular reactions.

Sensorimotor scheme See **Scheme**.

Sentence An utterance that interrelates the meanings of its component parts by means of structural devices, primarily word order and **prosody**. A child is said to be producing sentences if his or her multiword utterances exhibit word-order regularity even when they are not sentences from the perspective of adult grammar.

Sign A **signifier** whose **signified** is a specific thing or action rather than a **concept**. Contrasted with **Symbol**.

Significance See **Statistical significance**.

Signified A represented entity. See also **Signifier**.

Signifier An entity that represents another entity. See also **Signified**.

Spectogram A visual display of the characteristics of speech produced by a machine called a sound *spectograph*. A spectogram shows the temporal sequence of sounds on the horizontal axis, the sound frequency (in Hertz) on the vertical axis, and the intensity by the darkness of the tracings.

Spectograph A device that produces **spectograms**.

Speech The vocal aspect of language.

Stage 4 error The error that infants in Stage 4 of sensorimotor development make of searching for a hidden object in its previous hiding place even though they see it being hidden in a new place. See also **Search for vanished objects**.

Statistical significance A statistical test is said to be significant if the probability of the value obtained occurring by change is 5% or less, expressed as $p < .05$. The lower the probability the greater one's confidence in the results (i.e., the higher the significance level of the test). Thus, a test with $p < .01$ provides stronger evidence than one with $p < .05$. Simple, commonly used tests are the *t* **test** and the **correlation coefficient**.

Stimulus A source of physical energy that impinges on the senses. Objects, sounds, events, etc. are all potential stimuli.

Stops Consonants in whose articulation the airflow is brought to a complete halt and then released abruptly. The initial sound in *pin* is a stop. See also **Fricatives**.

Stress See **Phonetic stress**.

Structure dependence A characteristic of **transformational rules**, namely, that they operate on structurally defined entities (e.g., noun phrases) rather than on temporally defined entities (e.g., the third word in a sentence).

Subject The noun phrase about which the sentence speaks (e.g., *The scenery* in *The scenery is breathtaking*).

Subordinate category See **Superordinate category**.

Superordinate category A higher order category that subsumes lower order, subordinate categories. For instance, the category of fruit is superordinate to the subordinate categories of apple and orange.

Surface structure The analysis—within the framework of **generative transformational grammar**—of the sequence of words in a sentence into hierarchically organized structural components. The surface structure provides a basis for the prosodic patterns of sentences (see **Prosody**). It does not play an important role in the semantic analysis of sentences. See also **Deep structure**.

Symbol A **signifier** whose **signified** is a **concept**.

Symbolic capacity The intellectual capacity to deal with **symbols**.

Symbolic function Mode of psychological operation that involves the use of **symbols**.

Syntactic meaning The meaning that words and phrases take on when they become parts of sentences (e.g., the meanings of **subject** and **object**). Contrasted with **Lexical meaning**. The term is also used in the sense of **propositional meaning**.

Syntax The structure of sentences.

t **test** This test is used to compare two means. Assume, for instance, that you were interested in comparing the SAT scores in mathematics obtained by high school seniors in 1980 with those obtained in 1970. You found out that the mean in 1980 was 560 and in 1970, 550. Does the difference of 10 points represent a real improvement or is it due to random fluctuation? To answer this question, you would compute a *t* test (on the basis of the distribution of the individual scores in the two years), and if you obtain a value whose probability of occurring by chance is less than .05 you would be justified in concluding that the difference represents a genuine gain. The *t* test is checked for probability level as one-tailed or two-tailed. A one-tailed test yields higher significance levels than a two-tailed test but can be legitimately used only when there is a solid basis for predicting the direction of the results. See also **Statistical significance**.

Telegraphese Used to refer to children's early sentences. These sentences omit such elements as articles, prepositions, and inflections, and thus resemble telegrams.

Telegraphic speech See **Telegraphese**.

Test reliability Degree of accuracy of the measurements that a particular test yields.

Tokens Instances of linguistic units, counted without regard to **type**. Thus, "number of word tokens" refers to the number of words, including repetitions of the same words.

Transformational rules The grammatical rules of **generative transformational grammar** that transform **deep structures** into **surface structures** directly or indirectly (through intermediary structures).

Types Instances of different linguistic units. Thus, "number of word types" refers to the number of *different* words, counting separate occurrences of the same word only once. Contrasted with **Tokens**.

Verb phrase A phrase that has a verb and may also contain other sentential components, except the subject.

Voiced sounds Sounds in whose articulation the vocal cords vibrate.

Voiceless sounds Sounds in whose articulation the vocal cords do not vibrate.

VOT (voice onset time) The time (in milliseconds) between the release of air in the production of a **stop** consonant and the beginning of vocal cord vibration.

Vowels Sounds of speech whose articulation involves relatively little constriction in the way of the passage of the air through the mouth. See also **Consonants**.

Word sequence A succession of words that is more integrated semantically and structurally than a series of isolated words but less integrated than a sentence. The typical word sequence expresses semantic relations of the kind expressed in a sentence but has longer interword pauses and does not exhibit word-order regularities.

References

Akmajian, A., & Heny, F. W. *An introduction to the principles of transformational syntax.* Cambridge, Mass.: MIT Press, 1975.

Allport, G. W. *Pattern and growth in personality.* New York: Holt, Rinehart & Winston, 1961.

Anglin, J. M. *Word, object, and conceptual development.* New York: Norton, 1977.

Anisfeld, M. Disjunctive concepts? *Journal of General Psychology,* 1968, *78,* 223–228.

Anisfeld, M. Psychological evidence for an intermediate stage in a morphological derivation. *Journal of Verbal Learning and Verbal Behavior,* 1969, *8,* 191–195.

Anisfeld, M. Interpreting "imitative" responses in early infancy. *Science,* 1979, *205,* 214–215.

Anisfeld, M., & Gordon, M. On the psychophonological structure of English inflectional rules. *Journal of Verbal Learning and Verbal Behavior,* 1968, *7,* 973–979.

Anisfeld, M., & Klenbort, I. On the functions of structural paraphrase: The view from the passive voice. *Psychological Bulletin,* 1973, *79,* 117–126.

Appleton, T., Clifton, R., & Goldberg, S. The development of behavioral competence in infancy. In F. D. Horowitz (Ed.), *Review of child development research* (Vol. 4). Chicago: University of Chicago Press, 1975. Pp. 101–186.

Asch, S. E. *Social psychology.* Englewood Cliffs, N.J.: Prentice-Hall, 1952.

Aslin, R. N., & Pisoni, D. B. Effects of early linguistic experience on speech discrimination by infants: A critique of Eilers, Gavin, and Wilson (1979). *Child Development,* 1980, *51,* 107–112.

Barker, R. G., Dembo, T., & Lewin, K. Frustration and regression. In R. G. Barker, J. S. Kounin, & H. F. Wright (Eds.), *Child behavior and development.* New York: McGraw-Hill, 1943. Pp. 441–458.

Barrett, M. D. Lexical development and overextension in child language. *Journal of Child Language,* 1978, *5,* 205–219.

Bates, E. *Language and context: The acquisition of pragmatics.* New York: Academic Press, 1976.

Bates, E., Camaioni, L., & Volterra, V. The acquisition of performatives prior to speech. *Merrill-Palmer Quarterly,* 1975, *21,* 205–226.

Bell, S. M. The development of the concept of object as related to infant-mother attachment. *Child Development,* 1970, *41,* 291–311.

Belsky, J., Goode, M. K., & Most, R. K. Maternal stimulation and infant exploratory competence: Cross-sectional, correlational, and experimental analyses. *Child Development,* 1980, *51,* 1168–1178.

262 REFERENCES

Belsky, J., & Most, R. K. From exploration to play: A cross-sectional study of infant free play behavior. *Developmental Psychology*, 1981, *17*, 630–639.

Benedict, H. Early lexical development: Comprehension and production. *Journal of Child Language*, 1979, *6*, 183–200.

Berko, J. The child's learning of English morphology. *Word*, 1958, *14*, 150–177.

Berman, R. A. Regularity vs. anomaly: The acquisition of Hebrew inflectional morphology. *Journal of Child Language*, 1981, *8*, 265–282.

Blank, M. Mastering the intangible through language. *Annals of the New York Academy of Sciences*, 1975, *263*, 44–58.

Bloom, L. *Language development: Form and function in emerging grammars*. Cambridge, Mass.: MIT Press, 1970.

Bloom, L. *One word at a time: The use of single word utterances before syntax*. New York: Humanities Press, 1973.

Bloom, L., Hood, L., & Lightbown, P. Imitation in language development: If, when, and why. *Cognitive Psychology*, 1974, *6*, 380–420.

Bloom, L., Lightbown, P., & Hood, L. Structure and variation in child language. *Monographs of the Society for Research in Child Development*, 1975, *40*(2, Serial No. 160).

Blount, B. G., & Padgug, E. J. Prosodic, paralinguistic, and interactional features in parent-child speech: English and Spanish. *Journal of Child Language*, 1977, *4*, 67–86.

Bolinger, D. *Aspects of language* (2nd ed.). New York: Harcourt Brace Jovanovich, 1975.

Bower, T. G. R. *Development in infancy*. San Francisco, Cal.: Freeman, 1974.

Bowerman, M. *Early syntactic development: A cross-linguistic study with special reference to Finnish*. New York: Cambridge University Press, 1973.

Bowerman, M. Semantic factors in the acquisition of rules for word use and sentence construction. In D. M. Morehead & A. E. Morehead (Eds.), *Normal and deficient child language*. Baltimore, Md.: University Park Press, 1976. Pp. 99–179.

Bowerman, M. Systematizing semantic knowledge: Changes over time in the child's organization of word meaning. *Child Development*, 1978, *49*, 977–987.

Braine, M. D. S. The acquisition of language in infant and child. In C. E. Reed (Ed.), *The learning of language*. New York: Appleton-Century-Crofts, 1971. Pp. 7-95.

Braine, M. D. S. Children's first word combinations. *Monographs of the Society for Research in Child Development*, 1976, *41*(1, Serial No. 164).

Branigan, G. Some reasons why successive single word utterances are not. *Journal of Child Language*, 1979, *6*, 411-421.

Bretherton, I., Bates, E., McNew, S., Shore, C., Williamson, C., & Beeghly-Smith, M. Comprehension and production of symbols in infancy: An experimental study. *Developmental Psychology*, 1981, *17*, 728–736.

Bronckart, J. P., & Sinclair, H. Time, tense and aspect. *Cognition*, 1973, *2*, 107–130.

Bronstein, A. J. *The pronunciation of American English: An introduction to phonetics*. New York: Appleton-Century-Crofts, 1960.

Brooks-Gunn, J., & Lewis, M. "Why mama and papa?" The development of social labels. *Child Development*, 1979, *50*, 1203–1206.

Brown, C. J. Reactions of infants to their parents' voices. *Infant Behavior and Development*, 1979, *2*, 295–300.

Brown, R. *Words and things*. Glencoe, Ill: Free Press, 1958.

Brown, R. *A first language: The early stages*. Cambridge, Mass.: Harvard University Press, 1973.

Brown, R., Cazden, C., & Bellugi, U. The child's grammar from I to III. In J. P. Hill (Ed.), *Minnesota Symposia on Child Psychology* (Vol. 2). Minneapolis: University of Minnesota Press, 1969. Pp. 28–73.

Bruner, J. S. From communication to language: A psychological perspective. In I. Markova (Ed.), *The social context of language*. New York: Wiley, 1978. Pp. 17–48.

Bruner, J. S., Goodnow, J. J., & Austin, G. A. *A study of thinking*. New York: Wiley, 1956.

Bryant, B., & Anisfeld, M. Feedback versus no-feedback in testing children's knowledge of English pluralization rules. *Journal of Experimental Child Psychology*, 1969, *8*, 250–255.

Carew, J. V. Experience and the development of intelligence in young children at home and in day care. *Monographs of the Society for Research in Child Development*, 1980, *45*(6–7, Serial No. 187).

Carlson, P., & Anisfeld, M. Some observations on the linguistic competence of a two-year-old child. *Child Development*, 1969, *40*, 569–575.

Carter, A. L. Prespeech meaning relations: An outline of one infant's sensorimotor morpheme development. In P. Fletcher & M. Garman (Eds.), *Language acquisition: Studies in first language development*. New York: Cambridge University Press, 1979. Pp. 71-92.

Cazden, C. B. The acquisition of noun and verb inflections. *Child Development*, 1968, *39*, 433–448.

Chafe, W. L. Givenness, contrastiveness, definiteness, subjects, topics, and point of view. In C. N. Li (Ed.), *Subject and topic*. New York: Academic Press, 1976. Pp. 25–55.

Chomsky, N. *Syntactic structures*. The Hague: Mouton, 1957.

Chomsky, N. *Aspects of the theory of syntax*. Cambridge, Mass.: MIT Press, 1965.

Chomsky, N. *Language and mind*. New York: Harcourt, Brace & World, 1968.

Chomsky, N. *Reflections on language*. New York: Pantheon Books, 1975.

Chomsky, N. On cognitive structures and their development: A reply to Piaget. In M. Piattelli-Palmarini (Ed.), *Language and learning: The debate between Jean Piaget and Noam Chomsky*. Cambridge, Mass.: Harvard University Press, 1980. Pp. 35–52. (a)

Chomsky, N. The linguistic approach. In M. Piattelli-Palmarini (Ed.), *Language and learning: The debate between Jean Piaget and Noam Chomsky*. Cambridge, Mass.: Harvard University Press, 1980. Pp. 109–117. (b)

Chomsky, N. *Rules and representations*. New York: Columbia University Press, 1980. (c)

Chomsky, N., & Halle, M. *The sound pattern of English*. New York: Harper & Row, 1968.

Chukovsky, K. *From two to five*. Berkeley, Cal.: University of California Press, 1963. (Translation of 16th Russian ed. published, 1959.)

Clark, E. V. What's in a word? On the child's acquisition of semantics in his first language. In T. E. Moore (Ed.), *Cognitive development and the acquisition of language*. New York: Academic Press, 1973. Pp. 65–110.

Clark, E. V. Strategies for communicating. *Child Development*, 1978, *49*, 953–959.

Clark, E. V. Building a vocabulary: Words for objects, actions and relations. In P. Fletcher & M. Garman (Eds.), *Language acquisition: Studies in first language development*. New York: Cambridge University Press, 1979. Pp. 149–160.

Clark, E. V. Lexical innovations: How children learn to create new words. In W. Deutsch (Ed.), *The child's construction of language*. New York: Academic Press, 1981. Pp. 299–328.

Clark, R. A. The transition from action to gesture. In A. Lock (Ed.), *Action, gesture and symbol: The emergence of language*. New York: Academic Press, 1978. Pp. 231–257.

Condon, W. S. Method of micro-analysis of sound films of behavior. *Behavioral Research Methods & Instrumentation*, 1970, *2*, 51–54.

Condon, W. S., & Sander, L. W. Neonate movement is synchronized with adult speech: Interactional participation and language acquisition. *Science*, 1974, *183*, 99–101. (a)

Condon, W. S., & Sander, L. W. Synchrony demonstrated between movements of the neonate and adult speech. *Child Development*, 1974, *45*, 456–462. (b)

Cooper, W. E. The development of speech timing. In S. J. Segalowitz & F. A. Gruber (Eds.), *Language development and neurological theory*. New York: Academic Press, 1977. Pp. 357–373.

Corrigan, R. Language development as related to Stage 6 object permanence development. *Journal of Child Language*, 1978, *5*, 173–189.

Corrigan, R. Cognitive correlates of language: Differential criteria yield differential results. *Child Development*, 1979, *50*, 617–631.

Cross, T. G. Mothers' speech adjustments: The contributions of selected child listener variables. In C. E. Snow & C. A. Ferguson (Eds.), *Talking to children: Language input and acquisition*. New York: Cambridge University Press, 1977. Pp. 151–188.

Cross, T. G. Mothers' speech and its association with rate of linguistic development in young children. In N. Waterson & C. Snow (Eds.), *The development of communication*. New York: Wiley, 1978. Pp. 199-216.

Curtiss, S. *Genie: A psycholinguistic study of a modern-day "Wild Child."* New York: Academic Press, 1977.

Curtiss, S. Dissociations between language and cognition: Cases and implications. *Journal of Autism and Developmental Disorders*, 1981, *11*, 15–30.

Daehler, M. W., & O'Connor, M. P. Recognition memory for objects in very young children: The effects of shape and label similarity on preference for novel stimuli. *Journal of Experimental Child Psychology*, 1980, *29*, 306–321.

de Villiers, J. G., & de Villiers, P. A. A cross-sectional study of the acquisition of grammatical morphemes in child speech. *Journal of Psycholinguistic Research*, 1973, *2*, 267–278.

Dore, J. Conditions for the acquisition of speech acts. In I. Markova (Ed.), *The social context of language*. New York: Wiley, 1978. Pp. 87–111.

Dore, J., Franklin, M. B., Miller, R. T., & Ramer, A. L. H. Transitional phenomena in early language acquisition. *Journal of Child Language*, 1976, *3*, 13–28.

Drucker, J. Toddler play: Some comments on its functions in the developmental process. *Psychoanalysis and Contemporary Science*, 1975, *4*, 479–527.

Edwards, M. L. Perception and production in child phonology: The testing of four hypotheses. *Journal of Child Language*, 1974, *1*, 205–219.

Eilers, R. E., Gavin, W. J., & Wilson, W. R. Effects of early linguistic experience on speech discrimination by infants: A reply. *Child Development*, 1980, *51*, 113–117.

Eimas, P. D., Siqueland, E. R., Jusczyk, P., & Vigorito, J. Speech perception in infants. *Science*, 1971, *171*, 303–306.

Eimas, P. D., & Tartter, V. C. On the development of speech perception: Mechanisms and analogies. In H. W. Reese & L. P. Lipsitt (Eds.), *Advances in child development and behavior* (Vol. 13). New York: Academic Press, 1979. Pp. 155–193.

Epstein, W. The influence of syntactical structure on learning. *American Journal of Psychology*, 1961, *74*, 80–85.

Ervin, S. M. Imitation and structural change in children's language. In E. H. Lenneberg (Ed.), *New directions in the study of language*. Cambridge, Mass.: MIT Press, 1964. Pp. 163–189.

Escalona, S. K. *The roots of individuality: Normal patterns of development in infancy*. Chicago: Aldine, 1968.

Fagan, J. F. Memory in the infant. *Journal of Experimental Child Psychology*, 1970, *9*, 217–226.

Fagan, J. F. Infants' delayed recognition memory and forgetting. *Journal of Experimental Child Psychology*, 1973, *16*, 424–450.

Fagan, J. F. An attention model of infant recognition. *Child Development*, 1977, *48*, 345–359.

Farah, M. J., & Kosslyn, S. M. Concept development. In H. W. Reese & L. P. Lipsitt (Eds.), *Advances in child development and behavior* (Vol. 16). New York: Academic Press, 1982. Pp. 125–167.

Fein, G. G. Pretend play in childhood: An integrative review. *Child Development*, 1981, *52*, 1095–1118.

Ferguson, C. A. Baby talk in six languages. In J. J. Gumperz & D. Hymes (Eds.), *The ethnography of communication*. (Special publication of the *American Anthropologist*, 1964, *66*, 103–114.)

Ferguson, C. A. Learning to pronounce: The earliest stage of phonological development in the child. In F. D. Minifie & L. L. Lloyd (Eds.), *Communicative and cognitive abilities: Early behavioral assessment*. Baltimore, Md.: University Park Press, 1978. Pp. 273–297.

Ferguson, C. A. Phonology as an individual access system: Some data from language acquisition. In C. J. Fillmore, D. Kempler, & W. S-Y. Wang (Eds.), *Individual differences in language ability and language behavior*. New York: Academic Press, 1979. Pp. 189–201.

Ferguson, C. A., & Garnica, O. K. Theories of phonological development. In E. H. Lenneberg & E. Lenneberg (Eds.), *Foundations of language development: A multidisciplinary approach* (Vol. 1). New York: Academic Press, 1975. Pp. 153–180.

Ferrier, L. J. Some observations of error in context. In N. Waterson & C. Snow (Eds.), *The development of communication*. New York: Wiley, 1978. Pp 301–309.

Feuerstein, R. *The dynamic assessment of retarded performers: The learning potential assessment device, theory, instruments, and techniques*. Baltimore, Md.: University Park Press, 1979.

Fillmore, C. J. The case for case. In E. Bach & R. T. Harms (Eds.), *Universals in linguistic theory*. New York: Holt, Rinehart & Winston, 1968.

Flavell, J. H. On cognitive development. *Child Development*, 1982, *53*, 1–10.

Fremgen, A., & Fay, D. Overextensions in production and comprehension: A methodological clarification. *Journal of Child Language*, 1980, *7*, 205–211.

Fromkin, V., & Rodman, R. *An introduction to language* (2nd ed.). New York: Holt, Rinehart & Winston, 1978.

Fry, D. B. Phonological aspects of language acquisition in the hearing and the deaf. In E. H. Lenneberg & E. Lenneberg (Eds.), *Foundations of language development: A multidisciplinary approach* (Vol. 2). New York: Academic Press, 1975. Pp. 137–155.

Frye, D. Stages of development: The Stage IV error. *Infant Behavior and Development*, 1980, *3*, 115–126.

Garvey, C. Play with language and speech. In S. Ervin-Tripp & C. Mitchell-Kernan (Eds.), *Child discourse*. New York: Academic Press, 1977. Pp. 27–47.

Gleason, H. A. *An introduction to descriptive linguistics* (Rev. ed.). New York: Holt, Rinehart & Winston, 1961.

Glucksberg, S., & Danks, J. H. Effects of discriminative labels and of nonsense labels upon availability of novel function. *Journal of Verbal Learning and Verbal Behavior*, 1968, *7*, 72–76.

Goldin-Meadow, S., Seligman, M. E. P., & Gelman, R. Language in the two-year old. *Cognition*, 1976, *4*, 189–202.

Gottfried, A. W., Rose, S. A., & Bridger, W. H. Cross-modal transfer in human infants. *Child Development*, 1977, *48*, 118–123.

Gratch, G. A study of the relative dominance of vision and touch in six-month-old infants. *Child Development*, 1972, *43*, 615–623.

Gratch, G., Appel, K. J., Evans, W. F., LeCompte, G. K., & Wright, N. A. Piaget's Stage IV object concept error: Evidence of forgetting or object conception? *Child Development*, 1974, *45*, 71–77.

Greenberg, J. H. Some universals of grammar with particular reference to the order of meaningful elements. In J. H. Greenberg (Ed.), *Universals of language*. Cambridge, Mass.: MIT Press, 1963. Pp. 58–90.

Greenfield, P. M., & Smith, J. H. *The structure of communication in early language development*. New York: Academic Press, 1976.

Guillaume, P. *Imitation in children*. Chicago: University of Chicago Press, 1971. (Originally published in French, 1926.)

Guillaume, P. First stages of sentence formation in children's speech. In C. A. Ferguson & D. I. Slobin (Eds.), *Studies of child language development*. New York: Holt, Rinehart & Winston, 1973. Pp. 522–541. (Article originally published in French, 1927.)

Halliday, M. A. K. *Learning how to mean: Explorations in the development of language*. New York: Elsevier, 1975.

Harding, C. G., & Golinkoff, R. M. The origins of intentional vocalizations in prelinguistic infants. *Child Development*, 1979, *50*, 33–40.

Harnick, F. S. The relationship between ability level and task difficulty in producing imitation in infants. *Child Development*, 1978, *49*, 209–212.

Harris, P. L. Development of search and object permanence during infancy. *Psychological Bulletin*, 1975, *82*, 332-344.

Hayes, L. A., & Watson, J. S. Neonatal imitation: Fact or artifact. *Developmental Psychology*, 1981, *17*, 655–660.

Hebb, D. O. *Textbook of psychology* (2nd ed.). Philadelphia: Saunders, 1966.

Hockett, C. F. *A course in modern linguistics.* New York: Macmillan, 1958.

Horgan, D. Nouns: Love'em or leave'em. *Annals of the New York Academy of Sciences*, 1980, *345*, 5–25.

Horgan, D. Learning to tell jokes: A case study of metalinguistic abilities. *Journal of Child Language*, 1981, *8*, 217–224.

Huttenlocher, J. The origins of language comprehension. In R. L. Solso (Ed.), *Theories of cognitive psychology: The Loyola Symposium.* Hillsdale, N.J.: Lawrence Erlbaum Associates, 1974. Pp. 331–368.

Ingram, D. Fronting in child phonology. *Journal of Child Language*, 1974, *1*, 233–241. (a)

Ingram, D. Phonological rules in young children. *Journal of Child Language*, 1974, *1*, 49–64. (b)

Jackowitz, E. R., & Watson, M. W. Development of object transformations in early pretend play. *Developmental Psychology*, 1980, *16*, 543–549.

Jackson, E., Campos, J. J., & Fischer, K. W. The question of decalage between object permanence and person permanence. *Developmental Psychology*, 1978, *14*, 1–10.

Jacobson, S. W., & Kagan, J. Interpreting "imitative" responses in early infancy. *Science*, 1979, *205*, 215–217.

Jakobson, R. *Child language, aphasia and phonological universals.* The Hague: Mouton, 1968. (Originally published in German, 1941.)

Jakobson, R., Fant, C. G. M., & Halle, M. *Preliminaries to speech analysis: The distinctive features and their correlates.* Cambridge, Mass.: MIT Press, 1963.

Jakobson, R. *Six lectures on sound and meaning.* Cambridge, Mass.: MIT Press, 1978.

Jespersen, O. *Language: Its nature, development, and origin.* New York: Norton, 1964. (Originally published, 1922.)

Kagan, J. *The second year: The emergence of self-awareness.* Cambridge, Mass.: Harvard University Press, 1981.

Kagan, J., Kearsley, R. B., & Zelazo, P. R. *Infancy: Its place in human development.* Cambridge, Mass.: Harvard University Press, 1978.

Karmiloff-Smith, A. *A functional approach to child language: A study of determiners and reference.* New York: Cambridge University Press, 1979.

Kaye, K. Why we don't talk 'baby talk' to babies. *Journal of Child Language*, 1980, *7*, 489–507.

Keenan, E. O. Conversational competence in children. *Journal of Child Language*, 1974, *1*, 163–183.

Keller, H. *The story of my life.* New York: Doubleday, 1954. (First published, 1902.)

Kessen, W., Levine, J., & Wendrich, K. A. The imitation of pitch in infants. *Infant Behavior and Development*, 1979, *2*, 93–99.

Klenbort, I., & Anisfeld, M. Markedness and perspective in the interpretation of the active and passive voice. *Quarterly Journal of Experimental Psychology*, 1974, *26*, 189–195.

Labov, W., & Labov, T. The phonetics of *cat* and *mama. Language*, 1978, *54*, 816–852.

Ladefoged, P. *A course in phonetics* (2nd ed.). New York: Harcourt Brace Javanovich, 1982.

Langer, S. K. *Philosophy in a new key: A study in the symbolism of reason, rite, and art.* New York: New American Library, 1951.

Largo, R. H., & Howard, J. A. Developmental progression in play behavior of children between nine and thirty months. I. Spontaneous play and imitation. *Developmental Medicine and Child Neurology*, 1979, *21*, 299–310.

Lashley, K. S. The problem of serial order in behavior. In L. A. Jeffress (Ed.), *Cerebral mechanisms in behavior*. New York: Wiley, 1951. Pp. 112–136.

Latif, I. The physiological basis of linguistic development and of the ontogeny of meaning: Part I. *Psychological Review*, 1934, *41*, 55–85.

Lenneberg, E. H. *Biological foundations of language*. New York: Wiley, 1967.

Leonard, L. B. On differentiating syntactic and semantic features in emerging grammars: Evidence from empty form use. *Journal of Psycholinguistic Research*, 1975, *4*, 357–364.

Leonard, L. B., Newhoff, M., & Mesalam, L. Individual differences in early child phonology. *Applied Psycholinguistics*, 1980, *1*, 7–30.

Leonard, L. B., & Schwartz, R. G. Focus characteristics of single-word utterances after syntax. *Journal of Child Language*, 1978, *5*, 151–158.

Leonard, L. B., Schwartz, R. G., Folger, M. K., & Wilcox, M. J. Some aspects of child phonology in imitative and spontaneous speech. *Journal of Child Language*, 1978, *5*, 403–415.

Leopold, W. F. *Speech development of a bilingual child: A linguist's record* (Vol. 1): *Vocabulary growth in the first two years*. New York: AMS Press, 1970. (Originally published, 1939.)

Leopold, W. F. *Speech development of a bilingual child: A linguist's record* (Vol. 2): *Sound learning in the first two years*. New York: AMS Press, 1970. (Originally published, 1947.)

Leopold, W. F. *Speech development of a bilingual child: A linguist's record* (Vol. 3): *Grammar and general problems in the first two years*. New York: AMS Press, 1970. (Originally published, 1949.) (a)

Leopold, W. F. *Speech development of a bilingual child: A linguist's record* (Vol. 4): *Diary from age 2*. New York: AMS Press, 1970. (Originally published, 1949.) (b)

Leopold, W. F. Patterning in children's language learning. In A. Bar-Adon & W. F. Leopold (Eds.), *Child language: A book of readings*. Englewood Cliffs, NJ: Prentice-Hall, 1971. Pp. 135–141. (Article originally published in 1953.)

Levy, Y. *Gender in children's language: A study in first language acquisition*. Unpublished doctoral dissertation (in Hebrew), Hebrew University of Jerusalem, 1980.

Lewis, M., & Brooks-Gunn, J. *Social cognition and the acquisition of self*. New York: Plenum Press, 1979.

Lewis, M. M. *Infant speech: A study of the beginnings of language*. New York: Arno Press, 1975. (Originally published, 1936.)

Lewkowicz, D. J., & Turkewitz, G. Intersensory interaction in newborns: Modification of visual preferences following exposure to sound. *Child Development*, 1981, *52*, 827–832.

Liberman, A. M. The grammars of speech and language. *Cognitive Psychology*, 1970, *1*, 301–323.

Liberman, A. M. An ethological approach to language through the study of speech perception. In M. von Granach, K. Foppa, W. Lepenies, & D. Plaag (Eds.), *Human ethology: Claims and limits of a new discipline*. New York: Cambridge University Press, 1979. Pp. 682–704.

Liberman, A. M. On finding that speech is special. *American Psychologist*, 1982, *37*, 148–167.

Liberman, A. M., Harris, K. S., Hoffman, H. S. & Griffith, B. C. The discrimination of speech sounds within and across phoneme boundaries. *Journal of Experimental Psychology*, 1957, *54*, 358–368.

Lichtenberg, J. D. The development of the sense of self. *Journal of the American Psychoanalytic Association*, 1975, *23*, 453–484.

Lisker, L., & Abramson, A. S. A cross-language study of voicing in initial stops: Acoustical measurements. *Word*, 1964, *20*, 384–422.

Lisker, L., & Abramson, A. S. Some effects of context on voice onset time in English stops. *Language and Speech*, 1967, *10*, 1–28.

Lock, A. (Ed.). *Action, gesture and symbol: The emergence of language*. New York: Academic Press, 1978.

Luria, A. R. *Language and cognition*. New York: Wiley, 1982.

Macken, M. A. Aspects of the acquisition of stop systems: A cross-linguistic perspective. In G. H. Yeni-Komshian, J. F. Kavanagh, & C. A. Ferguson (Eds.), *Child phonology* (Vol. 1): *Production*. New York: Academic Press, 1980. Pp. 143–168.

Macken, M. A., & Barton, D. The acquisition of the voicing contrast in English: A study of voice onset time in word-initial stop consonants. *Journal of Child Language*, 1980, *7*, 41–74.

Macmurray, J. *Persons in relation*. London: Faber and Faber, 1961.

Macnamara, J. Cognitive basis of language learning in infants. *Psychological Review*, 1972, *79*, 1–13.

MacWhinney, B. Rules, rote, and analogy in morphological formations by Hungarian children. *Journal of Child Language*, 1975, *2*, 65–77.

MacWhinney, B. Hungarian research on the acquisition of morphology and syntax. *Journal of Child Language*, 1976, *3*, 397–410.

Mahler, M. S., Pine, F., & Bergman, A. *The psychological birth of the human infant*. New York: Basic Books, 1975.

Maratsos, M. Problems in categorial evolution: Can formal categories arise from semantic ones? In W. Deutsch (Ed.), *The child's construction of language*. New York: Academic Press, 1981. Pp. 245–261.

Markova, I. (Ed.). *The social context of language*. New York: Wiley, 1978.

Masters, J. C. Interpreting "imitative" responses in early infancy. *Science*, 1979, *205*, 215.

McCarthy, D. Language development in children. In L. Carmichael (Ed.), *Manual of child psychology* (2nd ed.). New York: Wiley, 1954. Pp. 492–630.

McCune-Nicolich, L. The cognitive bases of relational words in the single word period. *Journal of Child Language*, 1981, *8*, 15–34.

Mead, G. H. *Mind, self and society: From the standpoint of a social behaviorist*. Chicago: University of Chicago Press, 1934.

Meltzoff, A. N., & Moore, M. K. Imitation of facial and manual gestures by human neonates. *Science*, 1977, *198*, 75–78.

Mendelson, M. J., & Haith, M. M. The relation between audition and vision in the human newborn. *Monographs of the Society for Research in Child Development*, 1976, *41*(4, Serial No. 167).

Menn, L. Counter example to 'fronting' as a universal of child phonology. *Journal of Child Language*, 1975, *2*, 293–296.

Menyuk, P. *The acquisition and development of language*. Englewood Cliffs, N.J.: Prentice-Hall, 1971.

Menyuk, P., & Klatt, M. Voice onset time in consonant cluster production by children and adults. *Journal of Child Language*, 1975, *2*, 223–231.

Messer, D. J. The integration of mothers' referential speech with joint play. *Child Development*, 1978, *49*, 781–787.

Messer, D. J. The episodic structure of maternal speech to young children. *Journal of Child Language*, 1980, *7*, 29–40.

Miller, G. A., & Isard, S. Some perceptual consequences of linguistic rules. *Journal of Verbal Learning and Verbal Behavior*, 1963, *2*, 217–228.

Miller, G. A., & Johnson-Laird, P. N. *Language and perception*. Cambridge, Mass.: Harvard University Press, 1976.

Miller, M. *The logic of language development in early childhood*. New York: Springer-Verlag, 1979. (Translation of German book published, 1976.)

Mills, M., & Melhuish, E. Recognition of mother's voice in early infancy. *Nature*, 1974, *252*, 123–124.

Morse, P. A. The discrimination of speech and nonspeech stimuli in early infancy. *Journal of Experimental Child Psychology*, 1972, *14*, 477–492.

Muir, D., & Field, J. Newborn infants orient to sound. *Child Development*, 1979, *50*, 431–436.

Murphy, C. M. Pointing in the context of a shared activity. *Child Development*, 1978, *49*, 371–380.

Murphy, C. M., & Messer, D. J. Mothers, infants and pointing: A study of a gesture. In H. R. Schaffer (Ed.), *Studies in mother-infant interaction*. New York: Academic Press, 1977. Pp. 325–354.

Neisser, U. *Cognitive psychology*. New York: Appleton-Century-Crofts, 1967.

Nelson, K. Structure and strategy in learning to talk. *Monographs of the Society for Research in Child Development*, 1973, *38*(1-2, Serial No. 149).

Nelson, K. The conceptual basis for naming. In J. Macnamara (Ed.), *Language learning and thought*. New York: Academic Press, 1977. Pp. 117–136.

Nelson, K., Rescorla, L., Gruendel, J., & Benedict, H. Early lexicons: What do they mean? *Child Development*, 1978, *49*, 960–968.

Newport, E. L., Gleitman, H., & Gleitman, L. R. Mother, I'd rather do it myself: Some effects and non-effects of maternal speech style. In C. E. Snow & C. A. Ferguson (Eds.), *Talking to children: Language input and acquisition*. New York: Cambridge University Press, 1977. Pp. 109–149.

Nicolich, L. M. Beyond sensorimotor intelligence: Assessment of symbolic maturity through analysis of pretend play. *Merrill-Palmer Quarterly*, 1977, *23*, 89–99.

Ninio, A. Ostensive definition in vocabulary teaching. *Journal of Child Language*, 1980, *7*, 565–573. (a)

Ninio, A. Picture-book reading in mother-infant dyads belonging to two subgroups in Israel. *Child Development*, 1980, *51*, 587–590. (b)

Ninio, A., & Bruner, J. The achievement and antecedents of labelling. *Journal of Child Language*, 1978, *5*, 1–15.

Oller, D. K., Wieman, L. A., Doyle, W. J., & Ross, C. Infant babbling and speech. *Journal of Child Language*, 1976, *3*, 1–11.

Palermo, D. S. *Psychology of language*. Glenview, Ill.: Scott, Foresman, 1978.

Pavlov, I. P. *Conditioned reflexes: An investigation of the physiological activity of the cerebral cortex*. London: Oxford University Press: Humphrey Milford, 1927. (Translated from Russian.)

Pawlby, S. J. Imitative interaction. In H. R. Schaffer (Ed.), *Studies in mother-infant interaction*. New York: Academic Press, 1977. Pp. 203–224.

Piaget, J. *The child's conception of the world*. Totowa, N.J.: Littlefield, Adams, 1979. (Translated from French. First English ed. published, 1929.)

Piaget, J. *Play, dreams and imitation in childhood*. New York: Norton, 1962. (Translated from French. First English ed. published, 1951.)

Piaget, J. *The origins of intelligence in children*. New York: Norton, 1963. (Translated from French. First English ed. published, 1952.)

Piaget, J. *The child's conception of number*. New York: Norton, 1965. (Translated from French. First English ed. published, 1952.)

Piaget, J. *The construction of reality in the child*. New York: Basic Books, 1954. (Translated from French.)

Piaget, J. *Intelligence and affectivity: Their relationship during child development*. Palo Alto, Cal.: Annual Reviews, 1981. (Edited translation from original French ed. published, 1954.)

Piaget, J. Schemes of action and language learning. In M. Piattelli-Palmarini (Ed.), *Language and learning: The debate between Jean Piaget and Noam Chomsky*. Cambridge, Mass.: Harvard University Press, 1980. Pp. 164–167.

Piattelli-Palmarini, M. (Ed.). *Language and learning: The debate between Jean Piaget and Noam Chomsky*. Cambridge, Mass.: Harvard University Press, 1980.

Popova, M. I. Grammatical elements of language in the speech of pre-preschool children. In C. A. Ferguson & D. I. Slobin (Eds.), *Studies of child language development*. New York: Holt, Rinehart & Winston, 1973. Pp. 269–280. (Originally published in Russian, 1958.)

Preyer, W. *The mind of the child: Observations concerning the mental development of the human being in the first years of life* (Part 2): *The development of the intellect*. New York: Arno Press, 1973. (Reprint of original English translation from German published, 1889.)

Priestly, T. M. S. Homonymy in child phonology. *Journal of Child Language*, 1980, *7*, 413–427.

Putnam, H. *Mind, language and reality*. New York: Cambridge University Press, 1975. Pp. 139–152.

Quine, W. V. O. *The roots of reference*. La Salle, Ill.: Open Court, 1973.

Rader, N., Spiro, D. J., & Firestone, P. B. Performance on a stage IV object-permanence task with standard and nonstandard covers. *Child Development*, 1979, *50*, 908–910.

Ramer, A. L. H. Syntactic styles in emerging language. *Journal of Child Language*, 1976, *3*, 49–62.

Ramsay, D. S. Beginnings of bimanual handedness and speech in infants. *Infant Behavior and Development*, 1980, *3*, 67–77.

Reich, P. A. The early acquisition of word meaning. *Journal of Child Language*, 1976, *3*, 117–123.

Rescorla, L. A. Overextension in early language development. *Journal of Child Language*, 1980, *7*, 321–335.

Rheingold, H. L., & Adams, J. L. The significance of speech to newborns. *Developmental Psychology*, 1980, *16*, 397–403.

Ricks, D. Making sense of experience to make sensible sounds: Experimental investigations of early vocal communication in pre-verbal autistic and normal children. In M. Bullowa (Ed.), *Before speech: The beginning of interpersonal communication*. New York: Cambridge University Press, 1979. Pp. 245–268.

Rosch, E. H. On the internal structure of perceptual and semantic categories. In T. E. Moore (Ed.), *Cognitive development and the acquisition of language*. New York: Academic Press, 1973. Pp. 111–144.

Rosch, E. H., & Mervis, C. B. Family resemblances: Studies in the internal structure of categories. *Cognitive Psychology*, 1975, *7*, 573–605.

Rosch, E. H., Mervis, C. B., Gray, W. D., Johnson, D. M., & Boyes-Braem, P. Basic objects in natural categories. *Cognitive Psychology*, 1976, *8*, 382–439.

Rose, S. A., Gottfried, A. W., & Bridger, W. H. Cross-modal transfer in 6-month-old infants. *Developmental Psychology*, 1981, *17*, 661–669.

Ross, G. S. Categorization in 1- to 2-year-olds. *Developmental Psychology*, 1980, *16*, 391–396.

Ross, J. R. Three batons for cognitive psychology. In W. B. Weimer & D. S. Palermo (Eds.), *Cognition and the symbolic processes*. Hillsdale, N.J.: Lawrence Erlbaum Associates, 1974. Pp. 63–124.

Rumbaugh, D. M., & Savage-Rumbaugh, S. Chimpanzee language research: Status and potential. *Behavior Research Methods & Instrumentation*, 1978, *10*, 119–131.

Sachs, J., & Truswell, L. Comprehension of two-word instructions by children in the one-word stage. *Journal of Child Language*, 1978, *5*, 17–24.

Sakitt, B. Iconic memory. *Psychological Review*, 1976, *83*, 257–276.

Sapir, E. *Language: An introduction to the study of speech*. New York: Harcourt, Brace & World, 1921.

Sapir, E. Sound patterns of language. In M. Joos (Ed.), *Readings in linguistics I: The development of descriptive linguistics in America, 1925–56* (4th ed.). Chicago: University of Chicago Press, 1957. Pp. 19–25. (Article originally published, 1925.)

Sapir, E. The psychological reality of phonemes. In D. G. Mandelbaum (Ed.), *Selected writings of Edward Sapir*. Berkeley: University of California Press, 1951. (Article originally published in French, 1933.)

Schachter, F. F. *Everyday mother talk to toddlers: Early intervention*. New York: Academic Press, 1979.

Schaffer, H. R. (Ed.). *Studies in mother-infant interaction*. New York: Academic Press, 1977.

Schieffelin, B. B. Getting it together: An ethnographic approach to the study of the development of communicative competence. In E. Ochs & B. B. Schieffelin (Eds.), *Developmental pragmatics*. New York: Academic Press, 1979. Pp. 73–108.

Schlesinger, I. M. Relational concepts underlying language. In R. L. Schiefelbusch & L. L. Lloyd (Eds.), *Language perspectives: Acquisition, retardation and intervention*. Baltimore, Md.: University Park Press, 1974. Pp. 129–151.

Schlesinger, I. M. *Steps to language: Towards a theory of native language acquisition*. Hillsdale, N.J.: Lawrence Erlbaum Associates, 1982.

Schwartz, R. G., Leonard, L. B., Wilcox, M. J., & Folger, M. K. Again and again: Reduplication in child phonology. *Journal of Child Language*, 1980, *7*, 75–87.

Scollon, R. *Conversations with a one year old: A case study of the developmental foundation of syntax*. Honolulu: University Press of Hawaii, 1976.

Scollon, R. A real early stage: An unzippered condensation of a dissertation on child language. In E. Ochs & B. B. Schieffelin (Eds.), *Developmental pragmatics*. New York: Academic Press, 1979. Pp. 215–227.

Shatz, M. On the development of communicative understandings: An early strategy for interpreting and responding to messages. *Cognitive Psychology*, 1978, *10*, 271–301.

Shatz, M., & Gelman, R. The development of communication skills: Modifications in the speech of young children as a function of listener. *Monographs of the Society for Research in Child Development*, 1973, *38*(5, Serial No. 152).

Sherrod, K. B., Crawley, S., Petersen, G., & Bennett, P. Maternal language to prelinguistic infants: Semantic aspects. *Infant Behavior and Development*, 1978, *1*, 335–345.

Shotter, J. The cultural context of communication: Theoretical and methodological issues. In A. Lock (Ed.), *Action, gesture and symbol: The emergence of language*. New York: Academic Press, 1978. Pp. 43–78.

Shvachkin, N. Kh. The development of phonemic speech perception in early childhood. In C. A. Ferguson & D. I. Slobin (Eds.), *Studies of child language development*. New York: Holt, Rinehart & Winston, 1973. Pp. 91–127. (Article originally published in Russian, 1948.)

Sinclair, A., Jarvella, R. J., & Levelt, W. J. M. (Eds.). *The child's conception of language*. New York: Springer-Verlag, 1978.

Sinclair, H. The role of cognitive structures in language acquisition. In E. H. Lenneberg & E. Lenneberg (Eds.), *Foundations of language development: A multidisciplinary approach* (Vol. 1). New York: Academic Press, 1975. Pp. 223–238.

Skinner, B. F. *Verbal behavior*. New York: Appleton-Century-Crofts, 1957.

Slobin, D. I. The acquisition of Russian as a native language. In F. Smith & G. A. Miller (Eds.), *The genesis of language: A psycholinguistic approach*. Cambridge, Mass.: MIT Press, 1966. Pp. 129–148.

Slobin, D. I. On the learning of morphological rules: A reply to Palermo and Eberhart. In D. I. Slobin (Ed.), *The ontogenesis of grammar: A theoretical symposium*. New York: Academic Press, 1971. Pp. 215–223.

Slobin, D. I. Cognitive prerequisites for the development of grammar. In C. A. Ferguson & D. I. Slobin (Eds.), *Studies of child language development*. New York: Holt, Rinehart & Winston, 1973. Pp. 175–208.

Smith, E. E., Shoben, E. J., & Rips, L. J. Structure and process in semantic memory: A featural model for semantic decisions. *Psychological Review*, 1974, *81*, 214–241.

Smith, L. B., & Kemler, D. G. Developmental trends in free classification: Evidence for a new conceptualization of perceptual development. *Journal of Experimental Child Psychology*, 1977, *24*, 279–298.

Smith, N. V. *The acquisition of phonology: A case study*. New York: Cambridge University Press, 1973.

Snow, C. E. Mothers' speech research: From input to interaction. In C. E. Snow & C. A. Ferguson (Eds.), *Talking to children: Language input and acquisition*. New York: Cambridge University Press, 1977. Pp. 31–49.

Snow, C. E. The uses of imitation. *Journal of Child Language*, 1981, *8*, 205–212.

Snow, C. E., & Ferguson, C. A. (Eds.). *Talking to children: Language input and acquisition*. New York: Cambridge University Press, 1977.

Snyder, A. D. Notes on the talk of a two-and-a-half year old boy. *Pedagogical Seminary*, 1914, *21*, 412–424.

Snyder, L. S., Bates, E., & Bretherton, I. Content and context in early lexical development. *Journal of Child Language*, 1981, *8*, 565–582.

Sorce, J. F., & Emde, R. N. Mother's presence is not enough: Effect of emotional availability on infant exploration. *Developmental Psychology*, 1981, *17*, 737–745.

Spelke, E., & Owsley, C. J. Intermodal exploration and knowledge in infancy. *Infant Behavior and Development*, 1979, *2*, 13–27.

Stark, R. E. Prespeech segmental feature development. In P. Fletcher & M. Garman (Eds.), *Language acquisition: Studies in first language development*. New York: Cambridge University Press, 1979. Pp. 15–32.

Starkey, D. The origins of concept formation: Object sorting and object preference in early infancy. *Child Development*, 1981, *52*, 489–497.

Starr, S. The relationship of single words to two-word sentences. *Child Development*, 1975, *46*, 701–708.

Stern, D. N., Jaffe, J., Beebe, B., & Bennett, S. L. Vocalizing in unison and in alternation: Two modes of communication within the mother-infant dyad. *Annals of the New York Academy of Sciences*, 1975, *263*, 89–100.

Stern, W. *The psychology of early childhood: Up to the sixth year of age*. New York: Arno Press, 1975. (Reprint of original English translation from German published, 1924.)

Streeter, L. A. Language perception of 2-month-old infants shows effects of both innate mechanisms and experience. *Nature*, 1976, *259*, 39–41.

Sugarman-Bell, S. Some organizational aspects of pre-verbal communication. In I. Markova (Ed.), *The social context of language*. New York: Wiley, 1978. Pp. 49–66.

Svartvik, J. *On voice in the English verb*. The Hague: Mouton, 1966.

Trehub, S. E., Bull, D., & Schneider, B. A. Infant speech and nonspeech perception: A review and reevalutation. In R. L. Schiefelbusch & D. D. Bricker (Eds.), *Early language: Acquisition and intervention*. Baltimore, Md.: University Park Press, 1981. Pp. 9–50.

Trehub, S. E., & Rabinovitch, M. S. Auditory-linguistic sensitivity in early infancy. *Developmental Psychology*, 1972, *6*, 74–77.

Trevarthen, C. Communication and cooperation in early infancy: A description of primary intersubjectivity. In M. Bullowa (Ed.), *Before speech: The beginning of interpersonal communication*. New York: Cambridge University Press, 1979. Pp. 321–347.

Tulkin, S. R., & Kagan, J. Mother-child interaction in the first year of life. *Child Development*, 1972, *43*, 31–41.

Ungerer, J. A., Brody, L. R., & Zelazo, P. R. Long-term memory for speech in 2- to 4-week-old infants. *Infant Behavior and Development*, 1978, *1*, 177–186.

Uzgiris, I. C. Patterns of vocal and gestural imitation in infants. In F. J. Mönks, W. W. Hartup, & J. de Wit (Eds.), *Determinants of behavioral development*. New York: Academic Press, 1972. Pp. 467–471.

Uzgiris, I. C. Two functions of imitation during infancy. *International Journal of Behavioral Development*, 1981, *4*, 1–12.

Uzgiris, I. C., & Hunt, J. McV. *Assessment in infancy: Ordinal scales of psychological development*. Champaign: University of Illinois Press, 1975.

Valentine, C. W. The psychology of imitation with special reference to early childhood. *British Journal of Psychology*, 1930, *21*, 105–132.

Vygotsky, L. S. *Thought and language*. Cambridge, Mass.: MIT Press, 1962. (Originally published in Russian, 1934.)

Watson, M. W., & Fischer, K. W. A developmental sequence of agent use in late infancy. *Child Development*, 1977, *48*, 828–836.

Weir, R. H. *Language in the crib*. The Hague: Mouton, 1962.

Weir, R. H. Some questions on the child's learning of phonology. In F. Smith & G. A. Miller (Eds.), *The genesis of language: A psycholinguistic approach*. Cambridge, Mass.: MIT Press, 1966. Pp. 153–172.

Werker, J. F., Gilbert, J. H. V., Humphrey, K., & Tees, R. C. Developmental aspects of cross-language speech perception. *Child Development*, 1981, *52*, 349–355.

Werner, H., & Kaplan, B. *Symbol formation*. New York: Wiley, 1963.

White, B. L., Kaban, B. T., & Attanucci, J. S. *The origins of human competence*. Lexington, Mass.: Heath, 1979.

White, T. G. Naming practices, typicality, and underextension in child language. *Journal of Experimental Child Psychology*, 1982, *33*, 324-346.

Whorf, B. L. Science and linguistics. In J. B. Carroll (Ed.), *Language, thought, and reality: Selected writings of Benjamin Lee Whorf*. Cambridge, Mass.: MIT Press, 1956. Pp. 207–219. (Article originally published, 1940.)

Wieman, L. A. Stress patterns of early child language. *Journal of Child Language*, 1976, *3*, 283–286.

Wolf, D., & Gardner, H. On the structure of early symbolization. In R. L. Schiefelbusch & D. D. Bricker (Eds.), *Early language: Acquisition and intervention*. Baltimore, Md.: University Park Press, 1981. Pp. 287–327.

Wolff, P. H. The natural history of crying and other vocalizations in infancy. In B. M. Foss (Ed.), *Determinants of infant behaviour* (Vol. 4). London: Methuen, 1969. Pp. 81–109.

Yando, R., Seitz, V., & Zigler, E. *Imitation: A developmental perspective*. Hillsdale, N.J.: Lawrence Erlbaum Associates, 1978.

Yeni-Komshian, G. H., Kavanagh, J. F., & Ferguson, C. A. (Eds.). *Child phonology* (Vol 2): *Perception*. New York: Academic Press, 1980.

Author Index

A

Abramson, A. S., 193
Adams, J. L., 224
Akmajian, A., 122
Allport, G. W., 46
Anglin, J. M., 105
Anisfeld, M., 12, 43, 104, 116, 157,
    196–198, 205, 208, 213, 230, 231, 243
Appel, K. J., 36
Appleton, T., 45
Asch, S. E., 53, 55
Aslin, R. N., 221
Attanucci, J. S., 45
Austin, G. A., 13

B

Barker, R. G., 93
Barrett, M. D., 75
Barton, D., 232, 240
Bates, E., 57, 66, 69, 163, 171–172
Beebe, B., 227
Beeghly-Smith, M., 57
Bell, S. M., 49–50
Bellugi, U., 175
Belsky, J., 45–46, 60

Benedict, H., 70, 77, 79
Bennett, P., 225
Bennett, S. L., 227
Bergman, A., 46
Berko, J., 213
Berman, R. A., 213
Blank, M., 98
Bloom, L. M., 69, 72, 74, 92, 129–140,
    150–151, 156–157, 167–168, 178
Blount, B. G., 149
Bolinger, D., 118–119
Bower, T. G. R., 23, 31–33
Bowerman, M., 85, 89–90, 145–146, 163
Boyes-Braem, P., 10
Braine, M. D. S., 129, 133–138, 143–147,
    162–165
Branigan, G., 158
Bretherton, I., 57, 69
Bridger, W. H., 47
Brody, L. R., 25
Bronckart, J. P., 209
Bronstein, A. J., 191, 199
Brooks-Gunn, J., 53, 83
Brown, C. J., 227
Brown, R., 114, 118, 130–139, 142, 150,
    152, 175, 205–214
Bruner, J., 13, 94, 97, 172–173
Bryant, B., 213
Bull, D., 221

Subject Index

of word meaning
analogical, 77
correct followed by incorrect, 89–90
diffuse, 73–74
inappropriateness of term for early word
uses, 75
overextensions, 83–85, 88–89
personal, 74–75
underextensions (overrestrictions), 85
Extension (maternal), 174

F

Familiarity memory, *see* Memory, familarity
Fis phenomenon, 239–240
Formal-operational stage, 20
Frans, 237, 242
French
experiment on past tense, 209
Fricatives
defined, 191–193
marked in relation to stops, 230
as a subsystem, 196
acquired as a subsystem, 231–232
voicing assimilation of, 199, 204
Fronting of sounds by young children,
230–232
Function words
their absence from early sentences, 152–153
Functions of language
primacy of cognitive over instrumental
function
in sentences, 133, 139
in single-word utterances, 91–94
Functors, *see* Function words

G

Gender agreement
its overregularization in Russian, 215
Generative transformational grammar, 122–126
Genie, 183–184
German
in Hildegard's vocabulary, 75, 83, 86
Gia, 131, 133, 135, 137–140, 151
Glides, 190
Gradual assembly strategy, 161–165

Grammar, *see* Syntax
Grasping, *see* Action, manual
Growth spurt
in the acquisition
of plurals, 210–211
of syntax, 129–130
of vocabulary, 79–80
and the emergence of the syntactic
stage, 107–109, 128
and object permanence, 81

H

Habituation method, 218
Hebrew
drastic morphological changes in, 204
and English, differences in perceived sound
similarity, 197
Hebrew-English bilingual child, 213, 215
overextension in, 83
overregularization in, 212–213, 215
variable word order in, 142
Hierarchical organization
lack of in early vocabulary, 102–103
Hildegard, 75–77, 83, 85–88, 155, 157, 216,
236
Hindi
ability of American infants to discriminate
sounds of, 220
Holophrastic utterances, 77–78
Hopi, *see* Indian (American) languages
Hungarian
acquisition of locatives in, 210
acquisition of morphology in, 205

I

Identification, perceptual, 13–14, 23
Imitation
and acquisition of syntax, 177–179
causal, in infancy, 49
echoic, 238
echolalia, 237
and the emergence of the self, 54
its functions in infancy, 43–45, 228
of infants by mothers and mothers by infants
relative amounts of vocal and manual,
44–45

Language
functioning as a system
in the acquisition
of morphology, 215
of speech, 87, 229–232, 235–237
of vocabulary, 10, 87–88
in parts-of-speech classification, 118–119
in speech, 195–198
its functions, *see* Functions of language
universals of, 99–100, 119–121, 126, 182, 184
as a vehicle for cognitive development, 105–106, 179–181
Laurent, 29, 32–33, 38, 45, 62, 71, 73, 76
Learning, *see also under* Syntax; Vocabulary
and assimilation-accommodation, 16–18
constraints on the learning of vocabulary, 99–100
gradual, 17
habitual-associative, 40
through imitation, in infancy, 43–44
inferential, 40–43
mediated, 47
Lexical development, *see also* Syntax;
Vocabulary; Words, early
and the emergence of syntax, 107–109
and the socialization of the child, 106–107
Liquids, 190
Locatives
acquisition in Hungarian and Serbo-Croatian, 210
Locomotion
and the emergence of the self, 54
as facilitating exploration, 45–46
Lucienne, 29, 34–35, 57–59, 62, 71, 73

M

Magical efficacy, 33
Makeshift uses of words, *see under* Words, early
Mand, 91
Manner of articulation, 191–193
Marked-unmarked distinction
in phonology, 230
Marta, 183–184
Maternal role, *see also* Maternal speech;
Mother; Mother-Child interaction
in the development
of curiosity, 46–47
of the self, 54

of syntax, 171–181
of vocabulary, 94–98
Maternal speech, *see also* Baby talk
characteristics of, 94–98, 134, 149, 174–175, 181
to prelinguistic infants
adjusted to infants of different ages, 225
social class differences in amount of, 224–225
to verbal children
and the acquisition of syntax, 134, 175–177
and the acquisition of vocabulary, 96
Mathetic function, *see* Functions of language
Matthew, 91–92, 159, 179–180
Meaning
lexical, 66–105
Level 1, 67–72
Level 2, 72–79
Level 3, 79–90
and sensorimotor development, 80–81
propositional, 114, 134, 154
absence of in dummy constructions, 167–169
children learning how to express in sentences, 174
in word sequences, 156–158
referential vs. conceptual, 101–105
syntactic, 66
Memory, *see also* Discrimination, by infants
in infancy
of faces, 24
familiarity, 24–26, 28, 221
recognition, 24–26
sensorimotor, 20–26
of sentences, and the acquisition of syntax, 130–131
Meri, 108–109
Metalinguistic sensitivity and interests, 94, 171
in speech, 87, 239, 241–242
in syntax, 166
in words, 77
Michael, 237–238
Miriam, 88, 161, 170
Mirrors
infants' reactions to, 53
MLU (mean length of utterance)
defined, 107
progression in, 130
Modifier
in children's syntactic rules, 146